KU-607-798

Department of Criminal Science, Faculty of Law, University of Cambridge

ENGLISH STUDIES IN CRIMINAL SCIENCE

EDITED BY

L. RADZINOWICZ, LL.D.

VOLUME VIII

MENS REA IN STATUTORY OFFENCES

by

J. Ll. J. EDWARDS, M.A., LL.B., Ph.D.

MENS REA IN STATUTORY OFFENCES

BY

J. Ll. J. EDWARDS

M.A., LL.B., Ph.D.

OF THE MIDDLE TEMPLE, BARRISTER-AT-LAW;

READER IN LAW IN THE QUEEN'S UNIVERSITY OF BELFAST

LONDON

MACMILLAN & CO LTD

NEW YORK · ST MARTIN'S PRESS

1955

170036
KH 5

This volume is published under the auspices of the Department of Criminal Science of the Faculty of Law in the University of Cambridge. It must be understood that the Department does not necessarily agree with the views expressed by the author

MACMILLAN AND COMPANY LIMITED
London Bombay Calcutta Madras Melbourne

THE MACMILLAN COMPANY OF CANADA LIMITED
Toronto

ST MARTIN'S PRESS INC
New York

This book is copyright in all countries which are signatories to the Berne Convention

PRINTED IN GREAT BRITAIN

QUEEN MARY COLLEGE
LIBRARY
MILE END ROAD,
LONDON, E.1

CONTENTS

EDITORIAL NOTE

DR. Edwards's book may be regarded as the first comprehensive and critical examination of the judicial interpretation of the language which is used in the definition of statutory offences. It will be of considerable interest to the academic lawyer, providing as it does authoritative material for the current discussions of the theories of criminal liability.

It will also prove itself indispensable to practising lawyers, and through them to those whose task it is to determine the difficult issues of culpability, which arise whenever the language used leaves either the purpose of the legislature or the scope of the particular offence obscure.

Finally, this valuable monograph demonstrates the inconsistencies which have inevitably arisen in the interpretation of existing enactments, and so provides an indication of some of the difficulties to be avoided by the draftsmen of future legislation.

For all these reasons the Cambridge Department of Criminal Science welcomes the inclusion of this new volume in its *English Studies of Criminal Science.*

LEON RADZINOWICZ

DEPARTMENT OF CRIMINAL SCIENCE
UNIVERSITY OF CAMBRIDGE

PREFACE

In the entire field of criminal law there is no more important doctrine than that of *mens rea*, embedded as are its roots in the principle that no man shall be punished for committing a crime unless a guilty mind can be imputed to him. Since the turn of the last century this principle has been assailed in no uncertain manner by the legislature. Long before then, however, Parliament had been prepared to use the sanctions of the criminal law as a means of securing a well-ordered structure of social and economic conduct. Two world wars, with their vast output of regulations creating new offences, have served to foster and enlarge this practice, in which it has become increasingly common to by-pass the above cardinal principle. In its place there has arisen a theory of strict liability in which the question of a guilty mind is wholly irrelevant.

This departure from the earlier concept of criminal liability based upon a moral standard of wrong-doing is not the exclusive prerogative of Parliament. It has exercised a varying influence upon the judiciary, the present mood being manifestly suspicious of attempts to extend the field of strict liability in crime. This was not always so, and in this work an examination is carried out of the judicial interpretation of statutory offences founded upon such familiar epithets as "maliciously", "wilfully", "knowingly", "fraudulently", "permits" and "suffers". In carrying out this critical study I have been conscious of the difficulties confronting the judges, and where certain decisions are considered to be untenable I have endeavoured to analyse the reasons for such unsatisfactory decisions and to suggest alternative interpretations. Attention is also given to the application of the doctrine of vicarious liability in statutory offences, and to the question whether actual knowledge and connivance alone constitute the criminal degrees of knowledge or whether negligence also should be included. The various theories of liability for statutory offences have been considered against a fluctuating background of ethical, social and economic interests; and though appreciating the hazards of suggesting a guiding principle for adoption, I felt the attempt should be made. Perhaps I may be allowed to voice the hope that, whatever the deficiencies of this study, it will at least direct attention to the serious danger of the criminal law falling into disrepute if both the legislature and the courts allow statutory offences to be administered with scant regard for the doctrine of *mens rea*.

Originally, this work was written as a thesis for the degree of Doctor of Philosophy in the University of London, since when it has been expanded into its present form. For permitting me to incorporate certain articles which have previously been published in *The Modern Law Review* and in *Current Legal Problems* I wish to thank the respective editors. Finally, I should like to express my gratitude for the many helpful suggestions I received from my friends Professor Glanville Williams and Mr. A. Ll. Armitage, and for the constant support and encouragement that has been extended to me in preparing this book by Dr. L. Radzinowicz, Director of the Department of Criminal Science, and Mr. F. J. Odgers, then Assistant Director of Research.

J. Ll. J. E.

I

MALICE

PRE-EMINENT amongst words describing states of mind in criminal law is the term "malice" or "malicious", than which, according to Sir James Stephen, "there is no word in the whole range of criminal law which it is more important to understand correctly."[1] Perhaps best known of all is its use in the phrase "malice aforethought", which describes the manifold degrees of *mens rea* in the crime of murder. Another context in which malice appears is in relation to criminal libel. These two common law crimes are mentioned mainly as a matter of interest and, except where necessary for comparative purposes, no further reference will be made to them. As to offences created by statute, examination of the Malicious Damage Act, 1861, shows that out of fifty-four sections, defining various offences against property, only four omit the word "maliciously",[2] while in the Offences against the Person Act, 1861, twelve sections in all require proof of malice.[3] In sharp contrast, the term appears only once throughout the Larceny Act, 1916.[4] There are, of course, other minor statutory offences[5] in which the word "maliciously" appears, but inasmuch as the reported cases almost invariably arise under the two major statutes of 1861, it is inevitable that attention is principally directed to that fertile field of case law.

DEVELOPMENT OF STATUTORY MALICE

Before proceeding to classify the different kinds of malice to which the judges have given their attention, it will be advisable to trace very briefly the development of malice through the statute

[1] *General View of English Criminal Law*, p. 81.

[2] The exceptions are ss. 36, 47, 50 and 54. In his *History of Criminal Law*, II, p. 119, Stephen is guilty of an error in including, as exceptions, ss. 52 and 53. Both these sections contain the term "maliciously".

[3] These are ss. 16, 17, 18, 20, 23, 24, 26, 28, 29, 30, 32 and 33.

[4] In section 10, which deals with the malicious or fraudulent abstraction of electricity.

[5] E.g., Electric Lighting Act, 1882 (45 and 46 Vict. c. 56), s. 22; the Explosives Substances Act, 1883 (46 and 47 Vict. c. 3), s. 2; and the Post Office Act, 1953 (1 and 2 Eliz. 2, c. 36), s. 56.

law of the past seven hundred odd years.[1] The earliest mention of malice as a mental element in crime was in the middle of the thirteenth century, when Bracton, writing of arson, indicated the necessity for proving that the burning was done with evil design, *mala conscientia*.[2] Certainly arson owes its origin to the common law, but its importance in relation to malice becomes evident when it is realised that upon the law of arson was founded the entire structure of statutory offences dealing with malicious damage to property. Coke, writing in the seventeenth century, repeats Bracton's language and points to the form of indictment in arson which required that the burning be *voluntarie*, *ex malitia sua praecogitata*. "If it be done by mischance, or negligence,"[3] says Coke, "it is no felony".[4] What was written then remains true today, but there will be observed a considerable change in the interpretation of *malitia*.[5]

The first statute to punish injuries to property, passed in 1285,[6] contained no mention of the word "malice", but we find the expression in one of the earliest measures designed to punish crimes against the person. Enacted in 1403,[7] this statute made it a felony to cut out the tongue or put out the eyes of any person, by any malice prepense. In 1545, we find a more extensive enactment

[1] For a full account, see East, *Pl. of Cr.*, Vol. 2, pp. 1015–1017; Stephen, *History of Criminal Law*, III, pp. 109–113 and 188–190, and L. Radzinowicz, *A History of English Criminal Law*, Vol. I, pp. 49–73, 574–575, 630–631, 654–657.

[2] *De Legibus*, 146*b*.

[3] Yet 6 Ann, c. 31 made it an offence for any servant to *negligently* set fire to a house or outhouse.

[4] *Third Institute*, f. 67. One of the early statutes dealing with arson was in 1723, *viz.* 9 Geo. I, c. 22. Strangely, it contained no reference to the necessity for malice, but in *Susan Minton's Case* (East, *Pl. of Cr.*, Vol. 2, p. 1033) it was held that malice was still necessary.

[5] In Pollock and Maitland's *History of English Law*, Vol. 2, at p. 467, the view is put forward that it is rather the popular than the legal sense of the word that has changed. When it first came into use, they explain, *malitia* hardly signified a state of mind, some qualifying adjective such as *praemeditata* or *excogitata* was needed if much note was to be taken of intention or of any other psychical fact. Regarding *malice prepense* (see statute 5 Hen. 4, c. 5 referred to in the text above) they are of opinion that its earliest meaning was little more than intentional wrongdoing. This interpretation is not shared by East and Foster, for whose views see text above.

[6] 13 Edw. I, st. I, c. 46, which punished the throwing down of enclosures rightfully made by a person entitled to approve a common. Together with subsequent enactments, it provides an interesting commentary on the items of property considered sufficiently important to warrant legislation for their protection. To give only two examples, 37 Hen. 8, c. 6 dealt with "unlawful, wilful, malicious injuries to trees", and 22 and 23 Chas. 2, c. 11, s. 12, related to the "wilful" destruction of ships.

[7] 5 Hen. 4, c. 5.

dealing with offences against both the person and property.[1] Beginning with the preamble, "Where divers and sundry malicious and curious persons being men of evil and perverse dispositions, and seduced by the instigation of the devil . . . of their malicious and wicked minds have of late invented and practised a new damnable kind of vice," the statute then proceeded to list certain offences, including the burning of timber frames for houses, cutting out of beasts' tongues, cutting off the ears of the King's subjects and the barking of various kinds of trees.[2] The next enactment of any importance was the Coventry Act, 1670,[3] which provided that it shall be a felony "of malice, forethought and by lying in wait, to unlawfully cut out or disable the tongue, put out an eye, slit the nose, or cut off or disable any limb or member . . . with intention in so doing to maim or disfigure". Commenting on this statute, East writes that "if a corporal violence be intended, the more malignant the intention the more clearly it falls within the malice described by the Act".[4] Another statute,[5] closely following the Coventry Act, is cited by Foster to illustrate the frequent use of the terms "malice" and "maliciously" to denote "a wicked, perverse and incorrigible disposition".[6] The same writer later states that the words *per malitiam* and *malitiose* constantly mean an action flowing from a wicked and corrupt motive, a thing done *malo animo*, *mala conscientia*.[7]

If assistance is sought from the reports as to the early meaning of malice, it will be found that the cases mainly turned on the provisions of the Black Act, 1723.[8] Among other offences, this famous statute made it a felony maliciously to kill, maim or wound any cattle. In three cases decided in 1789,[9] it was held that to bring an offender within the statute it was necessary to show that the

[1] 37 Hen. 8, c. 6.

[2] Whereas the burning of timber frames was made a felony, punishable with death, all the other offences were punishable by a fine of £10!

[3] 22 and 23 Chas. 2, c. 1.

[4] 1 *Pl. of Cr.*, p. 400.

[5] 4 and 5 Wm. and M., which made it an offence to "maliciously command, hire or counsel any person to do any robbery".

[6] *Crown Cases*, p. 257, citing *Lord Raym*, 1487. This passage was cited, with approval, by Mellor, J., in *R.* v. *Ward* (1872) 1 C.C.R. 356, at p. 360. See, too, *R.* v. *Mawgridge*, Kelyng 119, at p. 127.

[7] *Ibid.*, p. 256.

[8] 9 Geo. I, c. 22. For a detailed survey of the provisions of this Act see (1945) 9 *Cambridge Law Journal*, pp. 56–81.

[9] *R.* v. *Pearce*, 1 Leach 527; *R.* v. *Hean*, 3 B. and C. 252, and *R.* v. *Shepherd*, 1 Leach 539.

maiming of the animal was done from some malicious motive towards the owner of it, and not merely from an angry and passionate disposition towards the beast itself. Some years later,[1] it was held by all the judges that it is not sufficient to prove malice even against a servant or relation of the owner; it must be against the owner of the cattle. As a result of these decisions, legislation was passed,[2] providing that it is immaterial whether the malice is conceived against the owner of the property in respect of which it shall be committed or otherwise. A similar provision has been retained in the Malicious Damage Act, 1861, s. 58.

Can it justifiably be argued, however, that in making this provision the legislature had in mind the extension of the law to cover cases involving malicious injury to the defendant's own animal or, as must follow, the defendant's personal but inanimate property. This astonishing interpretation was adopted by Lord Russell, C.J. (after consulting Grantham, J.), in the case of *R.* v. *Parry*,[3] where a man in a fit of drunken spite kicked and stabbed his own horse, and was convicted of maliciously wounding the animal. Such a case, it is suggested, falls more appropriately within the Protection of Animals Act, 1911. The logical extension of the decision in *R.* v. *Parry* would make a farmer liable, e.g., under section 15 of the Malicious Damage Act, who, incensed with his agricultural machinery which through some mechanical default had constantly failed to work smoothly, sets about destroying it. Unless there is some ulterior object in view by the

[1] *R.* v. *Austen* (1822) Russ. and Ry. 490. The same construction was adopted in *Curtis* v. *The Hundred of Godley* (1824) 3 B. and C. 248, in relation to the offence of maliciously destroying trees planted for ornament, shelter or profit, Bayley, J., referring to *R.* v. *Taylor* (1819) in which it had been unanimously held, by all the judges, that for such offence "malice against the owner was essential".

[2] (1823) 4 Geo. 4, c. 54, s. 2 and (1827) 7 and 8 Geo. 4, c. 30, s. 25. In the United States, however, the majority of cases still seem to require proof that the malice was directed against the owners of the property injured. This view is criticised by Miller, *Criminal Law*, p. 403.

[3] (1900) 35 L. J. Newsp. 456. See, too *R.* v. *Welch* [1875] 1 Q.B.D. 23, in which case there was no evidence to show that the prisoner was actuated by any ill-will towards the owner of the mare, nor by any spite towards the mare itself. In fact, the prisoner's only motive was the gratification of his own depraved tastes. He was convicted under the Malicious Damage Act, 1861, s. 40 (1). For Kenny's view, approving the decision in *R.* v. *Parry*, see *Outlines of Criminal Law* (15th ed.), p. 195, but doubts as to the correctness of the decision in *R.* v. *Parry* are expressed by the learned editor of the 16th edition of *Kenny* (at p. 190), Mr. J. W. C. Turner, who, in *Russell on Crime*, (10th ed.) p. 1908, suggests that the judges in that case were carried away by their natural feeling of indignation at the cruelty displayed.

accused, such as defrauding a third party[1] (e.g., an insurance company), there would appear to be no reason why the legislature should seek to punish a man under the Malicious Damage Act, 1861, for damaging his own property, whether animate or inanimate.

In the field of damage to property no further enactments of note were passed until 1827, when an attempt was made to secure some order out of the previous haphazard legislation. This had been designed solely to meet particular kinds of mischief which, from time to time, happened to require attention; a conclusion borne out by the fact that twenty-eight statutes in all[2] were repealed by the consolidating Act.[3] This was itself repealed and enlarged by the present governing statute, the Malicious Damage Act, 1861. So far as injuries to the person were concerned, Lord Ellenborough's Act of 1803[4] is generally regarded as the germ from whence sprang, through the medium of one intermediate statute,[5] the comprehensive Offences against the Person Act, 1861, which is still in force. It is with these two major statutes and the superimposed case-law that we are principally concerned.

Classification of statutory malice

The next task is to classify, if possible, the different degrees of *mens rea* which are said to fulfil the requirement of statutory malice. This can only be done by examining the language used by the judges. It will be found that such analysis indicates four different senses in which the term is applied, namely, express malice, implied malice, transferred malice, and, grouped together, general and particular malice. It is proposed to take each of these categories in turn.

Express malice[6]

This is sometimes referred to as actual malice[7] or malice in fact,[8] and indicates the commonly accepted meaning of malice,

[1] See, for example, section 3 of the Malicious Damage Act, 1861.

[2] For the full list, see Stephen, *Hist. of Cr. Law*, III, p. 190.

[3] Repealed by 7 and 8 Geo. 4, c. 27, the law was consolidated by 7 and 8 Geo. 4, c. 30.

[4] 43 Geo. 3, c. 58.

[5] (1828) 9 Geo. 4, c. 31, which repealed, so far as related to England, all the earlier Acts concerning personal violence.

[6] E.g., *R.* v. *Davies* (1858) 1 F. and F. 69, *per* Crompton, J., at p. 71.

[7] E.g., *R.* v. *Pembliton* (1874) 2 C.C.R. 119, *per* Lush, J., at p. 123.

[8] E.g., *Bromage* v. *Prosser* (1825) 4 B. and C. 247, *per* Bayley, J.

namely, wickedness, or a disposition to injure others without cause merely to procure personal gratification or from a spirit of revenge.[1] As we have already seen, this was the construction placed upon the old statutes dealing with malicious crimes. Today, its principal application in criminal law is in libel where, as in the law of tort, evidence of express malice is necessary to destroy the defence of qualified privilege or fair comment. Evidence is available, however, that at least up to the end of the last century many of the judges were imbued with the idea that it was necessary to prove malice in its natural sense in all crimes of malice. Thus, in 1839, we find a case[2] in which the accused was charged with maliciously killing a sheep, evidence being given that the intent of the prisoner was to steal the carcase. Both Alderson, B., and Parke, B., were agreed that killing with intent to steal came within the spirit of the term "maliciously to kill" which, they said, "ought to be construed to mean killing *malo animo*: any improper motive or bad intention would satisfy the statute". A slightly different twist was given by Parke, B., in *R.* v. *Prestney*,[3] to the offence of maliciously destroying any fence under the consolidating Malicious Injuries to Property Act 1827, s. 23. "To constitute the offence," Parke, B., declared, "the injury done . . . must be a wanton act of cutting or the like, with the object of doing damage to the thing injured. Here there was spiteful object in damaging the fence; it was done merely in prosecution of the intention to kill the game." In *Daniel* v. *James*,[4] decided in 1877, we find Lord Coleridge, C.J., expressing a similar opinion. In that case the accused was charged with maliciously killing a dog, contrary to section 41 of the Malicious Damage Act, a section which has recently been the subject of an unsatisfactory decision

[1] *Webster's Dictionary*. *The Oxford English Dictionary* defines malice as wrongful intention, that kind of evil intent which aggravates the guilt of certain offences. Miller, *Criminal Law*, p. 69 gives seven separate definitions commonly used which the learned author says, reflect an ascending scale of wickedness or malignity. They are:
(i) a wrongful act done intentionally without just cause or excuse;
(ii) a wrongful act done intentionally which the doer knows will injure another;
(iii) a disposition to injure another;
(iv) a wilful disregard of the rights or safety of others;
(v) a spiteful or malevolent design;
(vi) deliberate cruelty;
(vii) the expression of a wicked and depraved heart and mind.

[2] *R.* v. *Fordham* (1839) 4 J.P. 397. See, too, Lord Abinger, C. B., in *R.* v. *James* (1837) 8 C. and P. 131, at p. 132, a case which turned on the same statute, *viz.*, 7 and 8 Geo. 4, c. 30, s. 16.

[3] (1849) 3 Cox C.C., 505.

[4] [1877] 2 C.P.D. 351.

by the Divisional Court.[1] Referring to this particular section, Lord Coleridge declared that "it points to a wicked crime, the unlawfully and maliciously killing or maiming the animals referred to (in the section), simply for the purpose of indulging a cruel disposition."[2]

There is also the opinion of that eminent judge, Brett, J. in *R.* v. *Mathews and Twigg*,[3] in which case the accused were charged with maliciously stopping-up an airshaft with intent to obstruct a coal mine. "I think", said Brett, J., "that the act charged must be done not only wilfully but maliciously, that is to say, with a wicked mind, and if it is done under a bona fide claim of right it is not done maliciously according to our criminal law." This natural meaning of malice, as the motives which prompt a man's conduct, was approved by the Court of Criminal Appeal as recently as 1911, in the interesting case of *R.* v. *Syme*.[4] The accused, in that case, was charged with maliciously sending a letter to the late Ramsay MacDonald, then head of the Labour Party, threatening to murder a certain police inspector. The jury returned a special verdict to the effect that the threat was a bluff and was made to call attention to the prisoner's grievances. On his appeal against conviction, the Court of Criminal Appeal approved the trial judge's direction to the jury on the meaning of the word malicious, in which Darling, J., had stated: "There are many things which a man may do which are malicious if they are done from an improper and indirect motive. . . . The word malicious to my mind implies the doing of that which a person has no legal right to do, and his doing it in order to secure some object by means which are improper."

This interpretation of malice as signifying evil motive, with the consequent reliance on motive as the test of criminality, has been the subject of much criticism.[5] It has been pointed out that the

[1] *Gott* v. *Measures* [1948] 1 K.B. 234, discussed fully later at pp. 23–27.

[2] 2 C.P.D., at p. 353.

[3] (1876) 14 Cox C.C. 5, at p. 7. See, too, Mellor, J. (*arguendo*) in *R. v. Ward* (1872) L.R. 1 C.C.R. 356, at p. 360, where he uses the phrase *malus animus* to describe malice.

[4] 6 Cr. App. R. 257, *coram* Lord Alverstone, C.J., Avory and Pickford, JJ. This direction was approved again in *R.* v. *Johnson* (1913) 9 Cr. App. R. 57. The indictment was under the Offences against the Person Act, 1861, s. 16.

[5] See Stephen, *History of Criminal Law*, II, pp. 120–121, and compare with his views as quoted in the text, *post*, p. 8. This apparent inconsistency is explained by Stephen when he writes that lawyers are so fully sensible of the objections to motive as the test of criminality that they overcome them by resort to the fiction explained above. The result, he goes on, is to throw upon persons who commit acts of a particular class

main object of criminal law is to prevent certain acts which are injurious to society. In order, therefore, to overcome the difficulty of proving the accused's evil motives for any given act, there arose the practice of saying that certain unlawful acts are prima facie to be deemed wicked actions. By resort to one of the many legal fictions in our criminal law, the wickedness inherent in the meaning of malice is inferred from the wrongful act. Of course, circumstances may exist wherein the imputation of wickedness may be removed. The important point to note is that the original interpretation by the courts of *malo animo* is still the basis of the mental element signified by the terms "malice" and "maliciously". Indeed, no less an authority than Sir Fitzjames Stephen has expressed the view that "it is absolutely necessary that legal definitions of crimes should be based upon moral distinctions, whatever may be the difficulty of ascertaining with precision what those distinctions are; and it will be found in practice impossible to attach to the words 'malice' and 'malicious' any other meaning than that which properly belongs to them of wickedness and wicked".[1]

Implied malice

Several epithets including implied,[2] presumed,[3] inferred,[4] constructive,[5] and malice in law,[6] have been used to describe the

the burden of proving that they were not done under the circumstances contemplated by the legislature, but at the same time to permit them to give evidence to that effect. See, too, Sayre, (1932) 45 *Harvard Law Review*, p. 1019; Stallybrass, *Modern Approach to Criminal Law*, p. 409. Comparison may be made with the view of O. W. Holmes, *The Common Law*, p. 63, who defines malice in malicious crimes "as used in its popular sense, and imports that the motive for the defendant's act was a wish to harm the owner of the property, or the thing itself, if living, as an end, and for the sake of the harm".

[1] *General View of Criminal Law*, p. 84. In another passage, on the same page, Stephen says: "Malicious means wicked, and its truth can be denied by no one who is not prepared to contend that the word malicious in the statute referred to (the Malicious Damage Act, 1861) is mere surplusage". A similar opinion is expressed by Markby, *Elements of English Law*, p. 325, who says of "maliciously", and also words like "wilfully", "wantonly", "fraudulently", ". . . they more or less imply that the state of mind under consideration is, when tried by some standard which the person using the expression has in view, not what it ought to be. What this standard is it is not easy to discover, but is something in the nature of a moral standard."

[2] E.g., *Gott* v. *Measures* [1948] 1 K.B. 234, at p. 239. See, too, Foster, *Crown Cases*, p. 257.

[3] E.g., Sayre, *Mens Rea*, (1932) 45 *Harvard Law Review*, p. 916.

[4] E.g., *R.* v. *Shrimpton* (1840) 4 J.P. 508.

[5] E.g., *R.* v. *Pembliton* (1874) 2 C.C.R., at p. 123.

[6] E.g., *Bromage* v. *Prosser* (1825) 4 B. and C. 247, at p. 255.

second meaning in which the word "malice" is used in connection with statutory offences. Whichever adjective is used the meaning is always the same, namely, that malice, the guilty mind, is inferred from the wrongful act itself.[1] This fiction was first enunciated in 1825 in the leading case of *Bromage* v. *Prosser*, where Bayley, J., said: "There are two sorts of malice, malice in fact and malice in law, the former denoting an act done from ill-will towards an individual, the latter a wrongful act intentionally done, without just cause or excuse."[2] This distinction was approved in *R.* v. *Philip*,[3] in which case the accused was charged with maliciously setting fire to a vessel of which he was part owner. It was argued that the prisoner could not intend to mean malice to his part-owners in an act which was equally injurious to himself. The Judge, however, accepted the argument put forward by the prosecution, who maintained that, where the act is of such a nature as could spring from no other than a bad motive and is calculated to inflict injury without cause or justification, it is not necessary to prove express malice since the law implies malice from the act itself. Later we find a more elaborate explanation of the fiction being given by Coleridge, J., in *R.* v. *Weare*.[4] In that case a perfectly quiet and inoffensive bull was the object of a malicious maiming. It appeared that its owner had refused to let a field to the prisoner, but there was no evidence that the unfortunate animal had done anything to exasperate the accused. In his direction to the jury, the learned judge said that "if it were necessary for you to be satisfied of express malice, I think it would be scarcely safe to convict the prisoner. But however satisfactory it may be to a jury to have an adequate motive proved before them, and however much the absence of such motive may, in conjunction with other circumstances, weigh in favour of a prisoner, it is not necessary in point of law to prove such malice, or to give

[1] As is rightly pointed out by Miller, *Criminal Law*, p. 69, so far as the mental element itself is concerned the distinction between express and implied malice means nothing. Its only importance is, as a matter of the law of evidence, in the way in which malice is proved.

[2] *Loc. cit.* This lead was followed by Littledale, J., in *McPherson* v. *Daniels* (1829) 10 B. and C. 263; Tindal, C.J., in *The Bristol Riots* (1832) 3 St. Tr. (N.S.) 1, at p. 8; Taunton, J., in *R.* v. *Houghton* (1833) 5 C. and P. 559; and Campbell, C.J., in *Ferguson* v. *Earl of Kinnoull* (1842) 9 Cl. and F. 321.

[3] (1830) 1 Mood. 263.

[4] (1840) 4 J.P. 508, tried on assize. In a footnote to the report of *R.* v. *Weare*, it is stated that the same principle was laid down in *R.* v. *Shrimpton* (1840) which was concerned with a charge of malicious stabbing with intent to do grievous bodily harm.

any evidence of express malice. The law will imply malice from the unlawful act itself; it is sufficient if the act be performed wilfully and wantonly".

Considering the many centuries throughout which malice has played a prominent part in our criminal law, the doctrine of implied malice is of comparatively recent origin. Yet there is no denying the fact that long before the end of the last century the notion had become firmly embedded in the minds of the judiciary. Following the lead given in the earlier cases, Platt, B., in *R.* v. *Foster*[1] explained to the jury that "everything wilfully done, if injurious, must be inferred to be done with malice". A few years later, in *R.* v. *Davies*,[2] Crompton, J. declared that malice does not mean "particular spite against the prosecutor. If a man being in his right mind burns property belonging to another, a jury ought to infer malice from the act itself". Any doubts as to its importance in determining criminal liability were finally dispelled by the Court for Crown Cases Reserved in *R.* v. *Martin*.[3] The accused in that case, with the intention of causing terror in the minds of a theatre audience, put out the lights on a staircase and placed an iron bar across one of the exits. Panic ensued with the result that several people were thrown down and severely injured. At the trial of the accused, who was charged with maliciously causing grievous bodily harm under the Offences against the Person Act 1861, s. 20, the Recorder had intimated to the jury that if they thought the defendant's conduct amounted to nothing more than a mere piece of foolish mischief they might acquit him, but that if they believed the acts were done with a deliberate and malicious intention they ought to convict. On the accused's appeal against conviction, Stephen, J., criticised the Recorder's direction as being too favourable to the prisoner and went on to assimilate the two expressions "wilfully" and "maliciously". Lord Coleridge, C. J., said that the accused acted maliciously, "not that he had any personal malice against the particular individuals injured, but in the sense of doing an unlawful act calculated to injure". With this statement of the law, Field, Hawkins, Stephen and Cave JJ., concurred.[4]

Many cases will be found in the reports containing practically

[1] (1852) 6 Cox C.C. 25.
[2] (1858) 1 F. and F. 69.
[3] (1881) 8 Q.B.D. 54.
[4] It was expressly followed by Grantham, J., in *R.* v. *Chapin* (1909) 22 Cox C.C. 10.

identical language to describe what is meant by implied malice.[1] To cite only two more examples taken from cases decided, first, when the fiction was first introduced, and secondly, at the present day. In 1829, Littledale, J., in an oft-quoted sentence, said that "malice in its legal sense denotes a wrongful act done intentionally without just cause or excuse",[2] while in 1948 we find Lord Goddard, C.J., pithily stating the same idea in the words, "if an unlawful act is done wilfully the law implies malice."[3]

In using such language wherein no reference is made to the *mens rea* required, the danger is that stress will be laid more and more on the doing of the unlawful act and less and less on the mind of the accused. The tendency will be to approximate the language relating to malicious crimes with that relating to crimes of absolute liability. As to the latter, "it has been laid down over and over again", according to Avory, J.,[4] "that where a statute absolutely prohibits the doing of an act it is sufficient to show that the person accused did the forbidden act intentionally and that it is not necessary to go further and show what is commonly known as *mens rea* or any intention other than to do the thing forbidden." The similarity in language, used to describe two totally different classes of crime, is self-evident.

When it is said that the fact that the accused did the forbidden act intentionally in itself supplies *mens rea*, it is submitted that this use of the phrase *mens rea* is unreal[5] and bound to cause con-

[1] See *R.* v. *Upton and Gutteridge* (1851) 5 Cox C.C. 298 *per* Wightman, J. and *R.* v. *Ward* (1872) 1 C.C.R. 356, at p. 360, *per* Blackburn, J.: "I have always thought a man acted maliciously when he wilfully does that which he knows will injure another in person or property." In *R.* v. *Pembliton* (1874) 2 C.C.R. 119 we find malice defined by Lord Coleridge, C.J. (at p. 122) as "the wilful doing of an intentional act" and by Blackburn, J., (at p. 122) to be "where any person wilfully does an act injurious to another without lawful excuse". Bowen, L.J. in *R.* v. *Latimer* (1886) 17 Q.B.D. 359, at p. 362, adopted the definition put forward by Blackburn, J., (*supra*). Similar interpretations were adopted in such South African cases as *R.* v. *Mashanga* 1924 A.D. 11, and *R.* v. *Bhaya* 1953 (3) S.A. 143 (N).

[2] *McPherson* v. *Daniels* (1829) 10 B. and C. 263.

[3] *Gott* v. *Measures* [1948] 1 K.B., at p. 239. The learned editor of *Russell on Crime* (10th ed.), p. 1664, referring to this passage, denies the existence in modern law of the doctrine of implied malice, maintaining that "malice" no longer has any association with the idea of "wickedness". This view is shared by Glanville Williams, *Criminal Law*, p. 65, who considers that "it is now a commonplace that 'malice' in law means intention or recklessness" (p. 62). However, later in the same treatise, the learned author equivocates, saying "as the name 'malicious' implies, it is directed only against those who wantonly interfere with the right of others" (p. 405). See, too, Perkins *Rationale of Mens Rea* (1939) 52 Harv. L.R. 905, 916.

[4] *Law Society* v. *United Service Bureau Ltd.* (1939) 98 J.P. 33, at p. 36.

[5] For a similar opinion, see *Outlines of Criminal Law* (16th ed.) p. 39, and Glanville Williams, *Criminal Law*, p. 262. The subject is dealt with fully in Chapter xi of this book.

fusion with its established meaning at common law. Two other points so often overlooked are, first, that the wrongful or forbidden "act" generally consists of a number of constituent elements, and secondly, that a wrong is intentional only when the intention extends to all the elements of the wrong.[1] Failure to recognise or apply this rule has been one cause of several unsatisfactory decisions to be discussed in subsequent chapters.

Transferred malice

The principle of transferred malice is by no means a recent innovation. It was recognised by the old writers Hale and East, who confined themselves to its use in relation to murder and arson, both common law offences. Thus, in his *Pleas of the Crown*, Hale says:[2] "If *A* by malice aforethought strikes at *B*, and missing him strikes *C* whereof he dies, though *A* never bore any malice to *C* yet it is murder and the law transfers the malice to the party slain." East extends the principle in a very wide fashion. Referring to the rule that for arson the burning must be malicious and not by mischance, he draws a distinction between two persons who accidentally set fire to a house, in the one case whilst merely shooting at game, and in the other case whilst shooting with intent to steal the game. In the first example, East says, there is no malice because the burning was by mischance. In the second example, however, the original intent to steal being felonious the party must abide all the consequences.[3]

The application of the doctrine of transferred malice in statutory offences may be said to have originated in the decision of all the judges in *R.* v. *Hunt*[4] in 1825. Yet, in the previous year, the principle had been rejected by Bayley, J., in *Curtis* v. *The Hundred of Godley*,[5] where the accused was charged with maliciously destroying trees belonging to *A*., as the result of a fire kindled upon the ground of *B*, but which spread rapidly to *A*'s property, situated a considerable distance away. Imbued with the old notion that malice against the owner was essential, Bayley, J., declared

[1] See Salmond, *Jurisprudence* (9th ed.), pp. 519–520, and Glanville Williams, *Criminal Law*, pp. 113–114, 114–120 (for its application to crimes of wilfulness), and 131–133 (for its application to crimes involving the word "knowingly").

[2] Vol. I, p. 466. See, too, p. 569 for another illustration based on arson.

[3] *Pl. of Cr.*, Vol. 2, p. 1019. In *R. v. Ward* (1872) 1 C.C.R. at p. 360, Cockburn, C.J., following a somewhat similar line of argument, posed the question: "When a man does an act malicious of itself, but without intending larger consequences, are not the limited results sufficient to make him responsible for all?"

[4] (1825) 1 Mood 93.

[5] (1824) 3 B. and C. 248.

that although there may be ground for saying that the offender acted from malice towards *B*, it could not properly be said that he acted from malice against *A*. Accordingly it was held that no offence was committed against the statute. The prisoner in *R.* v. *Hunt*[1] in trying to stab *B* with a knife and being forcibly restrained made a desperate rush forward and, instead, cut *A*. Basing his case on the decision in *Curtis* v. *Hundred of Godley*,[2] the accused maintained there was no evidence of malice against *A*, but against *B* only, but the judges ruled that general malice was sufficient under the statute. The term "general malice" is used here to describe what is now termed transferred malice, the latter expression being preferred by Hale in his *Pleas of the Crown*. That the two expressions are, in fact, synonymous becomes even more apparent when reference is made later to the judgment of Lord Coleridge, C.J., in *R.* v. *Latimer.*[3]

Its introduction into the field of statutory offences having been established, another fifty years elapsed before the doctrine of transferred malice once more engaged the attention of the judges. On this occasion, in *R.* v. *Pembliton*,[4] the very broad principle advanced by East did not commend itself to the Court for Crown Cases Reserved. In that case the accused was charged under section 51 of the Malicious Damage Act, 1861, with having unlawfully and maliciously damaged a large plate glass window in the prosecutor's public house. It appeared that the prisoner was one of a large party who had been turned out of the inn for being disorderly. On reaching the street a general fight ensued, from which the accused disengaged himself. Crossing to the other side of the road, he picked up a large stone and flung it at the persons with whom he had been fighting. He missed, and instead broke a window in the public house. The jury found that the accused's intention was to strike his opponents but not to break the window. Nevertheless, he was found guilty of malicious damage to property.

In quashing the conviction, Lord Coleridge attempted to explain, with rather an unusual lack of clarity, the principles underlying the court's decision. His process of reasoning, it is suggested,

[1] (1825) 1 Mood 93. [2] (1824) 3 B and C. 248.

[3] (1886) 17 Q.B.D. 359. See, *post*, p. 17.

[4] (1874) 2 C.C.R. 119, *coram*, Lord Coleridge, C.J., Blackburn, Lush, JJ., Pigott and Cleasby, BB. In *Hall* v. *Richardson* (1899) 6 T.L.R. 71 the learned Chief Justice got confused as to the facts in *R.* v. *Pembliton*.

was along the following lines.[1] The Malicious Damage Act and the Offences against the Person Act are concerned, respectively, with totally different species of harm, the former with damage to property, the latter with injuries to the person. Where the accused is charged with malicious damage to property and is shown to have intended to cause damage to property, malice will be implied from his intentionally doing the unlawful act. The same applies if in place of "damage to property" we are concerned with "injury to the person". Where, however, the accused is charged with malicious damage to property and is shown to have intended injury to the person, or vice versa, malice will not be implied. On the other hand, where it cannot be shown that the accused intended the very kind of injury charged, but must have known that the natural consequence of his act would be to cause a different species of harm (i.e., damage to property instead of injury to the person, or vice versa), and was reckless[2] whether such injury was occasioned or not, he is liable for the malicious damage or injury actually caused. These questions being questions of fact, and the issue of recklessness as to the window never having been put to the jury in *Pembliton's Case*, the court was left with no alternative but to quash the conviction.

Four years later, in *R.* v. *Faulkner*,[3] a strong Irish Court for Crown Cases Reserved disapproved the trial judge's direction to the jury which was based upon East's wide interpretation of the doctrine of transferred malice. The accused was charged with maliciously setting fire to the *Semindar*, a ship carrying a cargo of rum, sugar and cotton worth £50,000. The prisoner, a member of the ship's crew, went into the hold for the purpose of stealing some rum. Unfortunately for himself, and the shipowners, he went about his task clumsily. In lighting a match to see what he was

[1] Acknowledgment is due to Prof. Kenny who, in the first edition of his classic work *Outlines of Criminal Law*, published in 1902, propounded a comprehensive definition of "malice" as requiring either (1) an actual intention to do the particular kind of harm that in fact was done, or (2) recklessness as to whether such harm should occur or not. This definition is accepted almost verbatim by Paton, *Jurisprudence* (2nd ed.), p. 247.

[2] This test appears in the judgments of both Lord Coleridge, C.J., and Blackburn, J., and, it is suggested, is used in the subjective sense of foresight of consequences. See the discussion of this particular state of mind, *post*, pp. 202–203, and also Glanville Williams, *Criminal Law*, p. 62, n. 1, and p. 63, suggesting that inadvertent negligence is not enough to constitute malice. A recent instance of the application of recklessness in malice is to be seen in *O'Driscoll* v. *Kildare County Council* (1953) 86 *Irish Law Times* 176.

[3] (1878) Ir. R. 11 C.L. 8; (1877) 13 Cox C.C. 550.

doing the rum caught fire, which soon enveloped and destroyed the entire ship. It was conceded that the accused had no actual intention of burning the vessel, but the jury were directed to find him guilty if they found that the fire originated whilst he was engaged in committing the felony of stealing rum. As East put it, "the original intent being felonious the party must abide all the consequences." On this direction a verdict of guilty was inevitable. It is fairly obvious that the decision in *R.* v. *Pembliton* was not known to at least one member of the Irish bench, for not until the second hearing of the appeal did the trial judge add a paragraph to his stated case adverting to the question of recklessness. Even then he makes the surprising statement that he "was not asked to leave any question to the jury as to the prisoner's knowing the probable consequences of his act, or as to his reckless conduct". With one dissenting voice, the full court rejected the trial judge's ruling on the application of transferred intent.

Further approval for the principles enunciated in *R.* v. *Pembliton* was given in the equally well-known case of *R.* v. *Latimer*.[1] Once again the scene took place in a public house with the unfortunate proprietress as the victim. The prisoner, in aiming a blow with his belt at his adversary, only managed to strike him slightly. The belt bounced off and struck the proprietress, who happened to be standing talking to the person assailed, cutting her face open and wounding her severely. The accused was charged under the Offences against the Person Act, 1861, s. 20, with maliciously wounding the proprietress. In answer to a question left them by the trial judge, the jury found that the striking of the prosecutrix was purely accidental and not such a consequence as the accused ought to have expected. Nevertheless, the judge directed a finding of guilty which was upheld by the Court for Crown Cases Reserved.[2]

The question naturally asked is how can the two decisions in *R.* v. *Pembliton* and *R.* v. *Latimer* be distinguished. The answer is dependent on the kind of harm intended and also the kind of harm in fact occasioned. Where, as in *Latimer*, *A* does an unlawful

[1] (1886) 17 Q.B.D. 359. Commenting on this case in (1886) 2 *L.Q.R.* 536, the learned editor writes: "Questions of this kind have given abundant exercise to Continental writers on the theory of criminal responsibility. The comparatively rough methods of our own criminal jurisprudence are perhaps sufficient for the common purpose of justice."

[2] Consisting of Lord Coleridge, C.J., Lord Esher, M.R., Bowen, L.J., Field and Manisty, JJ.

act intending to injure *B*'s person but accidentally injures *C*'s person, the express or implied malice against *B* is transferred against *C*. The species of harm is the same, namely, injury to the person, therefore the fact that *A* could not have foreseen the injury to *C* is immaterial. Where, as in *Pembliton*, *A* does an unlawful act intending to injure *B*'s person but accidentally damages *C*'s property, the express or implied malice against *B*'s person is not transferred against *C*'s property, unless it can be shown that *A* was reckless as to the damage to *C*'s property.

Little thought seems to have been given to determining the limits of this convenient theory.[1] One of the principal questions that suggests itself is this. Where the ultimate harm caused is of the same species as that originally intended, is a person to be held responsible however extended the chain of events which follow upon his unlawful act? Or is there to be introduced a set of rules similar to those on remoteness of damage in the law of tort. Take the following hypothetical situation. The defendant, annoyed with his bull, thrusts a pitchfork into its side. Incensed, the bull runs amok causing widespread damage, finally entering a prefabricated house where it upsets a table lamp resulting in the house being set on fire. Both kinds of damage, to the bull and the prefabricated house, fall within the Malicious Damage Act and are, therefore, presumably, to be considered the same species of harm to which the rule of transferred malice applies.[2] A glance at the sections in that enactment will indicate at once the widely different variety of things which are protected under the general heading of malicious damage to property. Fact is stranger than fiction is an old saying, and if the doctrine of transferred malice is as wide as seems apparent, it is impossible to conceive the strange turns through which the wheel of responsibility will lead a wrongdoer.

General and particular malice

Finally, there occasionally appears in the reports the terms "general" and "particular" malice. Particular malice is used to

[1] A notable recent exception is to be found in Glanville Williams' *Criminal Law*, pp. 101–110, where acknowledgment is made to the study of this subject by Wechsler and Michael in 37 *Col. L. Rev.* at pp. 1295–8.

[2] By virtue of the special provisions in the Malicious Damage Act, 1861, s. 7, an intent to commit malicious damage by fire to chattels in a house will not be transferred so as to support a conviction for arson (under s. 3) if the fire unintentionally spreads to the house. See *R.* v. *Child* (1871) 1 C.C.R. 307 and *R.* v. *Nattrass* (1882) 15 Cox C.C. 73.

describe the special form of statutory malice required; for example, under the Malicious Damage Act, 1861, the adjective refers exclusively to malicious damage to property.[1] General malice, on the other hand, is the phrase used by some judges to explain the principle of transferred malice. An instance of such use is seen in Lord Coleridge's judgment in *R.* v. *Latimer* when he said:[2] "It is common knowledge that a man who has an unlawful and malicious intent against another and, in attempting to carry it out, injures a third person, is guilty of what the law deems malice against the person injured, because the offender is doing an unlawful act and has that which the judges call general malice, and that is enough."

This alternative description of what is generally described as transferred malice is both inappropriate and unnecessary. Indeed, it is doubtful where there exists any necessity for the term "general malice".[3] At any rate, it is suggested that the adjective "general" should have a wider application and be synonymous with what Kenny describes as "universal malice". He uses it in relation to malice aforethought, saying it describes the case of a man who intends to kill, but who does not select any particular individual as the victim. In the case of statutory crimes, "general" or "universal" malice would describe the state of mind of a man bent on causing damage or injury to property or persons in general, having no particular individual or item of property as his prospective target.

Claim of right in malicious crimes

So much for the different senses in which the term malice is applied. The necessity for *mens rea* is universally accepted, though, as we have seen, there are certain dangers to be avoided, and some uncertainties still to be resolved. Attention must next be directed to another practical problem, namely, the significance of a bona fide claim of right in statutory crimes involving malice. To what extent does the existence of such a claim of right rebut proof of *mens rea*? This question has become of particular interest since the

[1] See Bowen, L.J., in *R.* v. *Latimer* (1886) 17 Q.B.D., at p. 362, and Blackburn, J. in *R.* v. *Pembliton* (1874) 2 C.C.R., at p. 120.

[2] At p. 361. Cf. *R.* v. *Hunt* (1825) 1 Mood. 93, discussed *ante* pp. 12–13.

[3] Jerome Hall in his *General Principles of Criminal Law*, pp. 450–2, describes the use of such terms as "transferred" and "general" intent as "cumbersome and hazardous to clear analysis, but defensible on grounds of policy".

recent decision of the Divisional Court in *Gott* v. *Measures* (1948),[1] which will be examined later.

At the outset it is essential to get quite clear the two different rôles in which a claim of right appears. It may serve either as a ground for ousting the magistrates' jurisdiction, or as a complete defence. The difference between these two functions is that where the plea of ouster of jurisdiction is successfully raised the magistrates merely refrain from adjudicating,[2] whereas in cases where a claim of right is upheld as a defence the accused is completely acquitted. Another difference, of course, is that the plea of ouster may only arise in cases which are heard before a court of summary jurisdiction,[3] whereas the defence of claim of right may be raised and determined by any court hearing a criminal trial. The importance of keeping the two rôles separate will become apparent when we discuss the rules governing claim of right as an ouster and as a defence respectively. The danger arises when the line of demarcation is either forgotten or ignored. It is proposed to examine both rôles in turn.

Claim of right as an ouster of jurisdiction

Such a plea may rest on either the common law or special statutory provision. Taking, first, the position at common law. In order to set up successfully a claim of right which will oust the jurisdiction of the justices, it is necessary to show that the right can exist in point of law and that it relates to a question of title to real property. It follows that if the right claimed is not within that class of rights which are recognised as being maintainable in point of law the jurisdiction is not ousted, and the magistrates may proceed to try the case.[4] Thus, in *Heaven* v. *Crutchley*[5] the

[1] [1948] 1 K.B. 234, discussed *post*, pp. 23–27.

[2] In *R.* v. *Holsworthy Justices* [1952] 1 All E. R. 411, Lord Goddard C.J. said (at p. 413) of the plea of ouster: "it does not mean that the justices should dismiss the summons because they have not power to hear and determine it. They must act as if the offence was one only triable on indictment, take the depositions, and commit for trial if they find a prima facie case made out."

[3] Mr. J. W. C. Turner in the 10th edition of *Russell on Crime*, p. 1903, referring to the application of ouster in courts of quarter sessions, concludes that there is no authority either way as to whether such courts have jurisdiction to try cases in which a question of title is involved.

[4] This rule was laid down as early as 1700 in *R.* v. *Speed*, 1 Ld. Raym. 583 and repeated in *Calcraft* v. *Gibbs* (1792) 5 Term. Rep. 19. It was upheld by Blackburn, J. in *Cornwell* v. *Sanders* (1862) 32 L.J.M.C. 6 and in *Hudson* v. *MacRae* (1863) 33 L.J.M.C. 65. A full discussion of the limitations of the rule appears in *Russell on Crime*, (10th ed.), pp. 1899–1903.

[5] (1903) 68 J.P. 53.

appellants, charged under the Malicious Damage Act, 1861, s. 23, with maliciously damaging certain plants and vegetables, maintained that they had acted in the bona fide and reasonable exercise of their customary right as members of the public at large to roam over certain lands, and of free access thereto for the purpose of recreation. The justices, being of the opinion that the right claimed did not and could not legally exist and was, therefore, absurd and unreasonable in point of law, proceeded to try the case and convict the defendants. The ruling of the magistrates was upheld as clearly right by the Divisional Court consisting of Lord Alverstone, C.J., Wills and Channell JJ. There is also a succinct but valuable statement of the true principle in *Croydon R.D.C.* v. *Crowley*,[1] where Jelf, J., declared: "In order to set up successfully a claim of right which will oust [the magistrates'] jurisdiction either by virtue of the common law principle or of the proviso [to section 52 of the Malicious Damage Act 1861] it is necessary that the claim should be one which has a foundation in law."

The artificial results obtained by applying these rules can best be judged by comparing the case of *A*, who claims a right as one of the public to fish in the non-tidal part of a river, and *B* who claims a similar right in respect of the tidal river. The law only recognises a public right to fish in that part of a river which is regarded as the tidal reach; consequently a difference in the *locus in quo* which may be a matter of yards only will enable *B* to succeed where *A* must fail.[2] Assuming the right claimed is maintainable in law, the next question for the justices is to decide whether the claim is honest and bona fide. Only if satisfied on this point also, will the summary jurisdiction be finally ousted.

It is, of course, open to the legislature to modify or curtail the common law rule. Concerned as we are with statutory crimes of malice it is to be noted that throughout the Malicious Damage Act, 1861, only one section provides expressly for a claim of right as an ouster of summary jurisdiction. That section, section 52,[3] creates the residuary summary offence of wilfully or maliciously injuring any real or personal property in any circumstances not

[1] (1909) 100 L.T. 441.

[2] Cf. *R.* v. *Stimpson* (1863) 32 L.J.M.C. 208 (tidal river) with *Hudson* v. *MacRae* (*supra*) (non-tidal river).

[3] Now repealed and replaced, with certain amendments, by the Criminal Justice Administration Act, 1914, (4 and 5 Geo. 5, c. 58), s. 14. The later enactment differentiates the punishment awardable according to the amount of damage occasioned. Cf. Offences against the Person Act, 1861, s. 46.

expressly provided for elsewhere in the Act, and declares that the section shall not apply "where the alleged offender acted under a fair and reasonable supposition that he had a right to do the act complained of". Three points need stressing here. First, this proviso does not constitute a defence in the true sense of the word—it is concerned with ouster of the magistrates' jurisdiction; secondly, it is confined to charges arising under section 52; thirdly, in its restricted application it supersedes the common law as to bona fide claim of right as an ouster.

These points appear clearly from the judgment of Blackburn, J., in *White* v. *Feast*,[1] in which the learned judge distinguished between "the well-established rule, that every statute giving summary jurisdiction has the implied restriction as to title, and that the justices must hold their hands if a bona fide claim of right is set up" and "another rule that wherever jurisdiction is given summarily to punish an offence, as there can be no crime unless there be *mens rea*, if the alleged offender bona fide thinks he has a right to do the act, that would be a *defence*". Referring next to the actual wording of section 52, Blackburn, J., said a man may be convicted of maliciously doing an injury under the section if, although he acted with a bona fide claim of right, he had no fair and reasonable ground for his supposition. As he put it, where "the proviso expressly says that the claim of right must be founded on reasonable grounds the ordinary proviso, usually implied as to mere bona fides, is superseded."[2] Cockburn, C.J., expressed the same view in the sentence: "The legislature . . . having expressly stated the limit, it is not for us to impose any other limit; the express restriction supersedes the implied restriction."[3]

To sum up, whether the accused bases his plea of ouster on a bona fide claim of right or a fair and reasonable supposition of right will be determined according to the section of the Malicious Damage Act under which he is charged. Two obstacles must be successfully surmounted. The first is the same in both cases, namely, that the right is capable of existing in law. The second differs according to the basis of the defendant's plea. To a charge under section 52 the accused must show that his supposition was

[1] (1872) L.R. 7 Q.B. 353. For a discussion of other cases in which section 52 has been interpreted by the courts, see *Russell on Crime*, (10th ed.), p. 1577 *et seq.*

[2] *Ibid.*, pp. 359–360. See, too, *Brooks* v. *Hamlyn* (1899) 63 J.P. 215; *Heaven* v. *Crutchley* (1903) 68 J.P. 53; and *R.* v. *Crowley* (1909) 100 L.T. 441.

[3] *Ibid.*, p. 357.

fair and reasonable judged by an objective standard; to a charge under any other section, the accused must show that he honestly and bona fide believed his claim of right to justify his action, the test here being subjective.

This discussion on ouster of jurisdiction has been introduced deliberately to point out that the law governing claim of right as a ground for ouster is totally independent of the law relating to claim of right as a defence.[1] Ouster of jurisdiction is a matter of criminal procedure, whereas the validity of a defence to a criminal charge is a matter of substantive law. The question of *mens rea* does not arise when a plea of ouster is raised, whereas it is the vital issue when claim of right is pleaded as a defence. Therefore, when it is said that summary jurisdiction will only be ousted if the right claimed is maintainable in law, it does not follow that the same rule applies where a claim of right is put forward as a defence.

Claim of right or mistaken belief as a defence

When we turn to consider the second rôle in which a claim of right appears, namely, as a defence, we are concerned solely with the common law. Unfortunately, the law is far from clear on the crucial point of what is the governing test. It is submitted that in any case where claim of right or mistaken belief is put forward *as a defence* to a statutory crime involving malice, the question is not whether the right or belief is maintainable in law or not, but whether the accused himself honestly believed he had a right to do what he did. The reasonableness of the claim of right or of the mistaken belief, or again of the steps taken to protect or enforce such right or belief, is a factor, but not the deciding factor, in determining whether the accused acted in good faith.

It will be well to examine the cases for and against the view put forward. One of the earliest exponents of the subjective test was Lord Abinger in *R.* v. *James*.[2] A dispute had arisen between the owners of adjoining mines and one of the owners, asserting that a certain airway belonged to him, directed his workmen to stop it up. The accused acting bona fide, and believing his employer to have a right to do so, assisted with the work and was duly charged with maliciously obstructing the airway. In the course of his

[1] The distinction between these two different concepts of claim of right was recently considered by the Queensland High Court in *Clarkson* v. *Aspinall* [1950] St. R. Qd. 79. A note on this case appears in (1951) 1 Queensland L.J., p. 62.

[2] (1837) 8 C. and P. 131, a case arising under 7 and 8 Geo. 4, c. 30, s. 6.

summing up, Lord Abinger said:[1] "If a man claims a right whic he knows not to exist, and he tells his servants to exercise it, an they do so acting bona fide, I am of the opinion that that is not felony in them even if in so doing they obstruct the airway of mine." The same eminent judge was concerned with the cas of *R.* v. *Day*,[2] in which the accused was charged with maliciousl maiming and wounding four sheep belonging to his neighbou The sheep having trespassed on his land, the defendant impounde them and demanded compensation. On his neighbour refusing t do so, the accused said: "Very well then, I'll go and prosecut the sheep and you shall not see them any more." Lord Abinger le it to the jury to say whether the prisoner had acted maliciousl or whether he had maimed the sheep under a mistaken claim c right to do the act complained of, for "it was no offence within th statute[3] for a man to do an act which he conceived himsel however erroneously, to be justified by his rights in carrying int execution". The accused was found not guilty.

In *R.* v. *Mathews and Twigg*,[4] another case of maliciousl stopping up an airshaft, we find Brett, J., saying that where th act charged is done under a bona fide claim of right, it is not don maliciously. Insomuch as the evidence showed that the prisone did the act after notice and openly, it was, he said, "preposterou to say that he did it otherwise than under a bona fide claim of righ Whether he had a right or not must be tried in a civil court." I other words, it is the good faith of the accused and not the rigl itself which is of prime consideration. Perhaps the best know among this series of cases is *R.* v. *Twose*,[5] in which the accused w

[1] *Ibid.*, p. 133. See, too, Lord Denman's judgment in *James* v. *Phelps* (1840) 11 and E. 483, at p. 489, in which the direction of Lord Abinger (*supra*) was approve The court, which also included Littledale and Williams JJ., rejected the contentic that "malicious" meant merely the intentional, as opposed to accidental, doing of wrongful act.

[2] (1844) 8 J.P. 186.

[3] This was the consolidating statute of 1827 (7 and 8 Geo. 4, c. 30), upon which w based the Malicious Damage Act, 1861.

[4] (1876) 14 Cox C.C. 5. See also *Watkins* v. *Major* (1878) 44 L.J.M.C. 164, at p. 16 where Lord Coleridge C.J. said: "where there must be *mens rea* to constitute offence, an honest claim of right, however absurd, would frustrate a summary co viction."

[5] (1879) 14 Cox C.C. 327. See too *Leyson* v. *Williams* (1890) 54 J.P. 631, and *R.* *Rutter* (1908) 1 Cr. App. R. 174. Likewise in the United States it has been held th there is no malice where the act is done in good faith under an honest claim of right in *Barlow* v. *State* 120 Ind. 56 it was said that the machinery of the criminal law was n to be set in motion to redress merely private grievances, or to settle questions of pr perty, where honest differences of opinion are involved.

charged with having maliciously set fire to some furze growing on a common. Her defence was that persons living near the common had occasionally burnt the furze to improve the growth of the grass, and she bona fide believed that she had a right to do likewise. In fact, no such right existed, but as Lopes, J., said, "If she set fire to the furze thinking she had a right to do so that would not be a criminal offence." The defendant was acquitted.

These cases, it is submitted, in which claim of right was put forward *as a defence*, show that the judges were not at all concerned with the legality or otherwise of the right under which the accused purported to act. In each case the decision hinged around the question whether the claim of right was honestly and bona fide held by the prisoner.[1] That question is essentially one of fact. When we turn to examine the decision in *Gott* v. *Measures*,[2] it is with considerable surprise that we read of the Divisional Court rejecting the accused's plea of a claim of right on the ground that the right was one which the law did not recognise. It has already been pointed out that in cases where the issue is one of ouster of jurisdiction, it is necessary to show that the right claimed was maintainable in law. But in *Gott* v. *Measures* that was not the issue before the court; instead, the question was whether a bona fide claim of right was a valid defence. How then can the decision be justified, particularly having regard to the body of authority discussed above?

It is necessary to look at the case a little closer. The accused was charged under the Malicious Damage Act 1861, s. 41, with maliciously killing a dog which was trespassing on land over which he had the full sporting rights. Having first torn a hen pheasant to pieces, the dog was chasing a hare when it was shot dead by the accused. Its owner had been warned several times about the dog trespassing. Lord Goddard felt no doubt as to the law under which, he said, "A person may be justified in shooting a dog if he honestly believes that it is necessary as being *the only way* in which he can protect his property. For example, if a farmer finds a dog chasing his sheep which may result in incalculable damage, and *the only way* in which he can protect his flock is by shooting the dog, he

[1] Specific reference to this question is made in both the Criminal Code of Western Australia, s. 22, and that of Queensland, s. 22 which declare: ". . . a person is not criminally responsible for an offence relating to property, for an act done or omitted to be done by him with respect to any property in the exercise of an honest claim of right and without intention to defraud."

[2] [1948] 1 K.B. 234.

would be justified in doing so."[1] Since the accused only had the sporting rights he had no property in the land nor in the game. His position in relation to wild game was identical with that of a landowner, neither had any property in the hare until he had shot it and taken it. Therefore, Lord Goddard, C.J., concluded: "Just as you cannot have a bona fide claim of right if the right is one which the law does not recognise, so it seems to me you cannot honestly believe that it is necessary to shoot a dog to protect your property when you have no property".[2] If this decision is correct, every landowner would appear to be amenable to a criminal charge every time he shoots a marauding dog which comes on his land in search of live wild game. Let the pheasant or the hare be dead before the landowner shoots and he can then plead a bona fide claim of right. Surely this is a remarkable interpretation of the law.

This statement of the governing principles, it is submitted, is defective in three separate respects. In the first place, it is a fallacy to proclaim that a claim of right is *only* maintainable where the accused has acted in defence of his property.[2] No such limitation is provided by statute or at common law. Take the case of a person who kills a dog under the honest but mistaken belief that he had received instructions from its owner to destroy the animal. There is no law which prevents him from successfully pleading a bona fide belief of his right to act as he did.

Secondly, it is inaccurate to state that if the accused has, in fact, acted in defence of his property the claim of right will only be deemed bona fide if he can show that there was *no other way* of doing so. It is significant that the Court of Appeal in *Cresswell* v. *Sirl*,[3] decided almost simultaneously with *Gott* v. *Measures*, rejected the harsh test propounded by the Divisional Court and, instead, accepted as a sufficient defence proof that the defendant's act in shooting a marauding animal was reasonably necessary in the circumstances. A few years later, in *Goodway* v. *Becher*,[4] the

[1] *Ibid.*, p. 239.

[2] See (1948) 64 *L.Q.R.*, p. 39, for a criticism of *Gott* v. *Measures*, based upon this particular ground. See, too, the discussion of this case in *Russell on Crime*, (10th ed.) pp. 1662–1664, and in Kenny's *Outlines of Criminal Law*, (16th ed.) pp. 191, 192.

[3] [1948] 1 K.B. 241, 249. See too *Hamps* v. *Darby* [1948] 2 K.B. 311, and *Thayer* v. *Newman* [1953] *The Times*, October 14. Opinion in the United States appears to follow similar lines, it being held in *People* v. *Kane*, 131 N.Y. 111 that it is a good defence to a charge of maliciously killing to prove that the killing of the animal was done to protect his crop and that the animal had a habitual proclivity for the commission of mischief.

[4] [1951] 2 All E.R. 349.

Divisional Court was presented with the opportunity of rectifying its earlier lamentable decision in *Gott* v. *Measures*. Since both cases turned on the same section of the Malicious Damage Act, it is particularly unfortunate that the earlier authority was apparently not even cited to the Divisional Court who may, therefore, plead that they were not given the opportunity to reconsider the decision in *Gott* v. *Measures*. Suffice it for the moment to say that the injustice done in that case was partly remedied by adopting the less stringent test laid down by the Court of Appeal. Examination of the facts in *Goodway* v. *Becher* indicates that little essential difference is discernible between the facts in the two criminal cases. On this occasion the offending dog had been seen on successive days worrying the defendant's fowls, and its owner had been warned that the dog would be shot if seen repeating its attacks. The following day the bitch was again caught in the act and the accused shot and killed it. Having regard to the unequivocal statement of the law in *Gott* v. *Measures* it is not surprising to find the justices in the present case, being of the opinion that while the defendant acted under considerable provocation he had not exhausted every practicable means of stopping the dog from attacking his fowls, convicted the defendant. To say of the magistrates' decision, as Lord Goddard C.J. did,[1] that they approached the case from a wrong point of view is, in effect, an admission that the court was itself wrong in *Gott* v. *Measures*. Without apparently realising the departure being created from their earlier ruling, the Divisional Court in *Goodway* v. *Becher* adopted the language of Scott, L.J., in *Cresswell* v. *Sirl*, requiring proof only that "the defendant, having regard to all the circumstances in which he found himself, acted reasonably in regarding the shooting as necessary for the protection of the animals against attack or renewed attack".[2]

[1] *Ibid.*, at p. 350.

[2] [1948] 1 K.B. 241 at p. 249. In the recently published Report (Cmd. 5746) of the Goddard Committee on the Law of Civil Liability for Damage done to Animals, the recommendation is made that when a farmer or other occupier sees a dog trespassing and shoots it, it should be a defence to prove (*a*) that the dog when shot was committing a trespass on land in the occupation of the defendant or his employer, (*b*) that he reasonably believed that cattle or poultry on that land had been or would be injured by reason of such trespass, and (*c*) that within 48 hours after the dog was shot he gave notice of the shooting to the nearest police station. These recommendations in substance follow the provisions of the Dogs Act (Northern Ireland) 1927. The Committee suggested that if their recommendations are adopted, consideration should be given to amending section 41 of the Malicious Damage Act, 1861, along similar lines. It is interesting to note that in 1952 over 5,000 sheep were killed and over 4,000 sheep

Finally, criticism is directed against the statement that a claim of right is only available if the right is one which the law recognises. It has already been pointed out that this may well be true in regard to a plea of ouster of jurisdiction, but, it is submitted, there is no such sweeping restriction so far as the common law defence is concerned. The essence of a bona fide claim of right is that it rebuts any presumption or proof of *mens rea*. In the case of malicious injuries that *mens rea* is malice; in the case of larceny that *mens rea* is *animus furandi*, i.e. a fraudulent intent to deprive the owner permanently. The definition of larceny in the Larceny Act, 1916,[1] which is declaratory of the common law, expressly provides that "a claim of right made in good faith" shall be a defence. Furthermore, it has been held by the Court of Criminal Appeal in *R.* v. *Bernhard*,[2] that an unbroken chain of authority supports the principle that "a person has a claim of right within the meaning of the section if he is honestly asserting what he believes to be a lawful claim, even though it be unfounded in law or in fact".[3] If that is so, why should the common law be different —as was suggested in *Gott* v. *Measures*—when a bona fide claim of right is pleaded as a defence to crimes requiring *mens rea* in the form of malice?

It is worth noting that none of the cases discussed earlier, in which the subjective test was applied, was apparently cited to the court in *Gott* v. *Measures*.[4] On the other hand, occasion was taken to doubt the correctness of Lord Coleridge's interpretation of the

were injured by dogs in Great Britain. In addition 17 cattle and over 20,000 poultry were killed by marauding dogs. The recommendations of the Goddard Committee were ignored in the Dogs (Protection of Livestock) Act, 1953 (1 and 2 Eliz. 2, c. 25), s. 1 (1) of which provides that the owner of a dog which worries livestock on any agricultural land, or the person in charge of such dog, shall be guilty of an offence. There is no offence where the livestock are trespassing on the land except, according to section 1 (3), where the occupier causes the dog to attack the livestock.

[1] Section 1 (i).

[2] (1938) 26 Cr. App. R. 137.

[3] *Ibid.*, p. 144, *per* Charles, J. One of the earliest instances of this principle, not cited in *Bernard*, is *R.* v. *Hall* (1828) 3 C. and P. 409.

[4] Nor, it would seem, were they cited in *Miles* v. *Hutchings* [1903] 2 K.B. 714, which case the court in *Gott* v. *Measures* purported to follow. The learned editor of *Russell on Crime* (10th ed.), Mr. J. W. C. Turner, criticising *Gott* v. *Measures* (at pp. 1662–1665), draws the same distinction (*supra*) between claim of right as an ouster and as a defence, and reaches the same conclusion as above, *viz.*, that where the defendant's belief is put forward as a defence "he may in law . . . put forward a bona fide claim of a supposed right which the law does not recognise". Likewise, Glanville Williams, *Criminal Law*, pp. 404–405.

law in *Daniel* v. *James*,[1] in which that judge said that section 41 of the Malicious Damage Act does not apply to an act done under an impression, right or wrong, that the party is justified in protecting his premises from a trespass by such means, especially after notice given. Such a rule, it was felt, was too wide. Reference was made to an earlier opinion[2] that the defence would not apply if the accused knew that much less violent measures would attain his object. This may well be true, but is not the position this, that the steps taken to uphold a claim of right are evidence, nothing more, which the jury must take into consideration when deciding the question of the accused's good faith? Certainly this was the attitude adopted by a very strong court in *R.* v. *Clemens*.[3] If this conclusion is correct, it seems that Lord Coleridge's language is fully in accord with the common law, and follows the earlier authorities in holding that the governing test of a bona fide claim of right is subjective.

Is the validity of such a defence to be judged objectively or subjectively?

Whether a defendant's claim not to have acted maliciously is to be judged by an objective or by a subjective standard is a vital question, and was directly involved in the latest case of *Goodway* v. *Becher*.[4] If the test is objective, to establish a defence on the grounds that he honestly believed he was entitled to do what he did the defendant must show that both his belief and conduct were reasonable. This, it would appear, is the prevailing view of the Divisional Court—at any rate where the *mens rea* involved is that of malice. If, on the contrary, the test is subjective, it follows that the reasonableness of the defendant's behaviour ceases to be a decisive condition and, instead, becomes only one of many factors to be taken into account when considering whether the accused acted bona fide and without malice.

In assessing the relative merits of these alternative tests it is

[1] [1877] 2 C.P.D. 351, at p. 353. This case was followed, albeit grudgingly, in *Smith* v. *Williams* (1892) 56 J.P. 840. Compare, too, *Bryan* v. *Eaton* (1875) 40 J.P. 213.

[2] Wills, J., in *Miles* v. *Hutchings* (*supra*), at p. 717.

[3] [1898] 1 Q.B. 557 (*coram*, Lord Russell of Killowen, C.J., Grantham, Wright, Bigham and Darling, JJ.), in which it was suggested that a proper direction to the jury would be that "if on the facts before them, the jury came to the conclusion that the defendant did more damage then they could reasonably suppose to be necessary for the assertion and protection of that right, then the jury may properly and ought to find the defendant guilty of malicious damage". On this case see Glanville Williams, *Criminal Law*, pp. 402–403.

[4] [1951] 2 All E.R. 349.

necessary to anticipate discussion later in this study of the recent decision in *Wilson* v. *Inyang*,[1] where the offence charged under the Medical Act 1858, s. 40, requires proof of *mens rea* in the form of "wilfully and falsely". In that case the Divisional Court consisting of Lord Goddard, C.J., Lynskey and Devlin JJ., recognised the subjective test as being the criterion for establishing a defence of honest belief. Unless, therefore, the court is prepared to withdraw from this new but altogether welcome attitude towards the reasonableness of the defendant's behaviour there exists an obvious conflict of principle according to whether the *mens rea* involved is that of wilfulness or, alternatively, malice. Such a position is ludicrous and should not be allowed to continue. It is suggested that whenever a crime requires proof of *mens rea* admitting of the possibility of a defence of mistaken but honest belief or claim of right, the lead given by the decision in *Wilson* v. *Inyang* should be followed and the validity of such a defence determined by reference to a subjective standard.

[1] [1951] 2 K.B. 799.

II

WILFULNESS

THE next task is to determine what part the basic principle of criminal law, that no man is guilty unless he has a guilty mind, plays in statutory offences based upon wilful conduct. It will become apparent that, as with crimes involving malice, there is some divergence of opinion among the judges as to the answer to this problem.[1] At the root of this conflict is the twofold interpretation given to the words "wilful" and "wilfully". On the one hand, the court will be found in certain statutory offences to interpret "wilfully" as requiring proof of a " knowingly wrongful act", that is to say, the accused did the prohibited act with knowledge of the circumstances which constitute the offence. Conversely, and less frequently, it will be found that the term "wilfully" is sometimes defined as simply requiring proof of the intentional doing of the forbidden act by the accused. It is impossible to predicate in advance which interpretation will be adopted by the courts, and it must be recognised that the presence of the epithet "wilful" in a statutory offence is not automatically understood by the judges as denoting the necessity for a guilty mind. It is a matter for consideration whether this two-fold interpretation is justified or desirable.

[1] The same conflict of opinion is manifest in the United States cases. Thus in *U.S.* v. *Murdock* (1933) 290 U.S. 389, in which the charge was that of wilfully failing to pay and to supply information for tax purposes, contrary to the Revenue Act, 1926, s. 1114 (*a*), Roberts, J., delivering the judgment of the Supreme Court said: "The word 'wilful' often denotes an act which is intentional or voluntary as distinguished from accidental. But when used in a criminal statute it generally means an act done with a bad purpose . . . without just excuse . . . ; stubbornly, obstinately, perversely . . . . The word is also employed to characterize a thing done without ground for believing it is lawful . . . ; or conduct marked by careless disregard whether or not one has the right so to act." A few years later in *Townsend* v. *U.S.* (1938) U.S. 664, however, the Supreme Court said it was clear that the Court in *Murdock* did not intend to limit the application of the word "wilful" in all cases to "acts done with a bad purpose". Generally, it was said, "wilful" means "no more than that the person charged with the duty knows what he is doing. It does not mean that, in addition, he must suppose that he is breaking the law". Other important U.S. cases to which reference should be made in this connection are: *Sinclair* v. *U.S.* 279 U.S. 263; *People* v. *O'Brien* (1892) 96 Cal. 171, 176–177; and *People* v. *McCalla* (1923) 63 Cal. App. 783. A selection of U.S. cases on the meaning of "wilfully" are also to be found in (1937) 50 *Harv. L.R.* 616, 644–646, and Miller, *Criminal Law*, p. 70.

SURVEY OF STATUTORY OFFENCES BASED ON THE EXPRESSION "WILFULLY"

Among the earliest statutes in which the epithet "wilfully" appears is the Uniformity of Service Act, 1548,[1] which made it an offence for any person, vicar or minister to "use, wilfully and obstinately . . . any other Administration of Sacrament or other open prayer than is mentioned and set forth in the Book of Common Prayer".[2] It is repeatedly used in the first Perjury Act of 1562,[3] and, thereafter, continued to make its appearance in such enactments as the Black Act, 1723,[4] the Royal Marriage Act, 1772,[5] the Licensing of Alehouses Act, 1822,[6] and the Licensing Act, 1828.[7] Among the varied list of statutes still in force wherein the terms "wilful" and "wilfully" are used as the basis of criminal offences are the Vagrancy Act, 1824,[8] the Perjury Act, 1911,[9] the Larceny Acts, 1861[10] and 1916,[11] the Solicitors Act, 1932,[12] the Marriage Act, 1949,[13] and the Pharmacy Act, 1954.[14] The Black Act, 1723, is of added interest because it used the term "wilfully" in conjunction with the word "maliciously" making it a felony (*inter alia*) to "wilfully and maliciously shoot at any person". This coupling of the terms is unusual,[15] but occasionally they are

[1] 2 and 3 Edw. 6, c. 1. [2] *Ibid.*, s. 9. [3] 5 Eliz. c. 9. [4] 9 Geo. I, c. 22.
[5] 12 Geo. 3, c. 11, s. 3. [6] 3 Geo. 4, c. 77, s. 18. [7] 9 Geo. 4, c. 58, s. 16.
[8] 5 Geo. 4, c. 83, s. 3. [9] 1 and 2 Geo. 5, c. 6, s. 1 (1). [10] 24 and 25 Vict. c. 96, s. 23.
[11] 6 and 7 Geo. 5, c. 50, s. 35. A similar provision is to be found in the Forgery Act, 1913, s. 11.
[12] 22 Geo. 5, c. 37, s. 46.
[13] 12, 13 and 14 Geo. 6, c. 76, s. 76 (3). Other statutes in which the term "wilfully" appears include the Children and Young Persons Act, 1933, s. 1 (1); Offences against the Person Act, 1861, ss. 26, 31 and 35; Companies Act, 1948, s. 71; Midwives Act, 1951, s. 15 (4), and the Registration Service Act, 1953 (1 and 2 Eliz. 2, c. 37), s. 15 (2).
[14] 2 and 3 Eliz. 2, c. 61, s. 18.
[15] Another example of its use is to be found in the Conspiracy and Protection of Property Act, 1875, s. 4, which deals with the wilful and malicious breach of contract of service by persons employed by municipal authorities etc. in the supply of gas or water. See, too, the Post Office Act, 1953 (1 and 2 Eliz. 2, c. 36), s. 56. There are occasions, too, when the two words have been considered interchangeable. Thus, in *Cox's Case*, 1 Leach 71, the accused was charged with perjury at common law, the indictment alleging that the offence was committed "falsely, maliciously, wickedly and corruptly". It was held by all the judges that those words implied that it was done wilfully. On the other hand, in *Davies's Case*, 2 Leach 556, the indictment, under the Black Act, 1723 (*supra*), read "unlawfully, maliciously, and feloniously" but omitted the word "wilfully". The indictment was held to be invalid by a majority of the judges, who considered that the words "wilfully and maliciously" were descriptive of the offence created by the statute; and that they were bound by former precedents in analogous cases (citing *Lembro* v. *Hamper*, Cro. Eliz. 147), however the sense and legal import of the words might be the same. See, too, *R.* v. *Bent* (1845) 1 Den C.C. 157 *per* Patterson, J., at p. 159.

found as alternative conditions of liability, as, for example, in the Supremacy of the Crown Act, 1562,[1] which, somewhat incongruously under such a title, made it a crime for any servant to wilfully or maliciously assault his master or mistress. Another illustration is to be found in the Malicious Damage Act, 1861,[2] and again in the Perjury Act, 1911.[3]

Liability based upon proof of *Mens Rea*

As already stated the meaning attributable to the word "wilfully", where it appears in statutory offences, depends largely on the attitude adopted towards the question of *mens rea*. That there should be a wide cleavage of opinion on the meaning of such an elementary expression is due, it is suggested, to at least three causes. First, to the trend of thought which happens to be current at the time when a particular case is decided; secondly, to the individual judge's attitude towards this vital principle, and thirdly, to the dubious meaning sometimes given to the expression *mens rea*. Which of the opposite points of view is correct? The answer must principally be tested on the basis of the principles adopted by the courts, and it is proposed to take each of the respective theories of liability in turn. Many cases will be found in the reports in which, whenever the offence depends upon the accused's conduct being wilful, *mens rea* has been held to be an essential element. In a case in 1856, *R.* v. *Badger*,[4] Lord Campbell, C.J., is found quoting Milton[5] in support of the view that "wilful" denotes "evil intention",[6] and ruling that where the accused had acted under an honest mistake he could not be convicted of "wilfully receiving a higher fee than that to which he was entitled".

[1] 5 Eliz. c. 1, s. 21. The full title of the statute reads: "An Act for the Assurance of the Queen's Royal Power over all Estates and subjects within her Dominions."

[2] S. 52, repealed and replaced by the Criminal Justice Administration Act, 1914, s. 14.

[3] S. 12 (1) (*b*).

[4] (1856) 25 L.J.M.C. 81, turning on the Metropolitan Buildings Act, 1844, s. 79.

[5] "Thou to me
Art all things under heav'n, all places thou
Who for my wilful crime art banish'd hence."
Paradise Lost, Book 12 1. 617–619.

[6] The interpretation "evil mind" was also adopted by Brett, J., in *R.* v. *Prince* (1875) 2 C.C.R. 154, at 161, when he said: "Wilfully is more generally applied when the prohibited acts are in their natural consequences not necessarily or very probably noxious to the public interest, or to individuals; so that an evil mind is not the natural inference or consequence to be drawn from the doing of the acts. The presence of the word requires somewhat more evidence on the part of the prosecution to make out a prima facie case, than evidence that the prisoner did the prohibited acts."

This meaning of the term "wilful" was approved by Coleridge, and Erle, JJ., the other members of the court. In another case, *Smith* v. *Barnham*,[1] the accused was charged with wilfully throwing rubbish into a certain river. The defendant, a tanner, had occupied the same premises for nearly twenty years and had constantly discharged refuse from his works into the same river. Referring to the epithet "wilfully", Bramwell, B., said he greatly doubted whether the defendant's conduct constituted a wilful throwing-in of rubbish within the statute. "What was done here," he added, "was done in the exercise of a supposed right, and the Act seems to me to point to a knowingly wrongful act on the part of the doer."

Lord Coleridge, C.J., was also a member of the court, together with Mathew, J., in *Hall* v. *Richardson*,[2] when the words "wilfully or maliciously" in the Malicious Damage Act 1861, s. 52, were held to necessitate proof of *mens rea*, no distinction being drawn between the two epithets. Lord Coleridge C.J., rejected the view put forward by counsel for the respondent that all that was required was proof that the act was done intentionally and an injury occasioned, saying, "it would be monstrous" to extend the operation of the Act to all such cases. According to the learned Chief Justice there must be an intention of doing harm to somebody, an interpretation which was severely criticised by a strong court of seven judges in *Roper* v. *Knott*.[3] In that case Lord Russell of Killowen, C.J., pointed out that the cardinal error made by Lord Coleridge, C.J., was in confusing between the damage to the property and the consequent loss or damage to the owner of the property. Section 52, it was explained, is not concerned with the

[1] (1876) 34 L.T. Rep. 774. The views of Bramwell, B., in that case were not accepted by Grantham and Kennedy, JJ., in *High Wycombe Corpn.* v. *R. Thames Conservators* (1898) 78 L.T. 463, which concerned the offence, under the Thames Conservancy Act 1894, s. 92, of wilfully causing or suffering any offensive matter to flow into the R. Thames. Grantham, J., whilst not questioning the authority of *Smith* v. *Barnham,* was not disposed to go as far as Bramwell B. did in that case. Nebulously, he said: "To establish a wilful suffering more must be proved than an omission to do something the evil of which science showed might have been mitigated." Kennedy, J. was more explicit, expressing the view that "wilful" did not mean wantonly or causelessly, and that "if you permit a thing, not under compulsion, you do it wilfully". The real key to this interpretation, it is suggested, is to be found in the rhetorical question put forward by Kennedy, J., in the course of argument, when he asked "Is not wilfully opposed to accidentally?" This meaning of the word "wilfully", advanced also by Maule, J. in *R.* v. *Holroyd* (1841) 2 Moo. and R. 339, is considered in the text above.

[2] (1889) 6 T.L.R. 71.

[3] [1898] 1 Q.B. 868.

latter damage, it being sufficient if wilful damage is done to property. It is, however, important to notice that no criticism was voiced in *Roper* v. *Knott* as to the opinion of Lord Coleridge, C.J., and Mathew, J., that the words "wilfully or maliciously" required proof of a guilty mind. The correct interpretation of this guilty mind, it is suggested, is that stated in *Roper* v. *Knott* by Wills, J., who declared:[1] "In my opinion, the act meant is a wilful doing of something which the man doing it knows must damage property." In other words, it is not enough to prove that the accused intentionally did the act which caused the damage, but in addition it must be shown that in doing the act he realised or must have realised that damage to property would ensue from his conduct. As Bramwell B. expressed the test in *Smith* v. *Barnham*, the offence points to "a knowingly wrongful act on the part of the doer". The same attitude was shown in *Morris* v. *Edmonds*[2] which arose under the Vagrancy Act,[3] 1824, s. 3 of which makes it an offence if a person, being able to maintain himself, his wife, and family, wilfully refuses or neglects to do so. It was held that the accused, who bona fide believed his wife to have committed adultery and had therefore refused to support his spouse, was not guilty of wilfully refusing to do so. In other words, the term "wilfully" signifies *mens rea* which, by reason of his bona fide belief, the accused did not have. The element of wilfulness is also the basis of the analogous offence in the Summary Jurisdiction (Married Women) Act, 1895,[4] s. 4, viz., that of wilfully neglecting[5] to provide reasonable maintenance for a wife, which was before the

[1] *Ibid.*, at p. 873.

[2] (1897) 77 L.T. 56. It is necessary, however, to point out that in *Roberts* v. *Regnart* (1921) 86 J.P. 77 and *Biggs* v. *Burridge* (1924) 89 J.P. 75, it was held to be no defence to the same offence under the Vagrancy Act, 1824, s. 3, that the husband bona fide but erroneously believed that he was not legally bound to maintain them in the circumstances. Lord Hewart C.J., in the later case, endeavoured to distinguish *Morris* v. *Edmonds* on the ground that a bona fide belief as to adultery was a mistake upon a question of fact, whereas in the present case it was a mistake upon a question of law, and, therefore, untenable. Where mistake or claim of right is put forward *as a defence* it has already been argued that the fundamental criterion is whether the accused's mistaken belief was bona fide and honestly held, and it is submitted that the reasoning upon which *Roberts* v. *Regnart* and *Biggs* v. *Burridge* were decided is erroneous.

[3] 5 Geo. 4, c. 83.

[4] 58 and 59 Vict. c. 39.

[5] Comparison may be made with the cases turning on the offence of "wilfully neglecting to provide adequate medical aid for his child"—Poor Law Amdt. Act, 1868, s. 37, and re-enacted in the Children and Young Persons Act, 1933, s. 1 (1). See *R.* v. *Downes* (1875) 1 Q.B.D. 25 and *R.* v. *Senior* [1899] 1 Q.B. 283, both of which, according to Glanville Williams, *Criminal Law*, pp. 115–118, involve faulty constructions of the particular section.

Divisional Court in the recent case of *Chilton* v. *Chilton*.[1] Accepting the fact that cases under the Vagrancy Act, 1824, were not directly in point, Lord Merriman, P., nevertheless, considered that the decision in *Morris* v. *Edmonds* was "a very strong indication" as to what the court's ruling should be and, with Pearce, J., concurring, held that the husband's bona fide belief, induced by the wife, that she had committed adultery was a good defence to the charge of wilful neglect to maintain.

A notable trio of recent cases has shown that the present members of the Judiciary are alive to the necessity of safeguarding the cardinal principle of criminal liability. In the first of these, *Younghusband* v. *Luftig*,[2] a strong Divisional Court of five judges[3] upheld the view that where the word "wilfully" appears in a statutory offence, a guilty mind must be shown. The case arose out of an information preferred by the Medical Defence Union charging the accused with wilfully and falsely using the description "M.D." thereby implying that he was registered under the Medical Act, 1858.[4] It was admitted by the accused that his qualification, as a doctor of medicine of Berlin University, did not entitle him to be, and that he was not in fact, registered under the Act of 1858. Until 1944, Luftig had described himself, on his note-paper and professional plate, as "M.D. Berlin" but, after certain unpleasant incidents, had abbreviated this to "M.D. BLN" so as to conceal the fact that his degree was obtained in Germany. The justices were satisfied that the degree diploma, produced by the accused, had been granted by a genuine university. The question before the court, therefore, was whether the accused had used the description "doctor of medicine" wilfully and falsely, thereby implying that he was a registered medical practitioner. The magistrates answered the question in the negative and dismissed

[1] [1952] 1 All E.R. 1322. Cf. the recent Court of Appeal decision in *Allen* v. *Allen* [1951] 1 All E.R. 724.

[2] [1949] 2 K.B. 354. See 14 *M.L.R.* p. 486.

[3] Lord Goddard, C.J., Oliver, Birkett, Lynskey and Sellers, JJ.

[4] This is made a summary offence under section 40 of the Medical Act, 1858, which provides that: "Any person who shall wilfully and falsely pretend to be or take or use the Name or Title of a Physician, Doctor of Medicine, Licentiate in Medicine and Surgery, Bachelor of Medicine, Surgeon, General Practitioner or Apothecary, or any Name, Title, Addition or Description implying that he is registered under this Act . . . shall, upon a summary conviction for any such offence, pay a sum not exceeding Twenty Pounds." Similar provisions are to be found in the Veterinary Surgeons Act, 1881, s. 11, and the Dentists Act, 1878, s. 3. In the latter enactment, however, the term "wilfully" is omitted.

the information, from which verdict the Medical Defence Union appealed. Lord Goddard, C.J., delivering the unanimous judgment of the Divisional Court, cited nine earlier cases[1] decided between 1860 and 1899, from which, he said;[2] "It will be seen that there is an unbroken line of authority—that to commit an offence (under section 40) the defendant must have acted wilfully and falsely, and that it is for the magistrates to decide whether he has done so; also that he does not commit an offence if he honestly believes that he was within his rights in describing himself as he did. He must, of course, have a reasonable ground for his belief." Summing up the court's view on the meaning of "wilfully and falsely", the Lord Chief Justice said,[2] "There must be *mens rea*, and the presence or absence of that state of mind must be tested on ordinary principles and in the light of common sense."

The disparity shown by different judges in interpreting the same statutory offence is well illustrated by reference to the earlier decision of the Divisional Court in *Jutson* v. *Barrow*.[3] In that case Lord Hewart, C.J., with whose views on *mens rea* we shall have special occasion later to be concerned, referred to section 40 in these words: "What is regarded is not the mind of the individual but the meaning likely to be conveyed by the words that are used."[4] Humphreys, J., speaking in the same strain, stated that "the prohibition against the use of the named words and titles or of any other titles having the same implication is absolute".[5] This construction of the offence as one of absolute liability, in spite of the words "wilfully and falsely" inserted by the legislature, was, it is suggested rightly, disapproved of by the court in *Younghusband* v. *Luftig*.[6] The interpretation adopted in *Luftig* was followed two years later in the leading case of *Wilson* v. *Inyang*,[7] which was concerned also with the same offence under the Medical Act 1858. When consideration is given later to the question of how

[1] *Ladd* v. *Gould* (1860) 1 L.T. 325; *Ellis* v. *Kelly*, 6 H. and N. 222; *Andrews* v. *Styrup*, 26 L.T. 704; *Carpenter* v. *Hamilton* (1877) 37 L.T. 157; *Davies* v. *Makenna* (1885) 29 Ch.D. 596; *R.* v. *Aston Justices* (1891) 8 T.L.R. 123; *Steel* v. *Ormsby* (1894) 10 T.L.R. 483; *R.* v. *Lewis*, 12 T.L.R. 415; *Humber* v. *Clare* [1899] 1 Q.B. 635.

[2] [1949] 2 K.B. 369.

[3] [1936] 1 K.B. 236, *coram*, Lord Hewart, C.J., Humphreys and Singleton, JJ.

[4] *Ibid.*, p. 241.

[5] *Ibid.*, p. 248.

[6] No doubt was expressed as to the correctness of the decision in *Jutson* v. *Barrow*, having regard to the particular facts in that case. The only member of the court in the latter case to even mention the words "wilfully and falsely" was Singleton, J., and then only in passing (see p. 252).

[7] [1951] 2 K.B. 799, *coram* Lord Goddard C.J., Lynskey and Devlin JJ.

far a mistaken belief negatives the element of wilfulness, detailed attention will have to be directed to the principles enunciated in that case. For the moment, it is sufficient to recognise the decision as supporting the view that where "wilfully" appears in a statutory offence there must be *mens rea*.

Finally, there is the recent decision in *Bullock* v. *Turnbull*[1] in which the principle firmly established in *Luftig* and *Wilson* v. *Inyang* was followed by a Divisional Court, composed of Lord Goddard, C.J., Finnemore and McNair JJ. The respondents in that case, both of them lightermen, were alleged to have boarded a motor-ship which, having newly arrived from a foreign port, was flying a yellow flag indicating that the vessel was in quarantine. The flag was not at the masthead but was flying from a prominent position, a foot or so above the bridge. The respondents approached the ship from opposite directions and neither saw the yellow quarantine signal, but the moment they noticed it they left the ship. They were charged with wilfully refusing to obey the regulation,[2] made pursuant to section 143 (5) of the Public Health Act, 1936, which prohibits any person, other than a pilot, customs or immigration officer, from boarding a vessel which is in quarantine. "Wilfully" in this connection, the appellant contended, meant "consciously" or "not inadvertently" but with the clear intention of doing the act of which complaint was made. In other words, if a person intentionally boarded a vessel in quarantine, knowledge of the fact that the ship was in quarantine was extraneous to the question of liability, which was incurred by the mere conscious act of going on board. Dismissing this construction of the word "wilfully", Lord Goddard, C.J. said:[3] ". . . the offence must be shown to have been committed wilfully. It is not one of those absolute prohibitions you find in some statutes, where if a person does the prohibited act he cannot be heard to say that he did not know it was a prohibited act. This section clearly shows that the element of *mens rea* must enter into the offence." Applying this principle to the offence charged against the respondents, the Lord Chief Justice concluded: "In my opinion, the words here show that before a person can be convicted of this offence he must at any rate know

[1] [1952] 2 Ll.L. Rep. 303.

[2] Article 16 (1) of the Port Health Regulations, 1933 and 1945: [1933] S.R. and O No. 38 and [1945] S.R. and O. No. 1282.

[3] [1952] 2 Ll.L. Rep. at p. 305.

the circumstances which will constitute the offence. He may very likely know the regulation, but the boarding of the ship is not prohibited. What is suggested here is boarding the ship when the quarantine flag was flying. He did not know that the quarantine flag was flying; therefore, under those circumstances, he was not guilty of wilful disobedience." Finnemore and McNair JJ. being in agreement with Lord Goddard C.J., the appeal was dismissed.

Each of the above cases, it is suggested, represents sound interpretation, achieved by regarding the word "wilfully" as the key which sets in motion the old maxim *actus non facit reum nisi mens sit rea.* There are other cases[1] and dicta[2] upholding the same principle but, for the moment, it is proposed to leave this theory of liability and move on to consider the alternative point of view.

Liability wherein the accused's state of mind is irrelevant

It has always been accepted that where the legislature has created, either expressly or impliedly, an offence of absolute liability, it is irrelevant to inquire into the defendant's state of mind. In such crimes, proof of a guilty mind is not necessary, and all that is required of the prosecution is to show that the accused intentionally did the prohibited act. Some judges have gone so far as to say that this in itself "gives full scope to the doctrine of

[1] E.g., *Steele* v. *Midland Railway Co.* (1869) 21 L.T. 387, 392.

[2] See *Swinfen* v. *Bacon* (1861) 6 H. and N. 846, *per* Cockburn, C.J., at pp. 848, 849; *Derbyshire* v. *Houliston* (1897) 66 L.J. Q.B. 569 *per* Hawkins, J., at p. 571; more recently, see *Reynolds* v. *G. H. Austin & Sons, Ltd.* [1951] 1 All E.R. 606, *per* Devlin, J., at p. 613. In *Horabin* v. *B.O.A.C.* [1952] 2 All E.R. 1016, Barry, J., was required to direct the jury in a civil action as to the meaning of "wilful misconduct" in the Carriage by Air Act, 1932, Sch. 1, Art. 25. He did so in these terms: "Wilful misconduct is misconduct to which the will is a party, and it is wholly different in kind from mere negligence or carelessness, however gross [it] may be. . . . As an example, if the pilot of an aircraft knowingly does something which subsequently a jury find amounted to misconduct, that fact alone does not show that he was guilty of wilful misconduct. To establish wilful misconduct on the part of this imaginary pilot, it must be shown, not only that he knowingly (and in that sense wilfully) did the wrongful act, but also that, when he did it, he was aware that it was a wrongful act, i.e. that he was aware that he was committing misconduct" (at p. 1019). See, too, pp. 1020, 1022. In another recent civil case, *Charles* v. *S. Smith and Sons* [1954] 1 All E.R. 499, Hilbery J., had occasion to interpret section 119 (1) of the Factories Act, 1937, which provides that "no person . . . shall wilfully interfere with or misuse any means, appliance or convenience provided." According to the learned judge the section required something more than mere intentional intermeddling. The words used "mean something in the nature of a perverse intermeddling with the appliance". Confining his remarks to the particular section, Hilbery J., drew attention to the variety of meanings accorded to the epithet "wilful" in criminal and domestic law.

mens rea".[1] This meaning of the expression *mens rea* is, as suggested earlier, spurious and unreal, but it is important to note the fact that it is used. Another way of expressing the same idea is to say that "the prisoner had done the thing which was forbidden by the statute and that it was not necessary to prove any further *mens rea*".[2]

In neither case, from which these dicta are extracted, did the word "wilfully" appear in the statutory offence before the court; in both cases the offence in question was deemed to be one of absolute liability. Yet we find the same language being used by some judges in relation to crimes based upon wilful conduct. Thus, for example, in *The Law Society* v. *United Service Bureau Ltd.*,[3] the defendant company were charged with wilfully pretending to be qualified to act as a solicitor, contrary to the Solicitors Act, 1932, s. 46.[4] To counsel's submission that the word "wilfully" involved some *mens rea*, Avory, J. replied:[5] "I am satisfied that the wilful pretence is satisfied by evidence that the person accused intentionally did that which the Act forbids", and later, in the same passage, he declared that "it is not necessary to go further and show what is commonly known as *mens rea*, or any intention other than do the thing forbidden".

Where the word "wilful" is interpreted in this fashion the court is merely stating a requirement common to all crimes, namely, that the accused's act must be intentional and not accidental. The act must be capable of being attributed to the accused. The conduct of the accused must be the result of the free and conscious exercise of his will.[6] It is in this sense, for

[1] *R.* v. *Prince* (1875) 2 C.C.R, 154, *per* Bramwell, B., at p. 175.

[2] *R.* v. *Maughan* (1934) 24 Cr. App. R. 130, *per* Avory, J., at p. 132. See, too, the same judge in *R.* v. *Wheat* [1921] 2 K.B., at p. 126. Surprisingly, the latest advocate of this meaning of *mens rea* is Lord Goddard, C.J. See, for example, *Kat* v. *Diment* [1950] 2 All E.R., at p. 661; *Reynolds* v. *G.H. Austin Co. Ltd.* [1951] 2 K.B. 135 at pp. 138, 140 where Lord Goddard declared: "I have always thought (rightly or wrongly) that where an act is absolutely prohibited the doing of it supplies the *mens rea*"; *Lamb* v. *Sunderland and District Creamery Ltd.* [1951] 1 All E.R. at p. 923; *Browning* v. *Watson* [1953] 2 All E.R. 778, at p. 778. It is instructive to compare the Lord Chief Justice's statement in *Harding* v. *Price* [1948] 1 K.B. 695, at p. 701: ". . . if a statute contains an absolute prohibition against the doing of some act, as a general rule *mens rea* is not a constituent of the offence".

[3] (1934) 98 J.P. 33.

[4] 22 Geo. 5, c. 37.

[5] *Ibid.*, p. 36. Charles and Lawrence, JJ., agreed with all that Avory, J., said on the question of *mens rea*. Cf. the direction given to the jury by Maule, J. in *R.* v. *Holroyd* (1841) 2 Moo & R. 339.

[6] See Kenny's *Outlines of Criminal Law* (16th ed.), pp. 23, 36 and 39.

example, that Lord Goddard, C.J., used the word "wilful" in his direction to the jury in *R.* v. *Craig*,[1] a case where the accused was charged with murder by killing in the course of resisting a lawful arrest by a police constable. According to the law of constructive murder, as the Lord Chief Justice explained to the jury, killing in those circumstances is murder provided the accused's *act* was wilful, that is to say, intentional. In such a case it is immaterial whether the *consequences* which ensued were intentional or accidental. If the meaning to be given to the word "wilful" is that suggested by Avory, J., in *The Law Society* v. *United Service Bureau Ltd.*, then it is submitted that its insertion in statutory offences is superfluous because it merely states what the law recognises as being an essential element in every criminal offence.[2] Furthermore, in so interpreting a statutory offence involving the element of "wilfulness", the construction adopted results in the offence being regarded as one of absolute liability in which no question of a guilty mind arises. It will be recalled that a similar interpretation was adopted by Lord Hewart in relation to section 40 of the Medical Act, 1858,[3] but this was strongly criticised in *Younghusband* v. *Luftig*.[4] Having regard to the decision in the latter case, it is submitted that the interpretation of Avory, J., above, is likewise no longer tenable.

The "obstruction" cases

The same interpretation of "wilful" as meaning intentional is to be found in a series of cases arising under the Highways Act, 1835, s. 72 of which creates the offence of wilfully obstructing the highway. Thus, we find Denman, J., in *Fearnley* v. *Ormsby*[5] saying: "The obstruction complained of is admitted to have been wilful in the sense of an act done purposely,"[6] and the same meaning was adopted by Lord Coleridge, C.J., the other member of the court. A few years later, in *Gulby* v. *Smith*[7] the Lord Chief Justice explained that whereas "an obstruction may not be in the first instance

[1] (1952) *The Times*, December 12. In so directing the jury Lord Goddard was following the direction of Brett, J., in *R.* v. *Porter* (1873) 12 Cox C.C. 444, which had been approved by the C.C.A. in *R.* v. *Appleby* (1940) 28 Cr. App. R. 1.

[2] *R.* v. *Larsonneur* (1933) 97 J.P. 206 stands on its own as a discreditable exception to the rule stated above.

[3] See *Jutson* v. *Barrow* [1936] 1 K.B. 236, at p. 241, discussed *ante*, p. 35.

[4] [1949] 2 K.B. 354.

[5] (1879) 4 C.P.D. 136.

[6] Cf. *Tunnicliffe* v. *Pickup* [1939] 3 All E.R. 297.

[7] (1883) 12 Q.B.D. 121.

wilful, yet when it is called to the notice [of the defendant], and he is required to remove it and does not, it remains there by an exercise of his will; in other words, leaving it there is a wilful act on his part".[1] More recently, the question of what constitutes a "wilful obstruction" has been considered by the Divisional Court in *Eaton* v. *Cobb*.[2] The appellant in that case, who was the driver of a motor car, opened the door on the off-side of the car while it was stationary and struck a cyclist who was passing. Before opening the door, the driver had looked in the internal mirror reflecting the view through the rear window of the car but had not seen any vehicle approaching. Referring to section 72 of the 1835 Act, Humphreys, J., declared: "It is true that [the appellant] wilfully opened the door and, if it were an offence to open the off-side door of a motor car, he would have committed it, but the offence here is wilfully obstructing the free passage of a highway . . . the test whether or not a person can be convicted of the offence of which the appellant has been convicted is whether or not the obstruction was intentional." The other members of the court, Lord Goddard, C.J., and Jones, J., being of the opinion that there was no evidence on which the justices could say that the appellant wilfully obstructed the highway, the conviction was quashed.

It will be seen that the court, in rightly placing the emphasis on the obstruction being intentional, distinguished between the physical act of intentionally opening the door (which is no crime in itself) and the consequences which result from that act, namely, the obstruction of the highway. To constitute the offence of wilful obstruction not only the initial act but the ensuing consequences must be intentional. Thus interpreted the offence is taken out of the category of crimes of absolute prohibition.[3] In comparison with *Eaton* v. *Cobb* the language used in *Gulby* v. *Smith* is ambiguous, but even in that case there seems to be recognition of the requirement of realisation of the consequences. In *Fearnley* v.

[1] Cf. *Walker* v. *Horner* (1875) 1 Q.B.D. 4.

[2] [1950] 1 All E.R. 1016. Cf. *Betts* v. *Stevens* [1910] 1 K.B. at p. 8, in which the offence of "wilfully obstructing the police in the execution of their duty" was interpreted as meaning not simply "wilfully obstructing" but intending to prevent the execution of the duty.

[3] Cf. *R.* v. *Senior* [1899] 1 Q.B. 283, in which Lord Russell of Killowen C.J. defined "wilfully", in the phrase "wilfully neglects" (Prevention of Cruelty to Children Act, 1894, s. 1), to mean "that the act is done deliberately and intentionally, not by accident or inadvertence, but so that the mind of the person who does the act goes with it".

Ormsby, on the other hand, according to the construction adopted by Lord Coleridge C.J. and Denman, J., liability is incurred by the mere intentional doing of the act which caused the obstruction. This is in direct conflict with the later construction in *Eaton* v. *Cobb* and, it is suggested, should not be followed.

Further evidence of the wider interpretation of "wilfully" is seen in *R.* v. *Ryan*,[1] in which the Court of Criminal Appeal held that "wilfully" meant "intentionally" in the sense of *mens rea*. In that case the appellant, a doctor, was charged under the Perjury Act, 1911, s. 4 (i) (*b*), with wilfully making false certificates of death purporting to be made under the Births and Deaths Registration Act, 1874.[2] The appellant had certified that he had attended certain persons in their last illnesses, and stated the cause of death in each case. In fact, he had not seen or attended these persons who were still very much alive and gave evidence at the trial. According to the appellant the certificates had been applied for by, and handed over to, the superintendent of an insurance company to enable the company to pay over the insurance money, and he argued that since "wilfully" in section 4 of the Perjury Act meant that the certificates must have been given intentionally for the purpose of registering a death, whereas they had only been issued as "cover" certificates, he could not be said to have committed the offence. Such a restricted interpretation was rejected by the court, Lord Reading stating:[3] ". . . the judge was right in the view he took that 'wilfully' means 'intentionally', and 'intentionally' means that he knew at the time of the making of these certificates that he was making false statements in relation to documents which purported to be made under the Act for the registration of births or deaths."

The "pigeon" cases

This leads us to consider section 23 of the Larceny Act, 1861,[4] out of which has arisen a series of cases calculated to dampen the most ardent advocate of our criminal law. This section deals with

[1] (1914) 10 Cr. App. R. 4. [2] 37 and 38 Vict. c. 88. [3] (1914) 10 Cr. App. R. 4. at p. 7.

[4] The full section reads: "Whosoever shall unlawfully and wilfully kill, wound or take any house dove or pigeon under such circumstances as shall not amount to larceny at common law, shall, on conviction etc." Cf. the recently created offence under the Protection of Birds Act, 1954 (2 and 3 Eliz. 2, c. 30), s. 1, which, save for certain exceptions, makes it an offence "wilfully to kill, injure or take any wild bird or attempt to do so, or to take, damage or destroy the nest of any wild bird while it is in use, or to take or destroy an egg of such bird".

the unlawful and wilful killing, wounding or taking of any house pigeon. Insomuch as all the earlier authorities were discussed in *Cotterill* v. *Penn*,[1] it is a convenient starting point for our discussion. In that case it appeared that the defendant was in his garden with the intention of shooting wild pigeons and magpies which had been damaging his crops. There was brilliant sunshine at the time, partly dazzling the accused. Suddenly he saw a solitary pigeon flying low. It remained visible for only a few yards before he shot it and killed it. Unfortunately, it was a house pigeon. The justices found that the accused honestly thought it was a wild pigeon, and that in shooting it he was exercising his right of protecting his crops from imminent danger. Both defences were held by the Divisional Court to be inapplicable.[2] It was admitted that if the accused could show a lawful excuse for his shooting his act would cease to be unlawful, and, therefore, outside the section. Lord Hewart, C.J., was of the opinion, however, that it would be an undue straining of the authorities to say that an apprehension of danger is a lawful excuse.[3] As we have seen, that view is no longer in keeping with the law recently laid down by the Court of Appeal in *Cresswell* v. *Sirl*[4] and *Hamps* v. *Darby*.[5] On this ground alone, it is suggested, the case of *Cotterill* v. *Penn* would be decided differently today.

Turning to the question of *mens rea* in relation to section 23 the then Chief Justice said that the state of mind of the person

[1] [1936] 1 K.B. 53, *coram*, Lord Hewart, C.J., Avory and Humphreys, JJ. This case, and that of *Horton* v. *Gwynne* (*infra*), are criticised by Glanville Williams, *Criminal Law*, pp. 118–119. The learned author points out that section 23, so construed, (1) requires a state of mind only in respect of the fact of killing, (2) creates an offence of strict responsibility in respect of the other ingredients of the *actus reus*. He concludes, it is submitted rightly, that where the word "wilfully" appears in the definition of an offence, it should be taken as requiring knowledge of all the ingredients of the *actus reus*, unless there are words in the statute dispensing with this necessity in respect of any particular ingredient.

[2] It is interesting to note that under the Defence (General) Regulations, 1939, Reg. 9, it was made an offence knowingly to kill, wound or take a racing or housing pigeon. The word "knowingly" was subsequently omitted, but a proviso was added which made it a good defence for the defendant to prove that he acted under the reasonable belief that the pigeon was not a racing or housing pigeon and that he forthwith handed it over to the authorities. This offence has since been revoked under the provisions of S.R. and O. 1945, No. 504.

[3] [1936] 1 K.B. 61.

[4] [1948] 1 K.B. 241.

[5] [1948] 2 K.B. 311. A later decision of the Court of Appeal is *Thayer* v. *Newman* [1953] *The Times*, October 14. However, under the Protection of Birds Act, 1954 (2 and 3 Eliz. 2, c. 30), s. 4 (2), it is only a defence to a charge of wilfully killing or injuring etc. a wild bird if the accused can satisfy the court that his action was necessary for the purpose of preventing serious damage to his property.

charged was irrelevant, and that the element of *mens rea* was not required beyond the point that the facts must show an intention on the part of the person accused to do the act forbidden.[1] Here, once more, an offence based upon wilful conduct is seen being interpreted in language peculiar to crimes of absolute liability. It follows the same pattern as that used by the same judge in construing section 40 of the Medical Act, 1858,[2] and rightly disapproved of in *Luftig's Case*. The same strictures, it is suggested, should apply to the interpretation of "wilfully" given in *Cotterill* v. *Penn*.

What of the other cases which have arisen under section 23? To what extent have they considered the term "wilfully" to require proof of *mens rea*, in the sense of a blameworthy mind? The earliest decision was that in *Taylor* v. *Newman*.[3] In that case the accused knew full well that he was shooting at a house pigeon. He had warned its owner to take steps to prevent his pigeons from doing further injury to the defendant's crops. Finding his warning ignored, the next time the defendant found them actually feeding on his crops he fired twice, killing one. It was held, on appeal, that insomuch as the accused had acted in defence of his property, his killing of the pigeon did not fall within the section. All the subsequent cases have based their attitude towards *Taylor* v. *Newman* on the report in *Best and Smith*. In that report, Blackburn, J., makes no reference to the question of *mens rea*, though Mellor, J. (the other member of the court), says that section 23 was not intended to apply to a case in which there was no guilty mind,[4] nor where the act was done by a person under the honest belief that he was exercising a right. If reference is made, however, to the

[1] [1936] 1 K.B. at p. 61.

[2] In *Jutson* v. *Barrow* [1936] 1 K.B. 236. It is interesting to note that Humphreys, J., also appeared in both cases.

[3] (1863) 4 B. & S. 89; 8 L.T. (N.S.) 424; 11 W.R. 752; 32 L.J.M.C. 186.

[4] 4 B. & S., at p. 94. In *Farey* v. *Welch* [1929] 1 K.B., at p. 392, Lord Hewart cites, with approval, this sentence from Mellor, J.'s judgment, but understands it to mean proof of a felonious intent to steal. (See the full wording of section 23 (*supra*).) In *Cotterill* v. *Penn* [1936] 1 K.B., at p. 61, the L.C.J.'s opinion undergoes a complete transformation when he says that, where an unlawful and wilful killing or wounding is alleged, no such felonious intent is required because the qualifying words (in section 23)—"under such circumstances as do not amount to larceny at common law"—are not apt words in reference to the words "kill" or "wound". If limited to the word "take", he says, the meaning of the qualifying phrase becomes obvious. It is, perhaps, worth adding that Avory, J., conceived an entirely different meaning to the qualifying words (see *Farey* v. *Welch*, at p. 392). Whichever meaning is preferred, this difference in interpretation lends added weight to the view that the reference in *Taylor* v. *Newman* to *mens rea* and wantonness was directed to the term "wilful".

other reports of the case it will be found that Blackburn, J., was firmly of the opinion that *mens rea* was required, stating that the section only applied to cases where the defendant does the act wantonly and without any colour of right.[1]

In the light of these views it is difficult to explain or reconcile the decision in *Hudson* v. *MacRae*,[2] decided the same year by the same two judges. That case was concerned with section 24 of the same Act, which deals with unlawful and wilful fishing in water where another person has a private right of fishery. The defendant claimed that, as the public had fished there for over sixty years, he honestly believed that he too was entitled to do so. This defence was rejected on the ground that, where the statute reads "unlawfully and wilfully", a guilty mind was not a necessary ingredient. The court said it would have been different if the word "maliciously" had been used. It is strange that no such argument had appealed to the same judges in *Taylor* v. *Newman*. One of the reasons[3] given for this *volte face* was that section 24 was directed mainly to the protection of property. But so was section 23, and many other sections in the same Act which require the accused's conduct to be wilful. Furthermore, to accept this argument is to say that any offence designed to protect property excludes the necessity for *mens rea* unless the word "maliciously" is used. That is not in keeping with the authorities.

[1] 8 L.T. (N.S.) 424 and 11 W.R. 752.

[2] (1863) 4 B. & S. 585; 33 L.J.M.C. 65 (by far the fuller report). On account of the apparent inconsistent attitude adopted in this case by Blackburn, J. (and Mellor, J.), both Lord Hewart and Avory, J., were of opinion that Blackburn, J.'s judgment in *Taylor* v. *Newman* had been misreported. (See [1936] 1 K.B. at pp. 61, 62, 63.) It would seem that, in making this criticism, reliance was placed on the one report, in 4 B. & S. 89. In his article in (1936) 52 *Law Quarterly Review*, pp. 60 *et seq.*, Dr. Stallybrass has made it abundantly clear that the criticism was unjustified. Reference to the other reports of the case show a remarkable degree of consistency as to what was said in *Taylor* v. *Newman*.

[3] We are not concerned here with the other point of difference which Blackburn, J., said distinguished the two cases, namely, that the basis of the decision in *Taylor* v. *Newman* was the absence of any proprietary interest in pigeons flying abroad which reasoning did not apply to *Hudson* v. *MacRae*. Assuming that to be the *ratio decidendi* in *Taylor*, it does not explain the subsequent radical change in the two judges' attitude towards *mens rea*. Moreover, the supposed basis of the decision in *Taylor* v. *Newman* depended on the validity of Croke's note to *Dewell* v. *Sanders* (1619), in Cro. Jac. 490. In *Hamps* v. *Darby* [1948] 2 K.B., at p. 320, Evershed, L.J., has shown that this note is unreliable in view of the further report of the same case in 2 Rolle Rep. 3, 30. The following authorities were also cited in support of the proposition that property in tamed pigeons remains so long as they retain an *animus revertendi*—Blackstone, *Commentaries*, (8th ed.), Vol. 2, at p. 391; Holdsworth, *H.E.L.* Vol. 7, p. 489; Williams, *Animals*, p. 252.

The facts and decision in the next case, *Horton* v. *Gwynne*,[1] bear a close resemblance to those in *Cotterill* v. *Penn*, which expressly followed the earlier case. At the time of the shooting the bird was sitting on the ground some forty yards away from the defendant. It may be thought that he had ample opportunity to decide whether or not it was a house pigeon. The justices, at any rate, were satisfied that the accused honestly mistook it for a wild pigeon and dismissed the case. On appeal to the Divisional Court this finding was reversed, on the ground that "a person who shoots a pigeon which turns out to be a house pigeon must take the consequences of his act".[2] Such language is the direct negation of *mens rea* which, as we have seen in *Taylor* v. *Newman*, was said to be vital to the offence. It comes as a shock, therefore, to find that same case cited in support of the view that *mens rea* is irrelevant. Referring to *Taylor* v. *Newman*, Avory, J., said that "but for the fact that the appellant was there acting in defence of his own property the court would have held that the mere act of killing a house pigeon was an offence if the defendant killed what he shot at".[3] This, of course, is pure surmise and does not tally with the passage in Blackburn, J.'s, judgment in which he said;[4] 'I do not think that the killing of a pigeon under a mistake—as, for example, where a man thought he was killing his own pigeon—would be a killing under this Act". Yet, if the views of the court in *Horton* v. *Gwynne* are the law, this man would undoubtedly be liable.

If, as has been argued in this chapter, *mens rea* is an essential element in the crime created by section 23, then surely a mistake of fact must always be a possible defence provided it is made in good faith. To draw a distinction, as Darling, J., suggested,[5] between the case of a man who shoots at a crow and accidentally kills a house pigeon, and of another man who shoots at what he believes to be a wild pigeon but kills what turns out to be a house pigeon, is unnecessary. Neither killing can be said to be the result of a "knowingly wrongful"[6] act or to have been made with the "evil intention" of killing a house pigeon. If that is so, neither case

[1] [1921] 2 K.B. 661.

[2] *Per* Darling, J., at p. 662.

[3] *Ibid.*, at p. 663.

[4] 11 W.R. 752.

[5] [1921] 2 K.B., at p. 662.

[6] Both these phrases were used by R. S. Wright, J., in *Sherras* v. *de Rutzen* [1895] 1 Q.B.D., at p. 921, when expounding the meaning of *mens rea*. They are to be found too in *R.* v. *Badger*, and *Smith* v. *Barnham* (*ante*, pp. 31, 32) where Lord Campbell, C.J., and Bramwell, B., adopted the phrases to explain the term "wilful".

is a wilful killing within the meaning of section 23 of the Larceny Act, 1861.

Conclusion

Can any conclusions be drawn from this survey of the manner in which the judges have interpreted the various statutory offences which include the terms "wilful" or "wilfully"? At the outset of this chapter the justification for the two-fold interpretation, manifested throughout the cases, was questioned. One view, of course, is to hold that the meaning attributable to such epithet may legitimately vary according to the statute and to the individual offence concerned. Certainly there are indications that such is the current practice, but where, it is suggested, the argument in favour of recognising such practice as satisfactory falls down is the manner in which occasionally *the same offence* is given conflicting interpretations by different judges. Moreover, when it becomes apparent that the tendency of certain judges is to consistently measure criminal liability—whatever the wording of the statute—by placing the accent on the mere intentional doing of the forbidden act, and this even in the face of earlier judicial opinion emphasising the element of a guilty mind, it is submitted that the real explanation of the variation in judicial interpretations is not so much the particular offence as the individual judge's attitude towards the application of the doctrine of *mens rea* in statutory offences.

Claim of right in wilful crimes

Consideration must now be given to the application of claim of right in relation to statutory offences based upon wilfulness.

Claim of right as an ouster of jurisdiction

It has already been pointed out that the special proviso of "fair and reasonable supposition of right", contained in section 52 of the Malicious Damage Act, 1861, applies equally whether the damage is caused wilfully or maliciously. Furthermore, where summary jurisdiction is exercisable in respect of any other statutory offence involving wilfulness, it is submitted that the accused may avail himself of the common law proviso as to bona fide claim of right.

To sustain this plea of ouster of jurisdiction it is, of course, necessary to show that the right claimed is one which is recognised as being maintainable in point of law and also that it relates to a question of title to real property. As in the case of malicious crimes, so, too, with respect to crimes involving wilfulness, the boundary line between this plea and that of claim of right as a defence has sometimes been lost sight of, and the case of *Foulger* v. *Steadman*[1] provides a good illustration of this. A railway company, who were the owners of a thoroughfare which had the appearance of being a public street, allowed certain cabs to stand in the thoroughfare on payment by the drivers of a weekly sum. The respondent, who had not paid his dues, refused to remove his cab when asked to do so by the company, and was charged with being a wilful trespasser under the Railway Regulation Act 1840, s. 16.[2] The respondent relied on the decision in *Jones* v. *Taylor*,[3] a case involving the same offence but in which no question of title to real property arose. Although the judgment, as reported, is very meagre it is clear that the court, consisting of Lord Campbell, C.J., Wightman and Hill, JJ., were of the opinion that where a man goes on to the land of another and remains there in pursuance of a claim of right, in the justice of which he *bona fide* believes, he is not a wilful trespasser. In *Foulger* v. *Steadman*, on the other hand, it is apparent that the respondent's claim to be entitled to remain on the railway premises rested on his belief that the property was a public thoroughfare,[4] but the court considered that upon the evidence no such right could exist in law and, therefore, that the magistrate's jurisdiction was not ousted. Delivering judgment, Blackburn, J., then went on to say: "but here the defence only amounted to this, that the respondent believed he had a right to stand his cab upon ground which was the premises of the company without their leave. This belief does not prevent the respondent from being a wilful trespasser." Notwithstanding the decision in *Jones* v. *Taylor*, it would seem that the court in *Foulger* v. *Steadman* were extending into the defence of claim of right the necessity for showing that the right is one which can exist in law.[5] To do so is to confuse the principles governing claim of right as an ouster of jurisdiction and as a defence.

[1] (1872) L.R. 8 Q.B. 65. See, too, *Simpson* v. *Wells* (1872) L.R. 7 Q.B. 214.

[2] 3 & 4 Vict. c. 97. [3] (1858) 1 E. & E. 20.

[4] Cf. *Walker* v. *Horner* (1875) 1 Q.B.D. 4, in which the question of claim of right, though raised by the defendant, was not discussed by the court.

[5] This conclusion is borne out by Hansen, J.'s remark: "Is not the trespass wilful if the person who commits it acts under a mistake as to what the law is?"

Claim of right or mistaken belief as a defence

What of the common law defence of claim of right? If the argument is accepted that "wilfully" imports *mens rea* into an offence, then surely it must be a good defence to show that the accused honestly, though mistakenly, believed himself to be entitled to do the act with which he is charged. If it be shown that he acted in good faith, how can it be said that the defendant acted knowingly with a wrongful intention? Such was the line of argument adopted in such cases as *R.* v. *Badger*,[1] *Smith* v. *Barnham*,[2] *Hall* v. *Richardson*,[3] *Morris* v. *Edmonds*,[4] *Taylor* v. *Newman*[5] and *Younghusband* v. *Luftig*[6] in which, as we have seen, the defence was allowed.

Is the defence to be judged objectively or subjectively?

Writing before the recent decision in *Wilson* v. *Inyang*[7] it was submitted by the writer[8] that when it is judicially stated, supposedly as a matter of law, that "the defendant must, of course, have a reasonable ground for his belief",[9] the judges are stressing what is, in fact, a matter of evidence to be taken into account when deciding whether the accused acted in good faith.[10] Proof of *mens rea* is a matter for the prosecution. Because of the difficulty experienced in showing exactly what was the accused's state of mind at the time of the alleged offence, such proof is generally judged by an objective standard. The dictates of expediency justify the adoption of such a standard. But where the accused himself puts forward evidence of his state of mind with a view to

[1] (1856) 25 L.J.M.C. 81.
[2] (1876) 34 L.T.Rep. 774.
[3] (1889) 6 T.L.R. 71.
[4] (1897) 77 L.T. 56.
[5] (1863) 4 B. & S. 89.
[6] [1949] 2 K.B. 354.
[7] [1951] 2 K.B. 799.
[8] (1951) *Current Legal Problems* at p. 281.
[9] *Younghusband* v. *Luftig* [1949] 2 K.B., at p. 369.
[10] The same attitude towards this question is taken by Glanville Williams, *Criminal Law*, pp. 163–167. Whereas the learned editor of *Russell on Crime* (10th ed.) p. 75, appeared to be in two minds as to the answer to this problem, in *Outlines of Criminal Law* (16th ed.) pp. 47–48, he categorically states that the reasonableness of mistake is fundamentally a matter of evidence, thus correcting an error perpetuated in earlier editions of *Kenny* (see e.g. 15th ed., p. 76). Other writers who had conceived this essential distinction are Keedy, *Ignorance and Mistake in the Criminal Law* (1908) 22 Harv. L.R. 75, 84, Nino Levi, *A Note on Mistake in Italian Criminal Law*, quoted in Michael and Wechsler's *Criminal Law and its Administration*, pp. 805–806, and Jerome Hall, *General Principles of Criminal Law*, pp. 330–343. Cf. Miller, *Criminal Law*, p. 156, and *Archbold* (33rd ed.) p. 23, who persist in maintaining that a mistake must be reasonable. For a recent statement indicating adherence to this view, *viz.*, that reasonableness of the defendant's belief is an essential condition for excluding liability, see *Reynolds* v. *G. H. Austin & Sons, Ltd.* [1951] 1 All E.R. 606, *per* Devlin, J., at p. 614.

rebutting *mens rea*, then surely a subjective test must be applied. If that is so, then even though the grounds for his belief be deemed unreasonable, may not the jury still be convinced that the defendant himself honestly and genuinely thought he was exercising a right to which he was entitled, and thus be satisfied that he had no guilty mind?

In what has been described by a learned writer[1] as "the most important contribution ever made to criminal jurisprudence by an English Divisional Court"[2] the decision in the recent case of *Wilson* v. *Inyang*[3] represents the repudiation "in general terms [of] the hoary error that a mistake to afford a defence to a criminal charge must be reasonable".[4] The respondent in that case was charged with wilfully and falsely using the title of physician, contrary to section 40 of the Medical Act 1858, i.e., the same offence as that involved in *Younghusband* v. *Luftig*. It was stated that the respondent, an African who had lived in England for about two years, had never been a medical practitioner but had obtained the diploma of the Anglo-American Institute of Drugless Therapy. Nevertheless, he inserted for publication in a weekly newspaper an advertisement which read: "Naturopath physician, N.D., M.R.D.P. Surgery for chiropody. For appointment." The magistrate, having seen the respondent and heard him cross-examined, was of the opinion that he genuinely believed that he was entitled to describe himself as a "physician" by reason of his diploma. Accordingly, the magistrate dismissed the summons.

Referring to the review of the earlier cases carried out in *Younghusband* v. *Luftig*, Lord Goddard C.J. cited the statement made in that case in which he had said that a defendant does not commit an offence under section 40 "if he honestly believes that he was within his rights in describing himself as he did. He must, of course, have a reasonable ground for his belief".[5] The reports are full of similar statements[6] acknowledging the necessity for a mis-

[1] Glanville Williams in (1951) 14 *Modern Law Review* 485.

[2] Consisting of Lord Goddard C.J., Lynskey and Devlin, JJ.

[3] [1951] 2 K.B. 799. [4] (1951) 14 *M.L.R.* 485. [5] [1949] 2 K.B. 354, 369.

[6] *R.* v. *Prince* (1875) L.R. 2 C.C.R. 154, at pp. 169–170, *per* Brett, J.; *R.* v. *Tolson* (1889) 23 Q.B.D. at pp. 181–182, *per* Cave, J.; *R.* v. *Rose* (1884) 15 Cox C.C. 540, *per* Lopes, J.; *Bank of N.S.W.* v. *Piper* [1897] A.C. 383, 390. Cf. *Derry* v. *Peek* (1889) 14 App. Cas. at p. 352, *per* Lord Bramwell, and *Knowler* v. *Rennison* [1947] K.B. 488 at p. 494, *per* Lord Goddard C.J. In Australia the courts frequently cite with approval the dictum of the Judicial Committee in *Bank of N.S.W.* v. *Piper* (*supra*) about "honest and reasonable belief"—see e.g. Dixon, J. in *Thomas* v. *The King* (1937) 59 C.L.R. 279 at pp. 303–304 and in *Proudman* v. *Dayman* (1941) 67 C.L.R. 536 at p. 541; *Bergin* v.

taken belief to be reasonable if it is to be a good defence. However, in *Wilson* v. *Inyang*, Lord Goddard, C.J., proceeded to explain that this condition of reasonableness is not an essential requirement laid down by law, but rather it is a factor which affects the credibility to be attached to the defendant's plea. Clarifying what was meant in the passage, quoted above, from *Younghusband* v. *Luftig*, the Lord Chief Justice said that "generally speaking, applying ordinary principles and in the light of common sense, he would say that, if a man had no reasonable ground for believing what he said he believed, he was not acting honestly. There may be exceptions. A man may believe that which no other man of common sense would believe, but he yet may honestly believe it".[1] A little later, he added: "If he [the accused] has acted without any reasonable ground and says: 'I had not properly inquired, and did not think this or that', that may be (and generally is) very good evidence that he is not acting honestly. But it is only evidence, . . . in considering whether he had acted honestly, the magistrate ought to take into account the presence or absence of reasonable grounds of belief".[1]

Here, at last, is a recognition of the true principle, but it remains to be seen whether the doctrine adopted in *Wilson* v. *Inyang* will permeate through the whole field of criminal liability, where the defence of mistake or claim of right is put forward by the accused in order to show that *mens rea* is negatived. The earliest indication, in *Goodway* v. *Becher*,[2] discussed at some length earlier in this study, is far from promising and it is to be hoped that an opportunity will soon present itself for extending into the field of malicious crimes the same subjective test as that accepted in *Wilson* v. *Inyang* in the case of crimes based on wilfulness.

Relating claim of right to the word "unlawfully"

Another source of confusion arises where the words of the section, in creating an offence, begin with the phrase, "Whosoever shall unlawfully and wilfully . . .", and the defence of claim of

Stack (1953) 88 C.L.R. 248. Furthermore the requirement of reasonableness is perpetuated in the Criminal Codes of Western Australia (s. 24), Queensland (s. 24) and Tasmania (s. 14), each of which provides a general defence of "honest and reasonable but mistaken belief". Recent South African cases manifest a conflict of judicial opinion on the necessity for reasonableness in the defence of mistaken belief—see, e.g., *R.* v. *Mbomela* 1933 A.D. 269; *R.* v. *Myers* 1948 (1) S.A. 375 (A.D.); *R.* v. *Milne and Erleigh* 1951 (1) S.A. 791 (A.D.); and *R.* v. *Bhaya* 1953 (3) S.A. 143 (N).

[1] [1951] 2 K.B. 799, 803. [2] [1951] 2 All E.R. 349. See *ante*, pp. 27–28.

right is related to the word "unlawfully"[1] instead of "wilfully". Take the following illustration. Where the accused can show a lawful excuse for his act—as, for example, in cases under the Larceny Act, 1861, s. 23, where the killing is done to protect the defendant's crops—it is said that his act ceases to be unlawful.[2] At the same time the lawful excuse negatives the mental element signified by the term "wilfully". The important point to observe is that where the defendant cannot show a lawful excuse but can, nevertheless, satisfy the jury that he acted bona fide, believing he had a right to do what he did, his act though unlawful is still not wilful. It is suggested that a more satisfactory attitude would be to relate the defence solely to the epithet "wilfully".

In his book on the *Advancement of Learning*, Bacon wrote that words were like a Tartar's bow, they shoot back upon the understanding of the wisest, and mightily entangle and pervert the judgment.[3] The truth of this adage has been shown in this examination of the part played in statutory crimes of the two simple words "maliciously" and "wilfully". It will continue until the principle is accepted that their presence in any statutory offence points clearly and unequivocably to the need for proving a guilty mind.

[1] For the interpretation of this epithet, see *Outlines of Cr. Law* (16th ed.), pp. 183–184.

[2] See *Cotterill* v. *Penn* [1936] 1 K.B. at p. 61.

[3] (5th ed.), Book 2, p. 163.

III
KNOWINGLY

Statutory offences involving guilty knowledge

Travellers along the Queen's highway will probably agree that a plethora of signposts can sometimes be as disconcerting and misleading as a complete absence of directions indicating what lies ahead. The same feeling of desperation may be experienced by examining the judicial interpretations during the past hundred and fifty years of statutory offences involving guilty knowledge. Bent on making knowledge on the part of the alleged offender an essential ingredient in a crime, the legislature, when defining an offence, has resorted with varying degrees of extravagance to the use of such words as "knowingly", "permitting", "suffering", "allowing", "causing", or double-barrelled expressions such as "knowingly permitting", "knowingly suffering" or "knowingly and wilfully permitting". Paying heed to these "signposts" or "danger signals",[1] it would sometimes appear, according to their personal predilections, different generations of judges have left cluttered up behind them a body of case-law which is badly in need of disentanglement. As a start, attention must be directed to the expression "knowingly".

Use of analogous expressions in early legislation

The necessity for some mental element in criminal offences was recognised in Roman law, and in Ortolan's reconstruction[2] of the Eighth Table "*de delictis*" the word "knowingly" appears twice, once in connection with the offence of "knowingly and maliciously burning a house"[3] and, later, in relation to the capital

[1] These striking phrases were used by Lord Hewart, C.J., in *Gaumont British Distributors Ltd.* v. *Henry* [1939] 2 K.B. 711, at p. 717.

[2] *Explication Historique des Instituts*, i, 114–118. Ortolan's work was published towards the end of the nineteenth century.

[3] Clause 10. Gaius's version of this clause (see Fontes, *Iuris Romani Antiqui* (1909)) reads: "*Qui aedes acervumve frumenti iuxta domum positum combusserit vinctus verberatus igni necari iubetur, si modo sciens prudensque id commiserit; si vero casu, id est neglegentia, aut noxiam sarcive iubetur, aut, si minus idoneus sit, levius castigatur.*"

offence of "knowingly and maliciously killing a free man".[1] However, Ortolan's and other reconstructions, being based upon fragments only of the Twelve Tables, are to a large extent conjectural and do not, therefore, constitute a satisfactory basis for comparison with modern legislation.

A study of the early statutes, on the other hand, does not suffer from a similar uncertainty and they reveal the legislature, in what appears to be a haphazard rather than a systematic manner, bent on making criminal liability dependent in most cases on proof of guilty knowledge. The particular epithet "knowingly" is of comparatively recent origin but there are innumerable instances to be found in the statute book of analogous expressions being used from the thirteenth century onwards.[2] Of these, the most frequently used were the words "wittingly" and "willingly", the former making its first appearance in 1343 in an Act[3] designed to repress the export of "money of good sterling" out of the realm, an offence created under the exigencies of an economic situation apparently bearing a close parallel to modern times. After languishing in idleness for the next hundred years it was next inserted in the Abduction of Women Act, 1486,[4] which made it a felony for any person "to wittingly receive any woman taken away against her will".

In succeeding legislation the term "wittingly" appears to have been forsaken and, instead, we find the word "willingly" used quite frequently during the greater part of the sixteenth century. Thus, beginning with the Increase of Horses Act, 1535,[5] it was inserted in such a variety of statutes as the Apothecaries Act, 1540,[6] the Burning of Frames Act, 1545,[7] the Export of Bell Metal Act, 1548,[8] and the Watermen's Act, 1555.[9] However, the epithet "wittingly" is seen restored to favour in the first Forgery

[1] Clause 24. The only certainty which can be stated is that some mental element is required in the offences defined in clauses 10 and 24, though without such particularity as is suggested by Ortolan.

[2] Markby in his *Elements of Law* (1905), p. 323 gives a list of adverbs which he has come across in codes and other legislative provisions. These include the following: fraudulently, dishonestly, maliciously, knowingly, intentionally, wantonly, malignantly, rashly, negligently, wilfully, wickedly, imprudently, wrongfully, unlawfully, illegally, unjustly. The learned author expresses the doubtful comment that most of these epithets originated with the judges.

[3] 17 Edw. 3, entitled the Money, Silver Act.

[4] 3 Hen. 7, c. 2, s. 2.

[5] 27 Hen. 8, c. 6, s. 4.

[6] 32 Hen. 8, c. 40, s. 4.

[7] 37 Hen. 8, c. 6, s. 2.

[8] 2 & 3 Edw. 6, c. 37, s. 5.

[9] 2 & 3 Ph. & M., c. 16, s. 8.

Act of 1562,[1] section 2 of which made it a felony for any person to "wittingly, subtilly, and falsely forge or make, or subtilly cause or wittingly assent to be forged or made, any false deed, character writing".

Not content with one word to define the necessary mental element the legislature, it will be noted, in the last example cited, sought to underline the emphasis on *mens rea* by using three expressions, a practice which was by no means uncommon at that time. Another example occurs in the Watermen's Act, 1555, which made it an offence for any waterman to "willingly, voluntarily and obstinately withdraw himself in time of Pressing".[2] A supreme illustration of this extravagant mode of defining an offence is to be found in the Burning of Frames Act, 1545,[3] it being made a felony to "maliciously, unlawfully, willingly and severly burn any frame of timber" required for building purposes. Occasionally, the legislature was content to rely upon a single expression, such as the forcible but significant word "obstinately" which appears in a variety of offences including, for example, that of "obstinately keeping a common alehouse without a licence",[4] or, in another statute, "any minister who obstinately uses any other administration of the Sacrament than is mentioned and set forth in the Book of Common Prayer".[5] Other epithets which began to make their appearance in sixteenth-century enactments and have since continued to flit across the pages of the statute book right up to the present day, include the words "advisedly" which made its debut in the Treason Act, 1562,[6] "corruptly", introduced in the first Perjury Act, 1562,[7] and "fraudulently"[8] which, if a count were taken, would probably come near the top of the list of epithets which form the basis of particular criminal liability.

Before leaving the penal statutes enacted during the sixteenth century it is interesting to note the appearance in two enactments of the terms "wittingly" and "willingly" side by side in the same offence. Thus, under the Bankrupts Act, 1570,[9] a penalty was incurred by any person who "willingly and wittingly helps to hide or keep secretly any bankrupt wanted for examination", and the

[1] 5 Eliz., c. 14, s. 2.
[2] 2 & 3 Ph. & M. c. 16, s. 8.
[3] 37 Hen. 8, c. 6, s. 2.
[4] 5 & 6 Edw. 6, c. 25, s. 4.
[5] 2 & 3 Edw. 6, c. 1, s. 9.
[6] 5 Eliz., c. 1, s. 10.
[7] 5 Eliz., c. 9, s. 3.
[8] An analysis of the authorities dealing with this word is to be found in Chapter VIII.
[9] 13 Eliz., c. 7, s. 9.

Jesuits Act, 1585,[1] made it an offence "to wittingly and willingly receive, relieve, comfort and maintain any Jesuit . . . knowing the same to be a Jesuit". Whether any difference in the meaning of these two words was intended is highly improbable, but they do serve as a pointer to the groping methods of draftsmanship displayed in the early statutes.

Early use of "knowingly"

Although, as will be seen later, the words "permitting" and "suffering" are to be found as early as 1604 in the Licensing Act[2] of that year, it is necessary to move forward to the end of the seventeenth century to discover what appears to be the earliest instance of the particular expression "knowingly" being inserted in a statutory offence. In the Suppression of Piracy Act, 1698,[3] it appears as an alternative to "wittingly", whilst in the Riot Act, 1714[4] the phrase used is "wilfully or knowingly". A touch of colour is provided by the Piracy Act, 1721,[5] which made it a felony for any master of a ship to "fit out any ship or vessel knowingly with a design to trade with . . . any pirate, felon or robber on the seas". Later, the terms "knowingly and wilfully" are seen used conjunctively in the Royal Marriages Act, 1772,[6] which confirmed the Crown's prerogative to superintend and approve of the marriages of the Royal Family.

Modern use of "knowingly"

Turning to the statutes of the nineteenth century there are increasing indications of the widespread use of the word "knowingly". To cite only a few examples, it appears as the basis of criminal liability in offences created by the Embezzlement of Public Stores Act, 1800,[7] the Prisoners of War Escape Act, 1812,[8] the Licensing Act, 1828,[9] the Coinage Offences Act, 1832,[10] the

[1] 27 Eliz., c. 2, s. 4. [2] 1 Jac. 1, c. 9, s. 2. [3] 11 Will. 3, c. 7, s. 9.
[4] 1 Geo. 1, st. 2, c. 5. [5] 8 Geo. 1, c. 24, s. 1.
[6] 12 Geo. 3, c. 11. For an elaborate discussion of this important statute, see (1951) 14 *M.L.R.* 53.
[7] 39 & 40 Geo. 3, c. 89. [8] 52 Geo. 3, c. 156, s. 1.
[9] 9 Geo. 4, c. 61, s. 13 and Sch. (*c*). This statute repealed in all seven earlier enactments. A sketch of the early history of the Licensing Laws is to be found in (1904) 20 *L.Q.R.* pp. 316–321. See, too, the *History of Liquor Licensing in England* by Sidney and Beatrice Webb (1903).
[10] 2 Will. 4, c. 34, s. 10.

Marriage Acts, 1823 and 1836,[1] the Forgery Act, 1861,[2] the Larceny Act, 1861,[3] and the Customs Consolidation Act, 1876.[4] A more up-to-date example occurs in the Post Office Act, 1953.[5]

Importing "knowingly" into a statutory offence

At the present time, the insertion of the crucial word "knowingly" in a newly enacted statute or regulation is a commonplace, though even such instances are probably considerably less in number than the veritable flood of offences of absolute prohibition, sometimes rather enigmatically described as public welfare offences. The task which constantly engages the attention of the Courts when construing nebulously worded statutory offences, namely, that of deciding whether or not to import *mens rea*, is by no means a recent innovation. From the beginning of the nineteenth century, there is evidence of the willingness of certain judges to effect judicial legislation by introducing into a statutory offence the necessity for proof of a guilty mind. A detailed investigation into the attitude adopted by individual judges, however fascinating the prospect may be, does not fall within the purview of this study, but attention must be directed to certain cases in which the courts have expressly inserted the epithet "knowingly" into a statutory offence.

One of the earliest examples in which this tug-of-war is seen manifesting itself is *R.* v. *Marsh.*[6] A carrier was charged in that case under the statute 5 Ann. c. 14, s. 2 with having game in his possession. Basing his defence on the ground that his agent was unaware that any game had been placed in the carrier's waggon, the accused claimed that he could not be convicted inasmuch as the information did not aver that the game was in his possession knowingly. This argument was soon dispelled by Abbott, C.J., who, pointing out that the statute contained no such word as "knowingly", fortified his opinion with the, by modern standards, odd remark:[7] "If it were necessary to aver that the defendant had actual knowledge it would cast on the prosecutor a burden of proof which could not easily be satisfied." When considering this case, it should be remembered that the doctrine of vicarious liability in criminal law was, at that time, undeveloped.

[1] 4 Geo. 4, c. 76, s. 21 and 6 & 7 Will. 4, c. 85, s. 39.

[2] 24 & 25 Vict. c. 98, s. 48.

[3] 24 & 25 Vict. c. 96, s. 91.

[4] 39 & 40 Vict. c. 36, s. 259.

[5] 1 & 2 Eliz. 2, c. 36, s. 63 (1) (*a*) and s. 63 (2).

[6] (1824) 2 B. & C. 717.

[7] *Ibid.*, p. 721.

Less certainty was displayed in *Burnby* v. *Bollitt*[1] when consideration was given to the statutes "*De Pistoribus et aliis Vitellariis*"[2] and "*Pillor et Tumbrel*",[3] under which victuallers, brewers and other common dealers in victuals who, in the course of their trade, sold provisions unfit for the food of man, were held criminally responsible. Whilst the court was of opinion that knowingly selling such provisions was clearly punishable, they also expressed the view that guilt was probably incurred even if no knowledge was shown.[4]

Symptomatic of the strong feelings sometimes engendered in certain of the judges of that period is the case of *Hearne* v. *Garton.*[5] The defendants, acting as forwarding agents and unaware of its true contents, innocently sent for carriage by rail a case containing oil of vitriol which was euphemistically marked on the outside "some stocks, seeds and a few corks", a description which had been affixed to the case by the original sender. Though clearly, on principles of present-day construction, the particular offence[6] was one of absolute prohibition the court was unanimous in importing the necessity for guilty knowledge. Lord Campbell, C.J., said that the question at issue was whether the legislature intended that a man should be liable who sent the goods with the most perfect innocence.[7] After saying that the justices were clearly right in acquitting the defendants, he added:[7] "What they have done is very satisfactory to me." Crompton, J., likewise wasted little time in construing the relevant section which, he declared, without any doubt should read "if a party shall knowingly send . . . he shall be liable to the penalty named".[8]

A year earlier in *R.* v. *Cohen,*[9] Hill, J. applying what he describes as common sense to the construction of section 2 of the Embezzlement of Public Stores Act, 1698,[10] under which it was a crime to be found in possession of naval stores marked with a

[1] (1847) 16 M. & W. 644. See, too, *R.* v. *Stevenson* (1862) 3 F. & F. 106; *R.* v. *Jarvis* (1862) 3 F. & F. 108; and *R.* v. *Crawley* (1862) 3 F. & F. 109.

[2] Statute Edw. 2. [3] 51 Hen. 3.

[4] Cf. *Hobbs* v. *Winchester Corporation* [1910] 2 K.B. 471, in which it was held that where meat intended for human consumption is exposed for sale and is condemned as unsound, the person in whose possession or on whose premises the meat is found is liable to conviction under the Public Health Act, 1875, s. 117, whether he is or is not aware of the unsoundness of the meat.

[5] (1859) 28 L.J.M.C. 216. [6] 5 & 6 Will. 4, c. 107, s. 168.

[7] *Ibid.*, p. 219. Cf. Lord Russell of Killowen, C.J., in *Parker* v. *Alder* [1899] 1 Q.B. 20, at p. 25.

[8] *Ibid.*, p. 220.

[9] (1858) 8 Cox C.C. 41 See, too, *R.* v. *Wilmett* (1848) 3 Cox C.C. 281.

[10] 9 Will. 3, c. 41.

broad arrow, held that no offence was committed without proof of knowledge on the part of the accused that the goods were marked with the arrow. In striking contrast to the attitude adopted in later cases, notably in *Cundy* v. *Le Cocq*,[1] the learned judge referred to the recital in the preceding section of the Act as clarifying his interpretation of the section before the court. This interpretation was upheld a few years later by a strong Court for Crown Cases Reserved in *R.* v. *Sleep*,[2] where Cockburn, C.J., said:[3] "It is true that the Act of Parliament says nothing about knowledge; but I think that must be imported into the statute."

This trend of construing statutory offences in favour of the accused was continued in *Cove* v. *James*[4] and again in the case of *Nichols* v. *Hall*[5] which, inasmuch as it formed the corner stone of the much criticised recent decision in *Harding* v. *Price*,[6] deserves more than a passing mention. By the provisions of an Order made under the Contagious Diseases (Animals) Act, 1869,[7] any person having in his possession an animal affected with a contagious disease is required to give notice of the fact to a police constable with all practicable speed. Both members of the Divisional Court were clearly of the opinion that knowledge was an essential ingredient of the offence, Keating, J., advancing the argument, which was repeated by Lord Goddard, C.J., in *Harding* v. *Price*: "I cannot understand how, on any reasonable construction of the words it can be said that a man can neglect to give notice with all practicable speed without knowledge of the fact of which he is to give notice."[8]

R. v. *Prince marks change in judicial outlook*

Bearing in mind the general consensus of judicial opinion as expressed in the above cases, that where a statute creates a crime the intention of the legislature should be presumed to include the requirement for *mens rea* unless a contrary intention is shown, the decision in *R.* v. *Prince*[9] represents a radical change in the judicial outlook. Of the sixteen judges constituting the Court for Crown

[1] (1884) 13 Q.B.D. 207, discussed *post* p. 62–63.

[2] (1861) 30 L.J.M.C. 170.

[3] *Ibid.*, p. 173.

[4] (1871) L.R. 7 Q.B. 135, *per* Lush, J., at p. 137. The charge was under 6 & 7 Will. 4, c. 37, s. 8.

[5] (1873) L.R. 8 C.P. 322.

[6] [1948] 1 K.B. 695, discussed *post* p. 78 *et seq.*

[7] Animals Order, 1871, made in pursuance of 32 & 33 Vict. c. 96, s. 75.

[8] (1873) L.R. 8 C.P. at p. 326.

[9] (1875) 2 C.C.R. 154. On this case see *Mod. App. to Criminal Law*, pp. 218, 219, 265.

Cases Reserved in that case, Brett J., alone stood his ground in maintaining the necessity for *mens rea* in the offence created by section 55 of the Offences against the Person Act, 1861. That section prohibits the unlawful taking of an unmarried girl, under the age of 16, out of the possession and against the will of her father and mother. The girl in the case, although only 14, looked very much older than 16 and the jury found that the accused bona fide believed the girl's statement that she was eighteen. This defence was rejected by the overwhelming majority of the court who construed the section strictly, holding that any person who takes an unmarried girl out of the possession of her parents does so at the risk of her turning out to be under 16.[1]

Although various lines of reasoning were advanced in support of this ruling, throughout all the majority judgments attention is constantly focused on that part of the offence which relates to the age of the girl. This, of course, is not surprising since it was to this end that the accused's defence was directed. In the first of these judgments, Blackburn, J., with whom nine other judges agreed,[2] considered that the sole question for determination was the intention of the legislature. Rejecting the suggestion that the word "knowingly" should be inserted into the section, Blackburn, J. said it was impossible to suppose that the legislature meant the crime to depend upon the knowledge by the prisoner of the girl's actual age.

The second judgment, which was delivered by Bramwell, B., with the support of seven other members of the court,[3] has long been considered as embodying the moral wrong doctrine as a basis of criminal liability.[4] This view is no longer generally supported, but in *R.* v. *Prince*, Bramwell, B., refused to insert the word "knowingly" into the section on the ground that "the act forbidden is wrong in itself, if without lawful cause; I do not say

[1] Cf. the Criminal Law Amendment Act, 1922 (12 & 13 Geo. 5, c. 56), s. 2, which provides that to a charge of unlawful carnal knowledge of a girl between 13 and 16 (Criminal Law Amendment Act 1885 (48 & 49 Vict. c. 69) s. 5) it shall be a defence to prove that the accused reasonably believed that the girl was over 16. This defence is only available to a defendant who is 23 years of age or under and only on the first occasion on which he is charged with the offence (see *R.* v. *Rider* [1954] 1 All E.R. 5). For reasons wholly illogical the defence is not available to a charge of indecent assault.

[2] Cockburn, C.J., Mellor, Lush, Quain, Denman, Archibald, Field and Lindley, JJ., and Pollock, B.

[3] Kelly C.B., Cleasby, Pollock and Amphlett, BB., Grove, Quain and Denman, JJ.

[4] See *Mod. App. to Crim. Law*, pp. 218–219, and Glanville Williams *Criminal Law*, pp. 151–154.

illegal but wrong".[1] What is wrong, said the learned Baron, is the taking of an unmarried girl under the age of 16, which he said "gives full scope to the doctrine of *mens rea*".[2] Continuing, Bramwell B. said: "If the taker believed he had the father's consent, though wrongly, he would have no *mens rea*; so if he did not know she was in anyone's possession, nor in the care or charge of anyone. In those cases he would not know he was doing the *act* forbidden by the statute."[2]

The dangers underlying this principle, *viz.*, that the doctrine of *mens rea* is fulfilled by the simple doing of the forbidden act, have been stated before in this study. Unfortunately, in recent years, those voices which have been strongest in condemning any unrestricted incursions into the fundamental maxim of criminal law, that there must be both a guilty act and a guilty mind, are often the very same voices which give support to this contrary explanation of *mens rea*.[3] If allowed to establish itself, the latter doctrine must inevitably tend to weaken the necessity for a guilty mind in criminal liability. Equally opprobrious, it is respectfully suggested, in the above passage from Bramwell B.'s judgment, is the adoption of the view that the *act* forbidden by the statute may concern only one out of the many elements which make up the offence. Earlier in this work it has been argued[4] that this theory is unjustified, and that the correct view is that the "*act*" forbidden by statute includes not only the primary act but also every condition in the statutory definition which relates to the consequences of such act, as opposed to the realisation or knowledge of such consequences which properly falls under the heading of *mens rea*.

This, it is submitted, was the principle adopted by the Court for Crown Cases Reserved[5] in *R.* v. *Hibbert*,[6] a decision which is frequently overlooked and more frequently not understood when it is compared with the later decision in *R.* v. *Prince*. The same offence was involved but the facts were somewhat different. Meeting the girl in the street on her way to Sunday School, the

[1] (1875) 2 C.C.R. 154, at p. 174. [2] *Ibid.*, p. 175.

[3] Compare, for example, Lord Goddard C.J., in *Brend* v. *Wood* (1946) 62 T.L.R. 462, 463, with the same judge's view in *Reynolds* v. *G. H. Austin, Ltd.* [1951] 2 K.B. 135 at pp. 138, 140.

[4] *Ante*, p. 42. See, too, *post*, pp. 90, 113–114.

[5] Consisting of Bovill C.J., Channell and Pigott, BB., Byles and Lush, JJ.

[6] (1869) 1 C.C.R. 184, following *R.* v. *Green* 3 F. & F. 274, a decision of Martin, B. In *R.* v. *Prince* only Brett, J., adverted to this case in his judgment, although Cockburn C.J. mentioned it in the course of the preliminary discussion.

accused induced her to accompany him to a neighbouring town where he seduced her. They returned together and having left the girl where he met her she immediately went home. No question of mistaken belief as to the girl's age arose in *R.* v. *Hibbert*, but the court quashed the conviction on the ground that there was no finding that the prisoner knew or had reason to believe that the girl was in the lawful care of her parents. This ruling amounts to a recognition by the court that knowledge that the girl was in the possession of her parents is an essential element in the offence. To establish such knowledge in the accused, it was open to the prosecution to show either actual knowledge or constructive knowledge in the sense that he had reason to believe but deliberately refrained from finding out.

It must be noticed, however, that the actual decision in *R.* v. *Hibbert* goes no further than requiring knowledge of *one* of the conditions of liability, namely, that the girl was in the possession of her parents. Moreover, in accepting, as sufficient, proof that the accused had reason to believe that the girl was in the possession of her parents the court, it is suggested, was merely acknowledging the principle that wilful blindness is equally culpable with actual knowledge. What is apparent, however, and difficult to reconcile, is the different application in the two cases of the basic requirement of knowledge. In *Hibbert* it was extended to the condition that the girl was in the possession of her parents, whereas in *Prince* it was rejected as having no application to the condition relating to the age of the girl. It may well be that different emphasis should be placed on these respective elements in the offence, but there can be no doubt that both are essential to the commission of the crime. The only possible line of reconciliation is that mooted by Bramwell, B., in *R.* v. *Prince*, *viz.*, that if the taker did not know that the girl was in anyone's possession, nor in the care or charge of anyone, he would not be liable because he would not know that he was doing the act forbidden by the statute.[1] If, on the other hand, this interpretation of the forbidden act is rejected, it follows that the two decisions are in conflict.[2] In practice, too much importance need not be attached to

[1] (1875) 2 C.C.R. at p. 175.

[2] Another way of reconciling the two cases is impliedly suggested by Glanville Williams, *Criminal Law*, pp. 260–261, who says that the same crime may be of strict liability in respect of one element and require fault (in the sense of knowledge) in respect of another. But this line of reasoning adds no greater attraction for the author than it does for the present writer.

this conflict, since the decision in *R.* v. *Prince* has long been accepted as the authoritative interpretation of section 55.

Despite the overwhelming rejection of his opinion, Brett, J.'s minority judgment is valuable for its wider consideration of *mens rea*, particularly with reference to the use of the word "knowingly" in statutory offences. In this connection, Brett J., classified together the three words "maliciously", "wilfully" and "knowingly", saying that they were "mere differences in form" all requiring proof of a guilty mind.[1] Of the expression "knowingly" he said that it is used "where the noxious character of the prohibited act depends upon a knowledge in the prisoner of their noxious effect, other than the mere knowledge that he is doing the acts. The presence of the word calls for more evidence on the part of the prosecutor".[2]

Furthermore, according to Brett, J., citing in support the judgments delivered in *R.* v. *Marsh*,[3] "the ultimate proof necessary to authorise a conviction is not altered by the presence or absence of the word 'knowingly' though by its presence or absence the burden of proof is altered."[4] Whether this statement was in the mind of Day, J., twenty years later is not known but in *Sherras* v. *de Rutzen*[5] we find the same proposition being maintained and it has since been repeatedly followed in several recent cases.[6] The accuracy of this rule was doubted by Devlin, J., in *Roper* v. *Taylor's Central Garages*[7] and it will be subjected to a detailed examination later,[8] so that it is unnecessary to discuss the question further at the moment.

With the decision in *R.* v. *Prince* marking, as it were, a prominent milestone along the path of cases in which the courts have construed offences as being of absolute liability, the decision in *Cundy* v. *Le Cocq*[9] is but the natural consequence of the stiffening

[1] (1875) 2 C.C.R. p. 160.

[2] *Ibid.*, p. 161.

[3] (1824) 2 B. & C. 717. For what, it is suggested, is the correct explanation of the views expressed in this case as to the shifting of the burden of proof, see *Newman* v. *Jones* (1886) 17 Q.B.D. 132, *per* A. L. Smith, J., at p. 136.

[4] (1875) 2 C.C.R. p. 161.

[5] [1895] 1 Q.B. 918, at p. 920.

[6] See *Gaumont British Distributors Ltd.* v. *Henry* [1939] 2 K.B. 711, at p. 721; *Harding* v. *Price* [1948] 1 K.B. 695, at p. 700; *Reynolds* v. *G. H. Austin Ltd.*, [1951] 2 K.B. 135, at p. 145.

[7] [1951] 2 T.L.R. 284, at pp. 287–288.

[8] See p. 90 *et seq.*

[9] (1884) 13 Q.B.D. 207. Cf. *Sherras* v. *De Rutzen* [1895] 1 Q.B. 918, discussed *post* p. 77. Comparison may also usefully be made with two recent decisions in Australia and Canada respectively. In *Maher* v. *Musson* (1934) 52 C.L.R. 100 the accused was charged under the Distillation Act 1901–1931, s. 74 (4), with having in his custody illicit spirits. Subsection 7 of the same section makes it an offence to purchase any

attitude of the judges. As is well known, in that case the Divisional Court, of which surprisingly Stephen, J., was the leading exponent of the new outlook, held that the words of the Licensing Act, 1872, s. 13, which made it an offence to sell any intoxicating liquor to any drunken person, amounted to an offence of absolute prohibition. It is no defence, according to the court, to show that the licensee acted under a bona fide mistake as to the condition of the person served. Undisturbed by the incongruous position created by the existence, side by side within the same section, of the offence of permitting drunkenness which requires proof of guilty knowledge, Stephen, J., explained the Court's decision by declaring that "it is necessary to look at the object of each Act that is under consideration to see whether and how far knowledge is of the essence of the offence created".[1]

Mens Rea AND BIGAMY

No discussion of the question of guilty knowledge as the basis of criminal liability would be complete without an analysis of the conflicting authorities dealing with the felony of bigamy. The attitude of the courts towards this particular offence has swung to and fro during the past sixty odd years, and the present trend of judicial opinion seems to point to a return to the original interpretation of bigamy as a crime involving proof of *mens rea*.

Originally, bigamy was treated as an offence against the canon law[2] and the earliest mention of bigamy in a statute was in the Statute de Bigamis[3] in 1275, where it is referred to as a capital offence. The law, as it stands today, is contained in section 57 of

illicit spirits knowing them to be illicit spirits. Despite the absence of any reference to knowledge in the subsection under which the accused was charged, the High Court of Australia (Rich, Dixon, Evatt and McTiernan JJ., Starke J. *dissentiente*) held that it was a good defence to prove that the accused neither believed nor had reason to believe that the spirits were illicit. By contrast, the Ontario Court of Appeal (Henderson, Laidlaw and Bowlby, JJ. A) in *R.* v. *Lawrence* [1952] O.R. 149 held that it was no defence to a charge of illegal possession of a narcotic drug, under s. 4 (1) (*d*) of the Opium and Narcotic Drug Act, 1929, that the accused did not know that the substance in his possession was a narcotic drug, For a strong criticism of this decision see (1952) 30 Can. B.R. 420–423.

[1] *Ibid.*, p. 210.

[2] Blackstone, *Commentaries*, Vol. 4, p. 163, n. (*b*). The meaning of bigamy in those early days was considerably different from the modern definition for, according to the canonists, bigamy consisted in marrying either two virgins successively one after the death of the other, or in once marrying a widow.

[3] 4 Edw. 1. The better opinion is that the common law courts had no jurisdiction in respect of bigamy until 1603, in the reign of James I. See 1 Jac. 1, c. 11.

the Offences against the Person Act, 1861,[1] which defines the crime of bigamy as follows: "Whosoever, being married, shall marry any other person during the life of the former husband or wife shall be guilty of felony." The statute then goes on to provide three exceptions which it is necessary to note carefully, for the offence is not committed by any person (1) who marries a second time[2] whose husband or wife shall have been continually absent from such person for the space of seven years then last past and shall not have been known by such person to be living within that time; or (2) who, at the time of such second marriage, shall have been divorced from the bond of the first marriage; or (3) whose former marriage shall have been declared void by the sentence of any court of competent jurisdiction.

It will be recalled that the offence in section 55 of the same enactment was construed in *R.* v. *Prince*[3] as embodying an absolute prohibition. Certainly, if the above section is read literally, no mention of the necessity for *mens rea* appears and prima facie, therefore, bigamy would appear to exclude any question of knowledge, with the exception of the first statutory defence indicated above.

Is bigamy a crime of absolute prohibition or is it based upon mens rea?

In 1889, in the leading case of *R.* v. *Tolson*,[4] this problem was considered at great length by the Court for Crown Cases Reserved consisting of fourteen judges.[5] In 1921, in *R.* v. *Wheat and*

[1] 24 & 25 Vict., c. 100, s. 57, re-enacting 9 Geo. 4, c. 31, s. 22 (c) and 10 Geo. 4, c. 34, s. 26. Some of the United States statutes call the crime "polygamy", some call it "bigamy", and some use the two words synonymously. For the various definitions of bigamy in the United States see Miller, *Criminal Law*, p. 424.

[2] In *R.* v. *Treanor* [1939] 1 All E.R. 330, it was held by the C.C.A. that the defence of seven years absence was not available to a person who married a third time. This decision was disapproved of in *R.* v. *Taylor* [1950] 2 K.B. 368, in which the court had little difficulty in showing the fallacy of the judgment in *Treanor*. It was pointed out that the words "second marriage" appear in the definition of bigamy in s. 57, so that on the interpretation given to similar words in the first proviso in *Treanor*, a person could never be convicted of bigamy in respect of a third marriage. In *R.* v. *Taylor* it was held that the second marriage referred to the second marriage charged in the count of the indictment, any other bigamous marriages, however many, being irrelevant. See *Bigamy and the Third Marriage* by Glanville Williams (1950) 13 *M.L.R.* 417.

[3] (1875) L.R. 2 C.C.R. 154.

[4] (1889) 23 Q.B.D. 168.

[5] Lord Coleridge C.J., Willes, Charles, Cave, Day, Smith, Stephen, Grantham, and Hawkins JJ. formed the majority of the court—Manisty, Denman, Pollock, Field, and Huddleston JJ. formed the minority.

Stocks[1] the Court of Criminal Appeal, composed of five judges,[2] directed their minds to the same question. It is with the views expressed in these two well-known cases that this study must inevitably concentrate. The facts in the respective cases are not, at this stage, important. Suffice it for the moment to say that the defence in *Tolson* was a bona fide belief in the death of the former husband, such belief preventing the accused from having any guilty intention, whereas in *Wheat* it was a bona fide belief that the accused had been divorced. In *Tolson* the defence was allowed, whereas in *Wheat* the defence was rejected.

Upon what grounds was this apparent divergent approach to the statutory definition of bigamy based? Delivering the unanimous judgment of the Court of Criminal Appeal in *R.* v. *Wheat*, Avory, J., said:[3] "It is true that the judgment in *Tolson* . . . proceeded mainly on the application of the maxim *actus non facit reum nisi mens sit rea* . . . but it was limited, in that case, to the belief in the death of the former husband. . . . In our opinion, the maxim, in its application to the statute, is satisfied if the evidence establishes an intention on the part of the accused to do the act forbidden by the statute, viz. 'Being married, to marry another person during the life of the former wife or husband'." The learned judge also made the observation that, in the opinion of the court, their decision to reject the defence submitted in *Wheat* was "not in conflict with the decision of the majority of the judges in *Tolson*, but was in accord with the principle of the judgment in *Prince*".[4]

Examination of the opinions expressed in *R.* v. *Tolson* indicate, it is respectfully submitted, that the explanation advanced by Avory, J., is both different from, and inconsistent with, the majority judgments in the earlier case. Those judges who constituted the majority in *Tolson* did not seek to limit the application of the maxim to a belief in the death of the former spouse but, on the contrary, indicated that in their view *mens rea* was an essential element in the crime of bigamy.

Thus, in the first of the majority judgments, delivered by Willes, J., with whose views Charles, J. concurred, referring to *R.* v. *Prince* as "a direct and cogent authority for saying that the intention of the legislature cannot be decided upon simple prohibitory words, without reference to other considerations",[5] the learned

[1] [1921] 2 K.B. 119.
[2] Avory, Bray, Shearman, Slater and Greer, JJ.
[3] [1921] 2 K.B. at p. 126.
[4] *Ibid.*, p. 125.
[5] (1889) 23 Q.B.D. at p. 180.

judge declared:[1] "The considerations relied upon in that case are wanting in the present case, whilst, as it seems to me, those which point to the application of the principle underlying a vast area of criminal enactment, that there can be no crime without a tainted mind, preponderate greatly over any that point to its exclusion."

The next judgment was that of Cave, J., with whose views Lord Coleridge, C.J., Day and A. L. Smith JJ. agreed. Reiterating the general principle underlying the fundamental maxim of criminal law, Cave, J., stated that "At common law an honest and reasonable belief in the existence of circumstances which, if true, would make the act for which a prisoner is indicated an innocent act has always been held to be a good defence".[2] The learned judge continued:[2] "So far as I am aware it has never been suggested that this exception does not equally apply in cases of statutory offences unless they are excluded expressly or by necessary implication." It is only right to state that in *R.* v. *Wheat* the Court, referring to this passage in the judgment of Cave, J., expressed the opinion that if the learned judge was laying this down as a principle applicable to all statutes they did not agree with him.[3] The principle, the Court of Criminal Appeal said, was stated too widely. But is it? By his own words, Cave, J., clearly did not intend that this common law principle should be applied "to all statutes" as he foresaw cases of statutory offences where the maxim "is excluded expressly or by necessary implication". Whether, in fact, the maxim is excluded in the case of bigamy is another matter, Cave, J., being firmly of the opinion that the maxim did apply. To the contention that the first part of the section was expressed absolutely, the learned judge considered that a case of insanity would not fall within its provisions. "If an exception is to be admitted" Cave, J. concluded,[4] "where the reasoning faculty is perverted by disease, why is not an exception equally to be admitted where the reasoning faculty, although honestly and reasonably exercised, is deceived?"

Stephen, J., likewise, accepted the competency of the legislature to define a crime in such a way as to make the existence of any state of mind immaterial. He considered that the case of *R.* v. *Prince* was distinguishable from that of the present case, for in *Prince* all the judges, with one exception, "considered that the object of the legislature being to prevent a scandalous and wicked

[1] (1889) 23 Q.B.D p. 180.

[2] *Ibid.*, pp. 181, 182.

[3] [1921] 2 K.B. at p. 126.

[4] (1889) 23 Q.B.D. at p. 182.

invasion of parental rights . . . it was to be supposed that they intended that the wrongdoer should act at his peril."[1] But Stephen, J., made it clear that he was not prepared to accept the proposition that the legislature, in enacting section 57, intended bigamy to be a crime of absolute prohibition. He said:[2] "It appears to me that every argument which shewed in the opinion of the judges in *R.* v. *Prince* that the legislature meant seducers and abductors to act at their peril, shews that the legislature did not mean to hamper, what is not only intended, but naturally and reasonably supposed by the parties to be a valid and honourable marriage, with a liability to seven years' penal servitude."

It must not be thought that the court were unanimous in their interpretation of the section defining bigamy. A minority of five judges were equally firm in their opinion that the language used by the legislature was plain and explicit and free from all ambiguity. That being so, it was said, "it is the imperative duty of the court to give effect to it, and to leave it to the legislature to alter the law if it thinks it ought to be altered."[3]

With the lead given in *R.* v. *Prince* it might have been expected that a different construction would have been adopted in *R.* v. *Tolson*, but whereas it is true that the ratio decidendi in *Tolson* was restricted to a bona fide belief in the death of the former spouse, it is submitted that the general reasoning of the majority judgments distinctly excludes any limitation of the doctrine of *mens rea* to such a belief.[4] Furthermore, it is submitted that bigamy is not a crime of absolute prohibition and that the common law maxim applies, making the absence of guilty knowledge a good defence.

Possible defences to bigamy at common law

This submission may be tested further, by considering the various possibilities which might arise in which a person marries again mistakenly believing the circumstances to be different from what they are in reality. These defences are, of course, exclusive of the three statutory defences contained in the proviso to section 57.

[1] (1889) 23 Q.B.D. at p. 190. [2] *Ibid.*, p. 191. [3] *Ibid.*, p. 196.
[4] Support for this view is found in the judgment of Latham C.J. in the Australian case *Thomas* v. *The King* 59 Commonwealth L.R. 279.

(1) *Belief in the death of the former spouse*

This belief was held to be a valid defence in *R.* v. *Tolson*, where the facts were, briefly, as follows. The accused, Mrs. Tolson, was married in 1880. In 1881 her husband deserted her. As a result of inquiries made about him from his brother, Mrs. Tolson was led to believe that her husband had been lost in a ship bound for America, which had gone down with all hands. In 1887 she married again, believing herself to be a widow. Later the same year, the first husband re-appeared on the scene.

There is no doubt that the case fell within the words of section 57.[1] The accused Mrs. Tolson, being married, married another person during the life of her former husband. Moreover, when she did so, he had not been continually absent from her for seven years as required to come within the first exception contained in the proviso. What then was the basis of the court's decision to quash the conviction? What difference was there, in the application of the general principle as to *mens rea*, from the decision in *R.* v. *Prince*? The answer, as has already been suggested, lies in the court's view as to the intention of the legislature. Whereas in *Prince* the court was of the opinion that the general principle requiring *mens rea* was excluded by the legislature's intention that if anyone does the wrong act of abducting a girl under 16, he does it at the risk of her turning out to be under 16; in *Tolson*, a majority of the court were of the opinion that the legislature cannot have intended in cases of bigamy a similar exclusion of the principle requiring a "guilty mind".[2]

[1] This being so, it is difficult to understand the view advanced by the learned editor of *Russell on Crime*, (10th ed.), p. 74, that the true explanation of *Tolson* is that the court allowed the defence of mistaken belief that the other spouse was dead, on the ground that it showed that there was no *actus reus*. Now, the *actus reus* of bigamy consists in "being married, marrying any other person during the life of the former husband or wife". When, therefore a person re-marries mistakenly believing the other spouse to be dead but who, in fact, is still alive, surely all the elements of the *actus reus* are fulfilled. On facts like those in *Tolson* the plea of mistaken belief is in reality a defence of absence of *mens rea* which view, it is maintained, was the basis of the majority judgments in that case. It was the accused's ignorance of the fact that she was still married which negatived her *mens rea*. A similar interpretation of *Tolson* is given by Glanville Williams, *Criminal Law*, pp. 5–6.

[2] In the United States, until recently, bigamy statutes have been interpreted to exclude *mens rea*. In the *Mass. Case* (1844) 7 Metc. 472 it was held that even a reasonable mistake regarding the death of the spouse was no defence. Commenting on this decision, the exact opposite of that reached in *Tolson*, Hall comments (*General Principles* p. 371): "Largely because of the influence of this case our law on bigamy can only be characterised as thoroughly disorganised." According to Hall bigamy, if interpreted soundly, requires a *mens rea*, viz., entry into a marriage with knowledge of an

(2) *Belief that the first marriage has been dissolved by divorce*[1]

This was the defence before the court in *R.* v. *Wheat and Stocks.* In that case the accused had been admitted as a poor person to bring divorce proceedings against his wife. On finding that the woman, Stocks, whom he wished to marry when divorced from his first wife, was about to become a mother, the prisoner sent an urgent telegram to his solicitors who wrote in reply, "We have your telegram and hope to send you papers for signature in the course of a day or two." Wheat, who was a man of little education, stated that on receipt of that letter he believed that he was divorced and consequently "married" the woman Stocks.

The jury were satisfied that the accused believed in good faith and on reasonable grounds that he had been divorced when he went through the alleged bigamous marriage. However, Sankey, J., directed the jury to return a verdict of guilty so that the question of law might be determined. The Court of Criminal Appeal found that, on the facts of the case, the belief of the accused was not reasonable and that, on that ground alone, the appeal should be dismissed. This doctrine has already been exploded, it being recognised now that absence of *mens rea* may satisfactorily be proved by either a reasonable or unreasonable mistaken belief, the only difference being the degree of success in convincing the jury that the accused had no guilty mind.[2] The court further held that even had there been reasonable grounds for the prisoner's belief, if in fact he had not actually been divorced, that is no defence in law to a charge of bigamy.[3]

The basis for the unanimous decision of the Court of Criminal Appeal rested on their interpretation of the second exception to section 57. Thus, Avory, J. stated:[4] "In the case of the second exception, there is no indication in the statute that any presump-

existing, binding union. Now, a few years ago in *Long* v. *State* (1949) 65 A. 2d. 489, there is a decision favouring the requirement of guilty knowledge in bigamy and this view has been welcomed in a note on the case in 62 *Harv. L.R.* 1393. On the earlier U.S. cases of bigamy see Trowbridge, *Criminal Intent and Bigamy*, 7 Calif. L.R. 1., and Michael and Wechsler, *Criminal Law and its Administration*, pp. 775–776.

[1] To come within the second exception contained in the proviso to section 57 a decree absolute is necessary, a decree nisi being insufficient.

[2] See *Wilson* v. *Inyang* [1951] 2 K.B. 799, and the discussion of this question, *ante*, pp. 28, 49–50.

[3] For an example where an honest belief that a prior marriage had been dissolved was held a good defence under a statute defining bigamy as "knowingly having a plurality of husbands or wives at the same time", see the United States case *Robinson* v. *State* 6 Ga. App. 69*b*.

[4] [1921] 2 K.B. at p. 125.

tion or belief is to afford any defence . . . the only defence under this head appears to be that the accused has, in fact, been divorced from the bond of the first marriage. If he has not, then at the time of the second marriage, he is a person who, being married, intends to do the act forbidden by the statute, viz., to marry during the life of the former wife."

The Court endeavoured to distinguish the case of *Wheat* from that of *Tolson* on the ground that in *Tolson* the accused, believing that her husband was dead, did not intend, at the time of the second marriage, to do the act forbidden by the statute, viz., to marry during her husband's life. But surely the same argument could be extended to cases where the accused husband, say, knowing his former spouse to be alive, nevertheless honestly believes his former wife to be no longer his wife. May it not be said that in the latter circumstances—no less than in *Tolson*—the accused did not intend, at the time of the second marriage, to do the act forbidden by the statute?

It has been suggested that the two cases, *Tolson* and *Wheat*, are reconcilable on the footing that a belief in death is a mistake of fact, whereas a belief in divorce is a mistake of law.[1] Such a convenient but, as will be shown later,[2] misguided distinction was not considered by the Court of Criminal Appeal in *R.* v. *Wheat*. Other academic writers have looked upon the decision in *Wheat* as good law,[3] and Lord Hewart, C.J., in a dictum in *R.* v. *Denyer*[4] stressed the importance of the court's observation upon *R.* v. *Tolson*.

On the other hand, there are at least two Dominion decisions—admittedly of persuasive authority only—one by the High Court of Australia,[5] the other by the High Court of New Zealand,[6] in

[1] Dr. Stallybrass, writing in 56 *L.Q.R.* pp. 64–67 and supported by Starke, J., in *Thomas* v. *The King* (1937) 59 C.L.R. 279. Cf. the equally forced distinction advanced in Williams, *Criminal Law*, pp. 142–144, which the author himself recognises is "very technical and not at all satisfactory".

[2] *Post*, pp. 74–76.

[3] Dr. R. M. Jackson, 6 *C.L.J.* 83 and Mr. J. W. C. Turner 6 *C.L.J.* 31. Cf. Glanville Williams, *Criminal Law*, p. 142 who says that in *Wheat* the *mens rea* doctrine reached its nadir.

[4] [1926] 2 K.B. 258, at pp. 265–266.

[5] *Thomas* v. *The King*, (1937) 59 C.L.R. 279 (majority of 3 to 2), in which the defence was that the accused reasonably and honestly thought that his marriage with his first wife was void, because the decree nisi which she had obtained from her previous husband had not been made absolute. In fact the decree had been made absolute. This case is discussed by G. W. Paton in (1939) 17 Can. B.R., pp. 94–104.

[6] *Carswell* (1926) N.Z.L.R. 321 (majority of 5 to 4). On the other hand *Wheat* was followed by the Supreme Court of Nova Scotia in *R.* v. *Morgan* (1942) 4 D.L.R. 321. A note on this case is in 16 Aust. L.J. 369.

which the limitation on the doctrine of *mens rea*, which *R.* v. *Wheat* advanced, has been rejected. Cases on the third possible defence, to which attention will next be directed, have also shown a disinclination to follow the principles expounded by Avory J. in *R.* v. *Wheat and Stocks*. Cumulatively, the decision in that case stands discredited, as needs must be if the emphasis is correctly placed on the necessity for proving a guilty mind.

(3) *Belief in the nullity of the first marriage*

It will be recalled that the third exception to section 57 states that the section shall not apply to any person "whose former marriage shall have been declared void by the sentence of any court of competent jurisdiction". Adopting the reasoning of the Court of Criminal Appeal in *R.* v. *Wheat*, and applying it to this particular defence, it would seem that since the statute makes no reference to any presumption or belief being a good defence, a mistaken belief as to the nullity of the first marriage will not excuse a person charged with bigamy. But was that the intention of the legislature, especially having regard to the undoubted fact that in certain circumstances a marriage may be treated by the parties as null and void without the necessity for any decree of nullity?

A distinction is drawn in law between void and voidable marriages. Thus, as was explained by Lord Greene M.R.:[1] "A void marriage is one that will be regarded by every court in any case in which the existence of the marriage is in issue as never having taken place, and can be so treated by both parties to it without the necessity of any decree annulling it; a voidable marriage is one that will be regarded by every court as a valid subsisting marriage, until a decree annulling it has been pronounced by a court of competent jurisdiction." The law, as it stands today, considers a marriage to be rendered void *ab initio* in various circumstances, of which the following are worth noting, viz., (i) if either party is under 16 years of age,[2] or (ii) if either party is already married, or (iii) if the parties are within the pro-

[1] *De Reneville* v. *De Reneville* [1948] 1 All E.R. 56, at p. 60. See, too, Dicey's *Conflict of Laws* (5th ed.) p. 295 where it is said: "Where marriage has never validly subsisted . . . the parties to it are in no wise bound by it and a declaration is not necessary to free them from the legal relationship as that does not exist." This distinction was also adverted to by Lord Goddard C.J. in *R.* v. *Algar* [1953] 2 All E.R. 1381, at pp. 1383–1384, a case concerning the competency of a wife to give evidence on the trial of her husband on a criminal charge.

[2] Marriage Act 1949 (12 & 13 Geo. 6, c. 76) s. 2.

hibited degrees of consanguinity or affinity.[1] Supposing, then, a husband or wife, mistakenly believing the other spouse to fall within one or other of the above categories, thus invalidating the first marriage, and marries again, would such a plea be a good defence to a charge of bigamy? The court in *R.* v. *Wheat* impliedly indicated that such a belief would afford no defence, but it is important to remember that what Avory, J., said was *obiter*, though, of course, carrying considerable weight, representing as it did the unanimous opinion of a strong court of five judges.

In considering the validity of the opinion expressed in *R.* v. *Wheat* it is essential to bear in mind the decisions on this particular point before *Wheat* was heard in 1921. There had been three reported cases in each of which a belief in the nullity of the first marriage was considered to be a good defence. Leading the way was the Common Serjeant in the case of *R.* v. *Thompson*,[2] whose direction was followed in *R.* v. *Cunliffe*[3] and *R.* v. *Conatty*.[4] But in *Wheat* the Court of Criminal Appeal expressed doubts whether the Common Serjeant's ruling in *Thompson*, which they said "was probably based on *R.* v. *Tolson*", could be "supported consistently with our present decision".[5] The crux of the whole matter is the patent conflict between the decisions in the two leading cases. If the reasoning of the majority judgments in *Tolson* is accepted, then the correctness of the direction given in *Thompson*, *Cunliffe* and *Conatty* must be acknowledged. If, on the other hand, the judgment in *Wheat* is preferred, it is doubtful if the earlier cases can be supported.

Subsequent to *R.* v. *Wheat* there have been three cases, all of which were tried on circuit, in which divergent rulings have been given to the jury, according to the individual judge's attitude towards the Court of Criminal Appeal's dictum that it was doubtful whether a belief in the nullity of the first marriage con-

[1] *Ibid.*, s. 1 and Parts I and II of the First Schedule to the Act. Other grounds rendering a marriage void *ab initio* are the insanity of either party or an invalid ceremony of marriage. For the statutory grounds under which a marriage may be rendered voidable, see the Matrimonial Causes Act, 1950 (14 Geo. 6, c. 25), s. 8; common law grounds include impotence and want of consent based upon mistake, fraud or duress. See, generally, Eversley, *Domestic Relations* (6th ed.) pp. 21–47.

[2] (1906) 70 J.P.6. The principle in the direction to the jury was approved by the Canadian Court of Appeal in *R.* v. *Sellars* (1905) 9 Can. Cr. Cas. 153.

[3] (1913) 57 S.J. 345.

[4] (1919) 83 J.P. 292.

[5] [1921] 2 K.B. at p. 127. The learned editors of Halsbury's *Statutes of England*, 2nd ed. Vol. 5, p. 810, whilst acknowledging the existence of the defence accepted in *Thompson* and *Conatty*, make no reference to the C.C.A.'s dictum in *R.* v. *Wheat*.

stituted a defence to bigamy. It was followed, after some hesitation, by Humphreys, J. in *R.* v. *Kircaldy*[1] where the prisoner, after marrying his first wife, discovered letters addressed to her from one Garst, a person in India, who wrote: "My dear wife . . . from your darling husband." The accused subsequently re-married. After his arrest, he wrote to India to make inquiries about the alleged marriage, and also made inquiries at the India Office, both inquiries proving fruitless. The prosecution contended that the prisoner had the necessary *mens rea* for bigamy in that, being married, his wife being alive, he did intend to marry another person. Kircaldy was convicted and it may well be that the jury were not convinced as to the genuineness of his belief. But it is submitted that if Kircaldy's belief had been correct he did not intend to marry another during the life of his former wife, since the so-called former wife had never been his wife. If this argument is accepted, Kircaldy did not have the necessary *mens rea* and should have been acquitted.

In *R.* v. *Weiow*,[2] Macnaghten, J. indicated that he was not prepared to accept the dictum of the Court of Criminal Appeal in *Wheat*, preferring to follow the Common Serjeant's direction to the jury in *Thompson*. Finally, there is the more recent decision of Streatfield, J. in *R.* v. *Dolman*.[3] The facts are not dissimilar to those in *Weiow*, the accused stating that, prior to the alleged bigamous marriage, his first wife had produced to him what appeared to be a genuine marriage certificate showing that she had been previously married. Later she showed the accused a photograph in which she appeared as a bride, telling him that it was a photo of the wedding group at her earlier wedding. Furthermore, on consulting the Army Legal Aid Department at his overseas station, he was advised that his belief as to his wife's earlier marriage had been confirmed. His wife denied the whole story and witnesses were called by the Crown to disprove the possibility of any such earlier marriage.

Having had the earlier authorities—*Tolson*, *Thompson*, *Wheat* and *Weiow*—brought to his notice, Streatfield, J., in directing the

[1] Tried at Manchester Assizes in 1929. The only report of this case is to be found in an article entitled "Is belief in prior marriage a defence to bigamy?" (1929) 167 *L.T.*, pp. 44–46.

[2] Tried at Nottingham Summer Assizes in 1945. The case is unreported, but a full account will be found in (1949) *Current Legal Problems*, pp. 62–63.

[3] [1949] 1 All E.R. 813.

jury said:[1] ". . . it has been held that bigamy, like many other offences, requires that there shall be what is known as guilty knowledge. There must be an appreciation that a crime is being committed. In many cases the law requires that in addition to an unlawful act there shall be a specific intention to do something or other. That does not apply here, but the person accused must have a culpable, guilty knowledge that he is doing something unlawful." Relating this doctrine to the facts in *R.* v. *Dolman*, Streatfield, J., ruled that if the jury were satisfied that the accused "had reasonable cause to believe, and did believe, that what he thought at the time to be a legal and subsisting first marriage had turned out not to be a legal and subsisting first marriage",[2] that was a good defence.

What conclusion can be drawn from this apparent change in judicial thought? In effect, it is submitted, both the learned judges in *Weiow* and *Dolman* accepted the argument that the doctrine of *mens rea* is not limited to the circumstances of *R.* v. *Tolson*, but is of general application to the crime of bigamy. To convict a person of bigamy there must, in other words, be an appreciation by the accused at the time of going through the alleged bigamous marriage that (1) he or she was already legally married to another person, (2) that such an earlier legal marriage was still subsisting, and (3) that such other person was still alive. A mistaken belief, honestly entertained by the accused, that one or other of the above three conditions did not apply should afford a complete defence to a charge of bigamy.

Mistake of law and mistake of fact

This question of mistake has given rise to some misapprehensions in its connection with bigamy. Mention has already been made of the view, expressed by Dr. Stallybrass, that *R.* v. *Tolson* and *R.* v. *Wheat* were perfectly reconcilable on the footing that a

[1] [1949] 1 All E.R. p. 814.

[2] *Ibid.*, p. 815. The learned judge's readiness to import guilty knowledge into the statutory definition is also seen in the passage where he said: ". . . although the statute itself does not say that a man shall not 'knowingly' or 'unlawfully' go through a form of marriage, it has for many years been held that a man does not commit the criminal offence of bigamy unless he realises that he is committing that offence" (pp. 814–815). It is very unlikely that Streatfield J. meant that the accused must have realised that he was committing the offence of bigamy, since knowledge or ignorance of the law is irrelevant to the question of liability. What, it is suggested, the learned judge had in mind was the principle that the accused must have realised he was fulfilling all the elements and which, if committed, the law declares to be the crime of bigamy.

belief in death is a mistake of fact, whereas a belief in divorce is a mistake of law. It is, of course, well recognised that ignorance of the law will not excuse from the consequences of guilt any person who has capacity to understand the law.[1] This maxim, it is suggested, is concerned essentially with ignorance of, if one may use the adjective, the "pure" criminal law of this country, where public policy justifiably requires that ignorance of the existence of an offence is no defence. It is perfectly obvious that no single member of the community can be expected to know the existence of every single criminal offence on the statute book, leave alone the mass of offences created nowadays by ministerial regulations. Nevertheless, public policy dictates, and rightly so, that such ignorance shall be no defence.

Mistake of law, on the other hand, as was seen in the discussion earlier of claim of right as a defence to malicious and wilful crimes, normally relates to mistake as to the accused's rights under the law to do a particular act or to pursue a particular course of conduct. An alternative way of expressing the principle is that mistake of law concerns mistakes as to the civil law, statutory or otherwise, which results in the commission of a crime.[2] In this sense, it has been shown already that there is no general proposition which ordains that mistake of law is no defence to a criminal charge. But what of bigamy? Is it permissible to plead mistake of law to such a charge? If Stallybrass is correct, and his view accepted as explaining *R.* v. *Wheat*, then the cases on belief as to the nullity of the first marriage require some further explanation. Is nullity of marriage a question of law, or of fact?

Proceeding by analogy from *Wheat*, where mistake as to divorce has been generally agreed to be a mistake of law, it would seem that a mistake as to the nullity of marriage would similarly be a mistake of law. But is that the correct answer?[3] A glance at the

[1] Blackstone, *Commentaries*, Vol. 4, p. 27, and Hale, 1 *P.C.* 42. For some interesting views on this seemingly harsh doctrine compare Holmes, *The Common Law*, pp. 47–48, Allen, *Law in the Making* (1946 ed.) pp. 390–391, Denning, *The Changing Law*, p. 37, and Jerome Hall, *General Principles of Criminal Law*, pp. 351–357.

[2] See "Ignorance and Mistake in the Criminal Law", 22 *Harvard L.R.* 76, and Glanville Williams, *Criminal Law*, pp. 429–432.

[3] Cf. the different points of view expressed in the Australian case, *Thomas* v. *The King* (1937) 59 C.L.R. 279. Starke, J. (p. 296) thought that divorce is not a mere matter of fact; Dixon, J. (pp. 306–307) said that a mistake as to the existence of a compound event consisting of law and of fact is in general one of fact and not a mistake of law (referring to Jessel M.R. in *Eaglesfield* v. *Marquis of Londonderry* (1876) 4 Ch. D. 693, 702, 703).

various grounds upon which the law considers a marriage to be void *ab initio* and, therefore, the proper subject for a decree of nullity, will surely convince the doubtful that nullity of marriage may well involve a mixed question of law and fact. Suppose, for example, that A marries B. Later A mistakenly discovers that B, his co-called wife, was under the age of 16 when the marriage took place. Assuming that A had good grounds for his belief that this was so, and that therefore his marriage to B was null and void, if it subsequently transpires that B was in fact over 16 when she married A, that is essentially a mistake of fact.[1] The same argument, it is suggested, might apply where A mistakenly believed that A and B, at the time of their marriage, were within the prohibited degrees of consanguinity or affinity.

Enough has been said to show the weakness of the proposed distinction between *R.* v. *Tolson* and *R.* v. *Wheat* which is based on the difference between mistake of fact and mistake of law. Certainly, in the two recent cases of *R.* v. *Weiow* and *R.* v. *Dolman*, no attempt was made to justify the direction to the jury on the ground that the accused's mistaken belief related to a question of fact. The position then may be summed up in two propositions. First, if the courts maintain the principle adopted in *R.* v. *Wheat*, viz., that the words of the statute do not admit of any qualification as regards any presumption or belief (other than in relation to the spouse's death), then the difference between mistake of fact and law is irrelevant. Secondly, if the courts prefer to follow the majority reasoning in *R.* v. *Tolson* and to hold that *mens rea* is a constituent element of bigamy, then the question of mistake of fact or law will be directed solely to determining whether such mistake negatives the guilty knowledge necessary for the commission of the crime.

Intention of the Legislature and the Presumption as to *Mens Rea*

The principle of construction which emphasises the need for looking at the object of a statute and which is so often relied upon by those judges prepared to exclude the necessity for *mens rea*, was

[1] These were the facts in *R.* v. *Johnston* (1940), a case heard before the Common Serjeant at the Old Bailey and reported in the *Journal of Criminal Law* (1940) Vol. 5, pp. 185–186. The learned judge considered himself bound by the decision in *R.* v. *Wheat*, and directed the jury to find the prisoner guilty irrespective of whether or not he had a bona fide belief on reasonable grounds that his first marriage was invalid.

rejected in the later case of *Derbyshire* v. *Houliston*[1] by R. S. Wright, J., one of the few judges to measure up to the stature of Stephen J., in the field of criminal law. Before the court in that case was the Sale of Food and Drugs Act, 1875, s. 27 (3) of which makes it an offence to give a false warranty in writing to any purchaser in respect of an article of food or drug sold. Distinguishing this offence from those created in the earlier subsections of section 27 in which the words "knowingly" and "wilfully" appear, counsel for the respondent argued that by this deliberate omission in subsection 3 the legislature intended that a person who deals in such commodities should be under an absolute duty to ensure that any written warranty which was given was in fact correct. This argument, propounded by Stephen, J., in the somewhat different circumstances which existed in *Cundy* v. *Le Cocq* was not accepted by the Divisional Court[2] in *Derbyshire* v. *Houliston*, who held that knowledge that the warranty was false must be proved in order to convict for the offence. Wright, J., referring to the presumption as to guilty knowledge, said:[3] "I think that the presumption is strengthened by the rule *noscitur a sociis* when the offence created by the clause is found embedded amongst others all requiring guilty knowledge. I think that, unless the language imports a contrast of statement,[4] it ought rather to be taken as importing a similarity in that respect." As to the necessity for having regard to the object of the statute, Wright, J.'s views are expressed thus:[5] "I do not know what the intention of the framers of the section may have been nor are we bound to consider that. We have to construe the section according to the ordinary rules of construction which have to be applied to a criminal act."

The same eminent judge was concerned in the earlier case of *Sherras* v. *de Rutzen*,[6] in which a similar problem arose of construing the offence of supplying liquor to a constable on duty, which is to be found in section 16 (2) of the Licensing Act, 1872,[7] alongside the offences of knowingly harbouring and knowingly suffering a constable to remain on licensed premises during his tour of duty. In what can fairly be described as a complete departure from the interpretation adopted in *Cundy* v. *Le Cocq*, and in apparent defiance of the legislature's intention indicated by the omission

[1] (1897) 66 L.J.Q.B. 569.
[2] *Coram* R. S. Wright and Hawkins, JJ.
[3] *Ibid.*, p. 572.
[4] Cf. the wording of the Licensing Act 1872, s. 13.
[5] *Loc. cit.*
[6] [1895] 1 Q.B. 918.
[7] Re-enacted in the Licensing Act, 1953 (1 & 2 Eliz. 2, c. 46), s. 142.

from section 16 (2) of the term "knowingly", the Divisional Court[1] held that such word must be imported into the statutory definition. Any doubts, however, which may exist as to the correctness of the judicial interpretation placed upon sections 13 and 16 (2) respectively of the 1872 Act, are resolved by referring to the Licensing (Consolidation) Act, 1910,[2] which, in repealing the earlier statute, preserved without any alteration[3] the statutory definitions considered in *Cundy* v. *Le Cocq* and *Sherras* v. *de Rutzen*.

Where Parliament inserts the word "knowingly" in one offence but excludes it in another offence which is defined within the same section or in an adjoining section of the same statute, strictly speaking the court is not concerned with the legislature's reasons for making such a distinction. Moreover, as the cases have already shown, the attitude of the judges towards the construction of such offences has been sharply divided. But when the word "knowingly" appears in a section of a statute which is repealed and replaced by another section in a new Act, wherein the expression "knowingly" no longer appears, it would seem safe to assume that Parliament intended to make the new offence a crime not requiring proof of guilty knowledge.

Such an assumption did not appeal to the Divisional Court in the recent case of *Harding* v. *Price*.[4] In that case the accused, the driver of a motor-lorry was convicted under section 22 (2) of the Road Traffic Act, 1930, with failing to report an accident whereby damage was caused to another vehicle. Owing to the noise made by his lorry the defendant was unaware that the trailer, which was attached to his lorry, had collided with the other vehicle. In support of the justices' finding that *mens rea* was not essential to the offence, counsel pointed out that in the corresponding section of the Motor Car Act, 1903,[5] it was provided that if any person "knowingly" acted in contravention of the section he should be guilty of an offence, while in the present section the word "knowingly" had been omitted. This argument made no impression on Lord Goddard, C.J., and Singleton, J., who held that the change in the wording of the two statutes only had the effect of altering the burden of proof. Humphreys, J., the third member of the court, supported the conviction but without giving any weight to the alteration effected by the omission of the word "knowingly"

[1] *Coram*, R.S. Wright, and Day, JJ.
[2] See s. 78 (1) (*c*).
[3] Likewise in the consolidating statute, the Licensing Act, 1953. See s. 142.
[4] [1948] 1 K.B. 695.
[5] 3 Edw. 7, c. 36, s. 6.

in the later enactment. As it is proposed to deal separately with the general question of knowledge and the burden of proof,[1] this aspect of the case can be temporarily put aside.

The Lord Chief Justice rested his judgment on the decision in *Nichols* v. *Hall*[2] in which, it will be recalled, the accused had been acquitted of the charge of failing to give notice that some of his animals were infected with a contagious disease because he was unaware that the animals were infected. The underlying principle in that and the present case, according to Lord Goddard, was that "in deciding whether *mens rea* is excluded as a necessary constituent of a crime, it is . . . always necessary to consider whether the offence consists in doing a prohibited act or in failing to perform a duty which only arises on the happening of a certain event. Unless a man knows that the event has happened, how can he carry out the duty imposed? If the duty be to report, he cannot report something of which he has no knowledge. . . . Any other view would lead to calling on a man to do the impossible".[3] Such forcible sentiments are undoubtedly prompted by the most admirable motive, namely, the maintenance of the general rule *actus non facit reum nisi mens sit rea*. It is, of course, trite to point out that impossibility may be either relative or absolute and, in this particular case, the impossibility of reporting the accident was only relative on account of the driver's ignorance that an accident had occurred. In expounding such a general principle Lord Goddard would seem to be denying the undoubted power of the legislature to penalise a person for failing to do what is relatively impossible, and where such circumstances arise through, for example, some neglect on the part of the driver. It is respectfully suggested that this is the true explanation underlying the vital omission of the epithet "knowingly" from the wording of the offence in the 1930 Act. To argue, as Humphreys, J., did, that whereas the offence in section 22 (2) imposes "an absolute duty to report to the police

[1] See p. 90 *et seq.* [2] (1873) L.R. 8 C.P. 322 discussed *ante*, p. 58.

[3] [1948] 1 K.B. at p. 701. Writing in 64 *L.Q.R.* 176, the learned editor agrees that stated in this form the argument is unanswerable, but suggests that the intent of the statute might be construed to be that a driver is required to drive in a sufficiently careful manner so as to be aware of any accident that has been caused by a collision with his vehicle. A similar problem, under the Pedestrian Crossings (London) Regulations 1951, reg. 4, came before the Divisional Court in *Leicester* v. *Pearson* [1952] 2 All E.R. 71, in which it was held that the regulation did not impose an absolute duty upon a motorist to afford precedence to a pedestrian on a non-controlled pedestrian crossing. See notes in 68 *L.Q.R.* pp. 464–468 and 16 *M.L.R.* 234 and correspondence in (1952) *The Times*, Dec. 1, 4.

... if, in fact, there has been an accident causing damage"[1] nevertheless a person is entitled to be acquitted if, as in the present case, he is "morally guiltless"[1] is to introduce a doctrine of *mens rea* which, it had been thought, was still-born in *R.* v. *Prince*.

Divergent approach to the construction of penal statutes

Enough has been said already to realise that the prevailing mood of judicial opinion on the question of *mens rea* in statutory offences has varied according to the era in which a particular case is heard. Further evidence will be forthcoming in the examination, which is to follow, of cases dealing with offences based on the words "permitting", "suffering", "causing" and "allowing", but it would be helpful at this stage to seek some more concrete explanation for the apparent readiness of some judges to construe an offence as being absolutely prohibited, which is in marked contrast with the reluctance of other judges to exclude or in any way minimise the application of *mens rea*. Considerable assistance is derived by studying the varied approach of judges to the construction of penal statutes, which approach, it is suggested, is closely linked with the attitude adopted to the presumption as to *mens rea*.

Examples of this divergent attitude are confined mainly to the past seventy-five years, which period corresponds with the era during which an ever increasing expansion has taken place in the legislative output of statutory offences dealing with matters of public welfare.[2] Take, for example, two cases decided in 1873 and 1874 respectively. In *Nichols* v. *Hall*[3] the Crown argued strongly in favour of excluding *mens rea*, pointing out that the Contagious Diseases (Animals) Act, 1869, was aimed at the prevention of a great public evil and that if it were necessary to prove knowledge it would be difficult or impossible to give effect to its provisions. Whilst this argument had been accepted fifty years earlier by

[1] *Ibid.*, at p. 703. Cf. *Green* v. *Dunn* [1953] 1 All E.R. 550 in which the driver of a motor-car, involved in a collision with a motor-cycle, gave his name and address and particulars of the car to the motor cyclist, as required by the Road Traffic Act, 1930, s. 22 (1). The driver of the car did not report the accident to the police. The Divisional Court held that the driver was not guilty of an offence under section 22 (2).

[2] For an excellent summary of the development of similar offences in the U.S.A., see the judgment of Jackson, J. in *Morissette* v. *U.S.* (1952) 342 U.S. 246–276. See, too, Sayre, *Public Welfare Offences* (1933) 33 *Col. L.R.* 55 and the same writer's *The Present Significance of Mens Rea in the Criminal Law,* (1934) Harvard Legal Essays, pp. 399–417. Also Hall, *General Principles of Criminal Law*, pp. 279–322.

[3] (1873) 5 L.R. 8. C.P. 322.

Abbott, L.C.J., in *R.* v. *Marsh*,[1] Keating, J., in the present case was not similarly impressed, saying[2] "... this is a penal enactment and we are bound, according to a well-established principle of interpretation, whatever the consequences, to construe it strictly."[3] Answering the contention that to import "knowingly" into the offence would render evasion of the order easy, Keating, J., boldly declared:[4] "... the Lords of the Privy Council have it in their power, under the Act, to make what order they may think expedient. They can so frame their orders as to prevent all doubt on the subject and obviate the possibility of evasion: our duty is only to construe the order according to the plain import of the language used without regard to the consequences." A year later, in *Mullins* v. *Collins*[5] the court was concerned with section 16 (2) of the Licensing Act, 1872,[6] which, it will be remembered, prohibits a licensee supplying liquor to a constable on duty. Whether this offence constitutes a greater public evil than failure to notify the existence of a contagious disease is certainly arguable, but Archibald, J., in construing the offence of supplying liquor as not requiring *mens rea* was impressed by the fact that section 16 was one of a series of clauses headed "offences against public order". It must, therefore, he said "be construed in the way most effective for maintaining public order".[7]

This principle of construction, which decrees that the objects of a statute must be considered and an interpretation adopted which gives effect to the intention of the legislature, was given powerful support by the decision of the Court for Crown Cases Reserved in *R.* v. *Prince*.[8] Before the court in that case, it will be recalled, was section 55 of the Offences against the Person Act, 1861,[9] which, Blackburn, J., pointed out, was one of a series of enactments, beginning with section 48 of the same statute, forming a code for the protection of women and the guardians of young women. In a judgment concurred in by nine other members of

[1] (1824) 2 B. & C. 717. [2] *Ibid.*, p. 326.

[3] Cf. *London Property Investments Ltd.* v. *A.G.* [1953] 1 All E.R. 436, *per* Upjohn, J. at pp. 441, 442, in which the learned judge placed great reliance on the principles laid down by Lord Esher, M.R. in *Tuck & Sons* v. *Priester* (1887) 19 Q.B.D. at p. 638.

[4] *Loc. cit.* [5] (1874) L.R. 9 Q.B. 292.

[6] Re-enacted in the Licensing Act, 1953 (1 & 2 Eliz. 2, c. 46), s. 142 (*b*).

[7] *Ibid.*, p. 295. [8] (1875) 2 C.C.R. 154.

[9] The section reads: "Whosoever shall unlawfully take or cause to be taken any unmarried girl, being under the age of sixteen years, out of the possession and against the will of her father or mother, or of any other person having the lawful care or charge of her, shall be guilty of misdemeanour."

the court,[1] Blackburn, J., summarised the argument in favour of the prisoner as entirely proceeding on the ground that, in general, a guilty mind is an essential ingredient in a crime, and that where a statute creates a crime the intention of the legislature should be presumed to include "knowingly" in the definition of the crime unless the contrary intention appeared. "We need not" Blackburn, J., commented,[2] "inquire at present whether the canon of construction goes quite so far . . . for we are of opinion that the intention of the legislature sufficiently appears to have been to punish the abduction unless the girl, in fact, was of such an age as to make her consent an excuse, irrespective of whether he knew her to be too young to give an effectual consent, and to fix that age at sixteen." The question of knowledge of the girl's age having been deemed irrelevant to criminal liability it followed that, notwithstanding the jury's finding that the prisoner bona fide believed the girl's statement that she was eighteen, his conviction was affirmed.

Examination of subsequent cases reveals the significant fact that whenever the courts decide to exclude the fundamental maxim of criminal liability from a statutory offence, it is the above principle of construction which, seemingly as a palliative, is invoked, with remarkable consistency. Thus, in *Cundy* v. *Le Cocq*,[3] Stephen, J., after referring to *R.* v. *Prince* and *R.* v. *Bishop*,[4] gives the lead by saying:[5] "In old time, and as applicable to the common law or to earlier statutes the maxim may have been of general application; but a difference has arisen owing to the greater precision of modern statutes . . . the substance of all the reported cases is that it is necessary to look at the object of each Act that is under consideration to see whether and how far knowledge is of the essence of the offence created." Having fortified himself with this panacea Stephen, J., proceeded to exclude all question of knowledge from the offence in section 13 of the Licensing Act, 1872. Yet, the same learned judge is seen in *Mallinson* v. *Carr*[6] executing what appears to be a complete somersault, for, in that case, Stephen, J., discussing the proper way to interpret a penal enactment, said:[7]

[1] Cockburn C.J., Mellor, Lush, Quain, Denman, Archibald, Field, & Lindley, JJ., and Pollock, B.

[2] (1875) 2 C.C.R., p. 171.

[3] (1884) 13 Q.B.D. 207.

[4] (1879) 5 Q.B.D. 259.

[5] (1884) 13 Q.B.D., p. 210.

[6] [1891] 1 Q.B. 48.

[7] *Ibid.*, p. 52. In the result, Stephen J., held that a person in possession of meat intended for human food and unfit for human consumption was liable under s. 116 of the Public Health Act, 1875, "whether he knows or does not know that the meat was unfit for human food."

"The true rule is to take the words used in their ordinary and natural sense and to construe them accordingly, without reference to any supposed intention of the legislature which cannot be gathered from the natural and ordinary meaning of the words." Another stalwart authority in the field of criminal law, R. S. Wright, J., adopted the same rule of construction in *Derbyshire* v. *Houliston*[1] in which he said:[2] "I do not know what the intention of the framers of the section may have been, nor are we bound to consider that. We have to construe the section according to the ordinary rules of construction which have to be applied to a criminal act."

Viewing the attitude of the courts at the end of the last century it must be realised that the latter method of interpretation was rarely expressed. Predominant in the minds of most judges was the need to ascertain the intention of the legislature. This process is well exemplified in *Parker* v. *Alder*[3] where Lord Russell of Killowen, C.J., posed the question: "Now, assuming that the respondent was entirely innocent morally and had no means of protecting himself from the adulteration of this milk in the course of transit, has he committed an offence against the Act?" Having given an affirmative answer to this question the learned Chief Justice justified his conclusion by saying:[4] "When the scope and object of these Acts [the Food and Drugs Acts] are considered it will appear that if he were to be relieved from responsibility a wide door would be opened for evading the beneficial provisions of this legislation." In the same case, Wills, J., expressed the opinion that "the legislation on the subject was intended to be drastic, and the offence was created quite independently of the moral charac-

[1] (1897) 66 L.J. Q.B. 569. [2] *Ibid.*, p. 572.

[3] [1899] 1 Q.B. 20, followed in *Andrews* v. *Luckin* (1917) 34 T.L.R. 33, in which an innocent milk vendor was convicted under the Food and Drugs Act, 1875, s. 6, for selling milk adulterated in the course of transit by *some person unknown*. But the principle accepted in those cases was ignored in *Reynolds* v. *G. H. Austin* [1951] 2 K.B. 135, in which the offence before the court was the Road Traffic Act, 1930, s. 72 (1) and (10). In the latter case, Humphreys J., expressed the opinion that the doctrine of vicarious liability "does not extend to the case of a defendant charged with having done an act lawful in itself but which had become unlawful as the result of some action entirely unknown to him by some person not his servant or agent" (p. 143). Lord Goddard C.J., was equally emphatic in stating that hitherto the doctrine of vicarious liability "has never been applied, as far as I know, to a case where the prohibited act is not that of the defendant but that of some person over whom he had no control and for whom he had no responsibility" (p. 145). Liability for the acts of strangers is discussed *post*, pp. 235–238.

[4] [1899] 1 Q.B. p. 25.

ter of the act".[1] Elaborating on this theme in *Korten* v. *West Sussex C.C.*[2] which dealt with the Fertilisers and Feeding Stuffs Act, 1893,[3] Wills, J., made great use of the fact "that there is a great body of modern legislation by which, for great public purposes and for the benefit of the community, offences are constituted to which the doctrine of *mens rea* either expressly or by necessary implication is not intended to apply".[4] Not content with this general statement the learned judge, in construing the relevant offence as one of absolute prohibition, found "strong ground" for support in the fact that the artificial compound "is probably bought on the largest scale . . . by small and poor people who cannot afford to have it analysed and would not know the process if they could afford it".[4] All this is undoubtedly true, but it is necessary to maintain a proper balance between the benefit to the community and the imposing of criminal punishment upon citizens who have no knowledge of the wrongfulness of their conduct. Perhaps the high-water mark in the movement towards construing statutory crimes as being based on a doctrine of absolute liability was reached in *Hobbs* v. *Winchester Corporation*[5] where Kennedy, L.J., declared:[6] "Taking the cases as a whole and admitting that some of them might give some ground for such an argument, I think there is a clear balance of authority that in construing a modern statute this presumption as to *mens rea* does not exist."

It is difficult to see upon what authority Kennedy, L.J., based his conclusion since, even in those cases in which a statutory offence has been construed as being of absolute prohibition, the court has frequently gone out of its way to pay, at least, lip-service to this presumption as to a guilty mind. Turning back to two cases already considered, in *Mullins* v. *Collins* it was said by Archibald, J., that "in construing this enactment adversedly to the appellant we are not interfering with the maxim that, before a person can be criminally convicted he must be shewn to have a *mens rea*".[7] Again,

[1] [1899] 1 Q.B., p. 26. [2] (1903) 72 L.J.K.B. 514.

[3] 56 & 57 Vict. c. 56, s. 3 (1) (6). This was repealed and replaced by an analogous section in the Fertilisers and Feeding Stuffs Act, 1926, s. 4 (3).

[4] *Ibid.*, pp. 521–522. [5] [1910] 2 K.B. 471.

[6] *Ibid.*, at p. 483. In this respect, as Kennedy, L.J. realised, he differed from Channell, J. in the court below. Commenting on this view in *Reynolds* v. *G. H. Austin Ltd.* [1951] 2 K.B. at p. 148, Devlin, J. said that the contrary view expressed by Wright, J., in *Sherras* v. *de Rutzen* [1895] 1 Q.B. 918 has consistently been followed.

[7] (1874) L.R. 9 Q.B. 292, at p. 295.

in *Korten* v. *West Sussex C.C.* we find Wills, J., prefacing his opinion that the offence was absolutely prohibited with the sentence: "I entirely agree that it is a sound principle, which ought not to be lost sight of in construing legislation of this kind, that prima facie an offence against the criminal law is not committed in the absence of what is commonly called *mens rea*."[1]

Kennedy, L.J., based his conclusion principally on the judgment of Stephen, J., in *Cundy* v. *Le Cocq*,[2] but seems to have overlooked the classic exposition as to *mens rea* in statutory offences delivered in *Sherras* v. *de Rutzen* by Wright, J., who declared:[3] "There is a presumption that *mens rea*, an evil intention, or a knowledge of the wrongfulness of the act is an essential ingredient in every offence; but that presumption is liable to be displaced either by the words of the statute creating the offence or by the subject matter with which it deals, and both must be considered." It is submitted, with respect, that this declaration embodies the correct approach to the interpretation of statutory offences. The objects of a statute and the intention of the legislature may properly be taken into account but should not be considered in isolation, apart from, and overshadowing, the basic principle of criminal liability. To do otherwise is to fall into the dangerous position whereby some judges, particularly during the earlier part of this century, readily displace or, at least, minimise the application of the presumption as to *mens rea* in modern statutory offences. The reality of this danger has led the present Lord Chief Justice to reiterate on several occasions recently the importance of maintaining in full vigour the rule as to *mens rea*. To cite only one passage, in *Brend* v. *Wood* Lord Goddard declared:[4] "There are

[1] (1903) 72 L.J.K.B. 514, at p. 520.

[2] Omitting to refer to the sentence in Stephen, J.'s judgment which reads: "I do not think that maxim has so wide an application as it is sometimes considered to have." The change in emphasis is important.

[3] [1895] 1 Q.B. 918, at pp. 921–922. The principal classes of exceptions in which *mens rea* is not an essential element, according to Wright, J., are as follows: (1) acts not criminal in any real sense, but which, in the public interest, are prohibited under a penalty—See *R.* v. *Marsh* 2 B. & C. 717; (2) public nuisances—see *R.* v. *Stephens* L.R. 1 Q.B. 702; (3) cases where, though the proceedings are criminal in form, it is really only a summary mode of enforcing a civil right—see *Marden* v. *Porter* 7 C.B.N.S. 641. This analysis is referred to with approval by both Lord Goddard C.J., and Devlin, J., in *Reynolds* v. *G. H. Austin Ltd.* [1951] 2 K.B. at pp. 145, 147. See, too, *Harding* v. *Price* [1948] 1 K.B. at p. 701. It was adopted also by the High Court in Australia in *Duncan* v. *Ellis* (1916) 21 C.L.R. 379. Cf. the analysis made in *R.* v. *Ewart* (1905) 25 N.Z.L.R. 709.

[4] (1946) 62 T.L.R. 462, at p. 463. With this declaration may be compared the view expressed by the learned authors of *An Introduction to Criminal Law in Australia* who write

statutes . . . in which Parliament has seen fit to create offences and make people responsible before criminal courts although there is an absence of *mens rea*, but it is certainly not the court's duty to be acute to find that *mens rea* is not a constituent part of a crime. It is of the utmost importance for the protection of the liberty of the subject that a court should always bear in mind that, unless a statute, either clearly or by necessary implication rules out *mens rea* as a constituent part of a crime, the court should not find a man guilty of an offence unless he has a guilty mind." Supplementing this warning in *Harding* v. *Price* the Lord Chief Justice added:[1] "In these days when offences are multiplied by various regulations and orders to an extent which makes it difficult for the most law abiding subjects in some way or at some time to avoid offending against the law, it is more important than ever to adhere to this principle." That such a fresh impetus was needed to restore the presumption to its proper place is unquestionable and with this lead it is not surprising to find other judges becoming imbued with the same refreshing outlook.[2]

Extent to which "knowingly" governs liability

Difficulties of interpretation are not entirely confined to the question whether or not *mens rea* is an essential requirement. Another problem which has engaged the attention of the courts concerns the extent to which the word "knowingly" in a statutory

of the position in that country (p. 22): "If a general statement may be hazarded it is that, at least in the High Court, the eclipse of *mens rea* has not proceeded so far as it has in England with reference to the interpretation of criminal statutes."

[1] [1948] 1 K.B. at pp. 700–701.

[2] Some examples are to be found in *Reynolds* v. *G. H. Austin Ltd.* [1951] 2 K.B. 135 *per* Humphreys, J., at p. 143, *per* Devlin, J., at pp. 147, 148; *Gardner* v. *Akeroyd* [1952] All E.R. 306, *per* Parker, J., at p. 308. Another recent instance of the emphasis placed on the presumption as to *mens rea* is to be found in *Bullock* v. *Turnbull* [1952] 2 Lloyd's List R. 303, at p. 305. Yet, even now, one learned writer—Friedmann, *Law and Social Change in Contemporary Britain*, pp. 261–262—will be found urging that the presumption as to *mens rea* should be discarded in the case of modern statutory offences which fall within the category of public law remedies. The attitude of the High Court of Australia was recently stated in *Proudman* v. *Dayman* (1941) 67 C.L.R. 536, at pp. 540–541 by Dixon, J. who said: "Indeed there has been a marked and growing tendency to treat the prima facie rule as excluded or rebutted in the case of summary offences created by modern statutes, particularly those dealing with social and industrial regulation. But although it has been said that in construing a modern statute a presumption as to *mens rea* does not exist . . . it is probably still true that, unless from the words, context, subject-matter or general nature of the enactment, some reason to the contrary appears, you are to treat honest and reasonable mistake as a ground of exculpation even from a summary offence." The same attitude was adopted in *Poole* v. *Wah Mi Chan* 75 C.L.R. 218.

offence governs the remaining conditions of liability. Where the offence is defined in a section which, in addition to prohibiting certain conduct, goes on to provide an escape clause, the question arises whether the element of knowledge applies not only to the commission of the forbidden act but also to the exculpatory provision in the section.

A good example of this is to be found in section 2 of the Intoxicating Liquors (Sale to Children) Act, 1901,[1] which renders any licensee liable who knowingly sells any intoxicating liquor to any child under 14 for consumption on or off the premises, excepting such intoxicating liquor is sold and delivered in corked and sealed vessels in the prescribed manner. In the light of the particular wording of this section, the question arises, what is the position of a licensee who knowing his youthful customer to be under 14, nevertheless, honestly but mistakenly believes when he delivers the liquor that the bottle is properly corked and sealed? Such a situation arose in *Brooks* v. *Mason*[2] where the court, in deciding that the word "knowingly" does not apply to the exception with the result that the licensee in the circumstances stated above has no defence, gave a lead which has been consistently followed in subsequent cases. This interpretation of the offence is unfortunate and it is worth noting that all three members of the court in that case, Lord Alverstone, C.J., Wills and Channell, JJ., were agreed that the point was doubtful. Giving judgment along lines strongly reminiscent of his effort the following year in *Korten* v. *West Sussex C.C.*,[3] Lord Alverstone, C.J., declared:[4] "... it would be altering the language of the statute, and departing from its intention, to read the word 'knowingly' into the exception. The effect would be to say that a defendant need only prove by way of defence that he believed the vessel to be secured as the Act directs, although in fact it was not so secured. I think the Act only intended to except intoxicating liquors sold or delivered in vessels which were in fact properly sealed and secured."

Earlier in his judgment Lord Alverstone stated that "what the

[1] 1 Edw. 7, c. 27, re-enacted in the Licensing Act, 1953 (1 & 2 Eliz. 2, c. 46), s. 128, which adopts the construction placed upon the earlier statute in *Brooks* v. *Mason* (*supra*), by making a separate proviso "that this subsection shall not prohibit the sale or delivery of intoxicating liquor to such a person ... (*b*) in corked and sealed vessels etc.".

[2] [1902] 2 K.B. 743, cited without disapproval by Devlin, J. in *Reynolds* v. *Austin* [1951] 2 K.B. at p. 152. See, too, the judgment of Lord Alverstone C.J., in *Emary* v. *Nolloth* [1903] 2 K.B. 264, at p. 269.

[3] (1903) 72 L.J.K.B. 514. See *post* pp. 112–114.

[4] [1902] 2 K.B. p. 747.

statute intended to stop was the sale or delivery of intoxicating liquor to children under 14".[1] Surely, if this were so, Parliament might have been expected to achieve that object by excluding all questions of knowledge as to the age of the child and, to use the words of Stephen, J., in *Cundy* v. *Le Cocq*, "throwing on the publican the responsibility of determining whether the person supplied comes within that category."[2] Instead, as the wording of section 2 shows, the word "knowingly" was expressly inserted and it has been held to be a good defence to prove that the licensee was honestly mistaken as to the age of the child served with intoxicating liquor. Thus, in *Groom* v. *Grimes*[3] which provides an illustration of this defence being upheld, Channell, J., was led to exclaim: "knowing the age of the child is the one thing the section clearly does mean, whatever else it may mean." Comparing the decisions in these two cases does it not seem strange that the legislature should be attributed with excusing a licensee from responsibility as to the age of the child whilst imposing responsibility as to the bottles being corked and sealed?

A more enlightened interpretation was forthcoming in *Gaumont British Distributors Ltd.* v. *Henry*,[4] where the same problem arose in connection with the Dramatic and Musical Performers Protection Act, 1925,[5] s. 1 (*a*) of which prohibits any person from knowingly making a record of a dramatic or musical work without the consent in writing of the performers. Substitute instead the words "excepting the consent in writing of the performers be obtained", which in no way alters the sense of the relevant section, and you have an exact parallel with the provision examined in *Brooks* v. *Mason*. Unlike the decision in that case, however, the Divisional Court in the *Gaumont British Case* held that the word "knowingly" applied to all the elements of the offence. As Lord Hewart, C.J. explained,[6] "Knowledge on the part of the alleged offender is described prominently as an essential ingredient of the offence. The other essential ingredient is that which he does must be knowingly done without the consent in writing of the performers. The knowledge, which is part of the essence of the offence, extends to knowledge of the absence of consent on the part of the performers." In passing, it should be mentioned that although *Brooks* v. *Mason* was referred to by Lord Hewart as "throwing light on the true interpretation of the present section" no comment,

[1] [1902] 2 K.B. 747.
[2] (1884) 13 Q.B.D. at p. 210.
[3] (1903) 89 L.T. 129.
[4] [1939] 2 K.B. 711.
[5] 15 & 16 Geo. 5, c. 46.
[6] *Ibid.*, p. 717.

adverse or otherwise, was made as to the decision reached in the earlier case. Nevertheless, it is respectfully submitted that the narrower interpretation adopted in *Brooks* v. *Mason* was motivated by a tendency—exhibited in other cases as well—to introduce the element of absolute prohibition, and this in the teeth of the legislature's express insertion of the word "knowingly".[1]

Linked with this problem is the precise meaning to be given to the word "knowingly". No consistent principle is to be found in the judicial interpretations expressed, and it will be seen that the courts have been guided to a large extent by the nature of the offence involved. Thus, in *R.* v. *Bannen*[2] where the accused was charged under the Coinage Act, 1832,[3] s. 10, with knowingly making a die without lawful authority, Tindal, C.J., said that "knowingly" must mean "with a design". A somewhat similar interpretation was suggested by Goddard, J., in *Van Dusen* v. *Kritz*[4] where an action for penalties was brought for infringement of copyright. Now, under the Copyright Act, 1911,[5] s. 2 (2) "copyright ... shall be deemed to be infringed by any person who ... by way of trade exhibits in public ... any work which to his knowledge infringes copyright." Adopting a liberal construction Goddard J., said:[6] "I do not think that the statute means that a person, directly he receives a notice that there is an infringement of copyright, must exhibit at his own risk. The Act seems to me to aim at a *deliberate infringement*[7] in the sense of deliberately continuing to use or exhibit a work which the defendant knows infringes a copyright."[8]

How very different all this appears when the case of *Att. Gen.* v. *Cozens*[9] is considered. There the statutory provision alleged to have been violated was section 40 (4) of the Licensing (Consolidation) Act, 1910,[10] which forbids any justice, declared by the Act not to be

[1] In his work on *Criminal Law*, p. 128, n. 8, Glanville Williams objects to the view that the insertion of the word "knowingly" prevents the crime being read as one of absolute prohibition, but only if this view implies that the absence of a statutory reference to knowledge justifies the court in reading the statute as creating absolute prohibition. Such implication is unfounded, certainly in the opinion of the present writer, and it is suggested that where the statute is silent, the court, guided by the presumption as to *mens rea*, is free to import into the offence the requirement of guilty knowledge. For the cases in which this course has been adopted see *ante* pp. 56–63.

[2] (1844) 1 Car & Kir. 295.
[3] 2 Will. 4, c. 34.
[4] [1936] 2 K.B. 176.
[5] 1 & 2 Geo. 5, c. 46.
[6] *Ibid.*, at p. 182.
[7] My italics.

[8] A somewhat similar interpretation was given to the Explosive Substances Act, 1883, s. 4, by Humphreys, J., in *R.* v. *Dacey* [1939] 2 All E.R. 641, 644.

[9] (1934) 50 T.L.R. 320.

[10] Re-enacted in the Licensing Act, 1953 (1 & 2 Eliz. 2, c. 46), s. 48 (6).

qualified to act thereunder, from knowingly acting as a justice for any of the purposes thereof. By virtue of his being a shareholder in a local firm of brewers the defendant magistrate was totally disqualified from acting as a licensing justice. Whilst fully realising that he could not form part of the licensing committee when applications for the grant of licences were heard, the defendant stated that he was unaware, and had not been advised otherwise by the clerk to the justices, that he was disqualified from sitting to adjudicate on such subsidiary applications as the "extension of hours" and "protection orders". Finlay, J., summed-up the case for the defence as amounting to a claim that "knowingly" in this section meant "deliberately", and since the defendant did not apply his mind to the question at all he could not be said to have acted deliberately. Rejecting this plea, Finlay, J., pointed out that the defendant had not only knowingly acted as a justice but had done so in licensing matters. The fact that he did not appreciate that those were matters on which he was not entitled to adjudicate was no answer to the charge. This, it is suggested, is yet another example of the failure to recognise the rule that where the wrongful "act" in a statutory offence, based on the word "knowingly", consists of a number of constituent elements the necessity for knowledge extends to *all* the elements of the wrong. It is only necessary to refer to some of the unsatisfactory decisions on crimes of wilfulness, such as *Horton* v. *Gwynne*,[1] *The Law Society* v. *United Service Bureau*,[2] and *Cotterill* v. *Penn*,[3] to realise that the same error of construction has been perpetrated in other fields of statutory crime.

"Knowingly" and the burden of proof

Where a principle of law is enunciated and, during the passage of over half-a-century, evokes no adverse comment its accuracy tends to become generally accepted. If such a pronouncement has been repeatedly cited with approval, any doubts which may be expressed as to its correctness are likely to be viewed with suspicion. Nevertheless, Devlin, J., in *Roper* v. *Taylor's Central Garages (Exeter) Ltd.*[4] took his stand on sure ground when expressing his doubts as to the accuracy of a well-known passage

[1] [1921] 2 K.B. 661. [2] (1933) 98 J.P. 33. [3] [1936] 1 K.B. 53.
[4] [1951] 2 T.L.R. 284, at pp. 287–288.

from the judgment of Day, J., in *Sherras* v. *De Rutzen*[1] relating to the burden of proof in crimes involving the presence or absence of the word "knowingly". That ground has been well trodden before by others concerned to point out the confusion caused by the failure to indicate in which sense the phrase "burden of proof" is used.[2]

The offence in *Sherras* v. *de Rutzen*, it will be recalled, was supplying a police constable on duty with intoxicating liquor, contrary to section 16 (2) of the Licensing Act, 1872.[3] The prosecution contended that the offence was one in which proof of *mens rea* was not necessary, pointing out that whereas section 16 (1) made it an offence to "knowingly harbour on licensed premises any constable on duty" the epithet "knowingly" was missing from section 16 (2). Rejecting this argument, Day, J., stated that the absence of "knowingly" from section 16 (2) only *shifted* the onus of proof so that it was for the defence to prove lack of knowledge and not for the prosecution to prove that there was knowledge.[4] R. S. Wright, J., the other member of the court, made no reference to the effect on the burden of proof.

It is worth noting that this was not the first occasion where the above principle had been put forward, for, as already indicated, Brett, J., in *R.* v. *Prince* stated that "the ultimate proof necessary to authorise a conviction is not altered by the presence or absence of the word 'knowingly', though by its presence or absence the

[1] [1895] 1 Q.B. 918, at p. 920.

[2] See, for example, *Presumptions and Burdens* by Lord Justice Denning (1945) 61 *L.Q.R.* 379, and an article under the same heading by Nigel Bridge (1949) 12 *M.L.R.* 273–289, in which Lord Justice Denning's reclassification of the conceptions involved under the general heading of burden of proof and presumptions is criticised and an alternative reclassification is suggested. Denning L.J. introduced his reclassification in *Emmanuel* v. *Emmanuel* [1946] P. 115 and in *Dunn* v. *Dunn* [1949] P. 98. References to the different senses in which burden of proof is used by text-book writers are collected in Nokes, *Introduction to Evidence*, p. 373.

[3] Now contained in the Licensing Act, 1953 (1 & 2 Eliz. 2, c. 46), s. 142 (*b*).

[4] A similar argument was advanced by Dixon, J. in the High Court of Australia case *Maher* v. *Musson* 52 C.L.R. 100. The accused in that case was charged under The Distillation Acts 1901–1931, s. 74 (4), which, if interpreted literally, makes an offence even the innocent possession of illicit spirit. The argument for the exclusion of *mens rea* was based on the fact that subsection 7 of the same section specifically required knowledge that the spirit was illicit and it was claimed that the legislature had directed its mind to the question of *mens rea*, the omission to require it in the relevant subsection being intentional. Dixon, J., however, rejected this line of argument saying: ". . . the absolute language of the statute should be treated as doing no more than throwing upon the defendant the burden of exculpating himself by showing that he reasonably thought the spirits were not illicit." Evatt and McTiernan JJ., it should be added, held that to suppose the legislature meant to expose an innocent possessor to the drastic penalties laid down was a "palpable and evident absurdity".

burden of proof is altered".[1] Although this rule was followed without hesitation by Humphreys, J., in *Gaumont British Distributors Ltd.* v. *Henry*,[2] the same judge is seen in *Harding* v. *Price*[3] taking up a more cautious attitude. In the latter case, it will be recalled, the Court was concerned with the wording of section 22 (2) of the Road Traffic Act, 1930, which replaced the corresponding section in the repealed Motor Car Act, 1903. Whereas under section 6 of the 1903 Act guilt depended on a person "knowingly acting in contravention of the section", section 22 (2) of the 1930 Act omits the word "knowingly", making it an offence simply to fail to report a road accident within twenty-four hours of its occurrence. According to Humphreys, J.,[4] the effect of the change was to render the offence one not requiring any proof of knowledge, leaving untouched the question whether proof of absence of knowledge on the part of the defendant affords in law a defence. The other members of the court invoked the words of Day, J., in *Sherras* v. *de Rutzen*, Lord Goddard, C.J., explaining[5] that the absence of the word "knowingly" *altered* the burden of proof, while Singleton, J., said[6] the effect was to *shift* the burden of proof. Insomuch as both judges laid no stress on their choice between the words "alter" and "shift" it may be assumed that they were intended to convey the same meaning.

This view is borne out by reference to *Reynolds* v. *G. H. Austin & Sons, Ltd.*[7] where Lord Goddard, in elaborating on the meaning which he attributed to the passage from *Sherras* v. *de Rutzen* (*supra*), said that the absence of "knowingly" in the statute only *shifted* the onus of proof. He went on to say:[8] "This affirms the principle that except in cases where the statute creates an offence of knowingly doing an act the prosecution can establish a prima facie case merely by proving the act was done.[9] Lack of knowledge must be proved by the defendant, as the burden of proving knowledge or the lack of it with respect to the act to be proved depends on the opportunities of knowledge which may be possessed by the respective parties":—for which proposition Lord Goddard referred to Stephen's *Digest of the Law of Evidence*.[10]

When considering the accuracy of the rule as stated in *Sherras* v.

[1] (1875) 2 C.C.R. 154, at p. 161. [2] [1939] 2 K.B. 711, at p. 721.
[3] [1948] 1 K.B. 695. [4] *Ibid.*, p. 703. [5] *Ibid.*, p. 700.
[6] *Ibid.*, p. 704. [7] [1951] 2 K.B. 135. [8] *Ibid.*, p. 145.
[9] As will be seen later (see p. 96), the Lord Chief Justice in *R.* v. *Cohen* [1951] 1 K.B. 505 disregarded this so-called exception.
[10] 12th ed. Art. 104.

de Rutzen and repeated in subsequent cases, the main difficulty arises in ascertaining in what sense the various judges used the expressions "*alter* the burden of proof" and "*shift* the burden of proof". There are, of course, two separate categories of burden of proof.[1] First, there is what has been conveniently described as the *legal* burden of proof[2] and which, in criminal cases (unless otherwise directed by statute) imposes upon the prosecution the duty of proving the accused guilty of the offence charged.[3] Any derogation from this well-established principle is apt to be regarded as a drastic and exceptional measure. But examination of the statute book reveals a considerable number of instances in which the legislature has imposed upon the accused the burden of proving his innocence. The formulae used by the draftsman vary and it may be useful to consider some of these. First, there is the phrase "without lawful excuse (the proof whereof shall lie on the defendant)". This is exemplified in the offences created by the Larceny Act 1916,[4] s. 28 (2), viz., unlawful possession of housebreaking implements, and by the Post Office Act 1953,[5] s. 63 (1) viz., unlawful possession of fictitious stamps. Secondly, there is the analogous but not wholly identical clause[6] "without lawful

[1] As Viscount Sankey L.C. said in *Woolmington* v. *D.P.P.* [1935] A.C. 462, at p. 479; "The word 'onus' is used indifferently throughout the books, sometimes meaning the next move or next step in the process of proving or sometimes the conclusion of the whole matter."

[2] 61 *L.Q.R.* p. 379.

[3] Finally established in *Woolmington* v. *D.P.P.* [1935] A.C. at p. 481.

[4] 6 & 7 Geo. 5, c. 50. See *R.* v. *Ward* [1915] 3 K.B. 696.

[5] 1 & 2 Eliz, 2, c. 36.

[6] The distinction between "lawful excuse" and "lawful authority" was considered by the Judicial Committee of the Privy Council in the recent case of *Wooh Pooh Yin* v. *Public Prosecutor* [1954] 3 W.L.R. 471. The accused, a former Chinese bandit, was convicted of carrying a revolver without lawful authority or excuse contrary to the Emergency Regulations 1951, Reg. 4 (1) (*a*), then operative in Malaya. The defence was that the appellant was intending to, and was on his way to, surrender at the time he was carrying the revolver, and that he was doing so in compliance with a pamphlet distributed by the Malayan Government appealing to armed terrorists to surrender. The Board (Lord MacDermott, Lord Cohen and Mr. de Silva) were of the opinion that while, in the circumstances, the appellant had no "lawful authority" for carrying the revolver, it did not follow that he had no "lawful excuse" for doing so. The Judicial Committee rejected the contention that as the appellant's possession of the revolver had been unlawful from the beginning no supervening event could give him a "lawful excuse" for carrying it. To accept such a proposition would be to confuse "lawful excuse" and "lawful authority". The Board held that if the evidence of the appellant were accepted it justified a finding that he was carrying the revolver in the course of complying with the Government's request, and such a finding would have warranted a verdict of lawful excuse within the terms of the regulation. The Board distinguished *Dickens* v. *Gill* [1896] 2 Q.B. 310 and *Winkle* v. *Wiltshire* [1951] 1 K.B. 684 as not touching upon the effect of a new situation arising after a period of unlawful possession.

authority (proof of which authority shall lie on the party accused)" which is instanced by the Public Stores Act 1875,[1] s. 4. Thirdly, a combination is sometimes used in the form "without lawful authority or excuse (the proof whereof shall lie on the person accused)". This formula appears, for example, in the Forgery Act, 1913,[2] ss. 8, 9 and 10, and in the Coinage Offences Act, 1936,[3] ss. 6, 7, 8, 9 and 10. Fourthly, a slight variation is introduced in the Prevention of Crime Act, 1953,[4] s. 1, which uses the clause "without lawful authority or reasonable excuse the proof whereof shall lie on the accused". Fifthly, there is the occasional phrase "shall be deemed . . . unless the contrary is proved" which is to be found in the Official Secrets Act, 1911,[5] s. 1 (2) and the Prevention of Corruption Act, 1916,[6] s. 2. Other variations which are used include such formulae as "unless the defendant proves that he acted without intent to defraud"[7] and "unless the defendant proves that he had no reason to suspect the genuineness . . ."[8] and "unless the defendant proves that he had reason to believe that the statements were accurate"[9] and "unless the defendant proves that he had it in his possession for a lawful object".[10] No matter what particular form of words are used[11] to impose upon the defendant the task of establishing his innocence, one thing is clear, namely, that used in this first sense the burden of proof is fixed. It cannot be altered, neither does it shift during the course of the trial. Furthermore, the question whether or not the legal burden has been dis-

[1] 38 & 39 Vict. c. 25. [2] 3 & 4 Geo. 5, c. 27. [3] 26 Geo. 5 & 1 Edw. 8, c. 16.

[4] 1 & 2 Eliz. 2, c. 14. [5] 1 & 2 Geo. 5, c. 28.

[6] 6 & 7 Geo. 5, c. 64. See *R.* v. *Carr-Briant* [1943] K.B. 607.

[7] Merchandise Marks Act, 1887 (50 & 51 Vict. c. 28), s. 2 (1).

[8] *Ibid.*, s. 2 (2). [9] Food & Drugs Act, 1938 (1 & 2 Geo. 6, c. 56), s. 85 (1).

[10] Explosives Substance Act, 1883 (46 & 47 Vict. c. 3), s. 4.

[11] See e.g. the Licensing Act, 1953 (1 & 2 Eliz. 2, c. 46), s. 124 (3), s.126 (8), s. 127 (4) and s. 136 (2). In addition to the examples given in the text above, attention may be drawn to a provision which is frequently inserted in new legislation. A typical illustration is to be found in the Borrowing (Control and Guarantees) Act, 1946, s. 4 (2), para. 3, sub-para. 4, which ordains that where a body corporate has been found to be an offender, then directors, general managers, secretaries, or other similar officers of the body corporate, including persons who are purporting to act in those capacities, are deemed to be guilty unless they prove the offence was committed without their consent or connivance. Commenting on this provision, Upjohn, J., in *London Property Investments, Ltd.* v. *A.G.* [1953] 1 All E.R. 436, at p. 441, declared: "I suppose that it represents the high water-mark of the Parliamentary invasion of the traditional rights of the subjects of this realm." Another example is to be found in the Adoption Act, 1950, s. 41, and throughout what might comprehensively be described as the "nationalisation" legislation. More detailed treatment of this important topic will be undertaken in the chapter devoted to vicarious liability.

charged does not arise until all the evidence, for the prosecution and for the defence, has been given.

Secondly, there is what has been called the *provisional* burden of proof.[1] Used in this sense the burden of proof rests on the party who, unless he is resigned to an adverse verdict, must either call further evidence or adduce arguments explaining away or rebutting an inference which the court may otherwise feel compelled to draw from the existing evidence. Admittedly difficult to pin down, and as often as not more apparent than real, burden of proof in this second sense is fluid and may shift to and fro during the course of the trial.

Turning now to *Roper* v. *Taylor's Central Garages Ltd.*,[2] it seems clear that Devlin, J., based his doubts as to the accuracy of the principle stated in *Sherras* v. *de Rutzen*[3] on the understanding that Day, J., and Lord Goddard in the later cases, were referring to the *legal* burden of proof. Accepting that, as an ordinary principle of the law of evidence, the statement from Stephen's *Digest* was correct, Devlin, J., continued[4] "... but Mr. Justice Day seems to me to be going further than that, and to be saying that the absence of 'knowingly' in the statute *as a matter of construction* shifts the burden of proof". After referring to statutes where the burden of proof is expressly shifted on to the defence, giving as an example the Merchandise Marks Act, 1887, Devlin, J., went on to relate the presence or absence of the word "knowingly" to the requirement of *mens rea*. The learned judge added:[4] "All that the word 'knowingly' does is to say expressly what is normally implied, and if the presumption that the statute requires *mens rea* is not rebutted I find difficulty in seeing how it can be said that the omission of the word 'knowingly' has, as a matter of construction, the effect of shifting the burden of proof from the prosecution to the defence."

This criticism, it is suggested, rests entirely on the assumption that the rule, as stated, refers to the legal burden of proof. To say that the burden of proof is altered (see Brett, J., in *Prince*[5] and Lord Goddard in *Harding* v. *Price*[6] (*supra*)) is certainly a pointer that such was the meaning intended. Added weight to this view is provided by reference to the judgment of the Lord Chief Justice in *R.* v. *Cohen*[7] where the offence was knowingly harbouring un-

[1] 61 *L.Q.R.*, p. 380.
[2] [1951] 2 T.L.R. 284.
[3] [1895] 1 Q.B. 918.
[4] [1951] 2 T.L.R. at p. 288.
[5] (1875) 2 C.C.R. 154.
[6] [1948] 1 K.B. 695.
[7] [1951] 1 K.B. 505.

customed goods contrary to the Customs Consolidation Act, 1876,[1] s. 186. Explaining the onus of proof in such a case, Lord Goddard said that where dutiable goods are found in the accused's house, that would establish a prima facie case that he knowingly harboured them.[2] By virtue of section 259 of the same statute the onus of proof is then on the accused to give some explanation of his possession from which a jury might infer that he did not know that duty had not been paid. Lord Goddard continued:[3] "It must be for him to give this explanation because the facts relating thereto must be exclusively within his knowledge. There is, in fact, a shifting of the burden of proof." Used in this connection where, it should be noted, the burden of proof is placed on the defendant by express statutory provision,[4] it is evident that the Lord Chief Justice was referring to the *legal* burden of proof. If reference is made to the language used by the court in relation to offences where the word "knowingly" is omitted—see, for example, *Reynolds* v. *Austin* (*supra*)[5]—the similarity is at once apparent. Moreover, it is not without significance that Lord Goddard in both *Cohen* and *Reynolds* v. *Austin* relied for support on the same passage from Stephen's *Digest of the Law of Evidence*.

This examination of the authorities, it is submitted, points to the following conclusions. First, where, as in *R.* v. *Cohen*,[6] the legislature has required the defendant to discharge a certain onus of proof, any reference to the shifting or altering of the burden of proof is concerned with the legal burden of proof. Secondly, where, as in *Reynolds* v. *Austin*[7] reference is made to the shifting of the burden of proof, if what is intended to be expressed is the shifting of the provisional burden, no occasion exists for criticism. But when it is seen that the language used is not materially different from that used in *R.* v. *Cohen* it is not surprising to find it interpreted as the shifting of the legal burden of proof. Thirdly, so far

[1] 39 & 40 Vict. c. 36. [2] See p. 92, n. 9 *ante*. [3] [1951] 1 K.B. p. 507.

[4] The most recent example occurs in the Prevention of Crime Act, 1953 (1 & 2 Eliz. 2, c. 14), s. 1, which makes it a crime to be found in possession of an offensive weapon without lawful authority or excuse. An elaborate definition of an "offensive weapon" covers three categories of articles (1) made for, (2) adapted for use for, and (3) intended for use, for causing injury to the person. To establish that the article, e.g., a bicycle chain, comes within the third category, the prosecution must satisfy the court that there were sufficient grounds for the belief that it was carried with intent to use it for causing injury—only then does the burden shift to the accused to prove lawful authority or excuse. See a note on this Act in (1953) 16 *M.L.R.* 482.

[5] See p. 92 *ante*. [6] [1951] 1 K.B. 505. [7] [1951] 2 K.B. 135.

as the judgment of Day, J., in *Sherras* v. *de Rutzen*[1] or any other judgment is intended to lay down that the absence of the word "knowingly" in an offence *ipso facto* affects the legal burden of proof, it infringes the irrefragable rule that the legal burden of proving the guilt of the accused rests upon the prosecution and cannot be altered except by express statutory provision. There is, therefore, no justification for the introduction or subsequent application of such a doctrine.

It will be seen that such divergence of opinion as exists is due to the unfortunate omission of any indication as to which particular sense of burden of proof is intended. Perhaps Devlin, J.'s expression of doubt as to the accuracy of the rule as stated in *Sherras* v. *de Rutzen* will help in drawing attention to a practice which has nought to commend it.

[1] [1895] 1 Q.B. 918.

IV

PERMITTING

Survey of Statutory offences based on the word "permits"

In tracing the earliest appearance of the word "permitting" in a statutory offence, it is necessary to turn back the pages of the statute book to 1548 to an apparently unimportant enactment entitled "an Act against the carrying of bell metal out of the realm".[1] This statute provided that "if any master, owner, purser, or boatswain of any ship do willingly permit or suffer any of the metals above said to be shipped contrary to this Act, or else perceiving any such metals to be shipped, do not disclose the same within three days after knowledge had" he shall commit an offence. When discussion is later centred on the question whether the use of the word "permitting" connotes the necessity for *mens rea*, it will be useful to recall that in this, its first appearance in a statutory offence, knowledge of the illegal shipment was the foundation of liability.

Another early example of the use of "permitting" appears in the Inns Act, 1604,[2] which, as quaintly described in the preamble, had as its object "the restraint of inordinate haunting and tippling in inns, alehouses and other victualling houses". To achieve this purpose the statute made it an offence for any innkeeper to "permit or suffer any person inhabiting and dwelling in any city, market town, village or hamlet to remain and continue drinking in the said inn", but certain well defined categories of customers were exempt from this provision.[3] Although this particular enactment initiated a minor deluge of legislation designed, for example, "to repress the odious and loathsome sin of drunkenness"[4] and, somewhat optimistically, "the reformation of alehouse keepers",[5] only the later Alehouses Act of 1625[6] resorted to the expression "permits" as the basis of criminal liability.

[1] 2 & 3 Edw. 6, c. 37, s. 5. [2] 1 Jac. 1, c. 9.

[3] S. 2, exempt from which (*inter alia*) were "such as shall be invited by any traveller and shall accompany him only during his necessary abode there, and labouring handicraftmen on the usual working days, for one hour at dinner time or take their diet in an alehouse" and "for urgent and necessary occasions to be allowed by two justices".

[4] 4 Jac. 1, c. 5. [5] 7 Jac, 1, c. 10. [6] 1 Car. 1, c. 4, s. 3.

Thereafter, until the beginning of the nineteenth century there is a singular absence of statutory offences prohibiting the permitting of certain conduct. When it reappears, as for example, in the Seditious Meetings Act, 1817,[1] and the Licensing Act, 1828,[2] the epithet "permits" is reinforced with the additional words "knowingly" or "wilfully or knowingly". A few years later, in the Highways Act, 1835,[3] it stands alone, only to revert to the formula "knowingly and wilfully permit" in the Betting Acts of 1853[4] and 1854.[5] An interesting statute, particularly from the standpoint of criminal degrees of knowledge, is the Criminal Lunatic Asylum Act, 1860,[6] which decrees that any officer or servant in a criminal lunatic asylum who through "wilful neglect or connivance permits any person confined therein to escape" shall be guilty of felony. Perhaps worth mentioning also is the Offences against the Person Act, 1861,[7] in which the expression appears only once and that in connection with the recently invoked crime of "knowingly and wilfully permitting a spring gun to be placed with intent to destroy or inflict grievous bodily harm upon a trespasser".[8] In the present century the verb "permits" has frequently been used by the legislature and it will suffice to draw attention to such diverse statutes as the Fertilisers and Feeding Stuffs Act, 1906,[9] the Protection of Animals Act, 1911,[10] the Road Traffic Act, 1930,[11] the Hill Farming Act, 1946,[12] the Adoption Act, 1950,[13] and the Customs and Excise Act, 1952.[14]

Divergence of views on the necessity for *Mens Rea*

Where the word "knowingly" is expressly inserted in a statutory offence, no doubt has ever been cast on the necessity for estab-

[1] 57 Geo. 3, c. 19, s. 28.

[2] 9 Geo. 4, c. 61, s. 13.

[3] 5 & 6 Will. 4, c. 50, ss. 70, 72. See *Croasdill* v. *Ratcliffe* (1862) 4 L.T. (N.S.) 834. Another enactment of the same period in which "permits" appears unsupported is the Copyright Act, 1842 (5 & 6 Vict. c. 45) s. 20. See *Monaghan* v. *Taylor* (1886) 2 T.L.R. 685.

[4] 16 & 17 Vict. c. 119, s. 3.

[5] 17 & 18 Vict. c. 38, s. 2.

[6] 23 & 24 Vict. c. 75, s. 12. Cf. Lunacy Act, 1890 (53 & 53 Vict. c. 5) s. 323, which makes it a summary offence to wilfully permit the escape of non-criminal lunatics.

[7] 24 & 25 Vict. c. 100.

[8] S. 31. The unusual circumstances in which this section was invoked occurred in the case of *R.* v. *Taylor* (1952) *The Times*, November 28, when the accused, though convicted of manslaughter as the result of killing a burglar by means of a spring-gun booby-trap, was given an absolute discharge by Finnemore, J.

[9] 6 Edw. 7, c. 27, s. 6 (1) (*b*). This statute was repealed and replaced by the Fertilisers and Feeding Stuffs Act, 1926 (16 & 17 Geo. 5, c. 45).

[10] 1 & 2 Geo. 5, c. 27, s. 1 (1).

[11] 20 & 21 Geo. 5, c. 43. E.g., ss. 19 and 72.

[12] 9 & 10 Geo. 6, c. 73, s. 19 (1).

[13] 14 Geo. 6, c. 26, s. 39 (1).

[14] 15 & 16 Geo. 6 & 1 Eliz. 2, c. 44, s. 9 (1) (*b*).

lishing *mens rea*. Where, on the other hand, the legislature has chosen to use the alternative expressions "permits" or "permitting", a careful analysis of the cases shows the inevitable cleavage of opinion among the judges as to the requirement of proof of a guilty mind. Earlier in this study several causes were tentatively suggested as underlying this constant divergence of views and it may, perhaps, be of assistance if they are restated. First, it is suggested, there is the trend of thought which happens to be current at the time a particular case is decided; secondly, there is the individual judge's attitude or approach to the wider question of the part to be played by *mens rea* in criminal law; and finally, there is the conflict which is created through the unreal meaning sometimes attributed to the phrase *mens rea*.

Bearing in mind these underlying causes, let us proceed to consider the merits and weaknesses of the different interpretations placed upon the words "permits" or "permitting". These interpretations fall conveniently into two groups and may, therefore, be considered separately.

Liability based upon proof of *Mens Rea*

Inasmuch as the expression "permits" has appeared more frequently in licensing offences than in any other class of statutory crime, it is not surprising to find most of the relevant cases dealing with this particular sphere of criminal liability. In the earliest instance of the word "permits" being inserted in a statutory offence the legislature, it will be recalled, made it abundantly clear that knowledge was an integral part of the crime concerned. And yet, not until prosecutions were brought under the Licensing Act, 1872,[1] did the courts have occasion to interpret the word "permit" in the light of the maxim *actus non facit reum nisi mens sit rea*. This, in itself, is a fact not without a certain measure of significance and is to be interpreted, it is suggested, as indicative of the general view that to permit, of necessity, requires proof of prior knowledge of the existing facts.

[1] 35 & 36 Vict. c. 94. In *Warden* v. *Tye* (1877) 46 L.J.M.C. 111, decided under the same section, it was held that a publican could not be convicted where the only person drunk was the publican himself. That "permitting" connotes some other person who is permitted was the basis also of the decision in *Mattison* v. *Johnson* (1916) 85 L.J.K.B. 741, which turned on the interpretation of the Criminal Law Amendment Act, 1885 (48 & 49 Vict. c. 69), s. 13.

"Permitting drunkenness on licensed premises"

In the earliest of these cases, *Ethelstane* v. *The Justices of Oswestry*,[1] a licensee was convicted under section 13 of the Licensing Act 1872,[2] with permitting drunkenness on his licensed premises. The Divisional Court, being of opinion that the question was one of fact and not of law, upheld the conviction upon evidence that a labourer who had been drinking on the licensee's premises was found, about an hour later, drunk in a ditch some hundred yards away. That knowledge on the part of the licensee was required is implied in the question posed by Cockburn, C.J., who asked:[3] "If a man goes into a public house sober and comes out drunk, surely that is some evidence that he got drunk within the house, and that his drunkenness was permitted by the publican?"

Although the facts in *Somerset* v. *Wade*[4] were different in important respects from those in *Ethelstane* v. *The Justices of Oswestry*, the same offence of permitting drunkenness on licensed premises was involved. The justices, in dismissing the information, found that the licensee was unaware that the woman, found on his premises, was drunk, and the Divisional Court were agreed that there was evidence to support that finding. In those circumstances, according to Mathew, J., an acquittal must follow because "where the defendant does not know that the person who was on his premises was in fact drunk, he cannot be said to permit drunkenness".[5] The other member of the court, Collins, J., was equally emphatic in requiring proof of knowledge on the part of the licensee, saying:[6] "The appellant does not contend that if a quarrel arose when the landlord was momentarily absent, and he stopped it on his return, he could be convicted under the same section of permitting quarrelsome or riotous conduct to take place.[7] He could not be convicted because while the quarrel went on he did not know of it, and the same observation applies here."

Principally significant for its application of the doctrine of vicarious liability, which is to be discussed later,[8] the case of *Worth* v. *Brown*[9] provides additional support for the view that *mens rea* is necessary in offences based on "permitting" defined

[1] (1875) 33 L.T. 339.

[2] 35 & 36 Vict. c. 94. This offence is now to be found in the Licensing Act, 1953 (1 & 2 Eliz. 2, c. 46), s. 136 (1).

[3] *Loc. cit.* [4] [1894] 2 Q.B. 574. [5] *Ibid.*, p. 577. [6] *Loc. cit.*

[7] See now the Licensing Act, 1953, s. 136 (1). [8] See Chapter X.

[9] (1896) 40 S.J. 515.

conduct. Interpreting the same offence of permitting drunkenness to mean "knowingly to allow a drunk person to remain on the premises", Grantham, J., might well have cited the analogous case of *Hope* v. *Warburton*[1] in which the licensee, in spite of his refusal to serve with liquor a person who was already drunk when he entered, was convicted for permitting drunkenness. According to Day and Charles, JJ., "it is perfectly clear that serving the man with drink is not material to the offence at all."[2] The important thing so far as the licensee was concerned in *Hope* v. *Warburton* was the fact that he was aware that the person was drunk when he entered. On this decision, it is clear that mere refusal to serve a person already drunk is no defence to the charge of permitting drunkenness. To escape liability the licensee must apparently exercise his statutory right of expelling the reveller.[3] It seems particularly hard on a publican that in order to carry on his business legitimately, without running the risk of losing his licence on account of a licensing conviction, he must keep a sharp look-out on all his customers and forthwith expel any of them if he thinks they have drunk too much. After all, the law does not, in express terms, impose a duty upon a licensee to evict, but rather a permissive discretion.[4]

"*Permitting a false invoice*"

Leaving these pioneering interpretations for the moment and turning to cases decided during the past fifty years, one of the important factors which must be borne in mind when considering the merits of these decisions, is that during the early part of this century the doctrine of *mens rea* lacked the invigorating support and emphasis accorded to it by the present members of the judiciary. An early example of this outlook, involving the interpretation of a statutory offence based upon the word "permits",

[1] [1892] 2 Q.B. 134. Cf. *Edmunds* v. *James* [1892] 1 Q.B. 18 and note in 184 L.T 268.

[2] *Loc. cit.*

[3] Under the Licensing Act 1872, s. 18 (re-enacted in the Licensing (Consolidation) Act, 1910, s. 80 (1) and now in the Licensing Act, 1953, s. 138 (1)), a licensee *may* turn out of the premises any person who is drunken, violent, quarrelsome or disorderly.

[4] It is worth noting that a new provision was inserted in the Licensing (Consolidation) Act, 1910, s. 75 (3), which is repeated in the Licensing Act, 1953, s. 136 (2), to the effect that if it is proved that any person was drunk on licensed premises and a charge of permitting drunkenness is brought against the licensee, it shall be a good defence to prove that he and his servants took all reasonable steps for preventing drunkenness on the premises.

occurred in the case of *Korten* v. *West Sussex C.C.*,[1] in which the majority of the court were of opinion that the intention of the Act concerned would be defeated if guilty knowledge was a necessary condition of liability. The views of the majority, consisting of Lord Alverstone, C.J., and Wills, J., will be considered carefully later,[2] but attention is now focused on the solitary but none the less powerful voice of Channell, J., which was raised in denunciation of the reasoning—not the actual decision—upon which his brethren rested their decisions. In that case, the defendant, managing director of a chemical company, was charged with permitting an invoice of fertilisers sold to a purchaser to be false in a material particular, which constitutes an offence under section 3 (1) (*b*) of the Fertilisers and Feeding Stuffs Act, 1893.[3] There was no evidence that the defendant saw the particular invoice or knew it to be false, but there was evidence to the effect that invoices with a guarantee, similar to the one in question, would not be sent out in the ordinary course of business without his knowledge. In expressing his conviction that *mens rea* was a necessary constituent of the offence before the court, Channell, J., put forward the following, it is suggested, incontrovertible argument:[4] "To my mind it is impossible, without contradiction in language, to say that a man can be convicted of permitting the invoice to be false if he believes it to be true; and if that view be sound then *mens rea* is an element of this offence."

Although satisfied that the managing director had no actual knowledge of the false statement in the invoice, viz., that the fertiliser contained 38 per cent of total phosphates whereas, in fact, it contained less than 38 per cent, Channell, J., supported the other members of the court in sustaining the conviction by attributing to the appellant constructive knowledge of the falsity. "It seems to me" said the learned judge, "that in the reasonable sense of the words he can be said to have permitted the invoice to be false, because he carried on the business in such a way that, though the invoice was not to his knowledge sent out with a state-

[1] (1903) 72 L.J.K.B. 514. [2] See *post* pp. 112–114.

[3] 56 & 57 Vict. c. 56. The analogous section 4 (3) of the Fertilisers & Feeding Stuffs Act, 1926 (16 & 17 Geo. 5, c. 45), contains no reference to causing or permitting, but s. 8 provides that if the seller gives the purchaser a statutory statement in which the particulars stated therein differ from the particulars marked on the article, it shall be a good defence to prove that he took all reasonable steps to avoid committing the offence and that he acted without intent to defraud.

[4] *Ibid.*, p. 522.

ment that in fact was incorrect . . . he took no steps whatever to ascertain whether or not the particular parcel of goods to which that invoice was to be applied contained the specified percentage of phosphates."[1] It will be noticed that, whilst invoking the recognised principle of constructive *mens rea*, Channell, J., considered that the crux of the offence was guilty knowledge by the accused, not merely of the false invoice having been issued or despatched, but of the very fact that the statement in the invoice was false. Failure to recognise this essential distinction, it will be submitted later, led Lord Alverstone, C.J., and Wills, J., to misinterpret the particular offence before the court.

Channell, J.'s stand was not in vain and received, as one might expect in a country with a strong liberal outlook, the unconscious approval of the Scottish High Court of Justiciary in the case of *Clydebank Co-op. Society* v. *Binnie*.[2] The appellants, owners of several motor-cars which, although not hackney carriages, they hired out for all sorts of special occasions, were convicted of permitting one of their cars to be used as a public service vehicle without the necessary licences. The appellants' transport manager, though well aware that passengers other than the actual hirer were being carried, did nothing to warn the driver except not to overload. The kernel of the decision of the Court of Justiciary, which decided to uphold the conviction, is to be found in Lord Fleming's statement that "if a person knows that a forbidden thing is happening, and is able to prevent it,[3] and does not, of course he 'permits' in law and in fact".

"*Permitting a motor-vehicle to be used as an 'express carriage' without a road service licence*"

Not for the first time are English and Scottish decisions seen to be in step on this perennial problem of *mens rea*, for in a series of cases based on the closely corresponding offence in the Road

[1] *Ibid.*, p. 523. [2] (1927) S.C. (J.) 117.

[3] Cf. the statement in *Goodbarne* v. *Buck* [1940] 1 K.B. 771 at p. 774, where Mackinnon L.J., declared "In order to make a person liable for permitting another person to use a motor-vehicle, it is obvious that he must be in a position to forbid the other person to use the motor-vehicle". The learned Lord Justice then went on to express the opinion that there was "no ground on which anyone can be in a position to forbid another person to use a motor-vehicle except where he is the owner of the car". The Divisional Court in *Lloyd* v. *Singleton* [1953] 1 All E.R. 291, considered the latter dictum as having been uttered *per incuriam*, and it will be necessary, later, to consider this difference of opinion in conjunction with certain other views which have been expressed on the same question.

Traffic Act, 1930,[1] and exhaustively considered in the recent case of *Reynolds* v. *G. H. Austin & Sons, Ltd*,[2] the English Divisional Court has upheld the necessity for guilty knowledge. Being of a somewhat complicated nature,[3] it may be advisable to set out concisely the requirements of the relevant offence in the 1930 Act which, in section 72, forbids any person to permit a motor vehicle to be used as an "express carriage" without a road service licence. It may be explained that the term "express carriage" is defined in section 61 (1) (*b*) as "a vehicle which carries passengers for hire or reward at separate fares". Furthermore, it is permissible to use an express carriage without a licence only "on a special occasion", and to fall within this description certain conditions have to be fulfilled,[4] amongst which is the requirement that "the journey must be made without previous advertisement to the public of the arrangements therefor".

In the first of these cases, *Webb* v. *Maidstone*,[5] the judgments lend air to an unfortunate ambiguity, it being possible to read into the language used by the court a construction which would make the offence one of absolute prohibition. To relate briefly the facts, a greengrocer, having hired a coach from the respondents who were to provide the driver and to take a party of people to the Derby, exhibited a notice advertising the proposed trip and booked in all thirty-one passengers who paid separate fares. No evidence was given as to any knowledge on the part of any of the officers of the respondent bus company. Nevertheless, in directing the justices to find the defendants guilty, Lord Hewart, C.J., declared that by failing to take adequate steps to prevent [the party to the Derby] the respondent company had permitted that to be done which the statute forbade. The case is only briefly reported, and anyone desirous of refuting the view that such reasoning leads to construing the offence as one of absolute liability can rightly point to the parallel argument advanced by Channell, J., in *Korten* v. *West Sussex C.C.*[6] in which the latter judge was firmly of the opinion that the offence of permitting an invoice to be false was a crime involving *mens rea*.

[1] 20 & 21 Geo. 5, c. 43.

[2] [1951] 2 K.B. 135.

[3] A neat summary of the relevant provisions is given by Devlin, J., *ibid.*, pp. 152–153.

[4] These conditions are laid down in the Road Traffic Act, 1934 (24 & 25 Geo. 5, c. 50) s. 25 (1). For an examination of these conditions from the point of view of the requirement of knowledge, see Lord Goddard, C.J. *ibid.*, p. 146, and Devlin, J., *ibid.*, p. 150.

[5] (1934) 78 Sol. J. 336.

[6] (1903) 72 L.J.K.B. 514, 522, *ante*, p. 103.

Any doubts which may have been entertained after the decision in *Webb* v. *Maidstone* were finally resolved by Avory, J., in *Goldsmith* v. *Deakin*.[1] The defendant in that case hired out his bus to the officers of a club in order to take members to a dance. According to the terms of the agreement the club was to pay £1 for the whole trip, and although separate fares were not paid in the coach they were subsequently collected by a club official during the dance. The magistrates were satisfied that the coach was used as a stage carriage but held that since the bus owner did not know it was so used, he could not have "permitted" its use. This view did not commend itself to the Divisional Court, and Avory, J., stated the governing principle as follows:[2] ". . . if a person hires out a vehicle in circumstances in which he ought to know that it probably will be or may be used as a stage carriage, and puts his servant in charge of that vehicle to use it in any way in which the hirer may choose to direct the servant to use it, then he is, within the meaning of this statute, permitting it to be used as a stage carriage without the proper and appropriate licence." In the opinion of Lawrence, J., the word "permit" means "intentionally allow in the sense that one has to consider the state of the defendant's mind".[3] The wide question of what degrees of knowledge are sufficient to establish criminal liability is to be discussed at a later stage,[4] but the above statements are important insofar as they remove any doubts which may have arisen in *Webb* v. *Maidstone* as to the inviolate need to show that the prohibited acts were being carried out with the knowledge, actual or constructive, of the person charged with "permitting" such conduct.

Some caustic remarks on the absurdity of this particular statutory offence were made in *Newell* v. *Cross and Cook*,[5] in which Lord Hewart, C.J., citing with approval the above passage from Avory, J.'s judgment in *Goldsmith* v. *Deakin*, seems to suggest that the words of the statute are sufficiently clear in themselves and to be in no need of interpretation. This point of view was not ap-

[1] (1934) 150 L.T. Rep. 157, following *Osborne* v. *Richards* [1933] 1 K.B. 283.

[2] *Ibid.*, p. 158. Cited with approval by Lord Hewart C.J., in *Evans* v. *Dell* [1937] 1 All E.R. at p. 352.

[3] *Ibid.*, p. 159.

[4] See Chapter IX.

[5] (1936) 52 T.L.R. 489, in which du Parcq, J. (as he then was), said (at pp. 491, 493): ". . . the best way of pointing out any . . . defect in an Act is that it should be rigidly enforced by the courts. The worst possible way of dealing with an absurdity in the law is to have an authority or the Court to exercise common sense in deciding whether it is to be enforced or not." The opposite viewpoint was expressed by Lord Russell, C.J. in *Parker* v. *Alder* [1899] 1 Q.B. 20, at p. 26.

parently shared by certain traffic commissioners who, in the case of *Evans* v. *Dell*,[1] asked the Divisional Court to reconsider the requirements in the offence of permitting a vehicle to be used as a stage carriage otherwise than under a road service licence. Not mincing his words, Goddard, J., declared:[2] "... it seems to me that when one comes to analyse the argument addressed to one ... it really comes to this, that the traffic commissioners desired this court to hold, or to see if they could get this court to hold, that *mens rea* is not part of the offence." The learned judge's answer was forthright and unhesitating. "With the complexity of modern legislation" said Goddard, J.,[2] "one knows that there are times when the court is constrained to find that, by reason of the clear terms of an Act of Parliament, *mens rea*, or the absence of *mens rea*, becomes material, that if a certain act is done, an offence is committed whether the person knew or did not know. When one gets complete vindication of the respondent, as in this case, so far as any knowledge of being guilty of using the coach wrongly, I gather there is nothing in this Act that constrains me to hold that, knowledge or no knowledge, he is guilty of the offence."

"Hope springs eternal in the human breast" is an oft-quoted saying, and in this instance it might pardonably be altered to include the Ministry of Transport which was not disposed to accept the ruling given in *Evans* v. *Dell*, following as that case did a series of consistent decisions on the interpretation of the same statutory offence. In *Reynolds* v. *G. H. Austin Ltd.*[3] yet another attempt was made to obtain the Divisional Court's approval to the exclusion of any question of *mens rea* in considering liability under the Road Traffic Act, 1930, s. 72. As might well have been expected this venture, like its predecessors, was doomed to receive an unfavourable ruling by the court. The facts, following the usual

[1] [1937] 1 All E.R. 349. [2] *Ibid.*, p. 354.

[3] [1951] 2 K.B. 135. In the course of the preliminary argument counsel for the appellant sought to distinguish the case before the court, in which the respondents were charged with unlawfully *using*, from *Evans* v. *Dell* in which the respondent was charged with *permitting* a vehicle to be used in contravention of section 72. The words in the Road Traffic Act, 1930, s. 72 (10) read: "If any person uses a vehicle or causes or permits it to be used ..." To the appellant's contention, Lord Goddard replied: "I will certainly be no party to holding a man guilty of this offence according to whether the informant charges him with using or with permitting the use. This would be reducing the law to an absurdity" (at p. 147). Yet precisely this distinction was drawn in relation to the Motor Vehicles (Construction and Use) Regs. 1951, reg. 101, by the full Divisional Court (Slade, J. dissenting) in *James & Son, Ltd.* v. *Smee* [1954] 3 W.L.R. 631 and *Green* v. *Burnett*, *ibid.* According to Slade, J., in the case of a company, the two expressions are tautologous.

pattern disclosed in the cases already discussed, showed that the respondents had arranged with a Women's Guild to provide a motor coach for a trip to the seaside at a fixed rate per head and with a minimum of 28 passengers. Having six unbooked seats still to fill, the committee of the guild inserted an advertisement in a shop window inviting members of the public to apply for the vacant seats. The justices dismissed the case on the grounds "that the advertisement was made without the knowledge or connivance of the respondents in any way, and as the respondents' place of business was ten miles away they had no reasonable means of knowing that it had been made". Humphreys, J., was content to rely on the decision in *Evans* v. *Dell* from which, he said "it is plain that in the case of permitting at least lack of knowledge may be a complete defence".[1] Lord Goddard, C.J., no doubt recalling his forcible views expressed fifteen years earlier in *Evans* v. *Dell*, pointed to the consequences which would ensue if *mens rea* formed no part of the offence. He said:[2] ". . . were a coach proprietor to require his customer to make a statutory declaration that the trip had not been advertised the owner would still be guilty if the declaration proved to be false, and that even if the declarant did not know of the falsity, as might be the case if one of the party, unknown to the promoter of the trip, had advertised it somewhere. Unless compelled by the words of the statute so to hold no court should give effect to a proposition which is so repugnant to all the principles of criminal law in this kingdom." The other member of the court, Devlin, J., whose judgment throughout is deserving of the closest study, was at one with Lord Goddard, C.J., and Humphreys, J., in deciding that *mens rea* was essential to the offence before the court. Observing that section 72 (10) of the 1930 Act deals "as it were in the same breath" with using the vehicle and causing or permitting it to be used, treating all as being subject to the same penalty, Devlin, J., declared:[3] "Inasmuch as there must be guilty knowledge in the last two cases, the lack of differentiation suggests that there must be guilty knowledge in all three and that it is assumed that the user will know of the facts which constitute the offence."

[1] [1951] 2 K.B. p. 143. [2] *Ibid.*, p. 144.

[3] *Ibid.*, p. 151. But see *James & Son Ltd.* v. *Smee* [1954] 3 W.L.R. 631 and *Green* v. *Burnett*, *ibid.*, in which the Div. Ct. took the view that the Motor Vehicles (Construction and Use) Regs. 1951, reg. 101 creates an absolute prohibition against using, but not against permitting to be used.

Were the position to be judged in the light of the foregoing authorities there could be, it is submitted, no possible doubt that *mens rea*, in the form of guilty knowledge, is an essential requirement of this particular offence. However, this conclusion was rudely shaken in an unreserved judgment of Lord Goddard, C.J., in the recent case of *Browning* v. *J. W. H. Watson* (*Rochester*) *Ltd.*[1] It appeared that on six Saturdays at fortnightly intervals the respondents' motor coach was hired to take members of the United Services Club, Rainham, to the Gillingham football ground to watch league football matches. On one occasion, two persons in the employ of the Ministry of Transport insinuated themselves among the members of the club and travelled on the coach to and from the football match. In consequence of this intrusion the party conveyed was not a "private party", and the occasion ceased to be a "special occasion", within the meaning of the proviso to section 61 (2) of the Act. Neither the respondents' servant, who was driving the coach, nor any member of the club were aware that the motor coach was carrying as passengers anyone who was not a member of the club.

The bus company was charged with the now familiar offence of permitting a motor-coach to be used as an express carriage without a road service licence. Acting, as they believed, in accordance with the decision in *Reynolds* v. *G. H. Austin Ltd.*, the justices dismissed the information on the ground that the respondents did not know of the presence of the two "strangers" among the members of the club in the coach. The Divisional Court,[2] however, sent the case back to the magistrates with a direction that the offence was proved.[3] Two contradictory grounds seem to have been advanced as the justification for this decision.

First, referring to the particular offence before the court Lord Goddard, C.J., declared:[4] "The prohibitions in the Act are absolute and, while it is true that in *Reynolds* v. *G. H. Austin Ltd.* we refused to impose vicarious liability and a good deal of dis-

[1] [1953] 1 W.L.R. 1172; [1953] 2 All E.R. 775.

[2] Consisting of Lord Goddard C.J., Parker and Donovan JJ.

[3] Reminding the justices that "no court in England has ever liked action by what are generally called *agents provocateurs* resulting in imposing criminal liability", the Lord Chief Justice drew the attention of the magistrates to their power to order an absolute discharge without payment of costs.

[4] *Ibid.*, p. 778. In the report of this case which appeared in [1953] *The Times*, July 29, Lord Goddard is quoted as saying "There was a duty on the coach proprietor to take precautions, and if people who were not members of the club travelled in the coach he was liable".

cussion took place about the doctrine of *mens rea*, in cases of absolute prohibition *mens rea* can be supplied by the simple doing of the forbidden act." Whether or not this dubious interpretation of the doctrine of *mens rea* is accepted, it is submitted, with respect, that the Lord Chief Justice's description of the prohibition in section 72 (1) of the Road Traffic Act, 1930, as absolute bears no relation to the earlier authorities. It is diametrically opposed to the same learned judge's construction of the identical offence in *Evans* v. *Dell*,[1] and of the entire Divisional Court's views in *Reynolds* v. *G. H. Austin Ltd.*[2] If the present view is to prevail, namely, that the offence can be committed by the simple doing of the forbidden act, it follows that the question of knowledge or means of knowledge is irrelevant and that the mere presence of the outsiders in the party would be enough to constitute the offence. Is this the law? It is respectfully suggested that this interpretation cannot stand, and closer examination of the Lord Goddard's judgment reveals that it is rather on the precise point of means of knowledge that the decision principally rested.[3]

Thus, the Divisional Court distinguished *Reynolds* v. *G. H. Austin Ltd.*, on the ground that in that case there were no practical means by which the proprietors of the coach could know of the illegal advertisement by the women's institute who, it was stressed, were not servants of the bus company. In the present case, said Lord Goddard, the coach driver certainly did not know that unauthorised persons had boarded the coach but his ignorance was caused through failure to take any precaution to see that only members were allowed to travel on the football excursion. "Of course," said the Lord Chief Justice, "this was not a wilful violation, but it is clear that the respondents should have taken some precaution."[4] In other words, having regard to all the circumstances, the Court imputed knowledge to the respondents through their servant, the coach-driver, thus subscribing to the consistently recognised view that this particular offence is one involving proof of *mens rea*. The suggestion, pervading the whole of Lord Goddard's judgment, that the respondents were liable because they ought to have

[1] [1937] 1 All E.R. 349. [2] [1951] 2 K.B. 135.

[3] This view is borne out by reference to *James & Son, Ltd.* v. *Smee* [1954] 3 W.L.R. 631, *per* Parker, J., at p. 639.

[4] [1953] 2 All E.R. at p. 778. Of course, if the offence was one of absolute prohibition, as suggested earlier in his judgment by Lord Goddard, no matter how stringent the precautions taken by the bus company the offence would still be committed by the unauthorised act of the intruders if they succeeded in boarding the coach.

known, a view which accepts negligence as adequate for incurring liability, will be treated fully later.[1]

There the position rests in relation to this frequently invoked offence under the Road Traffic Act, 1930, and whilst the construction of other crimes in other statutes must primarily depend on the wording used in the enactment before the court,[2] it is both justifiable and useful to point to the interpretations adopted in other penal statutes wherein the expressions "permits" and "permitting" form the key to criminal liability.

LIABILITY WHEREIN THE ACCUSED'S STATE OF MIND IS IRRELEVANT

The view has already been put forward that one of the principal reasons underlying the divergence of judicial opinion on the necessity for *mens rea* in statutory offences is traceable to the attitude of individual judges. Furthermore, evidence is available that the mood of a particular decade is to a large extent set by the Chief Justice of the day. Indeed, successive Chief Justices may be said to have achieved in retrospect either a renown for maintaining in full vigour the doctrine that criminal liability is based on a guilty mind—as leading exponents of this attitude Cockburn, C.J., Lord Coleridge, C.J., and the present Lord Chief Justice, Lord Goddard, may be cited as shining examples—or else, perhaps unfairly, a reputation for readily construing statutory offences as being of absolute prohibition thus displacing the fundamental maxim of criminal law—Lord Alverstone C.J., and Lord Hewart C.J., may, with some justification, be described as manifesting this attitude. The truth of this invidious classification has been made apparent already in the study of cases involving malice and wilfulness, and it is to be underlined in the examination which follows.

The views of Stephen, J., are of course, deserving of the greatest respect but it is open to consideration whether even that great master of the criminal law was infallible. Stimulating this doubt

[1] *Post*, pp. 205–216.

[2] In the light of the criticism voiced (*supra*) against the interpretation adopted by the Divisional Court in *Browning* v. *J. H. Watson Ltd.*, it is disturbing to note that in the later case of *Shave* v. *Rosner* [1954] 2 W.L.R. 1057, Lord Goddard C.J. used the same language in relation to the offence created by the Motor Vehicles (Construction and Use) Regulations 1951, Reg. 101, which prohibits any person from "using or causing or permitting to be used on any road a motor-vehicle in such condition as to cause danger to any person". Of that offence Lord Goddard C.J. declared (at p. 1069): "That is an absolute prohibition; there is no question of negligence." On the interpretation of this particular offence see further *post.*, p. 117.

is his judgment in *Bond* v. *Evans*[1] when, construing the offence of suffering gaming on licensed premises contrary to the Licensing Act, 1872, s. 17,[2] Stephen, J., declared:[3] "I can see no distinction between the word 'permits' which is used in some of the other sections, and the word 'suffers' which occurs in section 17. On general grounds I should entertain no doubt as to the intention of the statute. I think the meaning is that the landlord of licensed premises must prevent that which the Act prohibits from being done on his premises, and if he does not prevent it so much the worse for him. I wish to repeat with regard to section 17 what I said in *Cundy* v. *Le Cocq* with regard to section 13 that the statute imposes a prohibition." In *Cundy* v. *Le Cocq*,[4] it will be remembered, Stephen, J., expressed the opinion that the wording of section 13 amounted to an absolute prohibition of the sale of liquor to a drunken person, contrasting that section with others in the Licensing Act, 1872, in which knowledge was an element in the offence. By analogy, the learned judge, in the passage quoted above, would seem to suggest that in offences incorporating the words "permitting" or "suffering" they, likewise, dispense with the necessity for *mens rea*. In fact, it is extremely doubtful whether such was the view held by Stephen, J., for, earlier in his judgment in *Bond* v. *Evans* after referring to previous cases decided under section 17, he had declared: "I think . . . all the other cases show that the prohibition is not quite absolute, but is subject to this limitation, that in order to justify a conviction someone must know of or connive at the gaming."[5] The inappropriateness of his reference to the analogy afforded by *Cundy* v. *Le Cocq* is obvious, unless, perhaps Stephen, J., had in mind a similar limitation in respect to section 17 which would, of course, effect a radical alteration in the opinion held of that particular decision.

"*Permitting a false invoice*"

Next, we must turn to examine the views put forward in two cases by Lord Alverstone, C.J. The first of these cases is *Korten* v. *West Sussex C.C.*[6] to which brief reference has already been made in connection with the minority judgment of Channell, J. It will be recalled that in *Korten* a chemical company sold a quantity of fertiliser, and an invoice was sent to the purchaser stating that the

[1] (1888) 21 Q.B.D. 249.
[2] Re-enacted in the Licensing Act, 1953, s. 141 (1).
[3] *Ibid.*, p. 257.
[4] (1884) 13 Q.B.D. 207.
[5] (1888) 21 Q.B.D. p. 256.
[6] (1903) 72 L.J.K.B. 514.

fertiliser contained 38 per cent of total phosphates whereas, in fact, the goods contained less than 38 per cent. The managing director of the company was charged with permitting the invoice to be false in a material particular to the prejudice of the purchaser, contrary to the Fertilisers & Feeding Stuffs Act, 1893, s. 3 (1) (*b*).

As to the question of *mens rea* the Lord Chief Justice felt "the very gravest doubt" and reached his conclusion "with considerable hesitation". To that extent the importance of his judgment is minimised, and it is significant that he accepted the application of the presumption as to *mens rea* in all criminal offences. Having referred to the classic judgment of Wright, J., in *Sherras* v. *de Rutzen* in which the exceptions to the general rule are set out, Lord Alverstone, C.J., said of the statutory offence before the court:[1] "I have come to the conclusion that the word 'permits' was inserted in order to include the case in which a description false in fact has been sent out by the permission of the person whose goods are being sent out with it, or who is the manager of the works from which the goods are being sent out. It may be said that the appellant did not permit the description to be false. He did not permit it in the sense of allowing this particular description to be false, but to found an argument on the rather unusual form of that phrase would be to defeat the intention of the Act."

A careful study of the relevant section reveals at once, with respect, the fundamental mistake perpetrated by Lord Alverstone. It lies in his refusal to relate the word "permits" to the falsity of the invoice, and instead to relate it merely to the despatch of the invoice.[2] In so denying the necessity for guilty know-

[1] (1903) 72 L.J.K.B., p. 520. Cf. the interpretation adopted by Hawkins and Wright, JJ., in *Derbyshire* v. *Houliston* (1897) 66 L.J.Q.B. 569, in which the court construed s. 27 (3) of the Food and Drugs Act, 1875, which prohibits the giving of any false warranty, as an offence requiring proof of guilty knowledge. No reference is made in s. 27 (3) to "permitting" or "knowingly".

[2] Lord Alverstone's judgment may fairly be said to lack consistency. Having ruled that the appellant fell within the scope of section 3 (1) (*b*), he then concluded that there was evidence upon which the magistrate could find that the appellant aided or abetted the offence of causing or permitting the invoice to be false. Finally, having decided that *mens rea* was unnecessary he completes his judgment by saying (at p. 520) it was "too narrow a construction . . . to say that there must be greater evidence of guilty knowledge on the part of the person charged than is to be found in this case as to the part the appellant had to play and did play in the management of this business". Were it not for Lord Alverstone's earlier statements it would clearly be possible to assimilate this final opinion with that of Channell, J. in which the latter held that the managing director had constructive knowledge of the false invoice.

ledge on the part of the accused as to the falsity of the invoice, the learned Chief Justice acquiesced in a construction which made the offence to all intents and purposes one of absolute liability, and this, it is respectfully submitted, constitutes a serious error in interpretation. Moreover, it is suggested, had Lord Alverstone given effect to the words used in the section it would have been unnecessary for him to invoke the intention of the legislature as justification for his decision. By so doing, the Lord Chief Justice set an example for other judges who, occasionally with what appears to be an excess of zeal, have been prepared to rely upon the "objects of the Act" as a convenient umbrella beneath which to seek refuge when excluding the basic principle of criminal responsibility. It is true, of course, that where the words of a statute provide no indication as to the necessity for, or exclusion of, *mens rea* it is a matter for the court to decide whether or not to import it into the statutory definition. This task frequently poses a difficult problem for the court. But where, as in *Korten* v. *West Sussex C.C.*, the legislature has expressly inserted the vital word "permits" in its definition of an offence it is difficult to believe that Parliament intended to create an offence of absolute liability. As has already been argued when discussing the crime of "wilfully killing a house pigeon",[1] the mistake made in cases like *Cotterill* v. *Penn*[2] and *Horton* v. *Gwynne*[3] was to relate the epithet "wilfully" solely to the act of killing and to exclude it from the remaining elements of the offence. Precisely the same mistake in construction is seen being made by Lord Alverstone, C.J., in the present case, where the word "permits" is related only to the sending of the invoice and not to what, it is submitted, is the real gravamen of the offence, namely, the falsity of the invoice.

Equally erroneous, it is respectfully submitted, in his explanation of the true meaning of the word "permits" was Wills, J. who declared that the persons concerned in sending out such invoices "should not be able to shelter themselves simply by saying that the purchaser cannot show that they did not believe that the invoice was perfectly genuine and correct".[4] But, surely, as Channell, J., argued in his minority judgment, "it is impossible,

[1] Larceny Act, 1861 (24 & 25 Vict. c. 96), s. 23. See the discussion *ante* p. 41 *et seq.*

[2] [1936] 1 K.B. 53.

[3] [1921] 2 K.B. 661. For an example of what it is suggested, is the correct method of interpretation see Hawkins, J., in *Derbyshire* v. *Houliston* (1897) 66 L.J.Q.B. 569, at p. 571.

[4] (1903) 72 L.J.K.B. 514, at p. 521.

without contradiction in language to say that a man can be convicted of permitting an invoice to be false if he believes it to be true."[1] Pointing out that section 6 of the same statute, the Fertilisers & Feeding Stuffs Act, 1893, created an offence into which guilty knowledge would reasonably be supposed to enter as an ingredient, Wills, J., stressed the use of the words "knowingly and fraudulently" in that particular section. Thus fortified, the learned judge concluded that "it was the intention of the Act to give this remedy in case the statements in the invoice were untrue in fact".[2] The comparative argument has been used before, for example in *Cundy* v. *Le Cocq*,[3] where the legislature had omitted all reference to guilty knowledge, but that is certainly not true of the offence created in section 3 (1) (*b*) which uses the expression "permits" as a beacon to light the entire offence.

Three years later the same offence again engaged the attention of the Divisional Court in *Laird* v. *Dobell*,[4] but the opportunity which presented itself for reconsidering the earlier interpretation was made more difficult by reason of the fact that Lord Alverstone, C.J., again presided over the court, accompanied on this occasion by Lawrence, J., who merely delivered a concurring judgment. In this case, cake meal, described in the invoice as containing 58 per cent of oil and albuminoids but in fact containing only 51 per cent, was sold by the defendants. Samples of the same consignment had previously been analysed and certified as containing over 60 per cent of oil and albuminoids. In purposely reducing the percentage from that certified by the analyst, the defendants were acting on the safe side and believed the statement in the invoice to be true. In the teeth of the earlier decision in *Korten* v. *West Sussex C.C.*[5] the magistrates refused to convict, and Lord Alverstone, C.J., at the outset of his judgment, was moved to saying that it was a hard case. However, having expressed his sympathy for the defendants, the Lord Chief Justice proceeded to show himself an unrepentant adherent to the decision that the crime was one of absolute liability. Displaying on this occasion no inhibitions on the question of *mens rea*, the learned Chief Justice declared that in his opinion the view expressed by Wills, J., and himself in *Korten* was correct, namely, "that a person who causes or permits the invoice or description of the article sold to be false in any material portion, although he may have no personal knowledge of

[1] *Ibid.*, p. 522. [2] *Loc. cit.* [3] (1884) 13 Q.B.D. 207.
[4] [1906] 1 K.B. 131. [5] (1903) 72 L.J.K.B. 514.

the falsity, is, nevertheless, guilty of an offence under that section."[1] Lest there be any doubt as to his views, Lord Alverstone added that he considered the object of inserting the word "permits" in the section "was to protect the purchaser where the description of the article sold was in fact false, though not false to the knowledge of the vendor"[1] Accordingly, the case was returned to the justices with directions to convict.

"Permitting a motor-vehicle to be on the highway without a policy of insurance"

More recently, in *Lyons* v. *May*,[2] the Divisional Court, consisting of Lord Goddard C.J., Hilbery and Birkett JJ., perpetrated what, it is respectfully suggested, is the same error in interpreting the word "permits" as extending to only one of the constituent elements of an offence. For consideration by the court in that case was section 35 (1) of the Road Traffic Act, 1930, which prohibits any person from permitting a motor-vehicle to be used on the highway without the requisite policy of insurance against third party risks. The respondent had apparently sent his lorry to a garage to be repaired and, finding it inconvenient to fetch it when it was ready, asked the garage proprietor to drive it back. This the proprietor did, but without having an effective insurance policy which covered the lorry. Moreover, although the respondent had a third party policy it covered only himself and his employees.

[1] [1906] 1 K.B. 133. It is noted with some surprise that in *Needham* v. *Worcs. C.C.* (1909) 25 T.L.R. 471, Lord Alverstone C.J. abstained from deciding whether *mens rea* was a necessary element of the offence under s. 6 (1) (*b*) of the Fertilisers and Feeding Stuffs Act, 1906, which is worded precisely the same as s. 3 (1) (*b*) of the 1893 Act.

[2] [1948] 2 All E.R. 1062. The decision in this case was followed in *Morris* v. *Williams* (1952) 50 Local Govt. Reports 308, in which the Divisional Court was composed of Lord Goddard C.J., Slade and Devlin JJ. It is perhaps worth noting that the other case relied upon by the court in *Morris* v. *Williams* for construing the offence under s. 35 (*supra*) as one of absolute prohibition was *Churchill* v. *Norris* (1938) 158 L.T. 255. In that case the defendant was charged with permitting a lorry to be used on the highway with a load in excess of the permitted weight, contrary to the Motor Vehicles (Construction & Use) Regulations 1937, Reg. 64. Lord Hewart C.J. upheld the finding of the justices on the ground that the defendant had connived at a matter which might well lead to the commission of the offence charged. Humphreys, J., (at p. 257) went further and said that the evidence showed "sufficient carelessness on the part of the [defendant] to justify the justices in holding that he had permitted the offence to be committed within the meaning of the cases cited to the court, in the course of which cases it was made clear that the word 'permit' may mean no more than a failure to take proper steps to prevent". In the light of these views it is difficult to see the justification for relying on *Churchill* v. *Norris* as a case of absolute prohibition. See, too, *Prosser* v. *Richings* [1936] 2 All E.R. 1627.

Remitting the case to the magistrates with directions to convict, Lord Goddard C.J. said that "scienter is not necessary . . . a person who is ignorant of the fact that there is no policy of insurance covering a vehicle, may, nevertheless, be held to commit an offence if he permits the use of the vehicle".[1] This interpretation of the offence in section 35 (1), in effect, restricts the keyword "permits" to, simply, the user of the vehicle, and excludes from the remaining elements of the offence any question of *mens rea*. The net result is to construe the crime as one of absolute liability.

"*Permitting a motor-vehicle to be on the highway in a dangerous condition*"

This trend is seen continuing in *Shave* v. *Rosner*[2] which involved the offence under the Motor Vehicles (Construction and Use) Regulations 1951, Regs. 72 (*c*) and 101 of "using or causing or permitting a motor-vehicle to be used on the road in a dangerous condition". The facts showed that a motor-van had been left by its owner at a garage to have the brakes re-shoed. Having carried out the work the mechanics replaced the wheel but failed to tighten sufficiently the hub nuts. After the van had been re-delivered to the owner and when the latter was driving it, the wheel came off and injured a pedestrian. The garage proprietor was charged with "causing" the van to be used in a dangerous condition but was held not liable on the ground that once he had handed the vehicle back to the owner he, the garage proprietor, no longer had any control or dominion over it. But, according to Lord Goddard C.J. the regulation which creates the offence "is an absolute prohibition; there is no question of negligence". Therefore, said the Lord Chief Justice, had the owner, who was driving the car at the time, been summoned—either with causing or permitting the car to be on the road in a dangerous condition—"it is difficult to see that he would have had any defence in law." Liability, in other words, would follow from the mere fact that the van was on the highway and was in a dangerous condition. The question of knowledge of the defective condition of the car, on Lord Goddard's view, would appear irrelevant.

A very different interpretation of the analogous offence under Regs. 75 and 101 was given by a strong Divisional Court in *James & Son, Ltd.* v. *Smee*.[3] The appellants' lorry and trailer had left their premises with the connecting cable in position and in good work-

[1] [1948] 2 All E.R. 1062.
[2] [1954] 2 W.L.R. 1057 & cf. *Macdonald* v. *Wilmae Concrete Co.* [1954] *Crim L.R.* 621.
[3] [1954] 3 W.L.R. 631.

ing order. In order to load certain goods it was necessary to uncouple the trailer but the driver's assistant forgot to re-connect the brake cable. The appellant company were charged with permitting to be used on a road a trailer the brakes of which were not in efficient working order. Delivering the majority judgment,[1] Parker, J. indicated that a charge of "permitting" at once imports a state of mind and then proceeded to draw the vital distinction between (1) permitting the driver to use the vehicle, and (2) permitting the driver to use the vehicle in contravention of the regulation.[2] In the latter contingency it becomes necessary to prove knowledge of the facts constituting the breach of the regulation. Since there was no evidence that the appellants, by any responsible officer, had knowledge of the failure to connect the brake cable it could not be said that the company had permitted the vehicle to be used in contravention of the regulation. Accordingly, the appeal against conviction was allowed.[3]

Conclusion

The interpretation adopted in *James & Sons, Ltd.* v. *Smee* is irreproachable and is in striking contrast with that followed in the "pigeon cases" *Cotterill* v. *Penn*[4] and *Horton* v. *Gwynne*,[5] and in the "false invoice cases" *Korten* v. *West Sussex C.C.*[6] and *Laird* v. *Dobell*.[7] Furthermore, it is clear that the construction put forward in *Lyons* v. *May*[8] is directly contrary to that placed in cases like *Goldsmith* v. *Deakin*,[9] *Evans* v. *Dell*[10] and *Reynolds* v. *G. H. Austin Co. Ltd.*[11] upon the analogous offence, in section 72 (10) of the same Act, of permitting a motor-vehicle to be used as an express carriage without a road service licence. In proving the commission of the latter offence, as Devlin, J. explained in *Reynolds* v. *Austin*, it is essential that the person who permits the user "*will know of the facts which constitute the offence*".[12] In other words, the condition of knowledge,

[1] Lord Goddard, C. J., Cassels, Lynskey and Parker, JJ. [2] *Ibid.*, p. 639.

[3] In a dissenting judgment Slade, J. argued that the word "uses" means, in the case of a body corporate, "permits to be used" and since the word "uses" creates an absolute prohibition so also does the expression "permits to be used". This view did not commend itself to the majority of the court, who considered that "permitting" in the regulation must have the same meaning whether the defendant is a private individual or a company.

[4] [1936] 1 K.B. 53. [5] [1921] 2 K.B. 661.

[6] (1903) 72 L.J.K.B. 514. [7] [1906] 1 K.B. 514.

[8] [1948] 2 All E.R. 1062. See Glanville Williams, *Criminal Law*, pp. 130–131.

[9] (1934) 150 L.T. Rep. 157. [10] [1937] 1 All E.R. 349. [11] [1951] 2 K.B. 135.

[12] [1951] 2 K.B. 135, at p. 151. The writer's italics. See, too, the views of Lord Goddard C.J. in that case and in *Evans* v. *Dell* which have been noted *ante*. pp. 107

which is embodied in the epithet "permits", must extend to *all* the constituent elements in the statutory offence.

Those who would support the contrary view that the insertion in a statutory offence of the term "permits" does not connote the need for proof of guilty knowledge of all the conditions of liability must content themselves with the support provided by these four cases, *Korten* v. *West Sussex C.C.*,[1] *Laird* v. *Dobell*,[2] *Lyons* v. *May*,[3] *Morris* v. *Williams*[4] the dicta of Stephen, J., in *Bond* v. *Evans*,[5] which have already been shown to be open to a twofold interpretation, and the dicta of Lord Goddard C.J. in *Browning* v. *J. H. Watson Ltd.*[6] and in *Shave* v. *Rosner*.[7] Set up in opposition to this point of view is the wide range of decisions covering a variety of statutory crimes and culminating with the recent decision in *James & Son, Ltd.* v. *Smee*,[8] in which the word "permits" was recognised as a pointer to the requirement of *mens rea* throughout the whole definition of an offence. In view of the weight of authorities to the contrary, which it is realised involved different offences, it is respectfully submitted that the reasoning underlying the decisions in *Korten* v. *West Sussex C.C.*, *Laird* v. *Dobell*, *Lyons* v. *May* and *Morris* v. *Williams* cannot stand and should not, in any case, be extended beyond the confines of the criminal offences there involved.

"Knowingly permit"

Before leaving the section of this study devoted to the terms "permits" and "permitting" it is necessary to glance at the difficulties sometimes encountered by the courts in interpreting the

and 108. This divergence in interpretation was appreciated by Devlin, J. in *Morris* v. *Williams* (1952) 50 Local Govt. Reports, 308 at p. 313, where, with respect, an unsatisfactory (so far as the present writer is concerned) explanation was put forward. It was to the effect that although precisely the same form of wording is used by Parliament in the two offences it does not in the least follow that because *mens rea* is required in section 72 it is necessarily required in section 35. According to Devlin, J., "The [Road Traffic] Act is a comprehensive one, achieving many different objects, and it may well be that in some parts of it Parliament must be taken to have intended a more stringent duty to be imposed than in others." With respect, it might be expected that Parliament would signify the existence of a more stringent duty by excluding any words which normally act as a signpost for the requirement of guilty knowledge. No such step was taken by the Legislature in defining the offence under section 35 and it is regrettable that the Divisional Court in *Lyons* v. *May* and again in *Morris* v. *Williams* should have been led to denying the application of the general maxim of criminal law.

[1] [1903] 72 L.J.K.B. 514.
[2] [1906] 1 K.B. 514.
[3] [1948] 2 All E.R. 1062. See Glanville Williams, *Criminal Law*, pp. 130–131.
[4] (1952) 50 Local Govt. Reports 308.
[5] (1888) 21 Q.B.D. 249.
[6] [1953] 1 W.L.R. 1172.
[7] [1954] 2 W.L.R. 1057.
[8] [1954] 3 W.L.R. 631.

phrase "knowingly permit". Thus, in *Roper* v. *Taylor's Centra Garages* Devlin, J., recently declared:[1] "I think that there ar obvious difficulties about distinguishing between knowingl permitting and permitting simpliciter. I should have thought tha the two were the same." Having regard to the examination whicl has been carried out above Devlin, J.'s opinion would seem, a first sight, to be correct, it being tautologous to use the tern "knowingly" in conjunction with the already sufficient wor "permits". However, as will be seen later, circumstances exis in which both words, though existing side by side, may have separate function to perform. With these rare exceptions th continued use in statutory offences of the phrase "knowingl permits" is both unnecessary and undesirable. It may serve t emphasise the element of guilty knowledge but that, it is sub mitted, is already well established.

In the early statutes many instances will be found where th legislature resorted to what, in the light of more modern inter pretations, may be regarded as otiose combinations. Presumabl the object of the legislature was to stress the application of th maxim as to *mens rea*, and it is worth remembering that in th earliest example of the use of the word "permits" in a statutor offence it did not appear in isolation but coupled with the wor "willingly", a favourite expression of the draftsman until re placed at a much later stage by the word "knowingly". Present da legislation reveals infrequent use of the phrase "knowingl permits", among the statutes being the Licensing (Consolidation Act, 1910,[2] the Agriculture Act, 1948,[3] the Rivers (Prevention c Pollution) Act, 1951,[4] and the Pests Act, 1954.[5]

Separate functions of "knowingly" and "permits"

What of the occasional exceptions in which the term "know ingly", though part of a double-barrelled phrase like "knowingl permits" or "knowingly suffers", has a precise meaning of its own Perhaps the best known example is contained in the offence c knowingly permitting licensed premises to be the habitual resor of reputed prostitutes. Originally this anti-social crime forme

[1] [1951] 2 T.L.R. 284, at p. 287.

[2] 10 Edw. 7 & 1 Geo. 5, c. 24, s. 76. See, too, Criminal Law Amendment Act, 188 (48 & 49 Vict. c. 69), s. 13.

[3] 11 & 12 Geo. 6, c. 45, s. 50 (1) (*b*).

[4] 14 & 15 Geo. 6, c. 64, s.2.

[5] 2 & 3 Eliz. 2, c. 68, s. 9, and s. 12 which makes it an offence to knowingly permit th spreading of myxomatosis.

part of section 14[1] of the Licensing Act, 1872, section 13 of which prohibits a licensee from permitting drunkenness. Differentiating between the formulae used in these adjoining sections, Mathew, J., in *Somerset* v. *Wade*[2] said that the word "knowingly" in section 14 applies to the character of the persons who are permitted to resort to the premises, and Collins, J., added that the word "knowingly" is used because "without the use of that or some similar word it might possibly be contended that if women were knowingly permitted to resort to the premises, it would be no defence that it was not known that they were reputed prostitutes".[3] In *Allen* v. *Whitehead*,[4] in which a similar offence under the Metropolitan Police Act, 1839,[5] was involved, it was established that the manager of a refreshment house, for whose conduct the licensee was sought to be held vicariously liable, knew that the women congregating on the premises were, in fact, prostitutes. Consequently, no occasion arose for testing the validity of the interpretation tentatively put forward in *Somerset* v. *Wade*.

According to the reasoning advanced by Collins, J. in that case, "permitting" in section 14 of the Licensing Act, 1872, relates solely to allowing women to resort habitually to licensed premises, whilst the additional word "knowingly" goes further and requires proof that the licensee was aware of the women's notorious character. Assuming this construction of the offence is correct and is of general application, may it not place a different complexion on the views of Lord Alverstone, C.J. and Wills, J. in *Korten* v. *West Sussex* C.C.?[6] Presumably, in that case, if the managing director of the chemical company had been charged, not with simply permitting, but with knowingly permitting a false invoice to be sent to a purchaser, Lord Alverstone might have related the element "permitting" to the mere act of despatching the invoice, as the learned judge in fact did, and then related the

[1] Re-enacted in the Licensing Act, 1953, s. 139 (1).

[2] [1894] 1 Q.B. 574 at p. 578.

[3] *Loc. cit.* Comparison may usefully be made with the Australian case *R.* v. *Turnbull* (1943) 44 S.R. (N.S.W.) 108 in which the charge was one of having knowingly suffered to be upon premises then used as a house of ill-fame a girl under 18. The court held that "knowingly" referred to the whole charge, including the fact that the girl was under the age of 18 years.

[4] [1930] 1 K.B. 211. See, too, *Linnett* v. *Metropolitan Police Comm.* [1946] K.B. 290.

[5] 2 & 3 Vict. c. 47, s. 44, which uses the alternative formulae "wilfully or knowingly permit drunkenness . . . or knowingly permit or suffer prostitutes . . . to meet together and remain therein".

[6] (1903) 72 L.J.K.B. 514, discussed *ante* pp. 112–115.

word "knowingly" to the falsity of the invoice, thus achieving the result which Channell, J., maintained was achieved by the appearance of the word "permitting" alone. It has already been argued that the minority judgment of Channell, J., in that case is to be preferred, and consideration of the views stated by Mathew, J. and Collins, J., in *Somerset* v. *Wade* do nothing to alter that opinion. Of course, if the intention of Parliament is to forestall and close any possible loopholes which might be created by astute prosecutors, then resort to what might be described as the "double signpost" system may be excusable. However, by making it a common practice to insert the additional epithet "knowingly", difficulties rather than assistance is given to the courts and it is suggested that a more selective method of draftsmanship should be adopted.

That the insertion of the extra word "knowingly" does not in fact contribute any new element of liability when it is used in conjunction with "permitting" was accepted by the Divisional Court in *Lomas* v. *Peek*.[1] The appellant in that case, a licensee, had been convicted under section 39 of the Licensing Act, 1910,[2] with suffering his premises to be used in contravention of the Betting Act, 1853,[3] section 3 of which provides that any occupier of premises who shall knowingly and wilfully permit the same to be used for the purpose of betting shall commit an offence. Inasmuch as the words "knowingly and wilfully" were omitted from the particulars of the offence which charged him with simply permitting gambling, the appellant contended that the information did not disclose an offence known to law. The court refused to countenance any such argument, Lord Goddard, C.J., saying: "In my opinion, those words 'knowingly and wilfully' can properly be described as technical terms. If a man permits a thing to be done, it means that he gives permission for it to be done, and if a man gives permission for a thing to be done, he knows what is to be done or is being done and, if he knows that, it follows that it is wilful . . . the fact that the words 'knowingly and wilfully' are not inserted, to my mind, makes no difference."[4]

[1] [1947] 2 All E.R. 574.

[2] 10 Edw. 7 & 1 Geo. 5, c. 24. Now re-enacted in the Licensing Act, 1953 (1 & 2 Eliz. 2, c. 46) s. 141 (2).

[3] 16 & 17 Vict. c. 119.

[4] *Ibid.*, p. 575. Cf. *Waring* v. *Wheatley* [1951] W.N. 569 in which the Divisional Court allowed an appeal against conviction on the ground that the omission of the word "wilful" from an information laid under s. 21 of the Town Police Clauses Act, 1847, was bad.

V

SUFFERING

Survey of statutory offences based on the word "suffers"

Of all the various expressions used in the early statutes when creating new offences, the legislature appears to have been best acquainted with the word "suffers", to which attention is next directed. Its debut occurred in the Punishment for Unlawful Distress Act, 1267,[1] which is of added interest insomuch as the term is used in a negative form, the statute making it a crime "if any [person], of what estate soever he be, will not suffer summons, attachments, or executions of judgments given in the King's Courts to be done according to the law and custom of the realm". Shortly afterwards, in 1275, the Maintainers of Quarrels Act[2] was passed making it a grievous offence for any sheriff "to suffer barretors or maintainers of quarrels in their shires", whilst other undesirable characters, to wit forestallers, were also the subject of a special statute[3] which forbade any person from suffering such "oppressors of the poor", such "deceivers of the rich", to dwell in any town. Attention has already been drawn in the preceding chapter to the early practice of emphasising the necessity for guilty knowledge by resort to such combinations as "willingly permitting", "knowingly permitting" and "wilfully permitting". The same tendency is evident in relation to the analogous term "suffers", the first instance occurring in the Money and Silver Act, 1343.[4] That statute made provision for the appointment of searchers—presumably the forerunners of H.M.'s Customs and Excise officers—to be assigned to sea ports to prevent money of good sterling leaving England, and, to encourage devotion to duty, the statute added that if any searcher "shall wittingly suffer silver or money to be transported out of the realm, he shall have judgment of life and member". The same phraseology is to be found in the Exportation of Gold and Silver Act, 1381,[5] but, for

[1] St. Hen. 3, c. 3, s. 2.
[2] St. Edw. 1, c. 23.
[3] St. Hen. 3, Edw. 1 & 2, c. 10 (date is uncertain).
[4] St. 17 Edw. 3.
[5] 5 Ric. 2, c. 1, s. 10.

no apparent reason, in the Exportation of Sheep Act, 1425, it was made an offence to simply suffer any fleeced or shorn sheep to be shipped into Flanders without the King's licence. Thereafter, when special attention was intended to be drawn to the element of *mens rea*, the expression "willingly suffers" as opposed to "wittingly suffers", was used, as in the Increase of Horses Act, 1535,[2] and the Exportation of Bell Metal Act, 1548,[3] but it is doubtful whether any change of meaning was thereby achieved. A considerable period was to elapse before the modern equivalent "knowingly suffers" was introduced, but its appearance is certainly traceable back to the beginning of the nineteenth century, where it is found in the Licensing Act, 1828.[4] Subsequent legislation shows the terms "suffers" and "knowingly suffers" constantly being used in enactments dealing with licensing offences,[5] but that such legislation has no exclusive claim to these expressions is manifested, among other statutes, by the Metropolitan Police Act, 1839,[6] the Customs Consolidation Act, 1876,[7] the Criminal Law Amendment Act, 1885,[8] and the Water Act, 1945.[9]

Whether or not the addition of expletives like "wilfully" and "knowingly" serves a special purpose has already been considered in relation to the verb "permits", and it is unnecessary to re-open the question, there being no evidence that, in this respect, any difference exists between the two expressions "permits" and "suffers". Reference has also been made to the gradual change from the form of drafting, initiated in the Alehouses Act, 1604,[10] whereby "permits or suffers" was made an alternative basis of criminal liability in a single offence, to the modern practice of

[1] 3 Hen. 6, c. 2, s. 2.
[2] 27 Hen. 8, c. 6, s. 4.
[3] 2 & 3 Edw. 6, c. 37, s. 5 (2).
[4] 9 Geo. 4, c. 61, s. 13 and Sch. c.
[5] See Licensing Act, 1872 (35 & 36 Vict. c. 94), ss. 16 (1), and 17 (1), and the Licensing (Consolidation) Act, 1910 (10 Edw. 7, & 1 Geo. 5, c. 24), s. 69 (2), 79 (1).
[6] 2 & 3 Vict. c. 47, s. 44. An earlier example is to be found in the still operative Highways Act, 1835 (5 & 6 Will. 4, c. 50), s. 72—see *Croasdill* v. *Ratcliffe* (1862) 4 L.T. (N.S.) 834.
[7] 39 & 40 Vict. c. 36, s. 186.
[8] 48 & 49 Vict. c. 69, s. 6. Other instances occur in the Thames Conservancy Act, 1894, s. 92, which formed the subject of the charge in *High Wycombe* v. *Thames Conservators* (1898) 78 L.T. 463, and the Thames Navigation Act, 1866, s. 64—see *R.* v. *Staines* 60 L.T. 261.
[9] 8 & 9 Geo. 6, c. 42, Sch. 3, Part XIV, cl. 64 (1) and 71 (1). See, too, Partnership Act, 1890 (53 & 54 Vict. c. 39), s. 14 (1) which was interpreted in *Tower Cabinet Co.* v. *Ingram* [1949] 2 K.B. 397. In the Post Office Act, 1953 (1 & 2 Eliz. 2, c. 36), s. 58, there occurs the unusual combination "wilfully procures or suffers".
[10] 1 Jac. 1, c. 9, which is probably the first statute to create licensing offences.

eparating the two words and assigning each to particular conduct.[1] In doing so, it may be assumed that the legislature is motivated by a distinction in the meaning of these two familiar terms. What, then, if any, is the difference between the expressions "permits" and "suffers"? What are the respective elements embodied in these two all-important words?

Relationship between "suffering" and "permitting"

Stephen, J., was the first judge to advert to this question and in *Bond* v. *Evans*,[2] referring to their appearance in separate sections of the Licensing Act, 1872, he expressed the opinion that there was no distinction between the two terms. This opinion must, however, be related to the judgment of Stephen, J., as a whole, which makes it clear that what the learned judge had in mind was the necessity, in both cases, of proving either actual knowledge or connivance. The same explanation, it is submitted, applies to the statement by Mathew, J., in *Somerset* v. *Wade*[3] who said that "the word 'suffers' is not distinguishable from 'permits'". For a detailed analysis it is necessary to refer to the later case of *Rochford Rural Council* v. *P.L.A.*[4] which, though of little importance so far as the actual decision is concerned, provided Darling, J., with the opportunity of indicating what he considered to be the demarcation line dividing the respective terms. "Apart from decisions", said Darling, J.,[5] "one would have said that if, without committing a legal wrong, a person is in a position to stop a thing and does not stop it he 'suffers' it." Illustrating this thesis, the learned judge continued: "if a person is in a situation when he might, without committing any legal wrong, prevent a stream from flowing in a particular direction, and he does not prevent it, he 'suffers' it to flow in that direction; but he cannot be said to 'suffer' it if he is not in a position either physically to prevent it or if by law he ought not to prevent it." Relating this argument to the word "permitting" Darling, J., concluded:[6] "If a man knowingly permits a thing to happen he certainly suffers it to happen. A man who suffers a thing to happen does not necessarily permit it, as he may not have the physical power or the right to stop it: but if

[1] For example, in the Licensing Consolidation Act, 1910, s. 69 (2) and s. 79 (1) are based on "suffering", whilst "permitting" is the conduct aimed at preventing in ss. 75 (1), 76 and 77 (1).

[2] (1888) 21 Q.B.D. 249, at p. 257. [3] [1894] 1 Q.B. 574 at p. 576.

[4] [1914] 2 K.B. 916. [5] *Ibid.*, p. 922. [6] *Ibid.*, p. 924.

he has that power or right, and does not stop it, he suffers the thing to happen."

This analysis, it is respectfully suggested, is far from being entirely satisfactory. In the first place, Darling, J., in equating "suffering" with "knowingly permitting" rather than with "permitting" simpliciter, seems to deny the existence within the word "permits" of the element of knowledge. This is contrary to the vast majority of cases previously discussed, according to which guilty knowledge is clearly a constituent part of any statutory offence based on the words "permits" or "permitting". Secondly, Darling, J., basis his distinction between the respective words according to whether the defendant has the power or the right to stop the prohibited act or omission happening. According to the learned judge, a person suffers a thing to happen only if he is in a position to stop it and nevertheless remains passive. Darling, J., is surprisingly reticent in attempting a definition of "permitting", but other judges who have endeavoured to fill the gap are found to have used precisely the same test as that put forward by Darling, J., in respect of "suffering". Thus, in the Scottish case of *Clydebank Co-op. Society* v. *Binnie*[1] we find Lord Fleming declaring: "If a person knows that a forbidden thing is happening, and is able to prevent it, and does not, of course he 'permits' in law and in fact."

Similar language was used by Mackinnon, L.J., when delivering the Court of Appeal's judgment in the case of *Goodbarne* v. *Buck*.[2] That case, it may be recalled, turned on the construction of the penal section 35 of the Road Traffic Act, 1930,[3] which makes it an offence to permit[4] another person to use a motor-vehicle on the road without a current policy of insurance covering third-party risks. The action arose out of an accident in which a van recklessly driven by William Buck had killed the appellant's husband. Unable to recover the £2,000 damages awarded her in a claim against William Buck who was utterly impecunious, there being also no effective policy of insurance, the appellant

[1] (1927) Sc. J. 17. See, too, *R.* v. *Staines* 60 L.T. 261 in which Field, J. declared: "A man cannot be said to 'suffer' that which he has no right to prevent."

[2] [1940] 1 K.B. 771; [1940] 1 All E.R. 613, *coram*, Mackinnon and Clauson L.JJ., Charles, J. See *ante*, p. 104, n. 3.

[3] 20 & 21 Geo. 5, c. 43.

[4] Section 35 creates three separate offences, it being enacted that "it shall not be lawful for any person to *use* or *cause* or *permit* any other person to use a motor-vehicle on a road etc". The Court of Appeal in *Goodbarne* v. *Buck* considered the possible liability of the respondent for (1) permitting and (2) causing another to use the motor-vehicle without a proper insurance policy.

sought to make Henry Buck responsible for the payment of this sum under the principle laid down in *Monk* v. *Warbey*.[1] Considerable effort was made to establish that Henry Buck, who had lent his brother William £20 to buy the van, was really the owner of the van but, in the opinion of the Court of Appeal, the van was at all times the property of William Buck. Referring to the verb "permits" in section 35, Mackinnon, L.J., said:[2] "In order to make a person liable for permitting another person to use a motor-vehicle, it is obvious that he must be in a position to forbid the other person to use the motor-vehicle. As at present advised, I can see no ground on which anybody can be in a position to forbid another person to use a motor-vehicle except in a case where the person charged is the owner of the car." In the light of this reasoning, and having previously found that the van was not the property of Henry Buck, the Court of Appeal were bound to hold that the respondent was not liable for permitting the use of the van without a proper insurance policy.

For thirteen years this ruling of the Court of Appeal in *Goodbarne* v. *Buck* has been accepted and acted upon. In the recent case of *Lloyd* v. *Singleton*,[3] however, the Divisional Court[4] expressly repudiated the view that only the owner of a car can be convicted of "permitting" under section 35. Whilst in complete agreement with Mackinnon L.J.'s statement that permitting involves being in a position to forbid the other person using the motor-vehicle,[5] the Divisional Court refuted the view, which Lord Goddard, C.J., and Croom-Johnson, J. considered as having been uttered *per incuriam*, that only the owner of a car is capable of exercising the power of forbiddance. As an illustration, Lord Goddard instanced the case of a man who, owning a car, leaves it in the care of his chauffeur and, in the owner's absence, the chauffeur allows somebody else to drive it. In those circumstances, said Lord Goddard, the chauffeur, whether he is actually forbidden or not, is permitting the use of the car; "the master is not permitting

[1] [1935] 1 K.B. 75, which decided that where there has been a breach by the owner of a motor-car of the provisions of the Road Traffic Act, 1930, s. 35 (1), not only is the person committing a breach of that section liable in criminal courts to the penalty provided by that section, but he is also liable in damages civilly to a third person who has been injured as a result of his negligence.

[2] [1940] 1 K.B. at p. 774.

[3] [1953] 1 All E.R. 291.

[4] Consisting of Lord Goddard C.J., Croom-Johnson, J. (both of whom delivered separate judgments) and Pearson, J. (who merely concurred).

[5] Similar language was used in relation to "permitting a nuisance" in *Smeaton* v. *Ilford Corporation* [1954] 1 All E.R. at p. 927 *per* Upjohn, J.

the use of it because he does not know it is being used."[1] That may well be so where the employer has given no authority to the chauffeur as to the user of the car, but if such authority be delegated it is clear from such cases as *Redgate* v. *Haynes*,[2] *Bosley* v. *Davies*,[3] *Somerset* v. *Hart*[4] and *Allen* v. *Whitehead*,[5] as will be seen later, that the knowledge of the chauffeur may be imputed to the employer so as to involve the latter in liability for "permitting" under section 35. Another unsatisfactory feature of the Divisional Court's strictures on the passage relating to the owner's exclusive power of prohibition lies in the comment that Mackinnon, L.J.'s "observations were clearly *obiter*".[6] A careful study of that Lord Justice's judgment, which it must be remembered represented the unanimous opinion of the Court of Appeal, reveals quite the opposite. In fact, it will be found that the ruling as to the owner being the only person in a position to forbid user, so far as the offence of permitting was concerned, formed the plank upon which the decision in *Goodbarne* v. *Buck*[7] rested, and, as such, constitutes part of the *ratio decidendi* in that case. It may well be that Mackinnon, L.J., did not think of all the various permutations which could arise and, consequently, his pronouncement should be treated with reserve and, if necessary, distinguished. But to justify criticism on the ground that his views were only *obiter*, it is respectfully suggested, is wholly unwarrantable.

To return to Darling, J.'s analysis of the words "suffers" and "permits" in *Rochford R.D.C.* v. *P.L.A.*,[8] it will have been noticed that the definition put forward by Darling, J. exclusively in relation to "suffering" has, in subsequent cases, been used interchangeably to define the elements embodied in "permitting" wrongful conduct. Thus, whereas the court in *Lloyd* v. *Singleton*[9] were unable to accept the view that "permitting" came within the exclusive province of an owner, as was suggested in *Goodbarne* v. *Buck*, sight must not be lost of the fact that identity of views

[1] [1953] 1 All E.R., p. 293. Cf. too, the remarks of Lord Goddard C.J. in *Morris* v. Williams (1952) 50 Local Govt. Reports at p. 311, in *Shave* v. *Rosner* [1954] 2 W.L.R. 1057 at p. 1060, and Parker, J. in *James & Son, Ltd.* v. *Smee* [1954] 3 W.L.R. 631 at p. 639.

[2] (1876) 1 Q.B.D. 89.

[3] (1875) 1 Q.B.D. 84.

[4] (1884) 12 Q.B.D. 360.

[5] [1930] 1 K.B. 211.

[6] [1953] 1 All E.R. *per* Croom-Johnson, J. at p. 293, and, likewise, Lord Goddard at p. 292, who said "It was only a dictum, and obviously he went further than he need have done. . . ."

[7] [1940] 1 K.B. 771.

[8] [1914] 2 K.B. 916.

[9] [1953] 1 All E.R. 291.

were expressed on the necessity for establishing in the defendant power to forbid the other person from doing the forbidden act. The real answer, foreshadowed by Stephen, J., in *Bond* v. *Evans*[1] and by Mathew, J. in *Somerset* v. *Wade*,[2] it is suggested, is that the same conditions of liability pertain whether the offence is founded on suffering or on permitting.[3]

Necessity for *Mens Rea*

Looking back at the authorities dealing with the interpretation of "maliciously", "wilfully" and "permitting" in statutory offences, the position may be summed up by saying that the same story has unfolded itself of divergence of judicial views as to the application of the basic maxim of criminal liability. It is, therefore, almost astonishing to find in cases where the courts have had to construe statutory crimes based on the word "suffering" that, with the sole exception of Manisty, J., in *Bond* v. *Evans*,[4] whose judgment is capable of a two-fold explanation, the judges are agreed upon the necessity for proving *mens rea* in the form of guilty knowledge. Indeed, most of the discussion in the various cases has centred around the degrees of knowledge which will suffice to establish guilt, since it is rarely possible to bring home to the accused actual knowledge of the wrongful conduct. The important question whether, to establish the requisite *mens rea*, the minimum degree of knowledge to be established is connivance or mere negligence will be dealt with later,[5] but for the moment it may justifiably be asserted that when the court has directed its mind to this subsidiary problem it accepts, impliedly but in the clearest possible fashion, the need for a guilty mind.

This assertion is well illustrated by the case of *Bosley* v. *Davies*.[6] Although, as we have seen, the word "suffers" has a continuous association with statutory offences stretching back to the thirteenth century, it is a surprising fact that this case in 1875 was the first occasion in which the courts were required to advert to the actual meaning of the term. The manageress of a hotel was charged in that case under section 17 of the Licensing Act, 1872,[7] with

[1] (1888) 21 Q.B.D. 249.

[2] [1894] 1 Q.B. 574.

[3] See, too, Lord Goddard C.J., in *Ferguson* v. *Weaving* [1951] 1 All E.R. 412, at p. 414.

[4] (1888) 21 Q.B.D. 249.

[5] This question is discussed in Chapter IX.

[6] (1875) 1 Q.B.D. 84.

[7] It is worth noting that in section 13 of the Licensing Act, 1828 (which was repealed by section 17 of the Licensing Act, 1872) the words used were "knowingly suffering

"suffering" gaming to be carried on in licensed premises. The defendant's story was that she was unaware that anybody was playing cards which had not been supplied by herself. This statement was confirmed by the card-players who were found gaming in a private room of the hotel, and the justices accordingly acquitted the licensee. On appeal to the Divisional Court it was stated by Cockburn, C.J., delivering the only judgment, that "actual knowledge in the sense of seeing or hearing by the party charged is not necessary, but there must be some circumstance from which it may be inferred that he or his servants had connived at what was going on. Constructive knowledge will supply the place of actual knowledge".[1] The case was sent back to the magistrates with directions to reconsider the facts in the light of the above principle, which obviously emphasises the requirement of *mens rea* in that particular offence. In the following year, we find a differently constituted court in *Redgate* v. *Haynes*[2] unhesitatingly rejecting a construction which would have made the offence of suffering gaming a crime of absolute liability, Blackburn, J. saying:[3] "Gaming did, in fact, take place in the appellant's house, and the question is, whether she can be said to have 'suffered' it? I agree that the mere fact that gaming was carried on on her premises would not render her liable to be convicted, because that is not 'suffering' the gaming to be carried on . . ." The Court then proceeded to consider the degree of knowledge which had to be proved and, in this, followed *Bosley* v. *Davies*. In a manner to which he was accustomed, Lord Coleridge, C.J., put the same point of view very simply, but none the less effectively, in *Somerset* v. *Hart* when he asked the rhetorical question:[4] "How can a man suffer a thing to be done when he does not know of it?" The present Lord Chief Justice was to make forcible use of this opinion in the recent case of *Ferguson* v. *Weaving*,[5] discussed hereafter.

A decision which excited serious reflections in the mind of Sir Frederick Pollock, writing in one of the earliest numbers of the

gaming". A case turning on the earlier section is *Avards* v. *Dance* (1862) 26 J.P. 437, in which the conviction was quashed on the grounds that there was insufficient evidence to support the charge. The present enactment dealing with "suffering gaming" is the Licensing Act, 1953, s. 141 (1).

[1] (1875) 1 Q.B.D., p. 88.

[2] (1876) 1 Q.B.D. 89. See, too, *Crabtree* v. *Hole* (1879) 43 J.P. 799.

[3] (1876) 1 Q.B.D., p. 94.

[4] (1884) 12 Q.B.D. 360, at p. 362.

[5] [1951] 1 All E.R. 412, at p. 414.

Law Quarterly Review,[1] was *R.* v. *Webster*,[2] in which the appellant had been convicted under the Criminal Law Amendment Act, 1885,[3] s. 6, with, being the occupier of certain premises, knowingly suffering a girl under 16 years of age to be upon such premises for the purpose of being unlawfully and carnally known. A strong court, consisting of Lord Coleridge, C.J., Denman, Field, Hawkins and Wills, JJ. had upheld the conviction on facts which showed that the girl was the daughter of the appellant, the premises in question being the daughter's home. Sir Frederick Pollock considered it an open question whether on such facts the Act was violated for, as he wrote, "when a daughter comes back at night to her mother's home it is rather hard to assert that she is 'suffered to be upon the premises' for an immoral purpose." It may, on the other hand, be argued that since the facts showed a patent case of guilty knowledge in the appellant who was in a position to prevent the forbidden act, the court had no option but to uphold the conviction. Sir Frederick's comment that "moral indignation is apt to be the parent of bad law" can hardly in this case be justified, and in applying the law as laid down in the 1885 Act, the judges in *R.* v. *Webster* provided the perfect illustration for the principle advocated fifty years later in *Newell* v. *Cross & Cook*.[4] In that case it will be remembered du Parcq, J. declared:[5] ". . . if it ever does happen that Parliament, owing to the difficulty of drafting a law of general application, has spread the net too wide and has done something which on more mature deliberation it would say that it did not intend to do, then the best way of pointing out any such defect in an Act is that it should be rigidly enforced by the courts. The worst way of dealing with legislation of that kind is that any authority or any Judge should give sanction to the view that laws which the public do not like ought to be disregarded or improperly evaded." It is, of course, trite to point out that all the good intentions of the courts may so easily be nullified by apathy on the part of Parliament. However,

[1] (1886) 2 *L.Q.R.* pp. 287–288. Commenting on the statute in question, the learned editor considered that "from a legal point of view", it was open to very serious comment. "A statute" Sir Frederick writes "which itself invades (though possibly for sufficient cause) several sound legal principles may become a very serious matter if under the influence of sentiment the courts so construe its terms as to give the Act an extension not contemplated by Parliament".

[2] (1885) 16 Q.B.D. 134. An Australian case dealing with a similar offence is *R.* v. *Turnbull* (1943) 44 S.R. (N.S.W.) 108—see *ante* p. 121, n. 3.

[3] 48 & 49 Vict. c. 69. [4] (1936) 53 T.L.R. 489. [5] *Ibid.*, p. 493.

there are some grounds for supposing that the seed sown by Sir Frederick Pollock did not fall on barren ground, as is evidenced by the later decision in *R.* v. *Merthyr Tydfil Justices*[1] which involved the same offence as in *R.* v. *Webster*. What the mother did in the later case was not to prostitute her daughter but to lay a trap for the man who had seduced her daughter, thus enabling her to give conclusive evidence on a charge against the scoundrel. Refusing the application for a writ of mandamus to the justices to issue a summons against the mother under section 6 of the 1885 Act, Cave and Wright, JJ. considered that no offence had been committed by the girl's mother. Technically, as the court realised, the facts could be said to fulfil the elements of knowingly suffering unlawful carnal knowledge, but Cave, J. was certain that no jury could be found anywhere to convict the woman.

Affinity between "suffering" and aiding and abetting

Leaving the ethical problem created by the decision in *R.* v. *Webster*, and pausing only to draw attention to *Lee* v. *Taylor & Gill*[2] in which the court was principally concerned with the degrees of knowledge deemed sufficient to establish a case of suffering, we next find the Divisional Court in two recent cases pointing out the close analogy which exists between offences based on "suffering" a person to do an act and liability for aiding and abetting another to commit an offence. Consideration of the two cases, *Thomas* v. *Lindop*[3] and *Ferguson* v. *Weaving*,[4] is made easier by the fact that in both the defendant was charged with aiding and abetting the consumption of intoxicating liquor in licensed premises outside permitted hours, which is an offence under the Licensing Act, 1921,[5] s. 4. In *Thomas* v. *Lindop*, the justices had found that the licensee did not know that anyone was consuming drink on the premises and therefore, said the Divisional Court, on the principle that "a person who does not know of the acts which another person is doing cannot be charged with aiding and abetting him"[6] it could not be said that the defendant in this case aided and abetted the customers to consume the liquor. After referring to *Bosley* v. *Davies*[7] in which it will be

[1] (1894) 10 T.L.R. 375. [2] (1912) 77 J.P. 11. [3] [1950] 1 All E.R. 966.
[4] [1951] 1 All E.R. 412. See a note by the writer in (1951) 14 *M.L.R.* 334.
[5] 11 & 12 Geo. 5, c. 42. Now re-enacted in the Licensing Act, 1953, s. 100 (1) (*b*).
[6] *Ibid.*, p. 968. [7] (1875) 1 Q.B.D. 84.

recalled the court had held that actual knowledge or connivance was necessary to sustain a charge of "suffering gaming" under the Licensing Act, 1872, s. 17, Lord Goddard declared:[1] "It seems to me that considerations applying to a section which deals with the suffering of some act to be done apply with equal force to a charge of aiding and abetting a person to do an act, because that is suffering the person to do the act." The analogy is not entirely a happy one, for mere inactivity on the part of a passer-by who happens to see a crime actually being committed, though possibly describable as suffering the crime to be committed, is not such conduct as amounts to aiding and abetting.

Distinction between an absolute prohibition and a prohibition against "suffering" or "permitting"

This affinity between the two grounds of criminal liability was also drawn in the case of *Ferguson* v. *Weaving*,[2] in which the Lord Chief Justice, apparently oblivious to the earlier[3] decision in *Thomas* v. *Lindop* where not only the same offence was involved but the facts were identical, proceeded to deliver an even more convincing judgment in support of the principle that personal knowledge was necessary to sustain a charge of aiding and abetting.[4] In the course of his judgment Lord Goddard drew the clear distinction between offences of absolute prohibition and offences requiring proof of guilty knowledge.[5] As an example of the former, the learned Chief Justice cited the prohibition against selling liquor to a drunken person imposed by section 13 of the Licensing Act, 1872, in which "knowledge of the condition of the person served is not necessary to constitute the offence". As examples of the latter, Lord Goddard continued,[6] "there are many offences in which it is necessary to show either that the licensee

[1] *Loc. cit.* [2] [1951] 1 All E.R. 412.

[3] Decided only six months before *Ferguson* v. *Weaving*.

[4] See (1951) *14 M.L.R.* 334. Whereas, as will be seen later, the doctrine of vicarious liability operates in cases of permitting or suffering, the knowledge or connivance of a servant being attributed to his employer, the Divisional Court in *Ferguson* v. *Weaving* flatly refused to countenance any extension of the doctrine into the realm of aiding and abetting.

[5] See, too, *James & Son, Ltd.* v. *Smee* [1954] 3 W.L.R. 631, 638 *per* Parker, J. Failure to grasp this essential distinction, it is suggested with respect, leads Mr. J. W. C. Turner in the 16th edition of Kenny's *Outlines of Criminal Law*, pp. 38, 42, to include such offences as "permitting drunkenness", "knowingly permitting prostitutes to meet on licensed premises" and "suffering gaming" within the class of crimes for which liability is absolute.

[6] [1951] 1 All E.R. at p. 414.

suffered or permitted the offence to take place. . . . There is no material difference between permitting or suffering something and knowingly allowing it to take place, for, as was said in *Somerset* v. *Hart*,[1] 'How can a man suffer a thing to be done when he does not know of it?'" It will be observed that Lord Goddard treats the two words suffering and permitting as being synonymous and the same treatment is evident later when he explained:[2] "The difference between an absolute prohibition and a prohibition against permitting or suffering was pointed out by Collins, J., in *Somerset* v. *Wade*[3] where, under other words in the same section[4] as was under consideration in *Cundy* v. *Le Cocq*,[5] the licensee was prosecuted not for selling to a drunken person but for permitting drunkenness on licensed premises. As it was there proved that the licensee did not know that the person in question was drunk the court held he could not be convicted of permitting drunkenness, though they approved the decision in *Cundy* v. *Le Cocq* because the prohibition against selling to a drunken person was absolute." Although the Lord Chief Justice, in thus contrasting the two classes of prohibition uses an offence of permitting as his illustration, it is clear that an offence of suffering would have been equally appropriate.

Is "suffering gaming" an offence of absolute prohibition?

So far, the authorities have presented the picture of an united chorus but there is one apparently dissenting voice to which attention must now be directed. The voice is that of Manisty, J., in *Bond* v. *Evans*,[6] in which case the familiar offence of suffering gaming on licensed premises was again in issue. In each of the three cases already discussed, *Bosley* v. *Davies*,[7] *Redgate* v. *Haynes*[8] and *Somerset* v. *Hart*,[9] in which the defendant was charged with this same offence under section 17 of the Licensing Act, 1872, it will be recalled that the court held that *mens rea* was a necessary constituent of the crime. Delivering the first judgment in *Bond* v. *Evans*, Manisty, J. referred to the decision in *Cundy* v. *Le Cocq*[10] and, in particular, to the judgment of Stephen, J. in that case. Then he went on to say:[11] "In my opinion, the principle of that decision is applicable to the present case, for I think it was intended by

[1] (1884) 12 Q.B.D. at p. 362. [2] *Loc. cit.* [3] [1894] 1 Q.B. at p. 578.
[4] I.e., section 13 of the Licensing Act, 1872. [5] (1884) 13 Q.B.D. 207.
[6] (1888) 21 Q.B.D. 249. [7] (1875) 1 Q.B.D. 84. [8] (1876) 1 Q.B.D. 89.
[9] (1884) 12 Q.B.D. 360. [10] (1884) 13 Q.B.D. 207. [11] (1888) 21 Q.B.D., at p. 252.

section 17 *absolutely to prohibit gaming on licensed premises*,[1] and that the substantial effect is that the responsibility is thrown upon any person who keeps a licensed house to take proper precautions to prevent gaming on his premises." Such language does not admit of any equivocation and there is little doubt that Manisty, J. intended to exclude any question of *mens rea* from the particular offence before him. Developing his argument, Manisty, J. next analysed the use by the legislature in the adjoining sections of the same statute of the verbs "suffers", and "permits", and of the combinations "knowingly suffers" and "knowingly permits". It was worth noting, he pointed out, that whereas in section 14 the phrase "knowingly permits" appears and in section 16 "knowingly suffers" is used as the basis of the offence, in the particular section before the court, i.e. section 17, the legislature relied upon the word "suffers" alone. Of added significance, according to Manisty, J. was the fact that in the corresponding section 13 of the Licensing Act, 1828, which was replaced by section 17 of the 1872 Act, the phrase used was "knowingly suffering" gaming to take place on licensed premises. The inevitable consequence implicit in these divagations, according to the learned judge, was that knowledge or absence of knowledge played no part in determining liability.

Up to this point Manisty, J.'s judgment is a model of consistency, every argument being directed towards proving that the offence of suffering gaming was a crime of absolute liability. However, almost in the same breath he cites with approval the earlier decisions in *Bosley* v. *Davies*[2] and *Redgate* v. *Haynes*[3] in which Cockburn, C.J. and Blackburn, J. had declared that proof of either actual knowledge or constructive knowledge was necessary to make a licensee liable for suffering gaming on his premises. Without prejudging the discussion which is to follow on the degrees of guilty knowledge, it may be pointed out that in the opinion of both Cockburn, C.J., and Blackburn, J., constructive knowledge would be established if either the licensee or his servant, if left in charge of the premises, had connived at what was going on. In *Bond* v. *Evans*[4] there was no evidence of any knowledge or connivance on the part of the licensee, but there was evidence that the gaming had been carried on to the knowledge or with the connivance of the licensee's servant who was left in charge of the

[1] The writer's italics.
[2] (1875) 1 Q.B.D. 84.
[3] (1876) 1 Q.B.D. 89.
[4] (1888) 21 Q.B.D. 249.

premises. It was this latter fact which Manisty, J., undoubtedly had in mind when he declared, referring to *Bosley* v. *Davies* and *Redgate* v. *Haynes*: "It seems to me that those two cases, added to *Cundy* v. *Le Cocq*, constitute a series of authorities against the appellant's contention on which we ought to act."[1] Where, it is suggested, the learned judge erred is in his reference to *Cundy* v. *Le Cocq*,[2] a positive case of absolute prohibition, as supporting his decision that proof of connivance is sufficient to convict a licensee of suffering gaming. For, as will be seen later, connivance is only a lesser degree of knowledge than actual knowledge, and is accepted as adequate because of the difficulty of establishing actual knowledge. The important point to grasp is that connivance is still regarded as *mens rea*, and that the fundamental principle of criminal liability is not excluded where constructive knowledge is held to be a culpable substitute for actual knowledge. No clearer indication can be given of Manisty, J.'s mistake in treating the offence of suffering gaming as one of absolute prohibition, comparable with the offence in *Cundy* v. *Le Cocq* (supplying liquor to a person already drunk), than the opinion expressed by Stephen, J. in the same case of *Bond* v. *Evans*.[3] Referring to the earlier cases decided on "suffering gaming" Stephen J. declared:[4] "I think all the other cases shew that the prohibition is not quite absolute, but is subject to this limitation, that in order to justify a conviction someone must know of or connive at the gaming." Even Stephen J.'s description of the offence was not altogether felicitous, but it does lend strong support to the established view that *mens rea* is a necessary element in the offence of suffering gaming and in all statutory offences wherein the particular epithets "suffer" or "suffering" appear.

[1] *Ibid.*, at p. 253.

[2] (1884) 13 Q.B.D. 207.

[3] In the 16th edition of *Kenny*, p. 37, Mr. J. W. C. Turner treats this case as deciding that the offence of suffering gaming (he mistakenly describes it as permitting gaming) is one of absolute liability, citing Stephen, J. in support. A careful study of Stephen, J.'s judgment, however, reveals that the passage cited in *Kenny* does not correctly represent that judge's view which, it is submitted, is summarised in the passage quoted in the text above.

[4] (1888) 21 Q.B.D., p. 256.

VI

CAUSING

DIFFERENT CONTEXTS IN WHICH THE WORD "CAUSES" IS USED

INTERPRETATION of the words "causes" and "causing", to which attention must next be directed, is also fraught with difficulties, not the least of which is the element of confusion sometimes created by reference to theories of causation.[1] Examination of the statutory offences in which the term "causes" appears suggests that it is used in two different contexts. First, it is sometimes used as an alternative to such expressions as "induces", "counsels", "procures" or "encourages", which have long been associated with that degree of participation in crime described as an accessory before the fact. Secondly, it is occasionally to be found alongside the words "permits", "allows" or "suffers" or, less frequently, entirely on its own. In whichever context the epithet is used there appears to be one connecting link, and that involves the ever recurring question of *mens rea* in the form of guilty knowledge. Consideration of the words "causes" and "causing" may, therefore, be conveniently divided into two separate sections, in which an endeavour will be made to discover the attitude of the courts towards the requirement of a guilty mind.

"CAUSING" AS THE BASIS OF LIABILITY AS AN ACCESSORY

Many examples will be found scattered throughout the statute-book in which such phrases as "causes or encourages" and "causes or procures" are inserted by the legislature as the basis of criminal liability. One of the earliest instances occurs in the Licences for Retailing Beer Act, 1755,[2] under which it was made a capital felony "to cause or procure any vellum . . . to be marked with a counterfeit mark or stamp with intent thereby to defraud His Majesty". The same formula appears in the Prevention of Cruelty to Animals Acts, 1849[3] and 1911,[4] the Children and Young Persons Act, 1933,[5] the Betting and Lotteries Act,

[1] See *Benford* v. *Sims* [1898] 2 Q.B. 641, and cf. *Shave* v. *Rosner* [1954] 2 W.L.R. 1057, *per* Hilbery, J., at p. 1060, and *Lovelace* v. *D.P.P.* [1954] 3 All E.R. 481.

[2] 29 Geo. 2, c. 12, s. 21.

[3] 12 & 13 Vict. c. 92, s. 2.

[4] 1 & 2 Geo. 5, c. 27, s. 1.

[5] 23 Geo. 5, c. 12, ss. 4 (1), 6, 22 and 24.

1934[1] the Incitements to Disaffection Act, 1934,[2] and the Licensing Act, 1953.[3] In recent years, reference may be made to the Adoption Act, 1950,[4] which enacts that it shall not be lawful for any person, in connection with any arrangements made for the adoption of an infant who is a British subject, "... to cause or procure the care and possession of the infant to be transferred to a person who is not a British subject ... and who is resident abroad". Another recent statute, the Midwives Act, 1951,[5] is interesting for its unusual coupling of the epithets "knowingly or wilfully" with the phrase "causes or procures". The statute, which requires certified midwives, intending to practise, to notify their intention to the local supervising authority, makes it a criminal offence for any midwife to knowingly or wilfully make or cause or procure any other person to make a false statement in any such notice.

Guilty knowledge and aiding and abetting

In seeking to ascertain the mental requirement embedded in the word "causes", when used in the above context, it will be found that much assistance can be gleaned from a preliminary survey of the perhaps more familiar phrase "counsels or procures". Where the word "causes" is substituted for "counsels" it is not unreasonable to suppose that the meaning of the phrase remains unchanged. It is worth noting that Blackstone's definition[6] of an accessory before the fact, which was cited with approval by Lord Alverstone, C.J., in *Du Cros* v. *Lambourne*,[7] was "one who being absent at the time of the crime committed doth yet procure, counsel or command another to commit a crime". This apt phrase "counsels or procures" was subsequently incorporated in both the Summary Jurisdiction Act, 1848,[8] s. 5, and the Accessories and Abettors Act, 1861,[9] s. 8, which purport to lay down the circumstances governing liability as accessories before the fact. It is also incorporated in the recent Magistrates Courts Act,

[1] 24 & 25 Geo. 5, c. 58, s. 22.
[2] 24 & 25 Geo. 5, c. 56, s. 2.
[3] 1 & 2 Eliz. 2, c. 46, s. 126 (2).
[4] 14 Geo. 6, c. 26, s. 39 (1).
[5] 14 & 15 Geo. 6, c. 53, s. 15 (4).
[6] *Commentaries*, iv, 36.
[7] [1907] 1 K.B. 40, at p. 43.
[8] 11 & 12 Vict. c. 43.
[9] 24 & 25 Vict. c. 94. Whereas in the case of misdemeanours, section 8 provides for both those who aid and abet (i.e., principals in the second degree) and those who counsel or procure (i.e., accessories before the fact), in the case of felonies sections 1 and 2 are restricted to accessories before the fact only. No explanation can be found for this anomalous position.

1952,[1] s. 35 of which enacts that "any person who aids, abets, counsels or procures the commission by another person of a summary offence shall be guilty of the like offence". It is submitted that where the term "causes" is found in any particular statutory offence as a direct alternative to either "counsels" or "procures", the intention of the legislature is to prohibit such conduct as would amount, in the case of a felony, to being an accessory before the fact. If this conclusion is correct, the next question to consider is the extent to which guilty knowledge of the principal crime is an essential ingredient of liability. The various degrees of knowledge which will suffice in cases of aiding and abetting bear a close relationship to those deemed adequate in substantive offences of "knowingly", "permitting" and "suffering", but that is a subject on its own and will be treated fully later.[2] For our present purpose it is only necessary to note the principle, repeatedly enunciated[3] in recent years by the Divisional Court as, for example, in *Thomas* v. *Lindop*,[4] that "where anyone is charged with aiding and abetting a person to commit an offence it must, at least, be shewn that he knew what that person was doing. A person who does not know of the acts which another person is doing cannot be charged with aiding and abetting him because he does not know that he is doing acts which amount to an offence". It will be observed that in the passage quoted Lord Goddard, C.J., refers to aiders and abettors only. That the same principle is applicable to cases of "counselling or procuring" is, however, made clear in *Ferguson* v. *Weaving*,[5] in which it was pointed out that since *Re Smith*[6] was decided in 1858 all the words "aid, abet, counsel or procure" may be used together to charge a person who is alleged to have participated in an offence otherwise than as a principal in the first degree. Whatever other conditions distinguish aiders and abettors from accessories before the fact,[7] no suggestion was made in *Ferguson* v. *Weaving* that proof of guilty knowledge was not equally an essential element

[1] 15 & 16 Geo. 6 and 1 Eliz. 2, c. 55. [2] See Chapter IX.

[3] For example, see *Wessel* v. *Carter Paterson* [1947] K.B. 849; *Ackroyds Air Travel Ltd.* v. *D.P.P.* [1950] 1 All E.R. 933; *Johnson* v. *Youden* [1950] 1 K.B. 544; *Gardner* v. *Akeroyd* [1952] 2 All E.R. 306; *Sayce* v. *Coupe* [1952] 2 All E.R. 715; *Davies* v. *Brodie* [1954] 1 W.L.R. 1364.

[4] [1950] 1 All E.R. 966, at p. 968.

[5] [1951] 1 All E.R. 412. [6] (1858) 3 H. & N. 227.

[7] See note by the writer in 14 *M.L.R.* pp. 336–337, and also *Wessel* v. *Carter Paterson* [1947] 2 All E.R. 280, *per* Lord Goddard C.J. at p. 281.

in cases where the accused is charged with "counselling or procuring" an offence. By analogy it would appear to follow that in cases where the statute resorts to the phraseology "causes or procures", instead of the customary "counsels or procures", the prosecution must at least establish that the accused had knowledge of the essential matters which constitute the offence.

"*Cause or procure*"

So far as can be ascertained only one case is to be found in the reports in which this very problem arose for decision. In that case, *Benford* v. *Sims*,[1] a veterinary surgeon was charged under the Prevention of Cruelty to Animals Act, 1849,[2] s. 2, which made it an offence, *inter alia*, to cause or procure any animal to be cruelly beaten, ill-treated, abused or tortured. The respondent, after examining a mare belonging to a coal merchant, issued a certificate that the horse was free from pain and quite fit for work, and other evidence showed that the veterinary surgeon had indpendently advised its owner to work the mare. Some days later the horse was found being worked whilst "very lame, in great pain and suffering from long-standing disease of the feet". In dismissing the information, the magistrate held that although the respondent knowingly counselled the owner to cause the act of cruelty to be perpetrated he was not liable because his advice was the remote cause and not the proximate cause of the cruelty. The prosecution appealed against this decision but met with no greater success in the Divisional Court where Ridley, J., referring to section 2 of the 1849 Act, said:[3] "I think it is correct to say that the word 'cause' is used in a stricter sense than the words 'procure' or 'counsel' in section 5 of the Summary Jurisdiction Act, 1848, and that 'to cause' means 'to be the immediate cause' of the offence being committed." What the learned judge appears to have overlooked is the fact that the relevant section in the Act, then before the court, prohibits both causing or procuring an animal to be cruelly beaten. Unless, therefore, the interpretation of Ridley, J. is incorrect, the word "procure" in the Cruelty to Animals Act, 1849, would appear to have a different meaning from the word "procure" in the Summary Jurisdiction Act, 1848, which deals with aiders and abettors. To confuse matters still further, Ridley, J., went on to declare:[3] "It appears to me that the magistrate on his findings of fact might have convicted the respondent, he having

[1] [1898] 2 Q.B. 641. [2] 12 & 13 Vict. c. 92. [3] *Ibid.*, at p. 644.

. . . knowingly counselled *the owner to cause*[1] the act of cruelty." Where, it is submitted, both the magistrate and the Divisional Court were in error was in misconstruing the statutory offence to require proof that the act of cruelty was caused by the owner of the animal. Reference to the actual wording of section 2 of the Cruelty to Animals Act, 1849, indicates that two separate offences may be committed, viz., first, by the person who actually ill-treats the animal, secondly, by the person who causes or procures the animal to be ill-treated. In knowingly counselling the owner to work the mare when it was unfit the sensible deduction surely is that it was the respondent, the veterinary surgeon, who caused the animal to be cruelly ill-treated within the meaning of the statutory offence. It is further submitted that the use of the phrase "causes or procures" in section 2 of the 1849 Act,[2] and indeed in any other statute which adopts a similar terminology when defining a criminal offence, is synonymous with the phrase "counsels or procures" in the more general provisions to be found in the Summary Jurisdiction Act, 1848, s. 5, and in the Accessories and Abettors Act, 1861, s. 8. Before leaving the decision in *Benford* v. *Sims* it is perhaps worth drawing attention to the later Protection of Animals Act, 1911,[3] which, whilst exclusively restricting to owners of animals the offence of "permitting" acts of cruelty, makes no conditions as to the persons who might be held responsible for "causing or procuring" the same forbidden behaviour.

"Causing" as an alternative to "permitting", "suffering" or "allowing", or as the sole basis of liability.

Survey of statutory offences exemplifying this use of the word "causes"

The use of the words "cause" and "causing" in connection with statutory offences is of great antiquity. As early as 1267, in the Statute of Marlborough,[4] we find it enacted that "no one from

[1] The writer's italics.

[2] In *Elliott* v. *Osborne* (1891) 65 L.T. Rep. 378, the charge was one of actual ill-treating under the same section as in *Benford* v. *Sims*. In an interesting note in 184 *Law Times* 269, the suggestion is made that had the accused in *Elliott* v. *Osborne* been charged instead with "causing" ill-treatment the Divisional Court would have upheld the conviction.

[3] 1 & 2 Geo. 5, c. 27, s. 1, which consists of a number of separate offences all of which are drafted along the following typical lines: "if any person shall subject, cause or procure, or, being the owner, permit to be subjected, any animal to any operation which is performed without due care or humanity" (s. 1 (1)). See, too, s. 9.

[4] 52 Hen. 3, c. 4, s. 2.

henceforth shall cause any distress that he hath taken to be driven out of the country where it was taken, and if one neighbour do so to another of his own authority and without judgment, he shall make fine as for a thing done against the peace". Moving on to 1381 we see the legislature making it an offence[1] "to cause to be sent or carried beyond the sea any gold or silver", and in 1404 it was made a crime[2] "for any alien merchant or stranger to cause to be carried out of the realm any merchandise brought within the realm by the same merchants aliens". In the Burning of Frames Act, 1545,[3] a new development is noticeable, the expressions "maliciously, unlawfully, willingly and secretly" being inserted as prefixes to the offence of causing to be burned timber frames intended to be used for the making of houses. Although, as has already been shown, this practice was, and still is, frequently resorted to in the case of permitting and suffering it is rare to find any instances in which any epithet is attached to the word "causes". One or two examples can, however, be cited. Thus, in the Ready Money Football Betting Act, 1920,[4] the phrase "knowingly causes or procures" is used; in the Thames Conservancy Act, 1932,[5] liability is incurred by "wilfully causing or knowingly suffering" pollution of the River Thames; and in the Midwives Act, 1951,[6] there appears the double alternative "knowingly or wilfully causes or procures".[7] Innumerable illustrations could be given of the use of "causes" or "causing" untrammelled by any emphatic adverbs.[8] How very often one comes across the phrases "whosoever shall do or cause to be done", or "whosoever shall administer or cause to be administered", or again "any person who makes or causes to be made a false entry". Such liability is to be found in diverse statutes like the Unlawful Oaths Act, 1797,[9] the Malicious Damage Act, 1861,[10]

[1] 5 Rich. 2, c. 2, s. 5. [2] 6 Hen. 4, c. 4, s. 5.

[3] 37 Hen. 8, c. 6, s. 2. See, too, the Forgery Act, 1562 (5 Eliz. c. 14), s. 2 in which the expression "subtily cause" is used.

[4] 10 & 11 Geo. 5, c. 52, s. 1. [5] 22 & 23 Geo. 5, xxxvii, s. 123.

[6] 14 & 15 Geo. 6, c. 53, s. 15 (4). An instance where the phrase "negligently causes" is used appears in the Water Act, 1945, Sch. III, Part xiv, cl. 64 (1).

[7] Cf. the Post Office Act, 1953 (1 & 2 Eliz. 2, c. 36), s. 56 where the phrase "wilfully and maliciously causes . . ." is used.

[8] E.g. Highway Act, 1835 (5 & 6 Will. 4, c. 50), ss. 53, 72 and 78; Police Act, 1919 (9 & 10 Geo. 5, c. 46), s. 3; Sale of Food (Weights and Measures) Act, 1926 (16 & 17 Geo. 5, c. 63), s. 1.

[9] 37 Geo. 3, c. 123, s. 1.

[10] 24 & 25 Vict. c. 97, ss. 35, 36 and 50 are examples.

the Offences against the Person Act, 1861,[1] the Weights and Measures Act, 1878,[2] the Merchandise Marks Act, 1887,[3] and the Trade Marks Act, 1938.[4] Occasionally, as in the National Health Service Act, 1952,[5] the legislature uses the alternative formula "causes or knowingly allows", or, as in the Betting and Lotteries Act, 1934,[6] and the Rivers (Prevention of Pollution) Act, 1951,[7] "causes or knowingly permits". Yet another form is the phrase "causes or encourages" which is inserted, for example, in the Mental Deficiency Act, 1913,[8] and the Children and Young Persons Act, 1933.[9] These illustrations could be multiplied many times, but it is necessary now to turn to the cases in which the courts have been faced with the inevitable task of interpreting statutory offences in which the word "causes" is the hub around which the conditions of criminal liability revolve. As with the epithets already considered there exists a cleavage of opinion among the judges, and the same plan will be adopted of dividing the authorities into two groups.

LIABILITY BASED UPON PROOF OF *Mens Rea*

Notwithstanding the passage of seven hundred odd years during which the simple term "causes" has been appearing intermittently among the pages of the statute-book, it is not until the beginning of the nineteenth century that the courts apparently begin to be troubled with its exact meaning. Two of the earliest cases, *R.* v. *Glossop*[10] and *Parsons* v. *Chapman*,[11] shed little light on the matter. Both cases turned on the interpretation of the Plays Act, 1736,[12] s. 1 of which provided that any person who caused to be acted . . . any entertainment without a licence from the Lord Chamberlain was to be deemed a rogue and a vagabond and liable to a penalty of £50. In *R.* v. *Glossop* the defendant, who had engaged and paid an actor to perform in the production of Richard III, had been seen once or twice at rehearsals only. Nevertheless Abott, C.J., held that this evidence was sufficient to

[1] 24 & 25 Vict. c. 100, ss. 22, 26, 29, 31 and 58 are examples.
[2] 41 & 42 Vict. c. 49, ss. 27 and 58.
[3] 50 & 51 Vict. c. 28, s. 2 (1).
[4] 1 & 2 Geo. 6, c. 22, s. 56.
[5] 15 & 16 Geo. 6 & 1 Eliz. 2, c. 25, s. 6. See, too, the Workmen's Compensation (Supplementation) Act, 1951 (14 & 15 Geo. 6, c. 22), s. 4 (1).
[6] 24 & 25 Geo. 5, c. 58, s. 22.
[7] 14 & 15 Geo. 6, c. 64, s. 2 (1).
[8] 3 & 4 Geo. 5, c. 28, s. 56.
[9] 23 Geo. 5, c. 12, s. 2.
[10] (1821) 4 B. & Ald. 616.
[11] (1831) 5 C. & P. 33. Cf. *Monaghan* v. *Taylor* (1886) 2 T.L.R. 685.
[12] 10 Geo. 2, c. 28.

warrant the justices in drawing the conclusion that the defendant caused the play to be performed. The succeeding Chief Justice, Lord Tenterden, was likewise easily satisfied, being of the opinion in *Parsons* v. *Chapman* that evidence that the defendant was the acting manager of the theatre, in which capacity he paid the salary and dismissed one of the performers, was sufficient proof that he caused the illegal performance.[1]

A fuller discussion is reported in the case of *Harrison* v. *Leaper*,[2] in which Fitzjames Stephen, appearing in the unfamiliar role of counsel, argued in favour of a strict interpretation of section 70 of the Highways Act, 1835,[3] which imposes a penalty on any person who shall . . . erect or cause to be erected any steam engine within a distance of twenty-five yards from the highway. A thrashing machine had been lent on hire by its owner to a farmer, together with an employee who superintended the operation of the machine. On the directions of the farmer as to where the thrashing machine was to be placed, the driver erected it within the forbidden area. Fitzjames Stephen, in support of the conviction by the magistrates, contended that it was the duty of the appellant, the owner of the machine, to have given his servant orders not to place it in an improper position.[4] Such a principle did not meet with the approval of Cockburn, C.J., Crompton and Mellor, JJ., who quashed the conviction on the ground that the owner of the machine was not present at the time and place where the offence was committed, and there was nothing to show

[1] Cf. two recent decisions under the Theatres Act, 1843, s. 15, which is similar in terms to the earlier statute. In *Grade* v. *D.P.P.* [1942] 2 All E.R. 118, the appellant was away on national service and consequently not present at the theatre when the departure from the script was made. He had given instructions to his manager that the script was to be adhered to. Nevertheless, the Divisional Court held that the appellant was liable for causing the play to be presented. Humphreys, J., went further and said (p. 120) "I do not know of any section of any Act of Parliament, containing language in the least degree similar to the language of section 15 of this Act, when it has ever been held that proof of scienter is necessary". In *Lovelace* v. *D.P.P.* [1954] 3 All E.R. 481, the appellant, likewise, had taken every precaution to prevent what was done from being done, but the respondent argued that as the appellant caused the performance of the play he also caused the performance of that part of it which was unauthorised. Rejecting this argument Lord Goddard said there was "a long line of cases in which it had been held repeatedly that, although the prohibition of doing an act might be absolute so that *scienter* or *mens rea* was not necessary, different considerations applied where a person was charged with 'causing' or 'permitting', because one could not 'cause' or 'permit' unless one had knowledge of the facts".

[2] (1862) 5 L.T. 640.

[3] 5 & 6 Will, 4, c. 50.

[4] Citing in support *R.* v. *Fisher* 1 M. & M. 437; *R.* v. *Dixon* 3 M. & S. 11; and *Att. Gen.* v. *Siddon* 1 C. & T. 220.

that the engine was placed in that particular spot by the appellant's directions. Implicit in this decision is the necessity for establishing guilty knowledge in the accused. Certain observations by Cockburn, C.J., on the doctrine of vicarious liability strike a discordant note in the light of more modern cases, but this aspect of *Harrison* v. *Leaper* will be examined later.

Should guilty knowledge be equated with holding a position of responsibility?

Much stronger language is manifested in *Small* v. *Warr*,[1] in which Baron Huddleston described as "monstrous"[2] the decision of the justices who had convicted the manager of a colliery of unlawfully causing horses to be cruelly ill-treated[3] in spite of the fact that, according to their case stated, there was no proof of any notice or knowledge of the cruelty on the part of the appellant. Field, J., the other member of the court, in more conservative language declared:[4] ". . . the justices say that they thought [the appellant] had committed the offence because he was the certified manager, and because it was part of his duty to provide horses in a sound state. The question asked of us is, whether the mere fact of the appellant being the manager makes him liable to a penalty without any proof of knowledge. All I can say to that is that no criminal offence is committed, for the *mens rea* is an ingredient of the offence." Earlier in his judgment, the same learned judge criticised the assumption made by the justices that knowledge of the cruelty must be attributed to the manager by virtue of his failure to exercise daily control over the work in the mine.

Exactly seventy years later, in the recent case of *Rushton* v. *Martin*,[5] we find the present generation of judges rejecting, as emphatically as their Victorian predecessors, the prosecution's attempt to equate guilty knowledge with the mere holding of a position of managerial responsibility. In that case the defendant was charged with causing to be used on a road a motor-vehicle and trailer likely to endanger other users of the highway.[6] As general manager of Group 60 of the Road Haulage Executive, the

[1] (1882) 47 J.P. 20. See a comment on this case in 184 *L.T.* 268. In *Greenwood* v. *Backhouse* (1902) 66 J.P. 519, which involved the same offence, the Divisional Court (Lord Alverstone C.J., Darling and Channell JJ.,) held that a "suspicious amount of ignorance" was not sufficient evidence of guilty knowledge.

[2] *Loc. cit.*

[3] Under the Prevention of Cruelty to Animals Act, 1849 (12 & 13 Vict. c. 92), s. 2.

[4] *Loc. cit.* [5] [1952] W.N. 258.

[6] The information was laid under the Road Traffic Act, 1930, and the Motor-Vehicles (Construction and Use) Regulations, 1947, s. 67.

defendant was responsible for the operation of 160 vehicles which, distributed among five depots within the group, were driven and maintained by a large body of drivers, mechanics and fitters. Allowing the appeal against conviction, Oliver, J., with whose judgment Lord Goddard, C.J., and Byrne, J., agreed, declared:[1] "The justices had found that the defendant had not been personally aware of the condition of the vehicle and it was, therefore, difficult to understand how they could convict him of causing the vehicle to be on a road in an improper state. There was no vicarious responsibility;[2] the defendant had not been negligent and could not possibly have known that there was anything wrong with the vehicle." Although the case is only reported in the Weekly Notes where the judgments are reduced to a truncated synopsis, it is fairly obvious that the Divisional Court, in reaching its decision, was fully conscious of the absurd situation which would arise if a different construction had been placed upon the relevant offence.

Yet another decision, in the same tradition, laying stress on the necessity for establishing actual knowledge in the defendant of the prohibited state of affairs is that of *Hardcastle* v. *Bielby*.[3] Under the Highways Act, 1835,[4] s. 56, it is an offence for any surveyor "to cause to be laid any heap of stone upon any highway and to allow the same to remain there at night to the danger . . . of any person passing thereon". It will be noticed that "causing" and "allowing" are conjunctive not disjunctive elements in the offence, so that it is surprising to find Collins, J., treating the pertinent section as containing two separate offences. According to the learned judge the first offence, based on "causing" requires proof that the laying of the stones was occasioned by the authority of the surveyor; "the laying of the stones" he said "must be proved to have been

[1] *Loc. cit.*

[2] No reasons were given for this ruling, which may be questioned. Presumably the Divisional Court had in mind the fact that the defendant was only the general manager and himself a servant of the Road Haulage Executive. This raises the important question whether the doctrine of vicarious liability extends, or should extend, below the actual employer who might be an individual or a corporation. Certainly, in *Barker* v. *Levinson* [1951] 1 K.B. 342 (discussed *post* pp. 224–226 *et seq*) no strictures were placed on the liability of a manager of a block of flats for the illegal act of a rent collector whose duties he, the manager, controlled. The decision in that case turned on the acts of the rent collector being outside the scope of his authority, the question whether the manager could, in any circumstances, be held vicariously liable for the acts of lesser servants not being argued or discussed by the court.

[3] [1892] 1 Q.B. 709.

[4] 5 & 6 Will. 4, c. 50.

n some sort the act of the surveyor".[1] The facts showed that the tones had been laid there by a carter, who acted under the orders of a person to whom the surveyor had given general directions as o repairing the road. There was no evidence that the surveyor iimself knew that the stone had been laid on the road and, iccordingly, the offence was not proved. The same absence of :nowledge was relied upon by both Collins and Hawkins, JJ., n negativing the charge that the surveyor "allowed" the dangerous heap to remain on the highway at night. Giving vent to the ame explosive sentiments as those expressed by Baron Huddleston n *Small* v. *Warr*,[2] Collins, J. said:[1] ". . . it would be monstrous o hold that a man may be fined under the statute because an iccident has happened, which it was impossible for him to prevent or the simple reason that it was impossible for him to find out hat the circumstances which led to the accident had occurred. . . Any one would shrink from construing a statute in such a way is to make such a conviction possible." These remarks, of course, ire in fact directed to what Collins, J., erroneously believed to be he separate offence of "allowing" the danger to continue at iight, which, as a careful study of the wording of section 56 shows, only forms part of the offence of "causing and allowing".

Passive acquiescence or express authorisation?

Exceptional as this combination of terms is in the definition of a tatutory offence, it is equalled in unusualness by the presumption :reated in the Children Act, 1908,[3] s. 17 (2) of which provides hat "a person shall be deemed to have caused or encouraged the inlawful carnal knowledge of a girl under 16 years", which is an offence under section 17 (1) of the same Act, if "he has knowingly illowed the girl to consort with any prostitute or person of known mmoral character". Here, in the clearest possible terms, is an icknowledgment by the legislature that guilty knowledge is the ninimum requirement of such an offence based on "causing". Another fact worth noticing in this statutory presumption is that, vhereas in the earlier cases like *Harrison* v. *Leaper*[4] and *Small* v. *Warr*[5] the judges were apparently impressed by the positive import of the word "causing", and were not prepared to accept the view

[1] *Ibid.*, p. 712. [2] (1882) 47 J.P. 20.

[3] 8 Edw. 7, c. 67, as amended by the Children (Amdt.) Act, 1910, s. 1. These provisions are re-enacted in the Children and Young Persons Act, 1933 (23 Geo. 5, :. 12), s. 2.

[4] (1862) 5 L.T. 640. [5] (1882) 47 J.P. 20.

that a man may cause a thing to happen if he is in a position tc prevent its occurrence and takes no steps to obviate it, the legisla· ture in the above enactment is seen leading the way along a patl which the courts had previously shunned. Interpreting the offence it would seem with some reluctance, in accordance with the de clared intention of Parliament, the Court of Criminal Appeal ir *R.* v. *Chainey*[1] ruled that "If it was proved that a father, knowin; that his daughter was consorting with persons of known immora character, stood by and allowed such intimacies to continue wher it was in his power to prevent them, that *might furnish evidence*[2] o causing or encouraging her unlawful carnal knowledge".[3] Th interesting question next arises, was the lead given by the legis· lature, in adopting a wide interpretation of the word "causing" followed by the courts when construing other offences in whicl the same expression formed the key to criminal liability? In brief the answer is "No". Judicial opinion, whilst readily acquiescin; in the doctrine that a person could be said to "suffer" or "permit' a thing to happen if, being in a position to stop it, he does nothin; about it, refused to extend the same principle to statutory crime: involving "causing". Thus, in *Goldsmith* v. *Deakin*,[4] which ha: already been considered,[5] Avory, J. was prepared to concede that on the facts of that case, the garage proprietor "in hiring out hi: bus in circumstances in which he ought to know that it woul probably be used as a stage carriage [without a proper licence was 'permitting' his bus to be used in contravention of th statute;[6] nevertheless, he added[7] "it may well be that it coul not be said that the respondent 'caused' the vehicle to be so used" In distinguishing between the two offences it is suggested tha Avory, J., was guided by the same fundamental consideratio which guided the judges in the earlier cases, namely, that ir "causing" a thing to happen a person must be shown to hav expressly authorised the forbidden act, and that it is not enough tc prove merely that the accused failed to carry out his duty o exercising proper control.

The same need for proving positive conduct and not passiv acquiescence in order to substantiate a charge of "causing" wa:

[1] [1914] 1 K.B. 137.

[2] The writer's italics. According to the wording of the statute the presumption woul appear to be conclusive.

[3] *Per* Isaacs, C.J. at p. 142.

[4] (1934) 150 L.T. Rep. 157.

[5] *Ante* p. 106.

[6] Road Traffic Act, 1930, s. 72 (10).

[7] *Ibid.*, p. 158.

emphasised in the House of Lords case of *Houston* v. *Buchanan*[1] which was a civil action arising out of the familiar section 35 (1) of the Road Traffic Act, 1930.[2] That section, it may be recalled, forbids the causing or permitting any motor-vehicle to be used on the road without there being in force a proper policy of third-party insurance. "To cause the user" said Lord Wright, "involves some express or positive mandate from the person 'causing' to the other person or some authority from the former to the latter, arising in the circumstances of the case."[3] It is in this important respect that "causing" is to be distinguished from the word "permitting" which, according to Lord Wright is "a looser and vaguer term" and "may denote an express permission, general or particular, as distinguished from a mandate".[3] Although none of the earlier cases like *Harrison* v. *Leaper*,[4] *Small* v. *Warr*,[5] *Hardcastle* v. *Bielby*,[6] and *Goldsmith* v. *Deakin*[7] were apparently cited to the House of Lords, it will be observed that Lord Wright's interpretation follows closely the meaning attributed to the word "causing" in those cases by Cockburn, C.J., Crompton, Mellor, Field, Collins, JJ., and Huddleston, B., and, more recently, by Lord Goddard, C.J., Oliver and Byrne, JJ., in *Rushton* v. *Martin*.[8]

To adopt Lord Wright's phrase, "a positive mandate" is necessary which, it is submitted, presupposes knowledge on the part of the person charged with "causing" of the facts which constitute the particular offence. This necessity for proving *mens rea* was again approved in the recent case of *Reynolds* v. *G. H. Austin & Sons Ltd.*[9] which, it will be remembered, was concerned with the offence of using or causing or permitting a motor-vehicle

[1] [1940] 2 All E.R. 179 (*sub. nom. M'Leod* (*or Houston*) v. *Buchanan*).

[2] Another case turning on the same offence is *Goodbarne* v. *Buck* [1940] 1 K.B. 771.

[3] *Ibid.*, p. 187. This distinction between "causing" and "permitting" was approved in *Shave* v. *Rosner* [1954] 2 W.L.R. 1057. In that case the Divisional Court was concerned with the Motor Vehicles (Construction and Use) Regs. 1951, reg. 101 of which provides that any person who "uses or causes or permits to be used on any road a motor-vehicle in such a condition as to cause danger to any person" commits an offence. Hilbery, J. (at p. 1060) expressly followed the words used by Lord Wright (*supra*) and referred also to *Watkins* v. *O'Shaughnessy* [1939] 1 All E.R. 385, 387. Lord Goddard C.J. declared (at p. 1059): "When those two expressions 'causes or permits' are found in contrast or juxtaposition 'permits' means giving leave and licence to somebody to use the car, and 'causes' involves a person who has authority to do so ordering or directing someone to use it." Illustrating this distinction the Lord Chief Justice said: "If I allow a friend to use my motor-car, I am permitting him to use it. If I tell my chauffeur to bring the car round and drive me to the courts, I am causing the car to be used." See, too, *Lovelace* v. *D.P.P.* [1954] 3 All E.R. 481.

[4] (1862) 5 L.T. 640.

[5] (1882) 47 J.P. 20.

[6] [1892] 1 Q.B. 709.

[7] (1934) 150 L.T. Rep. 157.

[8] [1952] W.N. 258.

[9] [1951] 2 K.B. 135.

to be used as an express carriage without the requisite road service licence.[1] Humphreys, J., after citing *Evans* v. *Dell*[2] as authority for the proposition that in the case of permitting at least lack of knowledge may be a complete defence, added that the wording of section 72 (10) of the Road Traffic Act, 1930, did not suggest that the legislature intended that different considerations should apply to "using" and "causing" as opposed to "permitting". In other words, the learned judge was of the opinion that absence of knowledge was a good defence to a charge of "causing" a vehicle to be so used in contravention of the statute. The same view was taken by Devlin, J., in a notable judgment presaging, it is to be hoped, many future contributions to the field of criminal jurisprudence. "*Mens rea*" he declared, "is admittedly necessary for the offence of permitting the use. I think that it would also be necessary for the offence of causing the use."[3] Any doubts which may have existed in the judge's mind appear to have been quickly dispelled, for later on in his judgment Devlin, J., categorically stated that guilty knowledge is as essential for the offence of "causing" as it is for that of "permitting". This opinion, related, it is true, to an offence in which the word "causing" is used as a direct alternative to "permitting", is in line with the other authorities discussed wherein the courts have consistently accepted the application of *mens rea* when "causing" appears isolated from any other epithet.

LIABILITY WHEREIN THE ACCUSED'S STATE OF MIND IS IRRELEVANT

In the face of this formidable body of authorities we proceed next to consider what support exists for the contrary view, viz., that the appearance of the word "causes" in a statutory offence does not in itself denote the presence of a guilty mind, and that it is open to the court to construe such offences as being absolutely prohibited.

Detailed attention has already been given to the case of *Korten* v. *West Sussex C.C.*,[4] in which a majority of the Divisional Court held that the offence of unlawfully causing or permitting a false invoice, under the Fertilisers & Feeding Stuffs Act, 1893, s. 3 (1) (*b*), was one of absolute liability. So far as the problem of *mens rea* was concerned neither Lord Alverstone, C.J., nor Wills, J., who con-

[1] Road Traffic Act, 1930, s. 72 (10). [2] [1937] 1 All E.R. 349.

[3] [1951] 2 K.B. at p. 151. This assimilation of the two epithets was also adopted in *Lovelace* v. *D.P.P.* [1954] 3 All E.R. 481.

[4] (1903) 72 L.J.K.B. 514.

stituted the majority of the court on this question, drew any distinction between the two limbs of the section, the Chief Justice saying:[1] "I think that clause 3 (1) (*b*) was meant to be a wide clause embracing all the persons who in the course of business either cause or permit to be sent out an invoice which is in fact false". Earlier in his judgment Lord Alverstone had shown signs of grasping the true meaning of the word "causing", for, after saying that it was not the word "cause" which created any difficulty on the question of *mens rea*, he added:[1] "that word would prima facie refer only to a person taking a part in the act." This definition approximates closely to the test suggested in *Hardcastle* v. *Bielby*[2] in which, it will be recalled, Collins, J., said of the offence of causing any heap of stone to be laid upon the highway: "the laying of the stones must be proved to have been in some sort the act of the surveyor." This early glimpse of light was unfortunately overshadowed and almost obliterated by what, it has been suggested earlier in this study,[3] constituted some muddled thinking, in which the learned Chief Justice gives the impression of being in a most unhappy frame of mind so far as the vital question of *mens rea* was concerned. In *Laird* v. *Dobell*,[4] the same offence was involved and Lord Alverstone, who again participated, observed that "if it is necessary to prove guilty knowledge I can see no distinction between the words 'causes' and 'permits' in section 3 (1) (*b*)".[5] This grain of truth was, however, sandwiched between other statements purporting to emphasise the correctness of the interpretation given in *Korten* v. *West Sussex C.C.*

A few years earlier, in *Ashley* v. *Hawke*,[6] the Divisional Court had proceeded to rule out the necessity for *mens rea* in another offence based on the word "causing". In that case the proprietors of *The Sportsman* were charged with unlawfully causing betting advertisements to be published in their paper, contrary to the Betting Act, 1853,[7] s. 7. To the proprietors' plea that a guilty mind was an essential element in the offence charged, and of which they maintained there was no evidence, Lord Alverstone, C.J., answered:[8] "I do not accept the view . . . that there could not be an offence against the statute unless the owners of the paper who published the advertisement knew that illegal betting was going to be carried on. I think that if the case is one in which the

[1] *Ibid.*, p. 520.
[2] [1892] 1 Q.B. 709.
[3] See *ante*, pp. 112–115.
[4] [1906] 1 K.B. 131.
[5] *Ibid.*, p. 133.
[6] (1903) 89 L.T. 538.
[7] 16 & 17 Vict. c. 119.
[8] *Ibid.*, p. 541.

advertisement reasonably construed by the person to whom it is read indicates one of the two [betting] offences prohibited by section 1, then the offence under section 7 is complete." This line of reasoning excludes any consideration of the defendant's mind, and, as has been pointed out in the chapter devoted to wilfulness, the same method of construction was adopted by Lord Hewart, C.J., in connection with the offence of wilfully pretending to be a physician under section 40 of the Medical Act 1858. Speaking in *Jutson* v. *Barrow*,[1] Lord Hewart declared that "what is regarded is not the mind of the individual but the meaning likely to be conveyed by the words that are used".[2] The similarity in the interpretations adopted by Lord Alverstone and Lord Hewart, respectively, is self-evident and has the effect of making the offence one of absolute liability.

Further examination of Lord Alverstone, C.J.'s judgment in *Ashley* v. *Hawke*, however, reveals the learned Chief Justice apparently basing his decision on the concurrent, but totally different, ground that the proprietors must be deemed to have constructive knowledge of the illegal advertisements. "No newspaper proprietor" Lord Alverstone declared,[3] "can properly plead ignorance because he did not himself make inquiry as to what the advertisement indicated. . . . The proprietors of *The Sportsman* cannot possibly have thought that they did not know they were the advertisements of some kind of betting; and therefore, in that sense *mens rea* is not necessary." Although this use of the expression *mens rea* is not altogether appropriate, it would certainly seem that the learned Chief Justice, in this part of his judgment, considered the question at issue to be not so much the necessity or otherwise for a guilty mind, as the degree of knowledge which had to be proved against the proprietors. According to Lord Alverstone, knowledge that the advertisement related to illegal betting could be imputed to the defendants by virtue of their position of responsibility as proprietors of the newspaper. It may well be that the position of a newspaper proprietor is a peculiar one attaching to itself undesirable consequences, but it must be pointed out that the principle adopted by Lord Alverstone, C.J., is the exact antithesis of that followed in cases like *Harrison* v. *Leaper*,[4] *Small* v. *Warr*,[5] *Hardcastle* v. *Bielby*,[6] and *Rushton*

[1] [1936] 1 K.B. 236.
[2] *Ibid.*, p. 241.
[3] (1903) 89 L.T. at p. 541.
[4] (1862) 5 L.T. 640.
[5] (1882) 47 J.P. 20.
[6] [1892] 1 Q.B. 709.

v. *Martin.*[1] In each of those cases the court refused to attribute to the defendant knowledge of the facts constituting the offence merely on the ground that he occupied a position of authority. The earlier cases of *R.* v. *Glossop*[2] and *Parsons* v. *Chapman*[3] might be cited in support of the doctrine advanced in *Ashley* v. *Hawke*,[4] but the reports of both those cases are too brief to justify making any sound conclusions.

Another example of the "absolute liability" outlook frequently associated with Avory, J., is to be found in *Moses* v. *Midland Rly. Co.*[5] In that case the court had to consider the offence of "causing or knowingly permitting any substance to flow into any waters with the result that fish are poisoned or killed", under the Salmon Fishery Act, 1861, s. 5. Owing to a defect in a tank waggon travelling on the respondent's railway, creosote leaked through the permanent way into a river containing salmon, killing some of the fish. In the absence of any neglect or default on the part of the railway company, the magistrates dismissed the information which contained the word "causing" only, no reference being made to the alternative ground of liability under the same section, namely, "knowingly permitting". Before the Divisional Court, counsel for the railway company referred to Lord Alverstone's statement in *Korten* v. *West Sussex C.C.*[6] that the word "causes" prima facie refers only to a person taking a part in the act, and suggested that no offence was committed unless the act was an act done with intention in the sense of knowing. An additional argument might well have been founded on the actual formula used by the legislature when defining the offence, wherein the word "causing" is used in conjunction with "knowingly permitting". However, in the only substantive judgment delivered, Avory, J., referring to section 5 of the Salmon Fishery Act, 1861, stated:[7] "it appears to me to be one of those cases in which it is not necessary to prove *mens rea.* There is an absolute prohibition, and the person liable is the person who in fact 'causes' and I do not think that it is necessary to shew that the person was intentionally causing."

Such a categorical declaration would seem to exclude all consideration of guilty knowledge, but Avory, J., saw nothing

[1] [1952] W.N. 258.
[2] (1821) 4 B. & Ald. 616. [3] (1831) 5 C. & P. 33. [4] (1903) 89 L.T. 538.
[5] (1915) 84 L.J.K.B. 2181. *Coram* Lord Reading C.J., Low and Avory, JJ.
[6] (1903) 72 L.J.K.B. 514, at p. 520. [7] *Ibid.*, p. 2184.

incongruous in dismissing the appeal against acquittal on the ground that the creosote had escaped without the knowledge of the railway company or their servants and that no exercise of reasonable care on their part could have prevented it. The final words in the judgment of Avory, J., were that "a person cannot be said to cause liquid to flow when he is ignorant that it is flowing and could not by the exercise of reasonable care have prevented it".[1] The divagation reflected in the two passages quoted is striking and may justifiably be said to defy reconciliation. What appears at first sight to be a clear case illustrating the "absolute liability" mode of interpretation is, in effect, of dubious authority and care must be taken not to over-emphasise its importance. The view, implicit in Avory, J.'s concluding words, that negligence will suffice to establish liability is not without support, but that interesting aspect of *Moses* v. *Midland Rly. Co.* must be left until later.[2]

Reviewing the cases in which the opinion has been expressed that the accused's state of mind is irrelevant on a charge of "causing", the impression gained is that of lack of consistency or conviction, but no lack of conviction is evidenced in the case of *Cox & Sons, Ltd.* v. *Sidery*.[3] The defendants in that case were convicted for failing to cause a true record of the maximum load weight carried by one of their vehicles to be kept, contrary to regulations made under the Road and Rail Traffic Act, 1933. The Divisional Court considered the case to be a clear one, Lord Hewart, C.J., in a very brief judgment, declaring: "There have been many ingenious arguments upon the topic of *mens rea* in relation to the words of a particular statute, but here the words are imperative and plain . . . no words could be clearer and no question of *mens rea* can possibly arise." Two unreported cases, *Jackman* v. *Power Radiance Co.*[4] and *Nelson* v. *Coventry Swaging Co.*,[4] followed the decision in *Cox* v. *Sidery* but without any consideration of the legal arguments put forward in the earlier case. By a majority decision,[5] the same case was followed by the Scottish High Court of Justiciary in *Mitchell* v. *Morrison*,[6] in which Lord Moncrieff in the leading dissenting judgment, after reviewing a large number of cases involving the same problem of *mens rea*,

[1] *Loc. cit.* [2] See *post* pp. 211–212. [3] (1935) 24 R.C. & R.T.C. 69.

Cited in *Mitchell* v. *Morrison* (1938) S.C. (J) 64.

[5] Lord Justice-General (Normand), Lord Justice Clerk, Lord Wark and Lord Russell, *dissentiente* Lord Moncrieff, Lord Mackay and Lord Pitman.

[6] (1938) S.C. (J) 64.

proceeded to deliver a trenchant criticism of the English decision. One passage in particular deserves to be quoted, wherein Lord Moncrieff, commenting on the lack of explanation underlying Lord Hewart's judgment in *Cox* v. *Sidery*, declared:[1] "One is left to surmise whether ease of decision resulted from the exercise of a faculty of interpretation of which each for himself must be the finder yet may not disclose the processes, or from disregard of difficulties which, as disclosed *hinc inde* in the present case, may at least have been open to be discovered." Where the key to the decision in *Cox* v. *Sidery* lies, it is suggested, is in the peculiar form of the regulation which says:[2] "The holder of a licence shall keep or cause to be kept. . . ." Whereas in the other cases discussed above the legislature is concerned to *prohibit* a person from "causing" something to be done, in the present case "causing a true record to be kept" is the very thing which the legislature is concerned to *achieve* by means of the regulation. Moreover, it is a duty which does not permit of any qualification or exception and the intention of Parliament appears to be as stated by the Divisional Court. The decision in *Cox* v. *Sidery* and the majority decision in *Mitchell* v. *Morrison*, it is suggested, in no way minimise the principle, accepted by an impressive majority of judicial opinion, that guilt in statutory offences based upon the words "causes" or "causing" is dependent upon proof, first, of guilty knowledge of all the elements contained in the offence and, secondly, express authorisation of the forbidden event.

[1] *Ibid.*, p. 76.

[2] See Reg. 5 of the Goods Vehicles (Keeping of Records) Regs. 1934, made under the Road and Rail Traffic Act, 1933, s. 16

VII

ALLOWING

Survey of statutory offences based on the word "allows"

Unlike the epithets "permits", "suffers" and "causes" whose genealogy is traceable through many centuries, the word "allows" in statutory offences is very much a newcomer. Notwithstanding this fact it will be found that, in the spate of legislation dealing with the administration of nationalised industries and other bodies created by the Welfare State, this verbal suckling is, as often as not, the key to the new criminal offences. In such cases, the most elaborate definitions have sometimes been devised with a view to ensuring that criminal liability goes hand in hand with proof of a guilty mind.

Different formulae used by the legislature

Examination of statutory crimes which include the term "allows" indicates that three different formulae are used by the legislature. First, the verb "allows" appears as the only guide to the foundation of liability, such as in the Licensing (Consolidation) Act, 1910, s. 70,[1] which enacts that no person may allow to be made or used any internal communication between any licensed premises and any [other] premises which are used for public entertainment or resort. Another illustration is provided by the Children and Young Persons Act, 1933,[2] section 4 (1) of which makes it a crime for any person to cause or procure, or for any parent or guardian to allow, a child under 16 years to be in any street or other place for the purpose of begging or receiving alms. Furthermore, the statute goes on to provide that if it is proved that the person charged allowed the child to be in the street he shall be presumed to have allowed him to be in the street for the purpose of begging, unless the contrary is proved. Several other offences of a similar character in the same statute draw the significant distinction between parents or guardians who alone can commit

[1] 10 Edw. 7 and 1 Geo. 5, c. 24, re-enacted in the Licensing Act, 1953, s. 133 (1). See, also, the earlier Factory and Workshop Act, 1895 (58 & 59 Vict., c. 37), s. 9 (2) & (3).

[2] 23 Geo. 5, c. 12. The same framework for liability as quoted in the text above is seen in ss. 4 (2), 6, 22, 23, 24 & 25.

an offence by "allowing", and other persons who must "cause or procure" in order to incur liability. Secondly, there is the phrase "knowingly allow" which is frequently used in licensing statutes of which the Intoxicating Liquor (Sale to Children) Act, 1901,[1] the Licensing Act, 1902,[2] and the Licensing (Consolidation) Act, 1910[3] may be cited as examples. In these enactments it is usually sought to prohibit a licensee from "knowingly selling or delivering or allowing any person to sell or deliver intoxicating liquor" in certain defined circumstances. The third formula is found most frequently in recent legislation and takes several forms. One common factor is prominent, as will be seen in the following examples. In the National Health Service Act, 1952,[4] s. 6, for instance, it is an offence to "knowingly allow to be produced or furnished . . . any document or information *which* [*the defendant*] *knows to be false* in a material particular". Another form of defining an offence, exemplified in the Wages Councils Act, 1945,[5] s. 18, is "knowingly allowing false entries . . . to be made *which* [*the defendant*] *knows to be false*". Yet another formula in the same strain is that which constitutes an offence if any person "knowingly allows to be produced . . . any wages sheet or other document which is false in a material particular, *knowing the document to be false*", an example of which is to be seen in the Agricultural Wages Act, 1948,[6] s. 12 (7). In each of these definitions the significant phrase is that which is underlined, for it shows the legislature going to extraordinary lengths to ensure that the doctrine of *mens rea* is safeguarded. Assuming, as has been argued earlier in

[1] 1 Edw. 7, c. 27, s. 2. [2] 2 Edw. 7, c. 28, s. 6 (2) (*b*).

[3] 10 Edw. 7 and 1 Geo. 5, c. 24, s. 68. See, too, the Intoxicating Liquor (Sale to Persons under 18) Act, 1923 (13 & 14 Geo. 5, c. 28), s. 1.

[4] 15 & 16 Geo. 6 & 1 Eliz. 2, c. 25. Other instances of the same offence are to be found in the National Insurance Act, 1946 (9 & 10 Geo. 6, c. 67), s. 52 (1) (*c*) (ii); and in the National (Industrial Injuries) Act, 1946 (9 & 10 Geo. 6, c. 62), s. 67 (1) (*c*) (ii).

[5] 8 & 9 Geo. 6, c. 17. Cf. the Statistics of Trade Act, 1947 (10 & 11 Geo. 6, c. 39), which in sections 4 (3) & 6 (4) makes it an offence "if any person *knowingly or recklessly* makes a statement *which is false* in a material particular"; and also the Licensing (Consolidation) Act, 1910, s. 97 (2).

[6] 11 & 12 Geo. 6, c. 47. The same wording is used in the Coal Industry Nationalisation Act, 1946 (9 & 10 Geo. 6, c. 59), s. 58 (*a*). Cf. the wording in the Electricity Act, 1947 (10 & 11 Geo. 6, c. 54), s. 61 (1) which enacts: "If any person, in giving any information . . . makes any statement *which he knows to be false* in a material particular, or *recklessly* makes any statement *which is false* in a material particular," and this form is also used in the Iron and Steel Act, 1953 (1 & 2 Eliz. 2, c. 15), s. 30 (3). Cf. the Prevention of Fraud (Investments) Act, 1939 (2 & 3 Geo. 6, c. 16), s. 12 (*c*) (see p. 201 *post*, n. 4).

this study, that, where the words "maliciously" or "wilfully" or "knowingly" or "permitting" or "suffering" appear in the definition of an offence, the element of guilty knowledge extends to *all* the ingredients of the *actus reus*, it would appear that the mode of definition now under consideration is not only top-heavy but that the additional words underlined are superfluous. Any other construction of the terminology used in the above examples leads to the situation whereby, in the absence of the words underlined, a person charged with such an offence will have no defence if all he can prove is that he believed the information in the document was true. Such a plea, it will be recalled, was rejected by the majority of the court in *Korten* v. *West Sussex C.C.*[1] where the defendant was charged with permitting an invoice to be false in a material particular. Presumably, if the definition of that offence had added to it the phrase "which the accused knows to be false" or "knowing the invoice to be false", the views of Lord Alverstone, C.J., and Wills, J., in that case would have undergone a radical transformation. But such a view denies the existence of *mens rea*, in the form of guilty knowledge, in the word "permits" or, to relate the argument to the examples in recent legislation, in the words "knowingly allows".

Necessity for *Mens Rea*

The general consensus of judical opinion, it has been submitted, considers *mens rea* to be an essential ingredient in statutory offences founded on the alternative words "knowingly", "permitting", "suffering" and "causing". Our present task is to discover, if possible, the answer where the word "allows" is used instead by the legislature. The first case we must consider is *R* v. *Handley*[2] in which a contractor was charged under the Mines and Collieries Act, 1842,[3] ss. 8 and 13, with allowing females to have charge of the machinery whereby persons are carried up and down the vertical shaft of a mine. The only evidence adduced was that girls had been found so acting on one occasion, which the court rejected as insufficient to justify a conviction. According to Blackburn, J., the defendant was "not to be responsible if he had no knowledge of what was going on",[4] whilst Cockburn, C.J., declared that the employment [of the females] "must be with his knowledge or by his tacit acquiescence".[4] Crompton and Mellor, JJ., concurred

[1] (1903) 72 L.J.K.B. 514.
[2] (1864) 9 L.T. (N.S.) 827.
[3] 5 & 6 Vict. c. 99.
[4] *Ibid.*, p. 828.

with this opinion. A similar interpretation was adopted in *Hardcastle* v. *Bielby*,[1] a case already referred to, where the court was concerned with a charge against a surveyor of "causing a heap of stones to be laid upon a highway and allowing the same to remain there at night", contrary to the Highways Act, 1835, s. 56. Although Collins, J., on the hearing of the appeal in that case, mistakenly construed section 56 as containing two separate offences of "causing" and "allowing", his judgment, which has already been examined in the preceding chapter,[2] leaves no doubt as to his conviction that guilty knowledge of the circumstances was essential. Hawkins, J., the other member of the Divisional Court was of a like mind saying:[3] "If the appellant had been on the spot and had seen the dangerous heap lying on the road, and had then taken no pains to give warning of the danger, it might perhaps have been said that by his silence he had 'allowed' the dangerous heap to be there. But as it is clear that he did not know that the heap was there at all, I do not think that he can be said to have 'allowed' it to remain there." The learned judge emphasised that his judgment was confined to the circumstances before him and was not of general application.

Is personal knowledge necessary?

This warning is of particular importance when we turn to the only other decision to be reported on the interpretation of the word "allows" where it appears on its own in a statutory offence. That case, *Massey* v. *Morriss*,[4] was brought under section 28 of the Merchant Shipping Act, 1876,[5] which provides that "Any owner or master of a ship who allows the ship to be so loaded as to submerge in salt water the centre of the disc" shall be guilty of an offence. The magistrate, being of the opinion that the owner of the ship involved was responsible for the act of the master, convicted him despite the total absence of any knowledge of overloading on the part of the owner. Before the Divisional Court,[6] the appellant argued that he could only be said to have "allowed" the overloading on proof of personal knowledge, to which the respondent replied with the argument that where the Act requires personal knowledge on the part of the owner, as an ingredient in his liability, it says so by using, as in section 22 of the same statute, the words "knowingly allows". Reference was made to the

[1] [1892] 1 Q.B. 709. [2] *Ante*, pp. 146–147. [3] *Ibid.*, p. 712.
[4] [1894] 2 Q.B. 412. [5] 39 & 40 Vict. c. 80. [6] *Coram* Cave and Collins, JJ.

licensing cases, such as *Mullins* v. *Collins*[1] and *Bond* v. *Evans*,[2] in which the knowledge of a servant had been imputed to the licensee making him liable, a principle which, it was suggested, should be extended in the present case to hold the owner liable for the knowledge of the master. The Divisional Court, however, refused to draw the analogy suggested, accepting instead the distinction canvassed by the appellant, viz., that in the licensing cases the only person who is punishable is the licensee himself; consequently, unless the licensee is to be held liable for the act of his servant, to whom he has delegated the control and management of the house, the offences might be committed with impunity.[3] Unlike the licensing cases the relevant section in the Merchant Shipping Act, 1876, imposes liability upon the master of a ship as well as upon the owner of the vessel. According to Cave, J., the mere fact that the owner had appointed the master, who knew and nevertheless allowed the ship to be overloaded, was insufficient to establish an "allowing" by the owner. In other words, the Divisional Court held that in the particular section before them it was necessary to prove personal knowledge in the owner of the ship, and accordingly quashed the conviction.

"*Knowingly allows*"

So much for the authorities in which the term "allows" has been subjected to interpretation. We must now consider what difference, if any, is created by the prefacing of "allows" by the familiar epithet "knowingly". In the discussion of *Massey* v. *Morriss*, mention was made of the view that where a statute uses the phrase "knowingly allows" proof is required of personal, as opposed to vicarious, knowledge and it is necessary to examine this opinion a little further. Take, for instance, the Intoxicating Liquors (Sale to Children) Act, 1901, section 2[4] of which provides

[1] (1874) L.R. 9 Q.B. 292. [2] (1890) 21 Q.B.D. 249.

[3] This argument would no longer, as an universal rule, apply. In the Intoxicating Liquor (Sale to Persons under 18) Act, 1923, for example, s. 1 (1) provides: "The holder of a justices' on-licence shall not knowingly sell or allow any person to sell, *nor shall any servant of his knowingly sell* . . . ." S. 1 (2) of the same statute enacts: "The holder of a justices' on-licence shall not knowingly allow *nor shall any servant of his knowingly allow* any intoxicating liquor. . . ." These provisions are re-enacted in the Licensing Act, 1953 (1 & 2 Eliz. 2, c. 46), ss. 129 (1) and 129 (4) respectively. Cf. s. 128 (1) of the 1953 Act which, in the case of a sale to a person under 14, does not make it an offence in the servant to make such a sale. It is difficult to see any justification for this distinction.

[4] 1 Edw. 7, c. 27, re-enacted in the Licensing Act, 1953 (1 & 2 Eliz. 2, c. 46), s. 128.

for the punishment of every licensee who knowingly allows any person to sell intoxicating liquor to any person under 14 years. Such a sale took place in *Emary* v. *Nolloth*[1] by a barman when the licensee was himself present in the bar but did not see the child. Lord Alverstone, C.J., put the issue succinctly when he said:[2] "... the question is whether for the offence created by this statute, the knowledge of the person who is the seller in fact, and who is the agent of the licensee to sell, is sufficient to justify the conviction of the licensee?" Holding that what had happened did not amount to a breach of the law by the licensee, the Chief Justice, with whom Channell, J., concurred, based his decision on the ground that "the licensee himself kept charge of the premises, and did not delegate his authority". In similar circumstances, the same principle was applied by the Irish Divisional Court in *Conlon* v. *Muldowney*,[3] in which Lord O'Brien, C.J., declared:[4] "it is perfectly plain that the word 'knowingly' governs the words 'allows any person to sell or deliver' . . . that is to say, there must be knowledge, *mens rea*. But in this particular case knowledge is negatived. . . . It is not a case where the holder of a licence puts a man into a public house as his *alter ego*, to whom knowledge is brought home." When the doctrine of vicarious liability in relation to statutory offences involving knowledge is discussed later,[5] it will be found that in cases where the defendant, be he a licensee or any other person occupying a similar position, has delegated the management of his premises to a servant, who then becomes his *alter ego*, the knowledge of that servant is attributable to his employer who may be convicted of offences based upon "knowingly allowing" or "knowingly permitting" or, simply, "suffering" or "allowing", forbidden acts to take place. The short of it is that such expressions do not impose a condition of personal knowledge, which only becomes necessary where the defendant remains in control of his premises and where there has been no delegation of authority to any servant.

Relationship between "allowing", "suffering" and "permitting"

Earlier in this work it was suggested that "suffering" and "permitting", though often used in relation to different circum-

[1] [1903] 2 K.B. 264. The decision in this case was followed in *McKenna* v. *Harding* (1905) 69 J.P. 354, and *Allchorn* v. *Hopkins* (1905) 69 J.P. 355.
[2] *Ibid.*, p. 268. [3] [1904] 2 Ir. R. 498. [4] *Loc. cit.* [5] See Chapter X.

stances, possessed the same ingredients of liability, namely, knowledge of the particular event coupled with a power to prevent which is not exercised. Can it be said that the term "allows" or "knowingly allows" may be similarly defined? At least two Chief Justices appear to have been prepared to accept this view. Thus, in *Emary* v. *Nolloth*,[1] in the course of an attempt to classify the different types of cases constantly arising under the Licensing Acts, Lord Alverstone C.J. said:[2] "Then comes the class of case in which the licensee is charged with knowingly allowing, permitting or suffering an offence to be committed; in those cases knowledge is essential." The main emphasis, it will be noticed, is placed on the common factor of a guilty mind, and this same connecting link prompted Lord Goddard, C.J., in the recent case of *Ferguson* v. *Weaving*[3] to state: "There is no material difference between permitting or suffering something and knowingly allowing it to take place, for, as was said in *Somerset* v. *Hart*:[4] 'How can a man suffer a thing to be done when he does not know of it?'."

Both judges it will be observed chose to equate "knowingly allowing" rather than "allowing" with the expressions "permitting" and "suffering", but the correct view, it is suggested, recognises the word "allows" as being in itself synonymous with the terms "permits" and "suffers". Convincing support for this view is provided by the decision of a strong Divisional Court in *Crabtree* v. *Fern Spinning Co. Ltd.*.[5] In order to clean a machine in the respondents' factory a boy had to be in the space between its fixed and traversing position. Whilst he was still there the man in charge of the machine, thinking the boy was clear of the space, restarted the machine with the result that the boy was caught and received injuries from which he died. The respondents were prosecuted under the Factory and Workshop Act, 1895,[6] s. 9 (3), with "allowing any person to be in the space between the fixed and traversing portions of a self-acting machine otherwise than when the machine is stopped". The Attorney General, for the appellant, maintained that "shall not be allowed" in the relevant section meant "shall be prevented" from being in the

[1] [1903] 2 K.B. 264.
[2] *Ibid.*, p. 269.
[3] [1951] 1 K.B. 814 at p. 820.
[4] [1894] 1 Q.B. 574.
[5] (1901) 85 L.T. 549.
[6] 58 & 59 Vict. c. 37. See now Factories Act, 1937 (1 Edw. 8, & 1 Geo. 6, c. 67), s. 19 (1).

space, and if the person in charge of the machine fails to take proper means to prevent the boy being there the offence was made out. This construction, if adopted, would render the offence one of absolute liability, but it was rejected by Darling, J., who replied that "if the legislature had meant anything of that kind they would have said so . . . it seems to me that a man cannot be said to allow that of which he is unaware or that which he cannot prevent.[1]" This interpretation of the word "allows" was approved by both Lord Alverstone, C.J., and Channell, J., the other members of the court. It was, of course, the same judge, Darling, J., who, in *Rochford R.D.C.* v. *P.L.A.*[2] described the word "suffers" as covering the case of a person who, being in a position to stop a thing, does not stop it, a definition which has also been applied, for example, in *Goodbarne* v. *Buck*[3] and *Lloyd* v. *Singleton*,[4] to the word "permits". Is there then any difference in the constituent elements of these three respective words? All the evidence available suggests that each and all of the epithets "permits", "suffers" and "allows" is designed to embrace the same conduct. Unless, therefore, some hidden meaning, known only to the legislature or the parliamentary draftsman, has yet to be realised, the hope might be expressed that in future legislation the numerous permutations which we have already examined might, with advantage, be considerably reduced.

[1] *Ibid.* p. 552.
[2] [1914] 2 K.B. 916, at pp. 922, 924.
[3] [1940] 1 K.B. 771, at p. 774.
[4] [1953] 1 All E.R. 291 at p. 293.

VIII
FRAUDULENTLY

Reluctance to define fraud

This study of *mens rea* in statutory offences began with an examination of the terms "malice" and "maliciously" which, in their importance as embodying the basic element of criminal liability, are probably equalled only by the words "fraud", "fraudulently" and the phrase "intent to defraud". Whereas, however, in the case of malice many instances were cited where a general definition has been advanced by different judges, there has always been, as Sir Fitzjames Stephen wrote in 1883,[1] a great reluctance amongst lawyers to attempt to define fraud. "No judge" said Maugham, J., half a century later,[2] "has ever been willing to define fraud and I am attempting no definition." Irish judges are no more bold for O'Byrne, J., in a recent case before the Irish Court of Criminal Appeal, after stressing that fraud was the outstanding and characteristic element of many of the crimes dealt with in the Larceny Act, 1916, declared:[3] "It would be difficult, if not impossible, to define fraud in such a way as to provide for every case in which the term may be used, and I do not propose to attempt to do so." Perhaps on account of the fact that he was writing, rather than speaking in his judicial capacity, Fitzjames Stephen in his *History of the Criminal Law* ventured to set forth an analysis of the principal elements essential to the commission of any crime involving fraud. It is felt, however, that consideration of Stephen's analysis should be postponed until some indication is given of the expanse of statutory crimes wherein fraud is the constant *sine qua non* of liability.

Survey of statutory offences involving fraud

What is today regarded as familiar and commonplace was, in the legislation passed during the early part of the sixteenth century, of infrequent occurrence. But it is to the statutes enacted during that period that the beginning of the present-day constant

[1] *History of the Criminal Law*, Vol. 2, p. 121.
[2] *Re Patrick and Lyon Ltd.*, [1933] Ch. 786, at p. 790.
[3] *The People* v. *Grey* [1944] Ir. R. 326, at p. 331.

resort to the expressions "fraudulently" and "intent to defraud" can be traced. Thus, in the first statute to render embezzlement a criminal offence, enacted in 1529,[1] it was provided that "if any servant, to whom any caskets, jewels, money . . . by his master shall from henceforth so be delivered to keep, go away with the said caskets, jewels, money . . . to the intent to steal the same, and defraud his master . . . then the same false, fraudulent, and untrue act shall be adjudged felony". In the Bankruptcy Act, 1542,[2] the legislature sought by heavy penalties to curtail bankrupts from suffering other persons to recover any debts, goods, or chattels against them "with intent to delay or defraud their creditors deceitfully". Fraud and deceit[3] have, of course, long been associated as synonymous terms so that it is not altogether surprising to note that whereas the first statute against false pretences, passed in 1542,[4] used the phrase "falsely and deceitfully", this mode of defining the offence was replaced in 1757[5] by the formula "knowingly and designedly by false pretences to obtain money, etc., . . . with intent to cheat or defraud any person of the same". In passing, it may be noted that the old phrase "falsely and deceitfully" still makes an occasional appearance as in the Forgery Act, 1861,[6] the Admiralty Powers Act, 1865,[7] the False Personation Act, 1874,[8] and the Companies Act, 1929.[9]

Forgery and coinage offences[10] are two more crimes in the present

[1] 21 Hen. 8, c. 7. For a summary of the early legislation relating to this crime, see Stephen, *H.C.L.* Vol. 3, 152–160.

[2] 34 Hen. 8, c. 4. The first statute which punished fraudulent bankruptcy with any severity was 21 Jac. 1, c. 19, s. 7 (1623), which enacted that "the bankrupt that fraudulently concealeth his goods (to the value of £20) or rendereth not some just reason why he became bankrupt, shall be set upon the pillory (for 2 hours) and lose one of his ears". A full account of the statutes dealing with frauds by bankrupts is to be found in Stephen, *H.C.L.* Vol. 3, 229–233.

[3] See *Derry* v. *Peek* (1889) 14 A.C. 337, at p. 374 *per* Lord Herschell; *Nocton* v. *Ashburton* [1914] A.C. 932, at p. 963 *per* Lord Dunedin, and at p. 978 *per* Lord Parmoor; and, more recently, *Armstrong* v. *Strain* [1952] 1 All E.R. 139, *per* Singleton L.J., at p. 141.

[4] 33 Hen. 8, c. 1. See Halsbury's *Laws of England* (2nd ed.), Vol. 2, p. 564, n (*b*).

[5] 30 Geo. 2, c. 24, s. 1.

[6] 24 & 25 Vict. c. 98, s. 3. It also appears in the Forgery Act, 1870 (33 & 34 Vict. c. 58), s. 4.

[7] 28 & 29 Vict. c. 124, s. 8.

[8] 37 & 38 Vict. c. 36, s. 1, in which the phrase appears alongside the more familiar words "with intent fraudulently to obtain. . . .."

[9] 19 & 20 Geo. 5, c. 23, s. 7.

[10] To counterfeit the king's coin and to import false money from abroad resembling English money was made treason by the Treason Act, 1351 (25 Edw. 3, stat. 5, c. 2), but ceased to be a treasonable offence with the passing of stat. 2 & 3 Will. 4, c. 34. For an account of the history of coinage offences see Stephen, *H.C.L.* Vol. 3, 177–179.

calendar in which the element of fraud figures prominently. Although individual crimes of forgery were created before 1562, it was not until the Forgery Act of that year[1] that fraud was included in a general definition which made it a grievous crime for "any person by false conspiracy and fraud with others to wittingly, subtilly and falsely forge or make any false deed, character or writing". In the Forgery Act, 1913,[2] which is now the principal statute dealing with forgery, a distinction is drawn between an intent to defraud and an intent to deceive, the forgery of certain documents being made criminal only if an intent to defraud is proved, whilst in the case of public documents either an intent to defraud or to deceive will generally suffice. Attention has already been drawn to the Larceny Act, 1916,[3] in which an intent to defraud is an essential constituent of the crimes of demanding with menaces[4] and obtaining by false pretences,[5] whilst the element of fraud, signified by the epithet "fraudulently", is also apparent in the definitions of simple larceny,[6] abstracting electricity,[7] embezzlement,[8] and fraudulent conversion.[9] A seemingly tautologous section is section 32 (2) of the Larceny Act, 1916, which covers the case of every person who "with intent to defraud . . . fraudulently causes any person to execute any valuable security". Another interesting provision occurs in the Post Office Protection Act, 1884,[10] which makes it a misdemeanour for any person "whether with or without any intention to defraud . . . to forge or wilfully alter any telegram". It would be tedious to examine each statute in turn in which an intent to defraud forms part of an offence, but the following further examples may be cited: the Debtors Act, 1869,[11] the Falsification of Accounts Act, 1875,[12] the Law of Property Act, 1925,[13] the Coinage Offences Act,

[1] 5 Eliz. c. 14, s. 2. An account of the earlier legislation, and also of subsequent statutes, is given in Stephen, *H.C.L.* Vol. 3, 180–186.

[2] 3 & 4 Geo. 5, c. 27. For example, in the case of documents listed in section 2 an intent to defraud is necessary, whereas in section 3, containing another list of documents, principally public documents, an intent to defraud or to deceive will suffice. A similar alternative intent will suffice in the forgery of seals and dies (s. 5), whereas an intent to defraud is requisite for a charge under section 7 of demanding property on forged documents.

[3] 6 & 7 Geo. 5, c. 50. [4] *Ibid.*, s. 29 (2). [5] *Ibid.*, s. 32 (1). [6] *Ibid.*, s. 1 (1).

[7] *Ibid.*, s. 10, where it is used as an alternative to "maliciously".

[8] *Ibid.*, s. 17 (2). [9] *Ibid.*, s. 20 (1). [10] 47 & 48 Vict. c. 76, s. 11.

[11] 32 & 33 Vict. c. 62, s. 13 (1). See *R.* v. *Muirhead* (1908) 1 Cr. App. R. 189, and *R.* v. *Jones* [1898] 1 Q.B. 119 *per* Lord Russell C.J.

[12] 38 & 39 Vict. c. 24, s. 1. [13] 15 Geo. 5, c. 20, s. 183.

1936,[1] and the Companies Act, 1948.[2] Occasionally, the legislature has considered it desirable to make the absence of an intent to defraud a defence, a typical illustration occurring in the Bankruptcy Act, 1914,[3] s. 154 (6), which makes it an offence for "any person who has been adjudged bankrupt to make any material omission in any statement relating to his affairs, unless he proves that he had no intent to defraud". The same wording appears in several other crimes created by that particular enactment, and it is also to be found in the much discussed section 2 of the Merchandise Marks Act, 1887.[4]

Whether the word "fraudulently" bears a different meaning from an "intent to defraud" is one of the questions to be considered when we examine the cases on fraud. Little help, at any rate, is forthcoming from a survey of the statutory provisions wherein "fraudulently" acts as the signpost to criminal liability. Some examples have already been given and, in addition, we may note the following enactments in which the term is used in a straightforward fashion: the Larceny Act, 1861,[5] the Weights and Measures Act, 1878,[6] the Moneylenders Act, 1900,[7] the Post Office Act, 1908,[8] the Vehicles (Excise) Act, 1949,[9] the Representation of the People Act, 1949,[10] and the Post Office Act, 1953.[11] Furthermore, a comparison between two more statutes in which the word "fraud" is inserted in diverse offences emphasises well the difficulty of laying down any comprehensive definition of that noun. Thus, under the Gaming Act, 1845,[12] any person who "by any fraud or unlawful device or ill-practice" uses any money in playing with cards, dice etc. is deemed guilty of obtaining money by false pretences with intent to defraud. In totally different cir-

[1] 26 Geo. 5 & 1 Edw. 8, c. 15, s. 5.

[2] 11 & 12 Geo. 6, c. 38, s. 320.

[3] 4 & 5 Geo. 5, c. 59.

[4] 50 & 51 Vict. c. 28. See now the Merchandise Marks Act, 1953 (1 & 2 Eliz. 2, c. 48), s. 4 which merely purports to clarify the earlier enactment.

[5] 24 & 25 Vict. c. 96, ss. 82 and 84.

[6] 41 & 42 Vict. c. 49, as amended by the Act of 1889 (52 & 53 Vict. c. 21), s. 3.

[7] 63 & 64 Vict. c. 51, s. 4.

[8] 8 Edw. 7, c. 48, s. 58.

[9] 12, 13 & 14 Geo. 6, c. 89, s. 21.

[10] 12, 13 & 14 Geo. 6, c. 68, s. 52. See, too, the Fraudulent Mediums Act, 1951 (14 & 15 Geo. 6, c. 33), s. 1 (1).

[11] 1 & 2 Eliz. 2, c. 36, s. 55. Cf. the Food and Drugs (Amdt.) Act, 1954 (2 & 3 Eliz. 2, c. 67), s. 2, which provides the defence of showing that the operation in question was not carried out fraudulently.

[12] 8 & 9 Vict. c. 109. s. 17, In *R.* v. *Leon* [1945] K.B. 136 it was held that there is "fraud" within the meaning of section 17 if the defendant is proved to have made bets with no intention of paying if he lost.

cumstances, the Offences against the Person Act, 1861,[1] makes it a felony for any person "unlawfully, either by force or fraud", to take or entice away a child under 14 years.

Application of the doctrine of *Mens Rea*

Fitzjames Stephen's views

However many more instances of statutory crimes involving fraud might be cited, no further information is likely to be gleaned as to its meaning or, in particular, as to the application of *mens rea* in such offences. That the element of fraud in criminal law should be judged by reference to the mental attitude of the accused was indicated by Fitzjames Stephen when he wrote:[2] "Fraud involves, speaking generally, the idea of injury wilfully effected or intended to be effected either by deceit or secretly. It is essential to fraud that the fraudulent person's conduct should not be merely wrongful, but should be intentionally and knowingly wrongful." We shall see in the examination which follows of the cases on fraud, that however much judicial views may differ as to the precise meaning of fraud in different offences there is an almost universal acceptance of Stephen's opinion that fraud implies a guilty mind. That being so, it is not unnatural that the same writer should add:[3] "Fraud is inconsistent with a claim of right made in good faith to do the act complained of. A man who takes possession of property which he really believes to be his own does not take it fraudulently, however unfounded his claim may be." If, as there seems no reason to doubt was intended, this view was put forward as a rule of general application, the cases show that it has its adherents, its doubters and its opponents among the judiciary whose views appear to be largely determined by the crime involved. The Larceny Act, 1916, s. 1 (1), in its definition of larceny,

[1] 24 & 25 Vict. c. 100, s. 56. In *R.* v. *Bellis* 62 L.J.M.C. 155 (overruling a dictum of Montagu Smith, J., in *R.* v. *Barrett* 15 Cox C.C. 658) it was held that any fraud whereby the child is taken away or decoyed is within the section—it does not mean that fraud has to be practised on the child.

[2] *History of the Criminal Law*, Vol. 3, p. 124. In Vol. 2 of the same work, at pp. 121–122, Stephen wrote that "there is little danger in saying that whenever the words 'fraud' or 'intent to defraud' or 'fraudulently' occur in the definition of a crime, two elements at least are essential to the commission of the crime, namely: (1) deceit or an intention to deceive or in some cases mere secrecy; (2) either actual injury or possible injury or an intent to expose some person either to actual injury or to a risk of possible injury by means of that deceit or secrecy". In contrast, Bentham, *Collected Works*, Vol. 6, p. 292 n. thought that fraud simply embraced the idea of falsehood or mendacity.

[3] *Loc. cit.*

expressly provides for the defence of a bona fide claim of right made in good faith, which puts the crime of larceny into a special category. Consequently, it is proposed to treat of "fraudulently" in the definition of larceny separately.

Defence of "without intent to defraud"

As to other crimes involving fraud the question of *mens rea* is generally considered in conjunction with the precise meaning attributed by the court to the word "fraudulently" or the phrase "intent to defraud". In *Starey* v. *The Chilworth Gunpowder Co.*,[1] for example, the Divisional Court was concerned with the crime of applying a false trade description to goods within the meaning of the Merchandise Marks Act, 1887,[2] s. 2 (1) (*d*) which contains the exculpatory clause "unless [the defendant] proves that he acted without intent to defraud". The respondents, manufacturers of gunpowder, were under contract to supply powder to the government but being unable to produce any themselves, because of an accident, the respondents bought German powder and put it into barrels which carried labels bearing their own name and a description applicable to gunpowder of their own manufacture. Although no indication was given that the powder was manufactured elsewhere, it was acknowledged that the quality of the powder actually delivered was every bit as good as the respondents' own make. Adverting to the meaning of "defraud" in the Act of 1887, Lord Coleridge, C.J., said that the statute was directed against the abuse of trademarks and "the putting off on a purchaser of, not a bad article, but an article different from that which he intends to purchase and believes that he is purchasing".[3] The other member of the court, Mathew, J., accepted the fact that there was no intent on the part of the respondents to palm off inferior goods, but considered that the words "intent to defraud" meant more than an intent to cheat a customer and applied "to cases where a person uses a particular mark with[4] an intent in so doing to induce a buyer to accept goods which might otherwise be rejected".[5] Until very recently this was the only reported case in which the phrase "intent to defraud" in the Merchandise Marks

[1] (1889) 24 Q.B.D. 90. See, too, *Burgess* v. *Burgess* 3 De. G.M. & G. 896.
[2] 50 & 51 Vict. c. 28. [3] *Ibid.*, p. 96.
[4] The report quotes Mathew, J. as saying "without any intent in so doing . . .", but this does not make sense.
[5] *Ibid.*, p. 97.

Act, 1887, had been judicially considered. However, in the case of *Kat* v. *Diment*[1] the Divisional Court expressed the view that for the purposes of the same Act no real difference exists between a person who acts "without intent to defraud" under section 2 (1) (*d*) and a person who "acts innocently" under section 2 (2) (*c*). Little importance might be attached to this assimilation of the two phrases were it not for the fact that Lord Goddard, C.J., and other judges before him, have expressed the meaning of "acting innocently" in terms appropriate to crimes of absolute liability. Is it surprising, therefore, that the question is asked, does the doctrine of *mens rea* have no part to play in offences under the Merchandise Marks Act, 1887, wherein an intent to defraud is expressly stated to be an essential ingredient of liability?

Defence of "acting innocently"

Before examining the cases it will be well to state the particulars of the troublesome section 2 (2) of the above statute. That sub-section, in creating the offence of selling or exposing for sale goods to which any false trade description has been applied, enables the accused to prove by way of defence (*a*) that having taken all reasonable precautions he had no reason to suspect the genuineness of the trade description, *and* (*b*) that on demand made by the prosecutor he gave all the information in his power with respect to the persons from whom he obtained the goods, *or* (*c*) that otherwise he has acted innocently.[2] It will be observed that two separate defences are provided; the first is fulfilled on proof of the conditions in paragraphs (*a*) and (*b*), whereas the second defence consists solely in establishing "that otherwise [the defendant] acted innocently", within the terms of paragraph (*c*) in the sub-section. Moreover, it will be noticed that in providing this latter defence to a charge under section 2 (2) the legislature used quite a different form of wording from the defence of "acting without intent to defraud" which applies in cases brought under section 2 (1) of the same Act.

We have already considered the interpretation given to the latter phrase in *Starey* v. *The Chilworth Gunpowder Co.*[3] by Lord Coleridge, C.J., and Mathew, J., and the reports show that the

[1] [1951] 1 K.B. 34.

[2] By the provisions of the Merchandise Marks Act, 1953 (1 & 2 Eliz. 2, c. 48), s. 4, the above sub-section in the 1887 Act is deleted and replaced by a new sub-section. The net effect of this change is that conditions (*a*) and (*b*) (*supra*) are now combined whilst condition (*c*) remains as an alternative line of defence.

[3] (1889) 24 Q.B.D. 90.

same two judges were asked in *Wood* v. *Burgess*,[1] decided in the same year, to construe the phrase "acting innocently" in the subsection quoted above. The facts in this case, which were to be repeated in several later cases, disclosed the sale by the respondent of mineral water in bottles belonging to, and embossed with the name of, a rival manufacturer. Being of the opinion that the respondent had no intent to defraud the purchasers, members of the general public, the magistrate held that he had acted innocently within the meaning of section 2 (2) (*c*). On appeal against dismissal of the summons, both Lord Coleridge and Mathew, J., considered that the magistrate was wrong, the learned Chief Justice stating that "an intent to defraud the purchaser is *not* a necessary ingredient of the offence charged".[2]

A more elaborate consideration of the phrase "acting innocently" took place in *Christie* v. *Cooper*,[3] which case does not appear to have been cited to the court in *Kat v. Diment*.[4] This omission is most unfortunate since the views expressed in the earlier case by Channell, J., whom Lord Goddard, C.J., has described as "one of the most eminent judges before whom I ever had the good fortune to practice",[5] are in no way suggestive that the crime is one of absolute liability. Referring to the offence under section 2 (2) (*c*) Channell, J. declared:[6] "this is not one of those cases where, it being the object of the legislature to forbid a particular act from being done at all, the statute is so framed as to forbid the commission of the act absolutely, quite independently of any question of *mens rea*." Distinguishing between paragraphs (*a*) and (*b*) on the one hand, and paragraph (*c*) on the other hand, Channell, J., said that the defence "that otherwise he acted innocently" assumes that there must be other cases of innocence besides absence of knowledge or suspicion. The result of paragraph (*c*), according to the learned judge, was that "it is open to the defendant to set up *any absence of mens rea*".[7] In a passage which, it

[1] (1889) 24 Q.B.D. 162. [2] *Loc. cit.*

[3] [1900] 2 Q.B. 522. Another case which was based on the same offence is *Coppen* v. *Moore* [1898] 2 Q.B. 306, but the discussion in that case turned on the question of vicarious liability.

[4] [1951] 1 K.B. 34. [5] See *R.* v. *Kritz* [1950] K.B. 82 at p. 87.

[6] [1900] 2 Q.B., p. 527.

[7] *Ibid.*, p. 528. The writer's italics. In *Thwaites* v. *M'Evilly* [1904] 1 Ir. R. 310, at p. 317, the Master of the Rolls suggested that the following might amount to "acting innocently"—(1) if the vendor bona fide believed that he had the authority and consent of the owner of the trade mark; (2) if the vendor reasonably believed that the trade mark had been abandoned.

is submitted, has subsequently been taken out of its context and misconstrued, Channell, J. concluded:[1] "The innocence contemplated by the Act is innocence of any intention to infringe the Act of Parliament. . . . It seems to me quite clear that there may be innocence of any intention to infringe the Act, even although there may be suspicion of the genuineness of the article or trademark." The whole tenor of Channell, J.'s judgment is the necessity for *mens rea* in the sense of a guilty mind, and in this he was supported by Grantham, J., the other member of the court. The appellants, auctioneers, having been informed that there was a doubt as to the genuineness of the Dresden china which they were offering for sale, communicated their doubt to the purchaser and sold it for "what it is". This action, in the words of Grantham, J., was bona fide and the conviction was accordingly quashed.

Channell, J.'s optimistic remark,[2] that his view of the meaning of the relevant section would be sufficient in any future cases upon it, has not been realised. Followed by the Irish Court of Appeal in *Thwaites* v. *M'Evilly*,[3] Channell, J.'s interpretation was before the Divisional Court again in *Stone* v. *Burn*[4] where the facts resembled closely those in *Wood* v. *Burgess*.[5] Claiming that it had been the custom of the trade for the past thirty years for rival brewers to use one another's embossed bottles but with their own individual labels, this plea of claim of right by the appellant was not upheld. The words "acted innocently" said Lord Alverstone, C.J., "point to some misapprehension of fact".[6] Quoting Channell, J.'s statement in *Christie* v. *Cooper*[7] that "the innocence contemplated by the Act is innocence of any intention to infringe the Act of Parliament", Lord Coleridge, J., explained that "such innocence can only exist where the infraction was committed by inadvertence or mistake of fact".[8] Here then is the first sign of the narrowing down of the authority of *Christie* v. *Cooper*, for no longer is "any absence of *mens rea*" sufficient to prove that the defendant acted innocently. Where a person acts inadvertently no question of negativing a guilty mind arises, for it is well recognised that an involuntary or an unintentional act is a good defence even if the crime is one of absolute liability. In *Allard* v. *Selfridge*[9] Lord

[1] *Ibid.*, p. 529. [2] *Loc. cit.*

[3] [1904] 1 Ir. R. 321, approving the interpretation of the Master of the Rolls, *ibid.*, p. 310.

[4] [1911] 1 K.B. 927. [5] (1889) 24 Q.B.D. 162. [6] [1911] 1 K.B., p. 931.

[7] [1900] 2 Q.B. 522. [8] [1911] 1 K.B., p. 933. [9] [1925] 1 K.B. 129.

Hewart, C.J. purported to deliver the *coup de grace* to *Christie* v. *Cooper*, saying that the judgments in that case must be read strictly in relation to the special facts there being considered. According to the Lord Chief Justice the words "acting innocently" mean "innocence of an intention to do the act which is forbidden by the statute".[1] This interpretation is repeated in similar language by Shearman, J., who said:[2] "I think the plain meaning of this statute is that guilt or innocence is determined by the answer to the question whether intentionally an act has been done which is contrary to the words of the statute." Such a construction, it is submitted, is capable of one meaning only, namely, that the offence is one of absolute prohibition, to escape liability from which the defendant must prove that his doing of the *actus reus* was unintentional. Previously in this study attention has been drawn to the fact that certain judges during the earlier part of this century were strong exponents of the "absolutist" school of thought in relation to statutory offences, and a further example of this outlook is provided in Shearman, J.'s judgment in *Allard* v. *Selfridge*. In it the learned judge criticised the loose use of the expression *mens rea*, the true translation of which he said was "an intention to do the act which is made penal by statute".[3] Proof of intention in the present case, according to the three members of the court, consisted merely in the intentional selling of stockings as silk which were not in fact silk. Criticising Grantham J.'s ruling in *Christie* v. *Cooper*,[4] that where the defendant acts bona fide he does not commit the offence, Shearman, J., declared:[5] "That is clearly acting upon the fallacy that under this Act a person who has acted honestly cannot be convicted. That is, I think, wrong." Here is the crux of the matter. If the offence is one of absolute liability to which only an unintentional act constitutes a defence, then the proviso in section 2 (2) (*c*) is superfluous because it is well recognised that no criminal liability is ever incurred if the com-

[1] *Ibid.*, p. 136.

[2] *Ibid.*, p. 139. To the same effect is the judgment of Salter, J., the third member of the court.

[3] *Ibid.*, p. 137, adding: "It is true that under the old common-law breaches of the laws of morality and crime were much the same. In a mass of cases *mens rea* involved moral blame, and the result is that people have got into the habit of translating the words *mens rea* as meaning guilty mind, and thinking that a person is not guilty of a penal act unless in doing what he did he had a wicked mind. That to my mind is wrong." The learned judge would probably find much to criticise in the present attitude of the judiciary towards the doctrine of *mens rea*.

[4] [1900] 2 Q.B. 522.

[5] [1925] 1 K.B., p. 138.

mission of an offence is not the result of an intentional act on the part of the accused. If, on the other hand, the offence is one which permits of disproof of *mens rea* in the sense described by Channell, J., in *Christie* v. *Cooper*, the phrase "acting innocently" is a clear expression of the necessity to apply the fundamental maxim of criminal liability.

Recent cases have unfortunately pushed this latter interpretation further and further into the background. In *Mercer* v. *Pyramid Sand and Gravel Co.*,[1] all three members of the Divisional Court, Viscount Caldecote, C.J., Humphreys and Birkett, JJ., approved of the construction placed upon the defence of acting innocently by the same court in *Allard* v. *Selfridge*,[2] Birkett, J., saying:[3] "the act of selling the sand was quite intentional and deliberate, and if in that intentional act of selling the goods in question a false trade description is applied to them, then it would appear that the offence is complete." It was no defence, according to the court in that case, to show that the seller was innocent in that he believed at all times in the genuineness of the transaction. Finally, in *Slatcher* v. *George Mence Smith Ltd.*,[4] the Divisional Court, consisting of Lord Goddard, C.J., Lynskey and Devlin, JJ., held that the fact that the defendant had acted in good faith and had taken all precautions against committing an offence against the Act did not amount to proof that the defendant had "otherwise acted innocently". Following the interpretation adopted in *Stone* v. *Burn*,[5] *Allard* v. *Selfridge*[6] and *Mercer* v. *Pyramid Sand Co.*,[7] Lord Goddard declared that the phrase meant that the accused must have acted by inadvertence or mistake of fact.[8] This of course, was the meaning originally placed by Coleridge J., in

[1] (1944) 109 J.P. 54. The facts in this case are indistinguishable from those in *Thompson* v. *Howard* (1944) 108 J.P. Journal 246, in which Viscount Caldecote C.J., also presided, where the Divisional Court upheld the justices' finding of acquittal on the ground that the defendant had taken all reasonable precautions against committing the offence, and that he had no reason to suspect the genuineness of the trade description. No cases were cited to the court in *Thompson* v. *Howard*.

[2] [1925] 1 K.B. 129.

[3] (1944) 109 J.P., p. 57.

[4] [1951] 2 K.B. 631, and see a note by Glanville Williams in (1952) 15 *M.L.R.* 78, criticising the decision in this case. The difficulties created when construing the Merchandise Marks Act, 1887, led Lord Goddard to declare in that case: "Those who are responsible might well consider whether new legislation should not be introduced to set out the law on this matter in clear language which lay justices and others concerned with its administration could understand."

[5] [1911] 1 K.B. 927.

[6] [1925] 1 K.B. 129.

[7] (1944) 109 J.P. 54.

[8] [1951] 2 K.B. 638. The judgment, read by the Lord Chief Justice, was prepared by Lynskey, J.

Stone v. *Burn* on the statement in *Christie* v. *Cooper*[1] by Channell, J., that "the innocence contemplated by the Act is innocence of any intention to infringe the Act of Parliament". Read in its proper context, that is to say in the light of Channell, J.'s entire judgment in *Christie* v. *Cooper*, it is suggested that the result of the later cases is directly opposite to the meaning attributed by that judge to the phase "acting innocently" which, it will be recalled, Channell, J., said, allowed the defendant "to set up any absence of *mens rea*". Once the importance of a guilty mind is minimised, and the tale unfolded above is an excellent example of this, the eventual result is that the courts accept an offence as imposing absolute liability.

Assimilation of the defence "without intent to defraud" with the defence of "acting innocently"

Views may, of course, differ as to the desirability of this result in relation to the particular offence which we have been considering. Surprise, however, is certain to be registered when it is pointed out that the same line of reasoning, and the same authorities, were used in *Kat* v. *Diment*[2] to construe the offence of "applying any false description to goods unless the defendant proves that he acted without intent to defraud", under section 2 (1) of the same statute. Lord Goddard, C.J., than whom no greater champion of the doctrine of *mens rea* is generally to be found, failed to see in that case that, for the purposes of the Merchandise Marks Act, 1887, "there would be any real difference between saying that a person acted without intent to defraud and that he acted innocently."[3] Considerations, he said, which apply to the latter expression must apply to the former. The question may be permitted, if no difference exists why did the legislature choose to use different phrases for the respective defences? Where, it is respectfully submitted, the Lord Chief Justice failed to maintain his usual vigorous emphasis on the principle of *mens rea* was in his statement that "where a statute forbids the doing of a certain act, the doing of it in itself supplies *mens rea*. . . . By throwing an onus on the defendant of proving that he acted without intent to defraud, it seems to me that the statute assumes that the doing of

[1] [1900] 2 Q.B. 522.

[2] [1951] 1 K.B. 34. The construction adopted in this case is criticised, with justification, it is respectfully suggested, by Glanville Williams, *Criminal Law*, pp. 75–76.

[3] *Ibid.*, p. 42.

the act alone implies an intent to defraud, but that the person charged can escape if he shows that he did not do the act intentionally".[1] As shown already in cases dealing with the epithets "wilfully", "permitting" and "causing", this is the language used consistently when construing an offence as laying down absolute liability. It was eschewed by the same Lord Chief Justice in *Bullock* v. *Turnbull*[2] when the expression "wilfully" was the key to criminal liability and which, Lord Goddard, C.J., declared emphatically, required proof of a guilty mind. Is this not the position, too, where the intent to defraud must either be proved or disproved as an element in establishing criminal liability? The departure from this principle, evidenced in *Kat* v. *Diment*,[3] certainly cannot be reconciled with Fitzjames Stephen's view that "it is essential to fraud that the fraudulent person's conduct should not be merely wrongful, but should be intentionally and knowingly wrongful".[4] In *Kat* v. *Diment* the court held that the sole question for consideration was the intentional doing of the act which, meaning simply that the conduct of the accused must be the result of the exercise of his will, excludes any consideration of the defendant's realisation that his act was wrongful. This, it is submitted, is neither what the legislature intended nor what the authorities lead us to believe is embodied in the phrase "intent to defraud".

Classic definitions of "intent to defraud"

The detailed analysis which has been carried out above into the two defences provided for in the Merchandise Marks Act, 1887, is justified, not on account of the statute itself, but rather by reason of the light which it sheds on the weight attached by different judges to the basic maxim of criminal liability. We must now proceed to consider other meanings which have been given to the words "fraudulently" and "intent to defraud". A definition, often quoted, is that put forward in *Re London and Globe Finance Corpn., Ltd.*[5] by Buckley, J., who distinguished an intent to defraud from an intent to deceive in these words: "To deceive is to induce a man to believe that a thing is true which is false, and which the person practising the deceit knows or believes

[1] *Loc. cit.* Cf., however, the same judge's remarks in *Brend* v. *Wood* (1946) 175 L.T. 306.

[2] [1952] 2 Ll. L. Rep., 303.

[3] [1951] 1 K.B. 34.

[4] *History of the Criminal Law*, Vol. 3, p. 124.

[5] [1903] 1 Ch. 728, at pp. 732, 733.

to be false. To defraud is to deprive by deceit: it is by deceit to induce a man to act to his injury." That definition, which postulates the state of mind required of a person charged with intent to defraud as knowledge or belief that the statement which he makes is false, was approved by the Court of Criminal Appeal in *R.* v. *Bennett*[1] and again in *R.* v. *Bassey*.[2] Moreover, it was relied upon by Byrne, J., in *Kat* v. *Diment*[3], but that learned judge failed to explain how the facts in that case were brought within the definition.

Another direction to the jury as to the meaning of intent to defraud, which is closely akin to the definition suggested by Buckley, J., is that given by Channell, J., in *R.* v. *Carpenter*.[4] Expressly repeated to the jury in *R.* v. *Parker and Bulteel*[5] by Avory, J., this direction was described by the Court of Criminal Appeal in *R.* v. *Kritz*[6] as the *locus classicus* on the point. In *R.* v. *Carpenter*, which was a case arising out of the failure of the Charing Cross Bank, there were fifty-one different charges covering the three separate offences of obtaining by false pretences, obtaining credit by false pretences, and obtaining credit by fraud other than false pretences. In each of these crimes it is necessary that there should be an intent to defraud, which Channell, J., proceeded to define in these words:[7] "If the defendant made statements of fact which he knew to be untrue, and made them for the purpose of inducing persons to deposit with him money which he knew they would not deposit but for their belief in the truth of his statements, and if he was intending to use the money so obtained for purposes different from those for which he knew the depositors understood from his statements that he intended to use it, then we have the intent to defraud." It made no difference, said Channell, J., that the ac-

[1] (1913) 9 Cr. App. R. 146.

[2] (1931) 22 Cr. App. R. 160. Mr. Turner, in the 16th edition of Kenny's *Outlines of Criminal Law*, p. 301, criticises the application in this case of the test laid down in *Re London & Globe Finance Corpn.* The most recent application of Buckley, J.'s test is in *R.* v. *Wines* [1953] 2 All E.R. 1497, 1498. See, too, *Russell on Crime*, 10th ed. pp. 1485–1486 and Glanville Williams, *Criminal Law*, p. 77.

[3] [1951] 1 K.B. 34, at p. 43.

[4] (1911) 76 J.P. 158.

[5] (1916) 25 Cox C.C. 145. Earlier in his summing up, Avory, J. had said of an "intent to defraud": "The common—I was going to say the most vulgar—form of fraud of course, is where a man by fraud extracts money out of another's pocket for the purpose of putting it directly into his own. . . . But that kind of fraud is not exhaustive of the expression 'intent to defraud' in a case of the present character" (i.e., conspiracy to defraud).

[6] [1950] 1 K.B. 82, at p. 86.

[7] (1911) 76 J.P. at p. 160.

cused honestly believed that he would be able to repay the money, for the fraud is in the mode of getting the money. "You are defrauding the man" continued the learned judge, "because you are giving him something altogether different from what he thinks he is getting, and you are getting his money by your false statement. In such a case as that the false statement would not be honestly made, and this question as to the intent to defraud substantially comes to this: whether or not the statements were honestly made." Here, in a direction which the Court of Criminal Appeal in *R.* v. *Kritz* said should always be given to juries in cases of intent to defraud, is a categorical statement that fraud connotes a guilty mind in the sense of an absence of honest belief in the truth of statements made. This interpretation is in striking contrast with the "intentional doing of the forbidden act" meaning attributed by the court in *Kat* v. *Diment* to the intent to defraud in the Merchandise Marks Act, 1887. It may be suggested that the offences dealt with in that statute and similar enactments are intended to protect the public, and consequently require a different attitude on the question of the mental element necessary to constitute liability. This view is vigorously contested where the legislature has not seen fit to define the crime in such a way as to exclude *mens rea*, and it is submitted that where Parliament expressly includes in the definition of a statutory offence, whether it be a felony, misdemeanour or a summary offence, the element of "fraudulently" or "intent to defraud", the fulfilment of this condition should be determined according to the principle *actus non facit reum nisi mens sit rea.*

"Fraudulently" in larceny

Meaning given by old writers

In the Larceny Act, 1916, the following definition of larceny is given:[1] "A person steals who, without the consent of the owner, fraudulently and without a claim of right made in good faith, takes and carries away anything capable of being stolen with intent, at the time of such taking, permanently to deprive the owner thereof." Larceny is undoubtedly one of the oldest common-law crimes and the above statutory definition, in its requirement that the taking and carrying away must be fraudulent, repeats what was deemed necessary in the Roman law definition of

[1] Section 1 (1).

theft.[1] Certain differences from the Roman law are manifest in Bracton's definition of larceny which reads:[2] '*Furtum est, secundum leges, contrectatio rei alienae fraudulenta, cum animo furandi, invito illo domino cujus res illa fuerit. Cum animo dico, quia sine animo furandi non committur.*' Unlike the definitions to be found in the *Institutes* or the *Digest*, Bracton's formula includes the words *cum animo furandi*. In view of the importance attached to the mental attitude of the thief, as evidenced by the word *fraudulenta*, it is suggested by Fitzjames Stephen[3] that the phrase *cum animo furandi* in Bracton's definition is tautologous, though, Stephen adds, if it is construed as excluding from the definition of theft the case of a taking under a claim of right the phrase is by no means superfluous. A different attitude is adopted by Mr. J. W. C. Turner, in the latest edition of *Russell on Crime*,[4] where he suggests that the word *fraudulenta* became otiose in Bracton's definition when the words *cum animo furandi* were inserted for, the learned author explains, the word *fraudulosa* in the *Digest* seems clearly to have indicated that it was necessary that the offender should have a wrongful intention. Writers in the seventeenth, eighteenth and nineteenth centuries varied in their explanations of what constituted larceny. Thus, Hale,[5] in stressing that it is the mind that makes the taking of another's goods to be a felony, interpreted *animus furandi* as meaning simply felonious, and this was followed by Coke[6] who wrote of the taking that "it must be felonious, *id est, cum animo furandi*". Blackstone says the same.[7] Bracton's Latin definition of the crime, it will be noticed, used the word *fraudulenta* and not *felonia*, and Hawkins[8] resorted to both epithets defining larceny as "a felonious and fraudulent taking and carrying away".

Meaning given 100 years ago

Many of these varied interpretations were examined in *R.* v. *Holloway*[9] by Parke, B., who also referred to East's *Pleas of the Crown*[10] wherein larceny, he said, is defined "with perhaps greater accuracy than other writers" to be "the wrongful or fraudulent

[1] *Institutes*. iv, 1 and *Digest*, xlvii, tit. ii, 1, 3 which read: "*Furtum est contrectatio fraudulosa lucri faciendi gratia, vel ipsius rei vel etiam usus ejus possessionisve quod lege naturali prohibitum est admittere.*"

[2] Lib. iii (De Corona), c. xxxii, f. 150b.

[3] *H.C.L.* iii, p. 131.

[4] 10th ed., Vol. 2, p. 1162.

[5] *Pleas of the Crown*, Vol. I, p. 508.

[6] *Institutes*, iii, p. 107.

[7] *Commentaries*, Vol. 4, p. 230.

[8] *Pleas of the Crown*, p. 134.

[9] (1848) 1 Den C.C. 370.

[10] Vol. 2, p. 553.

taking and carrying away by any person of the more personal goods of another from any place with a felonious intent to convert them to his (the taker's) own use, and make them his property, without the consent of the owner". Parke, B. considered that this definition was deficient in that "the taking should be not only wrongful and fraudulent, but should also be without any colour of right".[1] In two other reports,[2] however, of the same case, Parke B. is reported as saying of East's definition: ". . . some further explanation is needed of the words 'wrongful and fraudulent'. They probably mean without colour of right." The distinction between these two versions of what the learned judge said is important, insomuch as modern writers have relied on *R.* v. *Holloway* for guidance upon the problem whether the word "fraudulently" in section 1 of the Larceny Act, 1916, adds anything to the phrase "without a claim of right". In a standard work on criminal law, *Russell on Crime*, the view is expressed[3] that the word "fraudulently" retains something of the old moral significance which originally attached to the word "felonious" and, therefore, "serves to indicate that the offender must know that he is doing what is contrary to the standards of social conduct prevailing in the community." Furthermore, it is the opinion of the learned editor that the word "fraudulently" adds nothing to the more precise expression "without a claim of right".

Meaning given in some recent cases

Whereas support for the former proposition is forthcoming in two recent cases, it is equally evident that the latter opinion will require to be revised in the next edition.[4] In the first of these cases, *Rose* v. *Matt*,[5] the facts revealed that M., the respondent, had bought some goods from S. but was unable to pay for them at once. Wanting to obtain immediate delivery of the goods, M. offered his travelling clock as security for the purchase price, which S. accepted on condition that unless M. paid for the goods in cash

[1] (1848) 1 Den. C. C., p. 375.

[2] (1849) 18 L.J.M.C. 60, at p. 62; (1848) 3 Cox C.C. 241, at p. 244. In yet another report of the case, (1849) 2 C. & K. 942, Baron Parke is reported as criticising East's definition in these words: "This is defective, in not stating what the meaning of 'felonious' in this definition is. It may be explained to mean that there is no colour of right to excuse for the act."

[3] 10th ed. pp. 1161, 1175.

[4] Cf. Glanville Williams, *Criminal Law*, p. 412.

[5] [1951] 1 K.B. 810. *Coram* Lord Goddard C.J. and Devlin, J.

within one month S. was free to sell the clock. Failing to raise enough money M., some time later, returned to S.'s shop and surreptitiously removed the clock, as he put it, to prevent S. from selling it but with no intention of charging S. with its loss. Although at the time of M.'s removal of the clock he was still its true owner, the Divisional Court held that, in the facts before them, S. had a sufficient "special property" in the clock to fall within the statutory interpretation of the word "owner" and could, therefore, successfully prosecute M., the true owner, for larceny.

The more difficult question was whether the taking was "fraudulent, without a claim of right made in good faith . . . and with intent permanently to deprive the owner thereof". Reference was made by Lord Goddard to the earlier authorities wherein the same problem arose, and in which the mental element in larceny was respectively deemed to have been fulfilled on proof of an intent to charge the bailee in an action of detinue,[1] of an intent to expose the bailee to a penalty payable under a bond,[2] and even of an intent to defraud the Crown.[3] In *Rose* v. *Matt* the court was content to say that the owner of goods who has entrusted them to another person, in such circumstances that that other person has a special property in the goods, is guilty of larceny if he fraudulently takes them away from that person. No indication was given as to the limits of such fraudulent intention, unless it be said to mean simply "acting dishonestly",[4] the expression used of the respondent's conduct in *Rose* v. *Matt*. In a note[5] by the present writer on this case, it was suggested that the fraudulent intent in larceny be principally tested with reference to the "intent permanently to deprive the owner", adopting whichever statutory interpretation of the word "owner" is applicable to the special

[1] Hale, *Pleas of the Crown*, Vol. 1, p. 513.

[2] *R.* v. *Wilkinson and Marsden* (1821) Russ. & Ry. 470.

[3] *Ibid.*, p. 472.

[4] [1951] 1 K.B., p. 814.

[5] (1951) 14 *M.L.R.* 215–219. See, too, *Larceny by an Owner and Animus Furandi* by Rupert Cross, (1952) 68 *L.Q.R.* 99 in which the writer also argues in favour of interpreting "fraudulently" as having a separate meaning distinct from "without a claim of right made in good faith". Expressing doubts as to the possibility of a master being able to commit larceny of his own goods from his servant (p. 103) the writer submits that the real impediment is the difficulty of meeting the argument that the master had lawful possession of the goods all the time. One answer to this obstacle is to point to the wide definition of the word "owner" in section 1 (2) (iii), which includes a person who has "control of" another's goods. Such a person, it is suggested, includes both servants and bailees at will.

facts of each case. Thus, where an owner steals his own goods from a bailee for value, as in *Rose* v. *Matt*, it must be shown that the owner's intention was to deprive the bailee of his legal possession and, in so doing, to prevent the bailee from exercising his rights under the conditions of the bailment. Furthermore, assuming the possibility exists that a master can steal his own goods from his servant, it is fairly obvious that the fraudulent intent would not be satisfied merely on proof that the master intended to determine prematurely and permanently the servant's custody of the goods. Otherwise, the door would be wide open to any servant, with a grouse against his employer, to charge his master with larceny should the master decide to discontinue entrusting his goods to the servant. May it not be then that the fraudulent intention of the master in such a case, or a bailor in the case of a bailment at will, will have to be proved against a third party, e.g., an intent to make a bogus claim for alleged theft to an insurance company? Moreover, in such circumstances it could hardly be said that the master or bailor, in retaking his goods, was exercising a bona fide claim of right, and yet his taking is surely fraudulent.

Has "fraudulently" a separate meaning from "without a claim of right made in good faith"?

Any doubts which may have existed upon the question, whether the word "fraudulently" was intended to have a meaning separate from the ensuing phrase "without a claim of right made in good faith", have now been settled by the affirmative answer given by the Court of Criminal Appeal in *R.* v. *Williams.*[1] The appellant in that case was a sub-postmistress at a general shop in which her husband carried on business. When the shop was in financial difficulties, the appellant took money from the till in the postal department which belonged to the Postmaster-General and used it for the business of the shop. On the basis of the appellant's expressed intention to repay the money out of the sales in the shop, two lines of defence were put forward, viz., (1) that she had not intended permanently to deprive the Postmaster-General of the property in the money, and (2) that she had not acted fraudulently.

The first defence was calculated to negative the necessary *animus furandi* but, as Lord Goddard, C.J., rightly stated, it was essential to appreciate that what was alleged to have been stolen was money. In the opinion of the court the appellant, by taking

[1] [1953] 2 W.L.R. 937.

the actual coins and notes, intended permanently to deprive the Postmaster-General of the property in them. Currency has always occupied a peculiar position in the law of larceny, creating special difficulties in connection with the difference between larceny by a trick and false pretences, and between larceny and fraudulent conversion. This aspect of the decision in *R.* v. *Williams* should, therefore, be considered strictly in relation to the particular facts in that case. No suggestion can be read into the decision that a person who wrongfully borrows any article[1] other than money, such as a book or a bicycle,[2] from another and intends eventually to return it,[3] is guilty of larceny.

The second line of defence raised the question, what is the meaning of "fraudulently" in the statutory definition of larceny? Repudiating the interpretation put forward by Parke, B. in *R.* v. *Holloway*, Lord Goddard, C.J., considered that the word "fraudulently" is intended to, and does, add something to the phrase "without a claim of right made in good faith". Prefacing the court's definition with the warning that the words used might not fit every case—an admission which surely weakens any definition—the Lord Chief Justice said that the term "fraudulently" meant that "the person who takes the property must know when he takes it that it is the property of another person, and he must take it deliberately, not by mistake, and with an intention to deprive the person from whom it is taken of the property in it".[4] Thus, explained Lord Goddard, if a person picks up a suitcase at a railway station in the mistaken belief that it is his own, he does not take it fraudulently. Such conduct, it is suggested, might equally well be described as manifesting a claim of right, as may also be said of the case where a finder believes that the owner cannot be discovered by taking reasonable steps, or has abandoned the article, and resolves to keep the

[1] It is now a statutory offence under the Road Traffic Act, 1930, s. 28, to take and drive away a motor-vehicle without the consent of the owner or other lawful authority. To this charge it is a good defence to prove that the accused had a reasonable belief in the existence of lawful authority to take away the vehicle, or that the owner would have given his consent if asked.

[2] Under the Criminal Justice Act (Northern Ireland), 1953, s. 16, it is made an offence to take away a pedal-cycle in circumstances similar to those already provided for in the case of motor-vehicles. See n. 1 (*supra*).

[3] *R.* v. *Phillips and Strong*, 2 East P.C. 662, is the earliest authority for the proposition that no larceny is committed where the intention falls short of an intention to deprive the owner permanently. See, too, *R.* v. *Webb* 1 Moo. C.C. 431, and *R.* v. *Holloway* (1848). 1 Den. C.C. 370.

[4] [1953] 2 W.L.R. at p. 941.

article for himself. These examples indicate the difficulty of dissociating the word "fraudulently" from what has hitherto been described as acting "without a claim of right made in good faith".

Later, in the course of his judgment, Lord Goddard said of the sub-postmistress and her husband, "they acted fraudulently because they knew they had no right to take the money,"[1] and their conduct made it clear that "they had acted dishonestly".[1] It is in this sense of acting dishonestly, it is submitted, lies the true explanation of the word "fraudulently", which may be tested principally with reference to the intent permanently to deprive the "owner". It is in this sense that the Divisional Court in *Rose* v. *Matt* spoke of the true owner's fraudulent taking of his own clock from the shopkeeper who had a special property in it. Moreover, it is in this general sense of dishonest conduct that the earlier cases involving an intent to charge a bailee in detinue or to defraud the Crown, are explicable.[2] This interpretation is basically the same as the "absence of honest intention" test which Channell, J., in *R.* v. *Carpenter* said was the yardstick with which to judge an intent to defraud in a case of obtaining by false pretences. Stating that Channell, J.'s test was just as apposite in cases of larceny, the court in *R.* v. *Williams* held that it is no defence for a person in the position of the appellant to prove that although not in a position to replace the money at the time of the taking she hoped and intended to be able to do so in the future. However, in the same breath, the Lord Chief Justice added that the taking would not be fraudulent if the person who dabbles with somebody else's money is an individual with good credit and with plenty of personal funds. Thus, what would appear to be laid down as a rule of law in *R.* v. *Williams* is, in effect, reduced to a question of fact, wherein the issue of honest or dishonest conduct is left for the jury to decide having regard to all the facts before them.[3]

Claim of Right in Fraudulent Crimes

Larceny

Where a person is charged with stealing it is provided by the Larceny Act, 1916, that a claim of right made in good faith is a good defence.[4] This provision is declaratory of the common law

[1] *Ibid.*, at pp. 939, 943. [2] See *ante* p. 181.
[3] Cf. *R.* v. *Medland* (1851) 5 Cox C.C. 292; and *R.* v. *Trebilcock* (1855) D. & B. 453.
[4] See the definition in section 1 (1).

and in the leading case of *R.* v. *Bernhard*[1] the Court of Criminal Appeal ruled that they were bound by a long and unbroken chain of authority[2] to hold that "a person has a claim of right within the meaning of the section if he is honestly asserting what he believes to be a lawful claim, even though it may be unfounded in law or in fact".[3] In this test it will be observed that the criterion by which the claim of right is judged is essentially subjective, and where it is upheld it must follow that the taking is not fraudulent. As Fitz-james Stephen wrote:[4] "Fraud is inconsistent with a claim of right made in good faith to do the act complained of." So far as larceny is concerned the position is today well established, but an investigation into the availability of this defence in other crimes of fraud shows that judicial opinion is divided. This is difficult to understand for if the effect of a bona fide claim of right is to negative *mens rea*, and the requisite guilty mind happens to be fraud, what difference should it make whether the words "intent to defraud" or "fraudulently" are contained in the definition of larceny, forgery, false pretences, fraudulent conversion or any other crime?

Forgery

Confusion is sometimes caused when studying cases of forgery by failure to realise that, whereas a bona fide belief by the accused in his authority as agent to sign a document on behalf of his principal is frequently accepted as a defence, as in *R.* v. *Parish*,[5] *R.* v. *Forbes*[6] and *R.* v. *Clifford*,[7] no decision exists in which a claim of right has been upheld as negativing an intent to defraud in forgery. On the contrary, in *R.* v. *Wilson*[8] where the accused was authorised by his master to fill up a cheque for a specified sum, and instead filled it up for a greater sum which he retained, as he claimed, in satisfaction of a salary which was due to him the conviction for forgery was upheld by all the Judges. This case, however, is far from satisfactory. In reserving the case for the opinion of the judges, the trial judge, Coltman, J., said that he had felt some doubt whether the question of the reality of the prisoner's

[1] (1938) 26 Cr. App. R. 137.

[2] Among the authorities relied upon were East, *Pleas of the Crown*, Vol. 2, p. 659; Stephen, *H.C.L.* iii, p. 124; *Halsbury's Laws of England* (2nd ed.) Vol. 9, p. 497; and the following cases: *R.* v. *Hemmings* (1864) 4 F. & F. 50; *R.* v. *Wade* (1869) 11 Cox C.C. 549; and *R.* v. *Clayton* (1920) 15 Cr. App. R. 45. In addition, reference may be made to *R.* v. *Hall* (1828) 3 C. & P. 409 and *R.* v. *Boden* (1844) 1 C. & K. 395.

[3] *Ibid.*, p. 145.

[4] *H.C.L.*, iii, p. 124.

[5] (1837) 8 C. & P. 94.

[6] (1835) 7 C. & P. 224.

[7] (1845) 2 C. & K. 202.

[8] (1847) 1 Den C.C. 284.

claim to the alleged amount of salary ought not to have been left to the jury. This aspect of the case was not touched upon by the judges, who dismissed the appeal on the narrow ground that there was no shadow of authority given to draw a cheque for a larger sum than the accused's master had expressly authorised. On the other hand there is the statement in *R.* v. *Parker*,[1] a case of demanding money on a forged document with intent to defraud, by Ridley, J., who said: "if a man insists upon payment of a debt due to him, or recovery of a chattel to which he is entitled and for this purpose resorts to a forged instrument, that would afford evidence of an intent to defraud."

Embezzlement and Conspiracy to defraud

A different opinion was expressed by Cresswell, J., in *R.* v. *Norman*[2] where the master of a ship was charged with embezzling five tons of cargo to which he claimed he was entitled according to a recognised custom between shipowners and captains. The learned judge, in his direction to the jury, declared that "if instead of denying his appropriation, a defendant immediately owns it, alleging a right . . . no matter how frivolous the allegation, and although the fact itself on which the allegation rests were a mere falsification . . . in my opinion it does not [amount] to embezzlement". Accordingly, the jury returned a verdict of acquittal. On a different charge but also involving an intent to defraud, namely, that of conspiring to cheat and defraud the public by circulating a false prospectus, Cockburn, C.J., in his summing up in *R.* v. *Gurney*[3] said that the question for the jury to determine was "whether there was a reasonable and honest belief—or rather, I should say, an honest belief—for the reasonableness of belief,

[1] (1910) 74 J.P. 208.

[2] (1842) C. & M. 501. See, too, *Aberdare Local Board of Health* v. *Hammett* (1875) L.R. 10 Q.B. 162, in which a bona fide belief that the wife had authority to put her husband's name to a voting paper was held to be a good defence to a charge of fabricating the voting paper under the Local Govt. Act, 1858, s. 13 (5). Quain, J. in that case said that the word "fabricate" implies fraud or falsehood, a false or fraudulent concoction, knowing it to be wrong and contrary to the Act.

[3] (1869) 11 Cox C.C. 414, at p. 467. A similar direction was given by the same judge in *R.* v. *Murch* (1880), *The Times*, May 6. Comparing this direction with the views stated in *Starey* v. *Chilworth Gunpowder Co.* (1889) 24 Q.B.D. 90, Herbert Stephen wrote in an article entitled *Intent to Deceive or Defraud* (1904) 20 *L.Q.R.* 186, that "a shareholder has a right by statute to have a true balance sheet published, and is defrauded if he does not get it". This view excludes consideration of any question of honest belief and judges the intent to defraud purely on the result which ensues from the conduct of the defendant.

though it may be one element of judging its honesty, is not conclusive—on the part of the persons who entered into this engagement . . . that this was an enterprise which, though the ship was stranded for the moment, she would be got off, and being relieved from the lumber of dead weight which had oppressed her, would again float upon the sea of commercial prosperity and success". In similar circumstances also involving the issue of a false prospectus and resulting in a charge of conspiracy to defraud, Avory, J., in *R.* v. *Parker and Bulteel*,[1] having quoted from Channell, J.'s summing up in *R.* v. *Carpenter* as to the meaning of intent to defraud, proceeded to direct the jury in terms analogous to those used by Cockburn, C.J., in *R.* v. *Gurney*. Thus, in both these cases honest belief in the truth of the statements contained in the respective prospectuses was accepted as a complete defence. In laying the emphasis on the subjective character of such a defence, Cockburn, C.J., and Avory, J., were following a long line of cases in other fields of *mens rea*, such as malice and wilfulness, in which a bona fide belief or mistake or claim of right on the part of the accused has been held to negative the requisite guilty mind.

Fraudulent conversion

Fraudulent conversion is another crime involving an intent to defraud, and here again there is authority for the proposition that an honest, bona fide claim of right is a good defence. In the recent Irish case of *The People* v. *Grey*,[2] the Irish Court of Criminal Appeal held that the principle enunciated in *R.* v. *Bernhard* in regard to larceny was equally applicable to the crime of fraudulent conversion. The appellant, Grey, was the secretary of a gas and fuel company which, under the terms of his appointment, supplied the appellant with gas for domestic purposes free of cost. When, owing to prevailing conditions, this free supply of gas became impossible, the appellant, without any attempt at concealment removed to his residence a number of batteries and connectors, the property of the company, with which to provide electricity for lighting his home. Delivering the judgment of the court, O'Byrne, J., said that "if the officer, who takes and applies to his own use,

[1] (1916) 25 Cox C.C. 145.

[2] [1944] Ir. R. 326. Cf. *Brend* v. *Wood* (1946) 175 L.T. 306, in which the Divisional Court, consisting of Lord Goddard C.J., Humphreys and Singleton, JJ. upheld the magistrates' acquittal of a defendant charged with a statutory offence involving an "intent to deceive" on the ground that he had acted in good faith.

property belonging to the company, honestly believes that he is entitled to do so, he is entitled to be acquitted of the offence under the section [i.e., fraudulent conversion] even though his claim is unfounded in law or in fact".[1]

False pretences

What is the position where a similar defence is raised to a charge of obtaining by false pretences with intent to defraud? Such scant authority as exists would appear to recognise a plea of claim of right as a good defence, the earliest case being *R.* v. *Williams*[2] in 1836. In that case, the accused, realising that his employer was unable to secure payment from a debtor, told a false tale to the debtor's wife and obtained goods which he took to his employer, his intention being to enable his employer to sell the goods and so discharge the debt. Directing the jury as to the law in such circumstances, Coleridge, J., said that if the accused intended only to put it in his master's power to compel the debtor to pay a just debt, it was their duty to acquit the prisoner, which they accordingly did. This direction was followed in *R.* v. *Strickland*,[3] but was distinguished in *R.* v. *Hamilton*[4] in which the trial judge rejected the defence that there was no intent ultimately to cheat the person handing over the money.[5] In the latter case, Pollock, C.B., explained the decision in *R.* v. *Williams* as turning on the fact that the defendant believed, however erroneously, that he had some sort of right to do as he did.

Conclusions

Reviewing the authorities it is suggested that several conclusions may be drawn. First, it is clear that where the defence of claim of right or mistaken belief has been accepted, the court has shown no concern with the legality or otherwise of the right or belief under which the accused has purported to act. Secondly, the cases suggest that where such a defence has been allowed it has

[1] *Ibid.*, p. 333. Glanville Williams, *Criminal Law*, p. 419, suggests that the reasoning in this case went astray.

[2] (1836) 7 C. & P. 354. [3] (1850) 14 J.P. 784. [4] (1845) 1 Cox C.C. 244.

[5] Cf. *R.* v. *Hunt* (1918) 13 Cr. App. R. 155, in which the Court of Criminal Appeal quashed the conviction for obtaining goods by false pretences with intent to defraud, on the ground that the trial judge failed to refer in his summing-up to the appellant's defence that he had a reasonable expectation of having the means of payment and a bona fide intention to pay. Compare the direction of Channell, J., in *R.* v. *Carpenter* (1911) 76 J.P. 158, and the other authorities collected in *Outlines of Criminal Law* (16th ed.) p. 287.

been tested according to the subjective standard of whether it is honestly and bona fide held by the prisoner. Nowhere has it been suggested that the criterion is reasonableness, though it is recognised that this is an important factor in convincing a jury of the genuineness of the defence. Finally, it is submitted, that with the exception of the two cases in forgery, which are far from being convincing authorities to the contrary, the consensus of judicial opinion is in favour of recognising a bona fide claim of right as a good defence to the more familiar crimes involving fraud. It is difficult to see why this principle should not apply throughout the whole field of fraudulent offences,[1] it being submitted that, the cases under the Merchandise Marks Act, apart, the insertion of the words "fraud", "fraudulently" or "intent to defraud" connote the necessity for a guilty mind.

[1] Consideration to the question whether claim of right is not in truth a general defence and is not restricted to crimes involving malice, wilfulness, and fraud, is made by Glanville Williams, *Criminal Law*, p. 421 *et seq.*, who concludes that the chief stumbling blocks to generalisation are bigamy, brawling in church, offences against the person, and cruelty to animals. With certain qualifications, the learned author would accept the general application of the defence.

IX
THE CRIMINAL DEGREES OF KNOWLEDGE IN STATUTORY OFFENCES

To establish criminal guilt it is often necessary to consider what degree of knowledge is sufficient to incur liability. In two branches of criminal law, namely, statutory offences involving knowledge and aiding and abetting, this question is of such practical importance that it is surprising to find little or no treatment of the subject in any of the standard works.[1] How very different this is compared with the attention given, for example, to the doctrines of constructive notice and connivance in books on equity and divorce respectively. Indeed, the kinship which exists on this topic between the field of equity and criminal law is one of the interesting features made apparent by a closer study of the problem. In the recent case of *Roper* v. *Taylor's Central Garages (Exeter) Ltd.*,[2] an attempt was made by Devlin, J., to categorise the various degrees of knowledge which are relevant in statutory crimes, but it is respectfully suggested that his conclusions must be treated with reserve since, with one exception, they were put forward without any apparent citation or examination of the relevant cases. So far as the requisite grades of knowledge in aiding and abetting are concerned there have also been several recent cases[3] in which the courts have sought to re-enunciate the correct principles. In both spheres of liability the principal doubt concerns negligence as a state of mind. Whereas on a charge of aiding and abetting it is reasonably clear that nothing less than actual knowledge or connivance is required,[4] the examina-

[1] A notable exception is Glanville Williams's recently published *Criminal Law*. See pp. 59–60, 85–88, and 125–127.

[2] [1951] 2 T.L.R. 284, at pp. 287–288. In *Morris* v. *Williams* (1952) 50 Local Govt. Reports 308, at p. 312, Slade, J., adverted to the same problem but refrained from expressing any opinion.

[3] See *Johnson* v. *Youden* [1950] 1 All E.R. 300; *Ferguson* v. *Weaving* [1951] 1 K.B. 814; and *Gardner* v. *Akeroyd* [1952] 2 All E.R. 306, at p. 310.

[4] We have already seen that in *Thomas* v. *Lindop* [1950] 1 All E.R. 966, where a licensee was charged with aiding and abetting the consumption of liquor by two customers outside permitted hours, contrary to the Licensing Act, 1921, s. 4, Lord Goddard C.J. drew attention to the close relationship which exists between aiding and

tion which follows reveals the significant fact that there is an impressive body of dicta which suggests that even negligence will suffice in a large number of statutory offences involving guilty knowledge.[1] It is proposed to consider each state of mind in turn, and in examining the authorities it will be found necessary to refer to many cases which have already been cited in connection with the preliminary question of the necessity for *mens rea*. Any such repetition as occurs hereafter is unavoidable.

Actual or direct knowledge

The doctrine of natural consequences

Foremost among the culpable states of mind is actual or direct knowledge of the forbidden event. Invariably, however, as Devlin, J., pointed out in *Roper* v. *Taylor's Central Garages*, it is impossible to prove the state of another man's mind[2] with the result that the defendant's knowledge is generally inferred from the nature of the act done.[3] There is, of course, nothing new in this doctrine which

abetting and the type of offence which is based on guilty knowledge in the form of permitting or suffering certain conduct. Just as actual knowledge or connivance is necessary in cases of suffering, so, too, the Chief Justice added, it is one of the essential ingredients of aiding and abetting. "It is necessary" he said (at p. 968) "to show either that the licensee in a case of this sort knew what was being done or connived at what was being done". Some of the cases on aiding and abetting in which the doctrine of connivance was applied are: *R.* v. *Antonelli and Barberi* (1905) 70 J.P. 4; *Johnson* v. *Youden* [1950] 1 All E.R. 300. The decision in the last case should be compared with that in *Carter* v. *Mace* [1949] 2 All E.R. 714, in which the Divisional Court appears to lay down a principle wherein liability as an aider and abettor arises independently of knowledge or connivance. The suggestion made by a learned writer in 66 *L.Q.R.* at p. 228, that *Carter* v. *Mace* is explicable as laying down a rule that a person may be liable for aiding and abetting if he fails to carry out such inquiries as a reasonable man would make, is, in effect, tantamount to saying that negligence will suffice. This doctrine was rejected in *Callow* v. *Tillstone* (1900) 83 L.T. 411 and in *Benford* v. *Sims* [1898] 2 Q.B. 641. Although the Div. Ct. in *Davies* v. *Brodie* [1954] 3 All E.R. 283 sought to explain *Carter* v. *Mace* as laying down no principle of law and as having been decided on its particular facts, it is significant that Lord Goddard C.J., in the present case, declared: "If a person shuts his eyes to the obvious, or, perhaps, refrains from making any inquiry where a reasonably sensible man would make inquiry, I think the court can find that he was aiding and abetting" (at p. 286). This view appears to accept negligence as a culpable state of mind in aiding and abetting, which doctrine, if extended to the entire realm of crime, is fraught with obvious dangers.

[1] Contrast the statement by Glanville Williams in (1953) 16 *M.L.R.* 231, in which he writes: "Hitherto English courts have made little use of the concept of criminal negligence. A statute absolute in its terms is construed either as impliedly requiring *mens rea* (that is, intention or subjective recklessness) or else as not requiring any fault and therefore as ruling out even the defence of inevitable accident. Courts have not taken the middle course of construing the statute as aimed against negligence."

[2] Cf. Bowen L.J., in *Angus* v. *Clifford* [1891] 2 Ch. 449 at p. 471.

[3] [1951] 2 T.L.R. at p. 288.

is sometimes expressed in the time-honoured maxim that a man is taken to intend the natural consequences of his own conduct.[1] Its application in the realm of *mens rea* was well explained in *Lee* v. *Taylor and Gill* by Channell, J., who said:[2] "In all cases where it is necessary to prove anything which depends upon the state of a man's mind, whether it is malice, whether it is intent, whether it is knowledge, whether it is suffering or conniving, which all depend upon what is in the man's mind, in any of those cases the way in which it certainly maybe and generally must be proved is by inferring it from other facts."

Opinion is divided as to whether the presumption expressed in the above maxim is one of law or fact,[3] but this would seem to be of less importance than the realisation that the inference is not necessarily conclusive. Generally, it takes the prosecution only part of the way towards establishing the particular intent or knowledge—failure on the part of the accused to provide any explanation of his conduct will, of course, provide the final push, but if the defendant calls contrary evidence he may defeat the inference which would otherwise be drawn. Where the offence is one of absolute prohibition and *mens rea*, in the sense of foresight of consequences, is excluded, the mere intentional doing of the forbidden act is sufficient to render the accused liable.[4] All that must be shown is that the *actus reus*, which in itself constitutes the offence, resulted from a voluntary act on the part of the prisoner, and in such cases it is obvious that the maxim has no application.

Application of the doctrine in crimes involving guilty knowledge

Bearing in mind then the boundaries of the doctrine of natural consequences it is with surprise that we read, in the words of Lord

[1] For the recent discussion of this maxim see *R.* v. *Steane* [1947] 1 K.B. at pp. 1004, 1006; *Hosegood* v. *Hosegood* (1950) 66 T.L.R. 735 at p. 738; *Kaslefsky* v. *Kaslefsky* [1951] P. 38 at p. 46; *Sinnasamy* v. *The King* [1951] A.C. 83, at p. 87, and note in 67 *L.Q.R.* 283; *Sayce* v. *Coupe* [1952] 2 All E.R. at p. 717; *Lang* v. *Lang* [1954] 3 All E.R. 571; *Outlines of Criminal Law* (16th ed.), pp. 30, 369, and Williams, *Criminal Law*, pp. 77–81, 705–706.

[2] (1912) 77 J.P. 66 at p. 69.

[3] Compare, for example, the views of Denning L.J. in *Hosegood* v. *Hosegood* (*supra*) at p. 738, with those of Lord Merriman, P. in *Simpson* v. *Simpson* [1951] 1 All E.R. at pp. 961–962. For some pungent remarks on the application of this presumption see the judgment of Jackson, J., in *Morissette* v. *United States* (1952) 342 U.S. 246, at pp. 273–276.

[4] For a recent exposition of this form of liability wherein the court says that the doing of the act itself supplies the *mens rea*, see Lord Goddard C.J. in *Lester* v. *Balfour Merchant Shippers Ltd.* [1953] 1 All E.R. 1146.

Goddard C.J., in *Reynolds* v. *G. H. Austin & Co. Ltd.*,[1] that, "except in cases where the statute creates an offence of knowingly doing an act the prosecution can establish a prima facie case merely by proving the act was done." No authority was given for this so-called exception to the general rule and, assuming for the moment that the exception exists, it was ignored by the Lord Chief Justice himself in *R.* v. *Cohen*,[2] decided only a few months earlier. That case, which provides a good illustration of the commonly accepted mode of proving actual knowledge, involved a charge of knowingly harbouring uncustomed goods with intent to defraud the Revenue, contrary to the Customs Consolidation Act, 1876, s. 186.[3] Customs officers, on producing their cards showing their authority, were invited by the accused, a jeweller, to look round his premises. Although the ground floor revealed nothing, varying quantities of uncustomed watches were found upstairs, some in cardboard boxes, some in wardrobe drawers and others in canvas bags under the bed. The prisoner's explanation at the time was that he had forgotten about them, but at the trial he sought to excuse the untruths by saying that he was frightened because he thought the Customs officers were robbers who had come to steal his property.

Indicating what has to be proved in order to establish a prima facie case, Lord Goddard said:[4] "Apart from an intent to defraud[5] . . . the offence consists in knowingly harbouring uncustomed goods. . . . To prove a conscious harbouring it would usually be enough to show that the goods which were subject to duty were found in the possession of the accused. If they are found in his house, warehouse or other place under his control, that would establish a prima facie case that he knowingly harboured them, though, no doubt, he could rebut this by proving that he did not know of their presence, for instance, by showing that someone had dumped them there without his knowledge or privity." How is one to reconcile the two opinions of Lord Goddard, C.J., except to say that the above model direction to the jury must have slipped his memory in the later case. As to the decision in *R.* v. *Cohen*, having regard to the evidence which pointed to a surreptitious hiding of the watches coupled with the palpable untruths

[1] [1951] 2 K.B. 135 at p. 145.
[2] [1951] 1 K.B. 505.
[3] 39 & 40 Vict. c. 36.
[4] *Ibid.*, at pp. 506–507.
[5] There is an obvious mistake on p. 506 which reads "Apart from an *attempt* to defraud. . . ."

told by the jeweller, the Court of Criminal Appeal had no difficulty in upholding the conviction.[1]

The same principle is seen operating in cases of receiving stolen goods in which guilty knowledge must be shown to exist at the time of receipt. In the "very hard-worked and very often misunderstood"[2] case of *R.* v. *Schama and Abramovitch*, Lord Reading, C.J., explained the position by saying:[3] "Possession of property recently stolen where no explanation is given is evidence which can go to the jury that the prisoner received the property knowing it to have been stolen but . . . if the prisoner gives an explanation which raises a doubt in the minds of the jury whether or not he knew . . . he is entitled to be acquitted." Despite the clarity of this passage, appeals against conviction for receiving on the ground of misdirection continue to be made successfully. In *R* v. *Garth*,[4] and again in *R.* v. *Aves*,[5] the Court of Criminal Appeal, not without a discernible taint of tartness provoked by the difficulty experienced by certain learned recorders in explaining the law correctly to juries, has had to re-enunciate the application of the principle laid down in *Abramovitch's Case*. Events being of such an infinitely varied character, it is obviously difficult to lay down in advance what constitutes suspicious circumstances, but a good test, advanced by Kenny,[6] of what would suffice to infer guilty knowledge was the offering of goods by an unlikely vendor for an unlikely price at an unlikely hour. Not content with the above presumption, the legislature has provided additional facilities which frequently assist the prosecution in proving guilty knowledge,[7] but as these provisions are of limited application and sufficiently well-known, they do not merit further attention.

Connivance or knowledge of the second degree

For well nigh a hundred years, it has been clear from the authorities that a person who deliberately shuts his eyes to an obvious means of knowledge has sufficient *mens rea* for an offence based on such words as "permitting", "allowing", "suffering" and "knowingly". This state of mind has generally been described as

[1] See, too, *Petty* v. *Biggerstaff* [1954] N. I. 70.

[2] [1946] W. N. at p. 102.

[3] (1914) 11 Cr. App. R. 45 at p. 49.

[4] [1949] 1 All E.R. 773.

[5] [1950] 2 All E.R. 330.

[6] *Outlines of Criminal Law* (16th ed.), p. 291.

[7] Larceny Act, 1916, s. 43 (1). A recent application of these provisions occurred in *R.* v. *Davies* [1953] 1 All E.R. 341, where the C.C.A. ruled that where there are counts for stealing and receiving and the charge is substantially one of stealing and not receiving, the statutory evidence under s. 43 (1) ought not to be given.

connivance or constructive knowledge, and approximates closely to the conception of recklessness. Disregarding the hackneyed term "connivance", Devlin, J., in *Roper* v. *Taylor's Central Garages* coined the new phrase "knowledge of the second degree".[1] Introducing new descriptions such as this do no harm provided they help to clarify and not to complicate the existing law. By failing, however, to explain that the same state of mind was involved, the learned judge's purported re-classification is apt to mislead for it suggests that an additional degree of knowledge, separate from connivance, will suffice. In the ensuing discussion, therefore, the term connivance will be used as best calculated to describe the second sort of knowledge which carries with it criminal liability.[2]

So far as can be discovered, the case of *R.* v. *Sleep*[3] was the first occasion in which judicial approval[4] was given to the notion that some lesser degree of knowledge than actual knowledge would suffice to establish *mens rea*. The accused in that case was charged with having been found in possession of naval stores marked with the broad arrow,[5] into which offence the court inserted the word "knowingly". In two earlier cases, *R.* v. *Wilmett*[6] and *R.* v. *Cohen*,[7]

[1] [1951] 2 T.L.R. at p. 288.

[2] Many statutes can be cited in which the word "connivance" is constantly used as an alternative basis of liability. This is particularly evident in provisions which, for example, enact that where an offence under a statute is committed by a body corporate "any director, general manager, secretary or other similar officer shall be deemed guilty unless he proves that the offence was committed without his consent, or connivance and that he exercised all such diligence to prevent the commission of the offence. . . ." Instances of such a provision are to be found in the Iron and Steel Act 1949 (12 & 13 Geo. 6, c. 72), s. 55; the Air Corporations Act, 1940 (12, 13 & 14 Geo. 6, c. 91), s. 36 (2); the Patents Act, 1949 (12 & 13 Geo. 6, c. 87), s. 93; and the Radio-active Substances Act, 1948 (11 & 12 Geo. 6, c. 37), s. 8 (5). A full list is given in the next chapter on vicarious liability.

[3] (1861) 30 L.J.M.C. 170. It is interesting to compare the following definition of "conniving" put forward, a few years later, by Lord Westbury L.C. in *Gipps* v. *Gipps and Hume* (1864) 11 H.L.C. 1, an action for divorce: "The word 'conniving' is not to be limited to the literal meaning of wilfully refusing to see, or affecting not to see or become acquainted with, that which you know or believe is happening, or about to happen. It must include the case of a husband acquiescing in, by wilfully abstaining from taking any steps to prevent, that adulterous intercourse which, from what passes before his eyes, he cannot but believe or reasonably suspect, is likely to occur." See, too, the definition advanced by Sir Cresswell Cresswell in *Glennie* v. *Glennie* (1862) 32 L.J. P.M. & A. 17, 20.

[4] Yet, a year earlier, the Criminal Lunatics Asylum Act, 1860 (23 & 24 Vict. c. 75), s. 12, made it an offence for any officer or servant in such an asylum to permit any person confined therein to escape through "*wilful neglect or connivance*".

[5] An offence under the Embezzlement of Public Stores Act, 1697 (9 Will. 3, c. 41), s. 2.

[6] (1848) 3 Cox C.C. 281.

[7] (1858) 8 Cox C.C. 41.

actual knowledge had been required but in *R.* v. *Sleep*, Willes, J., delivering judgment quashing the conviction, said:[1] "... the jury have not found that the prisoner either knew that the goods were government stores or wilfully shut his eyes to the fact." This suggests that if evidence had been forthcoming showing that the accused had wilfully shut his eyes to the marking on the stores the case might have been decided differently.

Another fourteen years were to elapse before the lead given by Willes, J., was followed.[2] In *Bosley* v. *Davies*,[3] it will be recalled, a hotel-keeper was charged under the Licensing Act 1872, s. 17,[4] with suffering gaming to be carried on in licensed premises. The card-players, who were in a private room, corroborated the licensee's story that not only did they not have the cards from her but she was quite unaware of what was going on. To the licensee's plea that, to support a conviction under section 17, actual knowledge must be shown, the Divisional Court, consisting of Cockburn C.J., Mellor and Quain JJ., answered that "actual knowledge in the sense of seeing or hearing by the party charged is not necessary, but there must be some circumstances from which it may be inferred that he or his servants had connived at what was going on".[5] Time after time in subsequent cases it will be found that the knowledge or connivance of a servant is attributed to his employer, the governing principle being that the doctrine of vicarious liability applies only in cases where the employer has delegated control and responsibility for the premises to the servant.[6]

Entanglement of connivance with vicarious liability

The evolution in criminal law of the doctrine of vicarious liability, which originated a little over a century ago, is to be

[1] (1861) 30 L.J.M.C. 170, at p. 174.

[2] In *Avards* v. *Dance* (1862) 26 J.P. 437, owing to the strong stand taken by Wightman, J., that there was not enough evidence to support a conviction for "knowingly suffering gaming" (Licensing Act 1828, s. 13), Blackburn, J., and Crompton, J. (see p. 438), who seemed prepared to approve the principle of connivance, did not press their views and the conviction was quashed.

[3] (1875) L.R. 1 Q.B. 84.

[4] Re-enacted in the Licensing (Consolidation) Act, 1910 (10 Edw. 7 & 1 Geo. 5, c. 24), s. 79, and repeated in the Licensing Act, 1953, s. 141 (1). Compare the same offence in the Licensing Act, 1828 (9 Geo. 4, c. 61), s. 13, in which the words "knowingly suffers" were used.

[5] *Ibid.*, at p. 88.

[6] See *Allen* v. *Whitehead* [1930] 1 K.B. 211; *Linnett* v. *Comm. of Metrop. Police* [1946] K.B. 290 at 294; *Ferguson* v. *Weaving* [1951] 1 K.B. 814, at p. 821; *Quality Dairies (York) Ltd.* v. *Pedley* [1952] 1 K.B. 275 at p. 279. This subject is dealt with in the next chapter.

considered in the next chapter of this study. However, in examining the development of connivance as a culpable state of mind it is necessary to turn to two cases, decided towards the end of the last century, in which the doctrine of vicarious liability is seen entangling itself around the application of connivance. The first of these cases is *Redgate* v. *Haynes*[1] which, though bearing a close resemblance to *Bosley* v. *Davies* in that the same offence was involved and the circumstances were similar, is distinguishable by the significant fact that the hall-porter, whose duty it was to attend upon customers, retired after closing-time to his own chair in a parlour beyond the bar, at the extreme end of the house. Not unnaturally, the justices drew the conclusion that the porter suspected what was going on and connived at it. The Divisional Court held that the evidence justified the conviction, Blackburn, J., putting forward two alternative grounds upon which a licensee might be held liable for suffering gaming. First, the learned judge said, if the licensee "purposely abstained from ascertaining whether gaming was going on or not, in other words, connived at it" he commits the offence, and secondly, if the licensee goes to bed leaving a servant "in charge of the house" who connived at the gaming, the licensee is also answerable for the conduct of such servant.[2] Succinctly, Lush, J., agreed that "it is not necessary that actual knowledge of the gaming should be proved. I think that connivance on the part of the landlady or the person in charge would be quite sufficient".[3]

A few years later, in *Somerset* v. *Hart*,[4] a differently constituted court appears at first sight to have gone awry in requiring proof of connivance on the part of the landlord *himself* in order to justify a conviction. Once again the charge was suffering gaming and this time it appeared that the servant, a potman, who took and delivered customers' orders, knew that gaming was going on in a private room but took no steps to prevent it or to inform the licensee, who had no actual knowledge of the gaming. It was a market day, trade was brisk and the licensee was engaged in the bar attending to his customers. On the ground that the magistrates had acquitted the landlord of any connivance or wilful blindness the court affirmed their decision. The apparent departure from the principle enunciated in *Redgate* v. *Haynes* arose in the course of Lord Coleridge, C.J.'s judgment when, after

[1] (1876) L.R. 1 Q.B. 89.
[2] *Ibid.*, at p. 94.
[3] *Ibid.*, at p. 96.
[4] (1884) 12 Q.B.D. 360.

referring to the earlier cases, he declared:[1] ". . . it appears to me, in all of them the judges say that there must be something from which connivance on the part of the licensed victualler may be inferred, at all events to necessitate a conviction. It is nowhere held in those cases that he can be said to suffer gaming where what takes place is not within his knowledge, but merely within that of one of his servants, and there is no connivance on his part." With this view Cave, J., concurred but a quick glance back[2] at the words of Cockburn, C.J., in *Bosley* v. *Davies*, and of Lush, J., in *Redgate* v. *Haynes* will indicate the discrepancy between the principles laid down in those cases and Lord Coleridge's interpretation of them in *Somerset* v. *Hart*.

As was to be expected, when the opportunity presented itself in *Bond* v. *Evans*[3] for reconsidering all the authorities on knowledge and connivance, Manisty, J., adverting to the case of *Somerset* v. *Hart*, said that he could not reconcile the statements in Lord Coleridge's judgment with the previous decisions, and added that insofar as that case militated against the other authorities he preferred to adhere to the earlier cases.[4] Stephen, J., on the other hand, ignored the conflict of principle and preferred to explain the decision in *Somerset* v. *Hart* as resting on the absence of any delegation of authority to the potman who was not, at the relevant time, in charge of the premises.[5] So understood, the case is not in conflict with the previous authorities and the odd fact is that this distinction was appreciated by both Lord Coleridge, C.J., and Cave, J. in the course of the preliminary argument.[6] It is all the more unfortunate, therefore, that when delivering judgment in *Somerset* v. *Hart* the Lord Chief Justice should have allowed himself to be led astray from the proper principles.

Leaving aside the doctrine of vicarious liability, it will be seen that by the turn of the century the concept of connivance or wilful blindness had become firmly embedded in the minds of the judges as an alternative to actual knowledge. In *Elliott* v. *Osborne*,[7] where the appellant had been charged with cruelly ill-treating and torturing a bullock by neglecting to loosen the head rope by which it had been tethered during the passage across the Atlantic, the conviction was quashed because the appellant neither knew nor "wilfully abstained from knowing the condition of the

[1] (1884) 12 Q.B.D. at p. 364.
[2] *Ante* pp. 196, 197.
[3] (1888) 21 Q.B.D. 249.
[4] *Ibid.*, at p. 255.
[5] *Ibid.*, at p. 256.
[6] (1884) 12 Q.B.D. 360 at p. 362.
[7] (1891) 65 L.T. Rep. 378

bullock nor shut his eyes to the fact, which . . . would be sufficient evidence that he did know of the animal's condition". The same result was forthcoming in *Emary* v. *Nolloth*,[1] and in *Conlon* v. *Muldowney*,[2] both of which cases arose under the Intoxicating Liquors (Sale to Children) Act, 1901, s. 2, which prohibits a licensee from knowingly selling liquor to a child under 14 years. In neither case was there any delegation of authority and, consequently, in the absence of "any knowledge, actual or constructive, or any wilful connivance" by the licensee, the charge was not established.

Despite this wealth of authority, especially in regard to the offence of suffering gaming, at least one "very experienced magistrate" found it necessary in 1912 to seek the ruling of the Divisional Court on this same question whether connivance was sufficient *mens rea*. Although satisfied that the licensee and his servants had ample opportunity of becoming aware that the public bar was used for betting purposes, the magistrate in *Lee* v. *Taylor and Gill*[3] dismissed the information. Criticising this finding Lord Alverstone, C.J., declared:[4] ". . . the magistrate in dismissing this case has not given effect to his finding that these people who ought to have known were shutting their eyes to what they ought to have known and were thereby conniving at what was going on." Proceeding, Lord Alverstone thought that "conniving" is really a better word than "knowledge" for the purpose of dealing with these cases, because of course it is quite easy for a man to say he did not know, but it is not easy for him to say "I ought not to have known" if there is evidence of frequent and regular acts in which he himself took part. Channell, J. and Avory, J., agreed that the case should be remitted to the magistrate with a direction to consider whether the licensee had connived at the betting, and that if he answered this question in the affirmative the licensee should be convicted.

Various formulae used to define connivance

Thereafter, up to the present day, no real doubt has been cast on the proposition that connivance is as culpable as actual knowledge. We have already seen the diverse fashions in which this state of mind has been defined, ranging from the original expression "wilful shutting of the eyes" and its closest counterpart "wilful blindness", to the less forceful but equally satisfactory formulae

[1] [1903] 2 K.B. 264. [2] [1904] 2 Ir. R. 498. [3] (1912) 77 J.P. 66. [4] *Ibid.*, at p. 69.

"purposely abstaining from ascertaining" and "wilfully abstaining from knowing". The remarkable facility of judges to formulate still more phrases defining the doctrine of connivance is exemplified in the case of *Evans* v. *Dell.*[1] The respondent in that case, it will be remembered, was charged under the Road Traffic Act 1930, s. 72 (1) (10) with permitting a twenty-seater motor-coach to be used as an express carriage[2] otherwise than under a road service licence. It is permissible, under the Act, to use an "express carriage" without a licence but only on "a special occasion", to fall within which proviso certain conditions have to be fulfilled including one which requires the journey to be made without previous advertisement to the public. The bus proprietor did not concern himself with the arrangements made by the organisers of the trip, and had no knowledge of a newspaper advertisement in which an announcement of the coach trip appeared. According to the traffic commissioners there was a duty on the proprietor to inquire whether there had been any press advertisement, but Lord Hewart, C.J., rightly explained the law when he declared:[3] "It is said that, on those facts, the inference, not only may, but must, be drawn that the respondent deliberately refrained from making inquiries, the results of which he might not care to have. I think that is putting the matter too high."

This statement is in accord with the view expressed by Lord Goddard, C.J., in *R.* v. *Garth*[4] and in *R.* v. *Cohen*,[5] and by Lord Reading, C.J., in *R.* v. *Abramovitch*,[6] namely, that the conduct of the accused in such cases, where knowledge is an essential ingredient of the offence, constitutes prima facie evidence only upon which a jury is entitled, but not bound, to find a verdict of guilty. Earlier in *Evans* v. *Dell* Lord Hewart, C.J., had laid down that, as a guiding rule, "in circumstances in which the owner of the vehicle is put upon inquiry, if he refrains from making the inquiry . . . the fair inference may be that he permitted the offence to be committed."[7] Insomuch as the other members of the court were agreed, as Goddard, J., put it,[8] that there was nothing "which suggests either that he did know or that he shut his eyes to the obvious" the appeal against dismissal of the information was disallowed. In several recent cases it will be found that the tests propounded by Lord Hewart, C.J., and Goddard, J., in *Evans* v.

[1] [1937] 1 All E.R. 349. [2] Defined in section 61 (1) (*b*). [3] *Ibid.*, at p. 353.
[4] [1949] 1 All E.R. at p. 774. [5] [1951] 1 K.B. at p. 507.
[6] (1914) 11 Cr. App. R. at p. 49. [7] [1937] 1 All E.R. at p. 353. [8] *Ibid.*, at p. 354.

Dell have gained favour and have been used repeatedly to describe this second degree of knowledge. Thus, in *Roper* v. *Taylor's Central Garages*, which arose under the same section of the Road Traffic Act 1930, Devlin, J., in defining what he described as "knowledge of the second degree" adopted the phrase "deliberately refraining from making inquiries the results of which he might not care to have". This definition was also used by McNair, J., in *Taylor* v. *Kenyon*[1] in which case Lord Goddard, C.J., introduced a slight but significant variation by omitting the word "deliberately" and deeming it sufficient if a man "refrains from getting information which he did not want to get".

As to the vivid expression "shutting his eyes to the obvious" it is only necessary to refer to the suggested model direction to the jury in *R.* v. *Cohen*,[2] repeated recently in *Sayce* v. *Coupe*.[3] In addition to providing a further example of the use of this particular phrase to describe connivance, the Court of Criminal Appeal's judgment in *R.* v. *Cohen* provides authority for the proposition that the doctrine of connivance extends into the field of fraudulent offences.[4]

[1] [1952] 2 All E.R. 726. In this case the Divisional Court held that the statutory prohibition of driving while disqualified (R.T.A. 1930, s. 7 (4)) is an absolute one. Writing in (1953) 16 *M.L.R.* 232, Glanville Williams suggests that on the facts of the case this sweeping decision was unnecessary, because the defendant had clearly brought himself within the doctrine of "wilful blindness"; but this, as we have seen, only applies where guilty knowledge is an essential ingredient in the offence charged. See, too, Slade, J. in *Morris* v. *Williams* (1952) 50 Local Govt. Reports 308, 312.

[2] [1951] 1 K.B. 505, at p. 508.

[3] [1952] 2 All E.R. 715, at p. 717. See, too, *James & Son, Ltd.* v. *Smee* [1954] 3 All E.R., 273, at p. 278, and *Davies* v. *Brodie* [1954] 3 All E.R., 283, at p. 286.

[4] In civil actions for fraud or deceit it is well established that liability is incurred, in the oft-quoted words of Lord Herschell in *Derry* v. *Peek* (1889) 14 App. Cas. 337, at p. 374, "when it is shown that a false representation has been made (1) knowingly or (2) without belief in its truth or (3) recklessly, careless whether it be true or false." The latter interpretation was adopted by the Divisional Court in *Williams Bros.* v. *Cloote* (1944) 60 T.L.R. 270, 272, where the charge was one of "recklessly making a statement false in a material particular" under the Rationing (General Provisions) Order 1942, Art. 30 (1). The underlying identity of mind embodied in the terms "recklessness" and "connivance" is discussed later, but attention may be drawn here to the interpretation placed in *R.* v. *Bates* [1952] 2 All E.R. 842 by Donovan, J., on section 12 (1) of the Prevention of Fraud (Investments) Act, 1939 (2 & 3 Geo. 6, c. 16). That section provides that any person who, by any statement, promise or forecast which he knows to be misleading, false or deceptive, or by any dishonest concealment of material facts, or by *the reckless making of any statement etc. which is misleading, false or deceptive*, induces another person to invest money, shall be guilty of an offence. Rejecting as a guide to construction the marginal note to section 12 which reads "Penalty for fraudulently inducing persons to invest money", Donovan, J. held that the word "reckless" in the offence was not restricted to recklessness involving dishonesty (i.e., fraud), and that it extended to carelessness without any taint of dishonesty. According to the learned judge the section covered not only the dishonest prophet but also the prophet

Adverting to the necessity for proving "an intent to defraud" which, together with the expression "knowingly", constitutes the mental element in the offence created by the Customs Consolidation Act, 1876, s. 186, Lord Goddard, C.J., declared that "as in all cases where an intent to defraud is a necessary ingredient, the intent must usually be inferred from the circumstances. If a jury are satisfied that the accused person knew that the goods were uncustomed, which would include a case where he has wilfully shut his eyes to the obvious, and he had them in his possession for use or sale, it would follow, in the absence of any other circumstances, that he intended to defraud the Revenue".[1]

Similarity between connivance and recklessness

Earlier in this chapter it was suggested that a close analogy exists between connivance and that state of mind known as recklessness. The latter, which has been judicially defined as "an attitude of mental indifference to obvious risks",[2] envisages the mind of a person who foresees the consequences of his conduct and, though not seeking those consequences, deliberately takes the risk of their happening. Aptly described as a "I don't care" attitude, recklessness has hitherto been considered principally in relation to murder[3] and manslaughter[4] in both of which the

who, honestly believing it to be true, recklessly made a false statement. This interpretation was upheld by the Court of Criminal Appeal, *sub. nom. R.* v. *Russell* [1953] 1 W.L.R. 77, at p. 80. It is strongly criticised by Glanville Williams, *Criminal Law*, pp. 121–122.

[1] [1951] 1 K.B. 505, at p. 508.

[2] Eve, J., in *Hudston* v. *Viney* [1921] 1 Ch. 98, at p. 104. See, too, Austin, *Jurisprudence*, 3rd ed., Vol. 1, pp. 440–442, and the 7th Report of H.M.'s Commissioners of Criminal Law (1843), pp. 25–26. Salmond (*Jurisprudence*, 7th ed., 411) distinguished between two kinds of negligence "according as it is or is not accompanied by inadvertence". "Advertent negligence" he wrote "is commonly termed wilful negligence or recklessness". The increasing adoption of recklessness as invoking criminal liability is exemplified by the offences created in the Coal Industry Nationalisation Act, 1946 (9 & 10 Geo. 6, c. 59), s. 58; the Electricity Act, 1947 (10 & 11 Geo. 5, c. 54), s. 61 (1); the Iron and Steel Act, 1949 (12, 13 & 14 Geo. 6, c. 72), s. 54; the Docking and Nicking of Horses Act, 1949 (12 & 13 Geo. 6, c. 70), s. 2 (3) (*b*) and s. 2 (4); and the Diseases of Animals Act, 1950 (14 Geo. 6, c. 36), s. 7 (1).

[3] Thus, where a person kills another intending only to inflict serious bodily harm he is, nevertheless, guilty of murder—see *R.* v. *Lumley* (1911) 22 Cox C.C. 635, and the directions to the jury in the recent cases of *R.* v. *Whybrow* (1951) 35 Cr. App. R. 141, *R.* v. *Bloom* (1952) *The Times*, February 7, and *R.* v. *Craig and Bentley* (1952) *The Times*, December 12. The basis of this principle, it is suggested, is that the accused by his intention to occasion grave personal injury, in fact exhibits recklessness as to the foreseen possibility of death—see *Russell on Crime*, (10th ed.), Vol. 1, p. 543, n. 69a.

[4] Despite trenchant criticism (see, e.g. Turner, *Modern Approach to Criminal Law*,

doctrine of constructive *mens rea* has become firmly established.[1] Take whichever definition of connivance you please—in particular the wilful shutting of the eyes to obvious means of knowledge—and the close affinity which exists between the two concepts becomes immediately evident.

Yet, surprisingly, throughout the cases discussed above no single reference to the term "recklessness" can be found. Indeed, it is possible to find only one instance in which the similarity of mind characterising both recklessness and connivance appears to have been grasped or, at least, to have been judicially expressed. That occasion arose in the recent civil case of *Houston* v. *Buchanan*[2] in which, construing the word "permits" which forms the basis of the penal section 35 (1) of the Road Traffic Act, 1930, Lord Wright stated:[3] "In order to give permission, it is not necessary to show knowledge of similar user in the past, or actual notice that the vehicle might be, or was likely to be, so used, or that the

pp. 209–211; Dean (1937) 53 *L.Q.R.* 380; Hall, *General Principles of Criminal Law*, pp. 221–225, and Glanville Williams, *Criminal Law*, pp. 49–51), judicial practice continues to define recklessness as a "high degree of negligence". See, in manslaughter cases, *Andrews* v. *D.P.P.* [1937] A.C. 576, *Bonnyman* (1942) 28 Cr. App. R. 131, *The People* v. *Dunleavy* [1948] Ir. R. 95; and, more recently, in connection with the Prevention of Fraud (Investments) Act 1939, s. 12 (1), Donovan, J., in *R.* v. *Russell* [1953] 1 W.L.R. 77, at p. 80. Cf. Lord Goddard C.J., in *Pentecost* v. *London District Auditor* [1951] 2 K.B. 759. Whereas criticism is directed against the recognition of negligence as a *state of mind* meaning blameful inadvertence it seems clear that judicial interpretation is directed to the *conduct* of the accused from which the necessary foresight of consequences, essential to the concept of recklessness, is more readily assumed. The forming of this assumption proceeds through various degrees of certainty according to the particular circumstances of each case, so that the more reprehensible the behaviour of the accused the readier will the assumption be reached that he must have foreseen the results of his conduct.

The necessity in each case, it is suggested, is to distinguish between the *conduct*, sometimes loosely termed objective recklessness, which goes to prove the matter in issue, and the *matter in issue* itself which is that particular state of mind described as subjective recklessness.

[1] It is noteworthy, however, that the Royal Commission on Capital Punishment in its recently issued Report (Cmd. 8392) recommends that the doctrine of constructive murder should be abolished, except in relation to accomplices who agree to the use of force by the principal offender. Cf. the view expressed by Devlin, J. in a lecture on "Criminal Responsibility and Punishment" and published in [1954] *Crim. L.R.* 661.

[2] [1940] 2 All E.R. 179.

[3] *Ibid.*, at p. 187. The close analogy between the two states of mind is also drawn by Parker, J. in the recent case *James & Son, Ltd.* v. *Smee* [1954] 3 All E.R., at p. 278, where the learned judge said: "Knowledge . . . includes the state of mind of a man who shuts his eyes to the obvious or allows his servant to do something in the circumstances where a contravention is likely not caring whether a contravention takes place or not."

accused was guilty of a reckless disregard of the probabilities of the case, or a wilful closing of his eyes." It so happens that in that case Lord Wright went on to express the view that negligence is sufficient to establish liability under section 35, and it will be necessary to consider that opinion later in the light of the other authorities on the topic. But the passage quoted remains a strangely isolated instance where the two states of mind were brought into harmony.

Judges are not alone in failing to grasp the synonymous nature of connivance and recklessness. Thus, successive editions of Kenny's *Outlines of Criminal Law*[1] have contained the statement, in relation to guilty knowledge in charges of receiving, that "negligence, or even recklessness, in not realising their having been stolen will not create guilt: he must have shut his eyes wilfully to facts which ordinary men would realise it clearly". The concept involved in the latter part of this statement is, of course, connivance which, as Lord Wright recognised, is indistinguishable from recklessness. Insomuch as the authorities clearly indicate that connivance is a culpable state of mind in statutory offences involving guilty knowledge, it is difficult to understand why recklessness is excluded in cases of receiving stolen goods.

Yet such was the ruling of the Court of Criminal Appeal in *R.* v. *Havard*,[2] which case is cited by Kenny as authority for the proposition quoted above. Delivering the short judgment of the court, consisting of Darling J., Bray, J., and himself, Ridley, J., declared:[3] "it is not sufficient to say that if a man is reckless and does not care he is just as guilty as if he received the property, knowing at the time that there was something wrong with it." "The proper direction," according to the court "is that the jury must take into consideration all the circumstances in which the goods were received, and must say if the appellant, at the time when he received the goods, knew that they had been stolen". In assessing the correctness of this ruling it is necessary to distinguish carefully between the method of proof, whereby guilty knowledge is usually deduced from the surrounding circumstances, and the matter to be proved which, it will be observed, the court said is actual knowledge that the goods had been stolen. According to the decision in *R.* v. *Havard*, belief that the goods may or may not have been stolen coupled with indifference as to the true

[1] See 15th ed. p. 292, n. 4, and 16th edition by Turner, p. 291, n. 7.

[2] (1914) 11 Cr. App. R. 2.

[3] *Ibid.*, at p. 3.

position is not enough. But is this not the interpretation to be placed upon the earlier direction in *R.* v. *White*,[1] not apparently cited in *Havard*, in which Bramwell B. had said to the jury it is sufficient "if you think the circumstances were such, accompanying the transaction, as to make the prisoner believe that it had been stolen"? The headnote to that case, it is suggested, accurately embodies the true principle which ordains that belief without actual knowledge is sufficient to establish guilt, provided, of course, that the accused refuses to pay heed to that belief and proceeds to receive the stolen goods. Such was the interpretation placed on *R.* v. *White* by Kenny, who did so in terms appropriate to connivance. Whether the state of mind is described as connivance or recklessness, it is submitted that this principle should be adopted in charges of receiving, thus bringing such cases into line with the other authorities examined above.[2]

Negligence

Negligence, in the sense of blameful inadvertence, occupies a major rôle in the field of tortious liability where the principal accent is on compensation. Not unexpectedly, when consideration is given to the rôle of negligence in criminal law the immediate reaction is usually one of violent antipathy, the view being widely held that liability arising out of negligence is incompatible with the deterrent nature of criminal punishment.[3]

Can negligence properly be designated as Mens Rea?

Furthermore, views continue to differ as to whether inadvertence can properly be designated a form of *mens rea*. Where the phrase *mens rea* is used to denote a state of mind it is possible to argue that the only state of mind which is pertinent is the

[1] (1859) 1 F. & F. 665.

[2] It is worth noting that Mr. Turner (see 16th ed. p. 287) adopts the suggestion made by Kenny that in obtaining by false pretences recklessness is sufficient to establish knowledge of the falsity of the pretence. On the other hand, Glanville Williams, *Criminal Law*, considers that the two concepts of connivance and recklessness are distinguishable, the former being merely "a special case of recklessness" (p. 59). According to the learned author (p. 127), before the doctrine of connivance, i.e., wilful blindness, applies, there must be realisation that the fact in question is probable, whereas for recklessness it is sufficient to prove realisation that the fact in question is possible, Cf. p. 53. This, it is suggested, places the standard of recklessness at too low a level.

[3] See Jerome Hall, *Principles of Criminal Law*, pp. 215–225, 235–239, 244–246, Turner, *Modern Approach to Criminal Law*, pp. 205–211, and Williams, *Criminal Law*, pp. 88, 99.

positive form known as advertence, i.e., realisation or foresight of consequences, in which event the ambit of *mens rea* is restricted to intention and subjective recklessness. Conversely. it is possible to argue that although inadvertence involves the negative form of absence of realisation or foresight of consequences, it too can justifiably be termed a state of mind[1] and therefore, as forming, in certain conditions, part of the doctrine of *mens rea.* So far as the particular field of criminal liability to be discussed in the ensuing section is concerned, the present writer is of the opinion that negligence may properly be designated as *mens rea.*

To those who would deny the validity of this conclusion it may come as a surprise to realise that there exists a wide range of judicial dicta in which the view is expressed that if a statutory offence is based upon proof of knowledge such crimes can be committed negligently, a conclusion denied by Devlin, J., in *Roper* v. *Taylor's Central Garages.*[2] Speaking of the states of mind relevant in statutory offences involving guilty knowledge, Devlin, J., stressed the vast distinction between connivance, or, as he described it, knowledge of the second degree, and the state of mind encompassed by the words "ought to have known" which he defined as "neglecting to make such inquiries as a reasonable and prudent person would make". According to Devlin, J., "the case of shutting the eyes is actual knowledge in the eyes of the law, the case of merely neglecting to make inquiries is not knowledge at all—it comes within the legal conception of constructive knowledge a conception which, generally speaking, has no place in the criminal law."[3]

[1] For the doubts which this question engenders among learned writers, see, e.g., Salmond's *Jurisprudence* (10th ed.) pp. 401–403, in which the conflicting views of Sir John Salmond (negligence is a state of mind) and Sir Frederick Pollock (negligence is a type of conduct) are considered and an attempt made at reconciling the two views. Amongst writers on criminal law see Turner, *Mod. App. Crim. Law*, p. 208, who recognises negligence as a state of mind but does not consider it as sufficient to amount to *mens rea* in common law crimes; Hall, *General Principles of Criminal Law*, p. 216, who considers it is essential to take account of "state of mind" in describing negligence since negligence means that the conduct in question was not intentional or reckless; and Williams, *Criminal Law*, pp. 88, 122 (cf. p. 29) who states that inadvertent negligence is not a form of *mens rea* because it is not by definition a state of mind.

[2] [1951] 2 T.L.R. at p. 289, and repeated by the same learned judge in *Morris* v. *Williams* (1952) 50 Local Govt. Reports, 308 at p. 313.

[3] *Loc cit.* Whilst making a similar classification of the degrees of knowledge, Slade, J. in *Morris* v. *Williams* (1952) 50 Local Govt. Reports, 308, 312 refrained from expressing an opinion as to "whether it is sufficient to constitute 'permitting' for the purpose of contravention of statutes involving punishment for that offence merely that one has failed negligently but honestly to take some steps which, if taken, would have brought to one's knowledge what the true situation was".

However, evidence is available as early as 1859 that negligence might be deemed sufficient in a statutory offence dependent on proof of knowledge of the forbidden act or default. Thus, in *Hearne* v. *Garton*,[1] the defendants, acting as forwarding agents, innocently sent for carriage by rail a case containing oil of vitriol. They were unaware of its true contents and had no reason to doubt the accuracy of the description "some stocks, seeds and a few corks", which had been affixed to the case by the original sender. Importing the word "knowingly" into the offence charged, a strong court, consisting of Lord Campbell, C.J., Wightman, Erle and Crompton, JJ., expressed great satisfaction with the justices' finding of acquittal. Referring to the absence of all proof of guilty knowledge, Lord Campbell, C.J., added, significantly, that the defendants "have proved that there was no negligence on their parts, for they used all due diligence by making inquiries to ascertain the contents of the packages".[2] This, at least, suggests that had the defendants been guilty of negligence the view of the court might well have been different and a direction given to the magistrates to convict.

A few years later, in *Croasdill* v. *Ratcliffe*,[3] the court was concerned with section 72 of the Highways Act, 1835, which makes it an offence, *interalia*, for any person to suffer filth or other noxious substances to flow into the highway. Interpreting this offence, and comparing it with the offence (under the same section) of wilfully obstructing the highway, Crompton, J., declared: "The section applies to cases of persons who are guilty of negligence in suffering . . . filth to run on to the highway." With this opinion, Wightman, J., agreed. Equally categorical was the opinion of Cockburn, C.J., in *Bosley* v. *Davies*[4] when he declared, in the course of argument, "A man may be said to 'suffer' a thing to be done if it is done through his negligence."[5] Notwithstanding this opinion, however, it must be pointed out that the short judgment of the court contains no reference to negligence, the case being returned to the justices with an intimation that actual knowledge or connivance was necessary. In adding that "constructive knowledge will supply the place of actual knowledge",[5] it is fairly obvious that the court was using constructive knowledge as descriptive of

[1] (1859) 28 L.J.M.C. 216. The offence involved was under 5 & 6 Will. 4, c. 107, s. 168.

[2] *Ibid.*, at p. 219.

[3] (1862) 4 L.T. (N.S.) 834.

[4] (1875) L.R. 1 Q.B. 84.

[5] *Ibid.*, at p. 87.

connivance, but we shall see, in later cases, that the expression has been used occasionally to cover negligence.

Uncertainty as to the boundaries between connivance and negligence

Indications are that judges of the late nineteenth century were far from clear as to the exact boundaries of connivance and negligence. This confusion becomes apparent on reading the case of *Crabtree* v. *Hole*[1] in which the familiar offence of suffering gaming was once more involved. Referring to section 17 of the Licensing Act, 1872, Cockburn, C.J., said:[2] "The duty imposed by the enactment is to take reasonable care that gaming is not suffered on the licensed premises" and earlier the same judge epitomised the position by saying that the licensee "must show reasonable diligence". This definition of the licensee's duty conforms with Cockburn, C.J.'s previous statement in *Bosley* v. *Davies* that a publican "suffers" gaming if it is done through his negligence. The other member of the court, Lush, J., agreed with the Chief Justice, adding that he could see no distinction between the case before him and *Redgate* v. *Haynes*,[3] in which Lush, J., had participated with Blackburn, J. Yet, in that earlier case it had been held that actual knowledge or connivance—in the sense of purposely abstaining from ascertaining whether gaming was going on or not—was necessary. This blurring of the distinction between the two degrees of knowledge is not very helpful, but it does not prevent the growing feeling that a licensee is equally liable for suffering gaming if his conduct amounts to either connivance or negligence. In subsequent cases, like *Somerset* v. *Hart*[4] and *Bond* v. *Evans*,[5] there is a reversion to the "actual knowledge or connivance" test, but it is noticeable that Manisty, J., in *Bond* v. *Evans* refers,[6] without dissent, to the observation of Cockburn, C.J., in *Bosley* v. *Davies*.[7]

An analogous offence to suffering gaming in the sense that *mens rea*, in the form of "allowing", is necessary is that already noted in the Highways Act, 1835, s. 35 of which provides that any surveyor who allows a heap of stones to remain on the highway at night to the danger of passers-by, shall be guilty of an offence. The question whether negligence is sufficient to establish liability for this offence arose in *Hardcastle* v. *Bielby*,[8] in which it appeared that the stone had been laid on the roadway by a carter acting

[1] (1879) 43 J.P. 799.
[2] *Loc cit.*
[3] (1876) L.R. 1 Q.B. 89.
[4] (1884) 12 Q.B.D. 360.
[5] (1888) 21 Q.B.D. 249.
[6] *Ibid.*, at p. 253.
[7] *Ante*, p. 207.
[8] [1892] 1 Q.B. 709.

under the orders of a person to whom the accused had given general directions as to repairing the road. The surveyor himself knew nothing about the heap of stones. Referring to the word "allows", Collins, J. said it "seems to admit the consideration whether or not the offence can be committed where negligence on the part of the surveyor has been proved, although he may not have been proved to have any personal knowledge that the acts which have caused the injury have taken place".[1] Tantalisingly, the learned judge left the matter there, it being unnecessary, he said, to actually decide the question as there was no evidence of negligence on the part of the surveyor. Had Collins, J., been forced to give his answer it is likely that he would have referred to the wording of section 35 which, in laying down the conditions of liability, adds ". . . all due and reasonable precautions not having been taken by the said surveyor to guard against the same".

Statutory provisions for negligence as a culpable degree of knowledge

This clause, strongly indicative that the offence can be committed negligently, is one of the earliest examples of a proviso—sometimes in a positive, sometimes in a negative, form—which has occasionally been inserted in the definition of statutory offences based on the epithets "knowingly", "permitting" and "suffering".[2] To cite two examples, in the Protection of Animals Act, 1911, s. 1 (2), it is provided that "an owner shall be deemed to have permitted cruelty within the meaning of this Act if he shall have failed to exercise reasonable care and supervision in respect of the protection of the animal. . . ." Again, in the recent Rivers (Prevention of Pollution) Act, 1951, which makes it an offence to "knowingly permit to enter a stream any poisonous or polluting matter", absence of negligence exonerates a defendant, for section 2 (3) (*b*) provides that it shall be a good defence to prove that "all reasonably practicable steps are taken to prevent the effluent being unnecessarily poisonous etc". More frequently, a similar

[1] *Ibid.*, at p. 712.

[2] See, e.g., Food and Drugs Act, 1950 (14 Geo. 6, c. 35), s. 8 (2), and the Agriculture (Misc. Provisions) Act, 1954 (2 & 3 Eliz. 2, c. 39), s. 9 (5). Comparison may be made with similar provisions in offences of absolute liability, e.g. Merchandise Marks Act, 1887 (50 & 51 Vict. c. 28), s. 2 (2) (*a*); Fertilisers and Feeding Stuffs Act, 1926 (16 & 17 Geo. 5, c. 45), s. 7 (1); Factories Act, 1937 (1 Edw. 8 & 1 Geo. 6), s. 130 (2); Vehicles (Excise) Act, 1949 (12, 13 & 14 Geo. 6, c. 89), s. 15 (3) and s. 19 (2); Food and Drugs Act, 1950 (14 Geo. 6, c. 35), s. 26 (3) (*a*) & (*b*); Diseases of Animals Act, 1950 (14 Geo. 6, c. 36), s. 78 (2) and s. 83.

proviso is inserted as an escape route for an employer or principal who is sought to be made vicariously liable for an offence of absolute prohibition,[1] but as this is not germane to the present discussion, it is not proposed to pursue the analogy further at the moment. These specific instances, in which the legislature has made express provision for negligence as a degree of culpability certainly lend colour to the view, propounded by Cockburn, C.J., that in statutory offences involving knowledge a person may be liable if the prosecution succeed in proving negligence.

It will have been noticed that as frequently as not the legislature and the courts appear to be concerned with negligence as a state of conduct, and it may be suggested that this bears no relation to negligence as a state of mind, in the sense of inadvertence. Certainly it is difficult to trace any consistency in the manner in which the legislature, in creating new offences, and the judges, in interpreting such offences, sometimes rely on negligence as a state of mind and sometimes as a state of conduct. The correct approach, it is suggested, is this. Where the offence makes no reference to any requirement of knowledge but seeks to punish carelessness or negligence,[2] then it is with negligent conduct alone that the court is concerned. Where, however, the offence is based on words like "permitting", "suffering", "allowing" or "causing", which indicate the necessity for guilty knowledge, the courts are prepared to attribute such knowledge to the accused if his conduct, in all the circumstances, indicates that he ought to have known. The difference between connivance and negligence in this respect is that where negligence is accepted as culpable then the court recognises a lower standard of conduct as manifesting the requisite guilty knowledge.

Additional evidence of the acceptance of inadvertence as suffi-

[1] Examples are to be found in: Truck Amdt. Act, 1887 (50 & 51 Vict. c. 18), s. 12; Betting and Loans (Infants) Act, 1892 (55 & 56 Vict. c. 4), s. 1 (2); Shops Act, 1912 (2 & 3 Geo. 5, c. 3), s. 4 (2) and (3); Factories Act, 1901 (1 Edw. 7, c. 22), ss. 140, 141; Sale of Food (Weights and Measures) Act, 1926 (16 & 17 Geo. 5, c. 63), s. 12 (5); Food and Drugs Act, 1938 (1 & 2 Geo. 6, c. 56), s. 83 (1), and the Licensing Act, 1953 (1 & 2 Eliz. 2, c. 46), s. 126 (3) (*a*).

[2] A recent example where negligence is stated as the basis of criminal liability, but not in relation to an offence involving knowledge, is in the Post Office Act, 1953 (1 & 2 Eliz. 2, c. 36) s. 59 (*c*), which is concerned with G.P.O. employees who are "guilty of carelessness, or negligence whereby the safety of postal packets are endangered". S. 59 (*f*) uses a different formula and seeks to punish any G.P.O. employee who "does not use due care and diligence safely to convey a mail bag or postal packet at the due rate of speed". The last condition is intriguing.

cient is forthcoming in the person of Mathew, J., who, in *Somerset* v. *Wade*,[1] summed-up the position by saying,[2] "It comes to this, that a licensed person cannot be convicted of suffering gaming in the absence of knowledge, or connivance, or carelessness on his part." Effect to this dogma was given by Grantham and Collins, JJ., in *Worth* v. *Brown*,[3] a case of permitting drunkenness on licensed premises,[4] in which the police had found a man sitting on a seat asleep, in full sight of the bar, very drunk. The barmaid, who was in charge at the time said that she had no knowledge that a drunken person was on the premises, but the court being of opinion that she must have been aware of the man's condition, remitted the case with direction to convict.

Divergence of views as to negligence in offences based on "causing"

So far we have been concerned with offences dealing with the "suffering", "allowing" or "permitting" of criminal acts. Another epithet which has been considered in this study and found to have been consistently interpreted as requiring proof of guilty knowledge is the word "causing",[5] and we proceed next to compare the views expressed in *R.* v. *Chainey*,[6] and *Moses* v. *Midland Railway*[7] on the application of negligence in offences based on this expression. Although the composition of the court in the two cases, decided within a year of each other, was completely different it is, nonetheless, at first surprising to note the disparity in the respective interpretations adopted. In *R.* v. *Chainey*, it may be recalled,[8] a father was charged with causing the unlawful carnal knowledge of his daughter under 16, contrary to the Children Act, 1908, s. 17,[9] which enacts that any person, having custody of a girl under age, who knowingly allows her to consort with any prostitute shall be deemed to have caused the unlawful carnal knowledge. Quashing the conviction, which was based on the

[1] [1894] 1 Q.B. 574. [2] *Ibid.*, at p. 576.

[3] (1896) 40 Sol. Jo. 515. Cf. *Greenwood* v. *Backhouse* (1902) 66 J.P. 519, in which a "suspicious amount of ignorance" was held not to amount to guilty knowledge in a case of causing cruelty under the Prevention of Cruelty to Animals Act, 1849 (12 & 13 Vict. c. 92).

[4] Licensing Act 1872, s. 17, re-enacted in the Licensing Act, 1953, s. 136 (1).

[5] Reference may be made to *Harrison* v. *Leaper* (1862) 5 L.T. 640; *Small* v. *Warr* (1862) 47 J.P. 20; *Hardcastle* v. *Bielby* [1892] 1 Q.B. 709; *Reynolds* v. *G. H. Austin & Sons, Ltd.* [1951] 2 K.B. 135; *Rushton* v. *Martin* [1952] W.N. 258; and *Lovelace* v. *D.P.P.* [1954] 3 All E.R. 481.

[6] [1914] 1 K.B. 137. [7] (1915) 84 L.J.K.B. 2181. [8] See *ante* p. 148.

[9] Re-enacted in the Children and Young Persons Act, 1933 (23 Geo. 5, c. 12), s. 2.

jury's finding of criminal neglect, Isaacs, C.J., declared that "negligence is not an offence under the enactment in question. The offence is causing or encouraging, and the evidence must at least amount to knowingly allowing. To allow knowingly would seem to include negligence, but negligence does not amount to conscious permission".[1] No discussion of any cases appears to have taken place and it is worth noting that the Chief Justice confined his remarks expressly to the statute under consideration.

An offence of quite a different character was involved in *Moses* v. *Midland Rly.*, a case also previously discussed[2] in which the defendants were charged under the Salmon Fishery Act, 1861, s. 5, with "causing or knowingly permitting any substance to flow into any waters with the result that fish are poisoned or killed". Due to a defect in a tank waggon which was travelling on the defendants' railway, creosote leaked through the permanent way into a river containing salmon killing some of the fish. The court dismissed the appeal against acquittal on the ground that the creosote had escaped without the knowledge of the railway company or their servants, and that no exercise of reasonable care on their part could have prevented it. The underlying principle, according to Avory, J., was that "a person cannot be said to cause liquid to flow when he is ignorant that it is flowing and could not by the exercise of reasonable care have prevented it".[3] From this, may it not fairly be deduced that had the company not taken reasonable precautions to discover the escape and thus be in a position to prevent the creosote flowing into the river, they would have been held liable on the grounds of negligence?

How to reconcile these conflicting views on the application of negligence is a difficult task. Limiting the opinions expressed to the respective offences is, of course, one way of disposing of the difficulty. On the other hand, there is no denying the fact that both defendants were charged with criminal offences arising out of the same formula of causing forbidden acts. The true explanation to the wider liability outlined in *Moses* v. *Midland Rly.* it is suggested, lies in the nature of the offence involved which, as Cockburn, C.J., once said of "suffering gaming" is "on the confines between a civil and criminal offence".[4] In the offence of causing the unlawful carnal knowledge of a girl under 16 or, to take another example with which we have been concerned, receiving stolen goods, the

[1] [1914] 1 K.B. at p. 143.
[2] See *ante*, pp. 153–154.
[3] (1915) 84 L.J.K.B. at p. 2184
[4] (1879) 43 J.P. at p. 799.

mens rea or guilty knowledge is more akin to the old *mala conscientia* or evil design, and carries with it a more severe punishment than in the case of offences like permitting drunkenness, suffering gaming, or knowingly permitting pollution of rivers which do not embody the same degree of moral blameworthiness. Hence, whereas in the case of the former, actual knowledge or connivance is required, in offences bent on maintaining a certain standard of behaviour for the protection of the public, negligence is more readily accepted.

"Ought to have known"

Another compendious expression sometimes used to describe negligence is the phrase "ought to have known" which, probably gleaned from the realm of tortious negligence, appears to have come to the fore during the last twenty years.[1] It was adopted by Avory, J., in *Goldsmith* v. *Deakin*[2] when considering the offence of permitting a motor-vehicle to be used as an express carriage without the requisite licence. In a passage which was subsequently cited with approval by Lord Hewart, C.J., in *Newell* v. *Cross and Cook*[3] and again in *Evans* v. *Dell*,[4] Avory, J. stated:[5]

[1] Cf. its use in *Lee* v. *Taylor and Gill* (1912) 77 J.P. 66 at p. 69 (*ante* p. 199) in which Lord Alverstone, C.J., appears to equate the phrase with connivance.

[2] (1934) 150 L.T. Rep. 157. Cf. *Clydebank Co-op. Society* v. *Binnie* [1937] J. C. 17 (Sc.).

[3] (1936) 53 T.L.R. 489, at p. 491.

[4] [1937] 1 All E.R. at p. 352. Lord Hewart's interpretation of the judgment in *Goldsmith* v. *Deakin* was adverted to by Slade, J., a member of the Divisional Court in *Morris* v. *Williams* (1952) 50 Local Govt. Reports, 308 at p. 312. Lord Hewart had said that "in circumstances in which the owner of a vehicle is put upon inquiry, if he refrains from making the inquiry and an offence is committed, the fair inference may be that he permitted the offence to be committed". Explaining what he thought Lord Hewart had in mind when he said "in circumstances in which the owner is put on inquiry" the learned Judge referred to what Lord Hewart had said earlier in his judgment, viz., "it is perhaps fair that the matter shall be decided on the footing that wrapped up in the contention that the respondent permitted the coach to be used as a stage carriage is the contention that he ought to have known and closed his eyes." It will be seen (*supra*) that no such qualification was introduced by Avory, J. in his judgment. Having posed the problem of connivance and negligence it is disappointing that Slade, J., felt it "unnecessary to decide whether Lord Hewart, C. J. had in mind in giving that result of the decision in *Goldsmith* v. *Deakin* the case, not of wilful abstention from ascertaining the facts, but of pure inadvertence or negligent omission". It is perhaps significant that in *Churchill* v. *Norris* (1938) 158 L.T. 255 (discussed *ante* p. 116, n. 1.) on a charge of permitting a vehicle to be on the highway carrying an excess load, Lord Hewart C.J. based his decision on connivance, whereas Humphreys, J., rested his judgment on carelessness, i.e., negligence.

[5] 150 L.T. Rep. at p. 158. Referring to this passage, Glanville Williams, *Criminal Law*, p. 130, n. 15, accepts the possibility that it might be understood as meaning that mere negligence in not finding out the proposed use of the vehicle is enough, but submits that this would be too stringent a rule. The learned author adds that "what is or should be required is not inadvertent negligence but a conscious adversion to the risk".

". . . if a person hires out a vehicle in circumstances which he ought to know that it probably will be or may be used as a stage carriage, and puts his servant in charge of that vehicle to use it in any way in which the hirer may choose to direct the servant to use it, then he is, within the meaning of this statute, permitting it to be used . . . without the appropriate licence." Although Avory, J. was content to rest liability, at its minimum, on negligence it is evident that Lawrence, J., the other member of the court, had different ideas, his view being that, in the absence of actual knowledge, it was necessary to establish recklessness. How otherwise is the passage to be explained in which Lawrence, J., said:[1] "although the respondent may not have known affirmatively the way in which the vehicle was being used, if in fact he allowed it to be used and did not care whether it was used in contravention of the statute or not, he did, in my view, permit the use."?

A further example of the reliance on negligence as involving liability for the same offence is afforded by the recent case of *Browning* v. *J. W. H. Watson Ltd.*,[2] in which two persons in the employ of the Ministry of Transport insinuated themselves among the members of a private club and travelled on the respondent's coach to and from a football match. Holding the coach proprietor liable, Lord Goddard C.J., said:[3] "although [the respondent] did not know that persons who were not members of the club got in the coach, that was because he did not inquire or take any precaution to see that only members were admitted. . . . Of course, this was not a wilful violation, but it is clear that the respondent should have taken some precaution."

With the natural antipathy which exists against introducing negligence into criminal liability, it is only to be expected that now and again certain of the more conventionally minded judges and writers affirm the principle that intention or recklessness, actual knowledge or connivance, present the very limits of

[1] 150 L.T. Rep., at p. 159.

[2] [1953] 2 All E.R. 775; [1953] 1 W.L.R. 1172. Discussed *ante* pp. 109–110.

[3] *Ibid.*, p. 778. Owing to the imprecise language used it is possible to argue that what the court had in mind was connivance and not negligence. But similar language used in cases of aiding and abetting, *viz.*, *Carter* v. *Mace* [1949] 2 All E.R. 714 and *Davies* v. *Brodie* [1954] 3 All E.R. 283 (see *ante*, p. 190, n. 4), points to the reliance on negligence as sufficient to constitute liability. See, too, Slade, J. in *James* v. *Smee* [1954] 3 All E.R. at p. 280. For an example of a conviction based on "failure to do what a prudent man would have done under the circumstances to satisfy himself" see (1954) 69 *Journal of Criminal Law*, pp. 3–4, in which the offence was the same as that involved in *Harding* v. *Price* [1948] 1 K.B. 695 (*ante* p. 78).

criminal responsibility. It is, of course, true that the phrase "ought to know" is capable of different shades of meaning and it may be questioned whether Avory, J., had in mind conduct amounting to mere negligence. In cases subsequent to *Goldsmith* v. *Deakin* which deal with the same offence, Lord Hewart, C.J., is seen repeating the test laid down by Avory, J., but it is noticeable that in *Evans* v. *Dell* Goddard, J., used the phrase "shutting his eyes to the obvious" as bearing the hallmark of liability.[1]

This view, that nothing less than recklessness or connivance will suffice, would appear to have been rejected by Lord Wright in *Houston* v. *Buchanan*.[2] That was a case, it will be recalled, in which the House of Lords were required to consider section 35 (1) of the Road Traffic Act, 1930, which makes it a criminal offence to permit another person to use a motor-vehicle on a road without there being in force a policy of insurance covering third party risks. "In order to prove permission" said Lord Wright "it is not necessary to show actual notice . . . or that the accused was guilty of a reckless disregard of the probabilities of the case, or a wilful closing of the eyes". Instead, "the practical way of stating the crucial question" was to ask the question ". . . did the defendant know or ought he to have known that the van was being or was likely to be used by his brother for his own private purposes?".[3] If the answer is in the affirmative, a case of permission is made out. The same test was applied by Lord Russell of Killowen,[4] and, it is submitted, is manifestly a test based on negligence.[5]

Conclusion

It is in the light of the considerable body of judicial dicta discussed above that the soundness of Devlin, J.'s analysis in *Roper* v. *Taylor's Central Garages* may be judged. Now that an exhaustive study has been carried out it becomes clear that his exclusion of negligence from this particular expanse of criminal liability, though deriving sporadic support, is in direct conflict with the majority of dicta dealing with offences of the very kind referred to in *Roper*, in which negligence has been stated to be a culpable state of mind. However, this rule, insofar as it may be said to exist, does

[1] [1937] 1 All E.R. at p. 354.

[2] [1940] 2 All E.R. 179. [3] *Ibid.*, at p. 187. [4] *Ibid.*, at p. 185.

[5] Having regard to his views on the test propounded by Avory, J. in *Goldsmith* v. *Deakin* (see note 4, p. 213) it is not surprising to note that Glanville Williams, *Criminal Law* p. 41, refuses to accept Lord Wright's dictum as correctly stating the present position in relation to negligence in statutory offences.

not extend to all statutory crimes in which *mens rea* is required. The sufficiency of negligence as *mens rea* would appear to be limited to that special class of offences, based on "permitting", "suffering" and other similar expressions, in which the degree of moral blameworthiness is of a lesser character than that involved in offences such as receiving goods knowing them to be stolen, or fraudulent crimes such as forgery and embezzlement, whose qualities are more emphatically criminal. So far as actual knowledge and connivance are concerned, on the other hand, it is submitted that no such dividing line exists, all statutory offences involving guilty knowledge or fraud being treated alike in this respect.

As shown earlier in this chapter it has long been a common expedient when creating a new statutory offence for the legislature to exonerate a defendant who shows that he has taken all reasonably practicable steps to prevent the consequences prohibited by statute. It seems a natural step for the legislature to adopt a form of definition wherein criminal liability is imposed only on express proof of negligence. Although, as yet, of infrequent occurrence there seems every likelihood that, with the rising volume of legislation directed towards establishing ordained standards of social and economic behaviour, this particular form of blameworthy conduct will appear increasingly as the basis of culpability. It is for precisely the same reason that the courts have expressed their readiness to recognise negligence as a blameworthy state of mind in statutory offences of the type described in this chapter. There are not lacking writers who condemn the modern legislative and judicial approach on the ground that the punishment of inadvertent adults has no proper place in criminal liability.[1] Certainly in common law crimes negligence has no part to play, but with the present wide range of statutory crimes the judges are faced with two forms of liability—on the one hand, knowledge or connivance and, on the other hand, absolute prohibition. Should Parliament and the courts be left to choose between these two exclusive forms of liability? As another alternative to absolute liability, it is submitted, there exists with justification an intermediate theory of liability based upon blameful inadvertence.[2]

[1] See, e.g., Jerome Hall, *General Principles of Criminal Law*, pp. 215–235, and the same writer in (1954) 33 *Nebraska L.R.* 3, 6, in which he refers with apparent approval to Devlin, J.'s analysis in *Roper's Case*.

[2] The present writer's views on the subject are elaborated *post*, p. 256 *et seq.*

X

VICARIOUS LIABILITY IN STATUTORY OFFENCES

NECESSARY DOCTRINE FOR THE ENFORCEMENT OF MODERN LEGISLATION

THE application of the doctrine of vicarious liability in criminal law may be described as actuated by necessity rather than desirability. Criminal responsibility is generally regarded as being essentially personal in character, and it is with considerable diffidence that the principle is accepted whereby a man may be found guilty and punished for an offence which is actually committed by another. Doubts engendered as to the wisdom of such a principle in criminal law are increased when it is realised that such guilt may be incurred notwithstanding the fact that the accused may have no knowledge that the offence was being committed, or may even have done his best to prevent it. Indeed the sole justification for the application of such a doctrine in criminal law would appear to be public policy and, whereas in 1916 the learned author of the leading work on vicarious liability[1] was led

[1] Baty, *Vicarious Liability*, p. 218, in which the learned author gives the following reasons for his dislike of the doctrine: (1) to make an employer an insurer of his servant's conduct may be to throw on him an exceedingly heavy liability upon him, beyond what Parliament would have intended; (2) although the results of summary process are not very serious, they involve in the minds of ignorant people a certain amount of discredit; (3) the employer is always liable to be arrested on a warrant, and (4) he may be forced to attend from a remote part of the country. With (2) above, may be compared the view of Wills, J., in *R.* v. *Tolson* (1889) L.R. 23 Q.B.D., 168, 177, who said: "There is nothing that need shock any mind in the payment of a small pecuniary penalty by a person who has unwittingly done something detrimental to the public interest." A similar opinion is expressed by Hanbury, *The Principles of Agency* (1952) p. 211, who considers it is impossible to allow acts which are really anti-social, rather than immoral, to be checked only by the precarious sanction of civil actions. See, too, Sayre, *Criminal Responsibility for the Acts of Another* (1930) 43 *Harv. L.R.* 689; Powell, *The Law of Agency* (1951), 230–234, and Goodhart, *English Law and the Moral Law*, p. 86. Glanville Williams, *Criminal Law*, pp. 275–289, argues unconvincingly in favour of confining vicarious responsibility to public licensees and concludes with the view that "if criminal law is to be tinted with the notion of justice it would seem to be going too far to punish the master for his failure to prevent the servant from committing unauthorised crimes". The present writer dislikes the doctrine equally intensely but

to exclaim that "the law is in a state which it is not too much to call discreditable to English Jurisprudence, vicarious criminal liability is imposed haphazard and with an arbitrary hand", the present view, recently expressed in the case of *Gardner* v. *Akeroyd*[1] by Lord Goddard, C.J., is that vicarious liability "is a necessary doctrine for the proper enforcement of much modern legislation, but it is not one to be extended". Another eminent judge has stated much the same point of view in *Reynolds* v. *G. H. Austin & Co. Ltd.*[2] where, in considering the reason why a man may be made responsible for the acts of his servants or even for defects in his business arrangements, Devlin, J., explained that it is "because it can fairly be said that by such sanctions citizens are induced to keep themselves and their organisations up to the mark". "Although in one sense" he continued, "the citizen is being punished for the sins of others, it can be said that if he had been more alert to see that the law was observed the sin might not have been committed."[3]

Present tendency to restrict the extension of vicarious liability

Whilst recognising the force of this reasoning, it must be viewed in conjunction with the modern judicial tendency to keep a tight hold on the use of the principle *respondeat superior* to establish criminal guilt. Thus, in two recent cases, *Ferguson* v. *Weaving*[4] and *Gardner* v. *Akeroyd*,[5] the Divisional Court left no doubt as to their opinion that to include cases of aiding and abetting and attempts, respectively, within the operation of this maxim would be an

recognises that so long as the criminal law is used as a means to securing the legislative standard of correct trading, business and social welfare behaviour, it is legitimate to have recourse to the principle of vicarious responsibility.

[1] [1952] 2 Q.B. 743, at p. 751. [2] [1951] 2 K.B. 135.

[3] *Ibid.*, p. 149. See, too, Pound, *The Spirit of the Common Law*, p. 52, to which reference was made by Devlin, J., in the course of his judgment.

[4] [1951] 1 K.B. 814. See a note on this case by the writer in (1951) 14 *M.L.R.* 334, and cf. *Bennett* v. *Hanks* [1954] *Crim. L.R.* 545. The statutory offence involved in *Ferguson* v. *Weaving*, viz., consuming liquor outside licensed hours, contrary to the Licensing Act, 1921 (11 & 12 Geo. 5, c. 42), s. 4, is now to be found in the Licensing Act, 1953 (1 & 2 Eliz. 2, c. 46), s. 100.

[5] [1952] 2 Q.B. 743. "Were it to be applied in cases of attempt," said Lord Goddard C.J. (at p. 751) "the consequences might be startling and unjust in the highest degree. For, once a servant had done an act amounting to an attempt, his master would be vicariously liable although he had intervened and frustrated the commission of the substantive offence". If the doctrine does not apply to an attempt, concluded Lord Goddard, "still less does it apply to the vague and unsatisfactory offence of doing a preparatory act" (with which the court was in fact concerned). See a note on this case in (1953) 16 *M.L.R.* 236.

unwarrantable extension of the doctrine of vicarious liability in criminal law. What is perhaps insufficiently recognised is the extent to which the legislature has mitigated the hardships so frequently associated with this doctrine, and it will be necessary later to examine the scope of what has become known as "third-party procedure", whereby in certain statutory offences a defendant may escape liability altogether on proving that the offence was in fact committed through the act or default of a third person, the defendant himself having exercised due care. This type of clause is to be found in a wide range of statutes dealing with public welfare offences and, manifesting as it does the legislature's concern not to punish a person who is morally innocent, it is in striking contrast with some of the judicial protagonists during the early part of the last century to whom the maxim *qui facit per alium facit per se* was an all too convenient formula with which to impose criminal liability upon an innocent employer or principal.

Uncertainty as to the exact limits of the doctrine

Hitherto, in this study of statutory offences only infrequent reference has been made to crimes of absolute liability. It is not the intention now to depart from this mode of treatment but insofar as there have been, from time to time, indications on the part of some judges that the doctrine of vicarious liability is confined to such offences, which view the cases show to be palpably inaccurate, it will be necessary to treat occasionally of this field of strict liability. Furthermore, it is not proposed to discuss the application of vicarious liability in relation to public nuisance[1] or criminal libel,[2] both of which constitute well established excep-

[1] Some of the cases in which an employer has been held liable for a public nuisance committed by a servant, include *R.* v. *Stephens* L.R. 1 Q.B. 702, and *R.* v. *Medley* 6 C. & P. 292. For an explanation of this exception see *Kenny* (16th. ed.) p. 34. Where, however, the prosecution is brought in respect of a statutory nuisance, the terms of the statute must be examined to see whether the doctrine of vicarious liability applies. See *Chisholm* v. *Doulton* (1889) 22 Q.B.D. 736 and cf. *Armitage Ltd.* v. *Nicholson* (1913) 108 L.T. 993; *Barnes* v. *Akroyd* (1872) L.R. 7 Q.B. 474.

[2] At common law the proprietor of a newspaper was liable criminally for libels published by his employees in conducting his newspaper even though he had not authorised their publication. See *R.* v. *Almon* (1770) 5 Burr. 2686; *R.* v. *Walter* (1799) 2 Esp. 21; and *R.* v. *Gutch* (1829) Moo. & Mal. 483. However, since the Libel Act, 1843 (6 & 7 Vict. c. 96), s. 7, a newspaper proprietor may avail himself of the defence that the libel was published without his authority and without lack of care or caution on his part. In the leading case of *R.* v. *Holbrook* (1878) 4 Q.B.D. 60, at p. 66, Mellor, J. said that the provisions of section 7 are not confined to newspapers but apply generally.

tions to the general rule that in common law offences[1] a master is not criminally responsible for an offence committed by his servant unless he has either expressly authorised or aided and abetted such an offence.

Consideration of this problem in connection with offences created by Act of Parliament appears to have first engaged the attention of the courts in 1814, and examination of the cases in the succeeding hundred and forty odd years shows the uncertainty with which the different judges have endeavoured to explain the underlying basis of vicarious liability. Reliance has sometimes been placed on the tort formula of "acts done within the course of employment" or, in the case of principal and agent, on the closely analogous test of "acts done within the scope of authority". Equally prominent is the "delegation of authority" principle which has come to the fore in the present century. What is unfortunate is the failure to accept and recognise a single all-embracing basis of liability which, it is considered, is readily available in the delegation principle, but this is to anticipate examination of the development of the general doctrine of vicarious liability. In carrying out this examination it is proposed to use the alternative tests as a natural division of the subject, combining the two formulae "acting within the course of employment" and "acting within the scope of authority" since it is clear from the earliest treatment of vicarious liability that no distinction was drawn between the relationship of master and servant and that of principal and agent.

Liability based on acts done "within the course of employment" or "within the scope of authority"

In the earliest case, *R.* v. *Dixon*[2] in 1814, the doctrine of vicarious liability appears to have been applied unconsciously, for no statement of principle is to be found in the judgments. A baker in that case was convicted of supplying bread containing alum, which had

[1] As long ago as 1730, in *R.* v. *Huggins* 2 Ld. Raym, 1574, the common law rule was laid down by Raymond C.J., in these terms: "It is a point not to be disputed but that in criminal cases the principal is not answerable for the act of his deputy, as he is in civil cases; they must each answer for their own acts, and stand or fall by their own behaviour."

[2] (1814) 3 M. & S. 11. Cf. *Cove* v. *James* (1871) L.R. 7 Q.B. 135 in which it was held that if a journeyman knowingly uses any unrecognised ingredients in making bread (see 6 & 7 Wm. 4, c. 37, s. 8) his master, though innocent, was liable to be convicted for the guilty act of the journeyman, his servant.

been mixed with the loaves by a foreman who stated that his employer knew nothing of what had happened. This version of the facts was severely shaken in cross-examination and, in its suggestion that the employer was an active participator, the case is, to this extent, unsatisfactory. The germs of vicarious liability are, however, to be found in Bayley, J.'s words that "if a person employed a servant to use alum, or any other ingredient, the unrestrained use of which was noxious, and did not restrain him in the use of it, such person would be answerable if the servant used it to excess, because he did not apply the proper precaution".[1] Lord Ellenborough, C.J., on the other hand, seemed to decide the case on the grounds of personal liability saying: "He who deals with a perilous article must be wary how he deals [with it], otherwise, if he observe not proper caution, he will be responsible."[1]

Unauthorised acts of a servant

Ten years later, in *R.* v. *Marsh*,[2] we find the principle of vicarious liability enunciated by Littledale, J., in these words:[3] "A master in some cases is answerable criminally for the act of his servant, when the act is done by the servant for the benefit of the master and in the course of his employment." The defendant in that case, charged with having game in his possession as a common carrier, pleaded his ignorance of the contents of the particular parcel. Abbott, C.J., refused to accept this plea, but went on to declare that "it might be a good defence to show that [the parcel] was put into the waggon by the servant for his own benefit, and contrary to the orders of, and in fraud of, his master".[4] Bayley, J., expressed the position in similar terms. The innovation of applying the principle *respondeat superior* for the first time in a criminal case is revealed in the restrictive conditions which were imposed on the general test whether the servant was acting in the

[1] *Ibid.*, p. 14.

[2] (1824) 2 B. & C. 717. Cf. *Harrison* v. *Leaper* (1862) 5 L.T. 640.

[3] *Ibid.*, p. 723. It is significant that Littledale, J., to illustrate this rule, referred to the position existing in criminal libel, which has long been recognised as an exception to the rule relating to common-law offences.

[4] *Ibid.*, p. 721. Earlier in his judgment, Abbott C.J., had said of the plea that "knowingly" was an ingredient in the definition of the offence: "If it were necessary to aver that the defendant had actual knowledge it would cast on the prosecutor a burden of proof which could not easily be satisfied, particularly as the carriers . . . cannot have any actual knowledge of that which may be done by their servants. . . ." As we shall see later, subsequent cases indicate acceptance of the principle that the knowledge of a servant may be deemed to be that of his master.

course of his employment. These conditions played a less prominent rôle in *R.* v. *Siddon*,[1] where a trader was charged with harbouring smuggled goods which his servant had concealed in an endeavour to prevent discovery. This offence rendered the defendant liable to a penalty only, a fact which led Alexander, L.C.B., to hesitate as to how far the rule that "whatever a servant does in the course of his employment with which he is intrusted, and as a part of it, is the master's act" extended to criminal proceedings.[2] The Lord Chief Baron considered, however, that the rule had to a certain extent been applied in *R.* v. *Dixon*, in which the offence charged was a misdemeanour.

By the time the tort formula was next applied in the *Commissioner of Police* v. *Cartman*[3] the alternative test of delegation of authority had been frequently invoked, but the unwillingness of judges to discard the "course of employment" test is seen in the judgment of Lord Russell of Killowen, C.J., in that case. The respondent, a licensee, had given orders to his servants that no drunken persons were to be served. However, during his absence, his orders were disobeyed and the licensee was charged under the Licensing Act, 1872, s. 13,[4] with selling intoxicating liquor to a drunken person. In the opinion of the learned Chief Justice, a licensee who deputed the actual direct control of his business was liable for such an offence *provided* the acts of the servant were within the scope of his employment.[5] It will be noticed that Lord Russell considered this test to be an essential qualification which must be proved if the licensee was to be held liable for the act of his manager to whom he had delegated control. Treating the formulae "course of employment" and "scope of authority" as interchangeable, the learned judge concluded that "it was intended that the responsibility should be upon the licensee for acts done by an employee within the scope of his authority".[5] R. S. Wright, J., concurred in this statement of the law which also included a repudiation of the view, originally expressed in *R.* v.

[1] (1830) 1 Cr. & J. 220. At the trial, Alexander L.C.B. had told the jury that the defendant was liable for the act of his agent in the conduct of his business.

[2] *Ibid.*, p. 225, Bayley, J., who was also a member of the court in *R.* v. *Dixon* and *R.* v. *Marsh*, stressed the fact that the servant, in concealing the goods, had acted to save his master, thus bringing his act within the ordinary scope of the authority which he had received from his master.

[3] [1896] 1 Q.B. 655, followed recently in *Bennett* v. *Hanks* [1954] *Crim. L.R.* 545.

[4] Re-enacted in the Licensing Act, 1953 (1 & 2 Eliz. 2, c. 46), s. 136 (3).

[5] *Ibid.*, p. 658.

Marsh, that it would be a good defence for the master to show that his servant had acted against his orders. Were it otherwise, said Lord Russell, the object of the section would be entirely defeated.

Confronted with the same problem two years later in *Coppen* v *Moore*,[1] Wright, J., found himself in a dilemma, for his attention had been drawn to the statement of Pollock, B., and Charles, J., in *Budd* v. *Lucas*[2] that "there is nothing in the present Act [the Merchandise Marks Act, 1887] to alter the general rule of law that a master is not criminally responsible for the unauthorised acts of his servants". Notwithstanding his acquiescence in Lord Russell, C.J.'s renunciation of this same rule in *Cartman's case*, Wright, J., in the present case had considerable doubts as to the correct position, which doubts were shared by Darling, J., the other member of the court. Accordingly, the case was remitted to a full Divisional Court[3] consisting of Lord Russell of Killowen, C.J., Sir F. H. Jeune, P., Chitty, L.J., Wright, Darling, and Channell, JJ., who upheld the view expressed in the *Commissioner of Police* v. *Cartman*. Referring to the earlier cases decided under the Licensing Acts, the court considered that "having regard to the language, scope and object of those enactments, the legislature intended to fix criminal responsibility upon the master for acts done by his servant in the course of his employment, although such acts were not authorized by the master and might even have been expressly prohibited by him".[4] Thereafter, no doubt has ever been entertained as to the correctness of this ruling insofar as a servant acting contrary to his master's orders are concerned. It was accepted in cases like *Boyle* v. *Smith*,[5] *Buckingham* v. *Duck*,[6] and *Pearks Dairies Ltd.* v. *Tottenham Food Controller*,[7] all involving statutory offences of absolute liability and in each of which the underlying principle of the employer's vicarious liability was expressed in terms of whether the act of the servant was performed within the scope of his

[1] [1898] 2 Q.B. 300. [2] [1891] 1 Q.B. 408.

[3] This is reported under the heading *Coppen* v. *Moore* (No. 2) [1898] 2 Q.B. 306.

[4] *Ibid.*, p. 312. In his judgment, Lord Russell treated cases of public nuisance and cases arising under the Licensing Acts alike, as constituting exceptions to the general rule.

[5] [1906] 1 K.B. 432. *Coram*, Lord Alverstone, C.J., Lawrance and Ridley, JJ.

[6] (1918) 88 L.J.K.B. 375. *Coram* Darling, Coleridge and Avory, JJ. Reference was made to *Mackenna* v. *City and Suburban Dairies* [1918] 2 Sc.L.T. 155, which was criticised as being inconsistent with the law laid down by the English courts.

[7] (1918) 88 L.J.K.B. 623. See, too, *James & Son, Ltd.* v. *Smee* [1954] 3 All E.R. 273, *per* Slade, J. at p. 280. Other decisions along similar lines include *Warrington* v. *Windhill Industrial Co-op. Society* (1918) 88 L.J.K.B. 280, and *Griffiths* v. *Studebakers, Ltd.* [1924] 1 K.B. 102.

employment or authority. Preference for this test was also exhibited by Avory, J., in the well-known case of *Allen* v. *Whitehead*,[1] where a licensee was charged under the Metropolitan Police Act, 1839, s. 44, with knowingly permitting prostitutes to meet together and remain on his premises. The licensee had expressly instructed his manager, who was responsible for running the refreshment house, that no prostitutes were to be allowed to congregate on the premises. Despite the absence of any personal knowledge on the part of the licensee his conviction was upheld, Lord Hewart, C.J., basing his decision on the delegation principle but Avory, J. whilst agreeing with the Chief Justice, put the position in a different form, saying:[2] "... the manager in this case, although acting contrary to his instructions in doing what he did, was acting in the course of his employment, and that being so, the employer is responsible for his acts." More recently, in *Brentnall* v. *L.C.C.*,[3] Humphreys, J. adopted the same test when he declared, in relation to an offence[4] construed as excluding *mens rea*, "a person is responsible for the actions of his agent within the scope of his authority, just as much as he is responsible for the acts of his servants, and, indeed, a servant is merely a specific case of an agent of a particular sort".[5]

Attempt to equate the "course of employment" test with the "delegation of authority" test

An attempt was made by Lord Goddard, C.J., in *Barker* v. *Levinson*[6] to equate the two tests of "delegation" and "acting within the course of employment". At least, so it appears from a study of the All England Reports, but in the Law Reports it will be found that all reference to the scope of the servant's employment has been deleted. Involved in that case was the offence, under the Landlord and Tenant (Rent Control) Act, 1949,[7] s. 2 (1), of requiring a premium as a condition of the grant of a tenancy, which offence was construed as one of absolute prohibition. Such an illegal premium had been collected by a rent-collector employed by the respondent, the manager of a block of flats. The duties to be performed by the collector were limited to satisfying himself as to the suitability of prospective tenants, and no authority was given him to negotiate the terms of a new tenancy. According

[1] [1930] 1 K.B. 211. [2] *Ibid.*, p. 221. [3] [1944] 2 All E.R. 552.
[4] Weights and Measures Act, 1889 (52 & 53 Vict., c. 21), s. 29 (2). [5] *Ibid.*, p. 556.
[6] [1951] 1 K.B. 342; [1950] 2 All E.R. 825. [7] 12, 13 & 14 Geo. 6, c. 40.

to Lord Goddard, C.J., the principle underlying the cases which deal with the criminal responsibility of a master for the act of his servant can be stated in this way:[1] "The master is responsible for a criminal act of the servant if the act is done within the general scope of the servant's employment. In other words, if a master chooses to delegate the conduct of his business to a servant, then, if the servant, in the course of conducting the business, does an act which is absolutely prohibited, the master is liable, which is really only another way of saying that the act done must be within the general scope of the servant's employment." Applying this test to the facts before them the court held that the rent-collector's illegal act was outside the scope of his employment and consequently the respondent was not vicariously liable.[2] Whether the two tests referred to in the passage above are identical in character is doubtful, but this problem must await an examination of the cases in which the delegation test has been applied.

The court's application in *Barker* v. *Levinson* of the tort formula when deciding a case of criminal vicarious liability was criticised by Denning, L.J., in *Navarro* v. *Moregrand Ltd.*,[3] where the learned judge said that if this were the correct principle it would equate the master's criminal responsibility with his civil responsibility "which would be an innovation against which I would issue a caveat". In the authorised Law Report of *Barker* v. *Levinson*, however, the governing test is stated to be not whether the agent was acting in the course of his employment, but whether he was a

[1] [1950] 2 All E.R. at p. 827.

[2] Glanville Williams, *Criminal Law*, p. 284, suggests that the actual decision "furnishes yet another example of a refusal to extend (what he describes as) the public licence cases". With respect, it does nothing of the sort. Had the conduct of the rent collector been within the scope of his authority there is little doubt that the manager would have been held liable. It is certainly questionable whether the doctrine of vicarious liability should be extended to cover relationships other than "head" employer and employees. Is it proposed, for example, to extend liability to managers or supervisors or foremen for the acts of minor servants? Although no express statement was made on this point, the decision in *Rushton* v. *Martin* [1952] W.N. 258, lends support to the view that what might loosely be described as "sub" employers (i.e., managers, supervisors, foremen and the like) are not subject to the doctrine of vicarious liability. This view is also supported by the recent decision of the High Court of Justiciary (Lord Justice-General, Lords Carmont and Russell) in *Shields* v. *Little* (1954) 23 S.L.T. 146. In *Crabtree* v. *Hole* (1879) 43 J.P. 799 the licensee was held liable for the conduct of a servant even though he had employed a manager who was responsible for running the premises. Cf. *Allchorn* v. *Hopkins* (1905) 69 J.P. 355, *Morris* v. *Williams* (1952) 50 Local Govt. Reports, 308, 310 *per* Lord Goddard C.J., and *James & Son, Ltd.* v. *Smee* [1954] 3 All E.R. 273.

[3] [1951] W. N. 335, at p. 337; [1951] 2 T.L.R. 674, at p. 681. See, too, a note on *Barker* v. *Levinson* by the writer in (1951) 14 *M.L.R.* 338–339.

general agent acting within the general scope of his authority, and this Denning, L.J., found satisfactory. However, in stating as the basic reason[1] for the decision in *Barker* v. *Levinson* that the manager had in no way authorised, expressly or impliedly, the agent to take a premium Denning, L.J., came perilously near to accepting the old test laid down in *R.* v. *Marsh*[2] and which has been repeatedly rejected in later cases. Authorisation or prohibition *of the particular illegal act* is in no way the criterion for establishing vicarious liability in criminal law. Notwithstanding Lord Goddard's discarding of the tort formula in the authorised law report of *Barker* v. *Levinson*, this same test, *viz.*, whether the servant was acting in the course of his employment, was re-introduced by the Lord Chief Justice in the subsequent case of *Gardner* v. *Akeroyd*.[3] Citing as examples of offences wherein the doctrine of vicarious liability applies, the sale of adulterated food or of goods with a false trade description or at a price in excess of a statutory maximum, Lord Goddard said:[4] "the master will be liable notwithstanding that the sale was effected by his servant and without his knowledge, provided only that the sale was in the course of the servant's employment."

Where, on the other hand, in offences under the Licensing Acts a servant sells, for example, drink to a drunken person in the course of his employment it has been held in several cases[5] that unless the licensee has in fact delegated the control of the premises to his servant no vicarious liability is incurred by the master. Here is the conflict, mentioned earlier, between the alternative tests. In many cases it will be found that either test is equally satisfactory, in the sense that when applied the same result is achieved. To enable a proper assessment of the merits of the respective tests to be carried out it is necessary to consider next the development and application of what may be described as the delegation principle.

Liability based on the delegation principle

This principle appears to have been first enunciated in *Redgate* v. *Haynes*[6] in 1876, over fifty years after the alternative test discussed above was introduced in *R.* v. *Marsh.* The appellant in the

[1] The real basis of the court's decision is to be found in Lord Goddard's words: "If, in the case now before us, the respondent had put [the rent collector] into the position of being a *general agent in respect of the flats and had left the management to him*, and [the rent-collector] had done an illegal act, it may be that the respondent would have been liable."

[2] (1824) 2 B. & C., 717. [3] [1952] 2 Q.B. 743. [4] *Ibid.*, p. 749.

[5] See *post*, p. 227 *et seq.*

[6] (1876) L.R. 1 Q.B. 89. Delivering judgment in *Somerset* v. *Hart* (1884) 12 Q.B.D 360, at pp. 362–363, Lord Coleridge C.J., sought to explain the decision in *Mullins*

later case was charged with suffering gaming on licensed premises, contrary to the Licensing Act, 1872, s. 17.[1] On closing the house at 11 p.m. the licensee had gone upstairs to bed and the hall-porter, who was left in charge and whose duty it was to attend upon customers, retired to his parlour beyond the bar, at the extreme end of the hotel. The justices drew the inference that the porter had so acted in order that he might not hear what passed, and Blackburn, J., than whom no greater advocate of the doctrine of vicarious liability was to be found in his day,[2] stated the principle governing the decision to be that "where the [licensee] goes to bed she is still answerable for the conduct of those whom she leaves in charge of the house, and if those persons connive at the gaming, she is responsible".[3] Lush, J., likewise considered that "connivance on the part of the landlady or the person in charge would be quite sufficient".[4] The same principle was applied in *Crabtree* v. *Hole*[5] where, in circumstances similar to those existing in *Redgate* v. *Haynes*, Cockburn, C.J., declared:[6] "The duty imposed by the enactment is to take reasonable care that gaming is not suffered on the licensed premises, and if the licensed holder employs one who does not do his duty, it is the same as if he himself did not do the duty."

Where a licensee, on the other hand, retains actual control of the premises and does not delegate charge of the house to a servant no vicarious liability is incurred. Such was the decision in *Somerset* v. *Hart*,[7] in which the earlier cases of *Redgate* v. *Haynes* and

v. *Collins* (1874) L.R. 9 Q.B. 292 on the ground that the liquor was served by a woman who was the appellant's wife and entrusted by him with the management of the house. If that were the case, said Lord Coleridge, the decision would be brought within the principle of the other cases which were decided on the delegation principle. See too, *Avards* v. *Dance* (1862) 26 J.P. 437, in which Blackburn, J., seems to have been prepared to hold a licensee liable for permitting gaming if he left his wife in charge of the house.

[1] Re-enacted in the Licensing Act, 1953 (1 & 2 Eliz. 2, c. 46), s. 141 (1).

[2] Baty, *Vicarious Liability*, p. 205 comments: "Blackburn, J.'s mentality was saturated with the contractual conception of agency with which, as a great commercial judge, he was familiar. It is hard to avoid the opinion that he carried the *qui facit* maxim far beyond its proper sphere." Early cases in which Blackburn, J. is seen taking the lead in invoking the principle of vicarious liability are *Avards* v. *Dance* (1862) 76 J.P. 437; *R.* v. *Handley* (1864) 9 L.T. N.S. 827, *Barnes* v. *Akeroyd* (1872) L.R. 7 Q.B. 474; *Davies* v. *Harvey* (1874) 9 Q.B. 439; and *Redgate* v. *Haynes* (1876) L.R. 1 Q.B. 89. Another critic of Blackburn, J.'s embracing of the doctrine of strict liability to the exclusion of *mens rea* is Jerome Hall—see his *General Principles*, p. 287, n. 27.

[3] *Ibid.*, p. 94. [4] *Ibid.*, p. 96. [5] (1879) 43 J.P. 799. [6] *Loc. cit.*

[7] (1884) 12 Q.B.D. 360. This decision was followed in *Somerset* v. *Wade* [1894] 1 Q.B. 574, for the same reasons, i.e., the servant was not in charge of the premises. See, too, *Sherras* v. *de Rutzen* [1895] 1 Q.B. 918, per Wright, J. at p. 922.

Crabtree v. *Hole* were distinguished. The same offence of suffering gaming was involved and it was proved that a potman, whose task it was to take and deliver customer's orders, was aware of what was going on but never communicated this knowledge to the licensee, his employer. "It is true" said Coleridge, C.J., "that a man may put another in his position so as to represent him for the purpose of knowledge, but there is no evidence of such delegation here."[1] Later in the same case the Chief Justice described the underlying test as requiring proof that the gaming took place "with the knowledge of some person clothed with the landlord's authority".[2] It will be observed that in all three cases the element of knowledge was a fundamental requisite of liability, and that emphasis was placed on attributing knowledge to the master *only* where the servant is in control of the premises. As Lord Coleridge, C.J., indicated in the course of argument: "The mere fact that a servant knows a thing cannot be evidence that his master knows it."[3]

Stephen, J., after reviewing all the earlier cases, applied the same principle in *Bond* v. *Evans*[4] where the appellant's servant was in charge of a skittle-alley in which the gaming took place. The fact of his being placed in charge of the premises was sufficient to attribute his knowledge of the gaming to the licensee whose conviction was therefore upheld. The distinguishing feature in *Somerset* v. *Hart*, according to Stephen, J. was the fact that the servant who knew of the gaming was only a potman and "there had been no delegation of authority" to him.[5]

Attention has already been drawn[6] to the next case, *Commissioner of Police* v. *Cartman*,[7] in which Lord Russell of Killowen, C.J., introduced a qualification to, not an explanation of, the customary test whether actual direct control of a business had been deputed to another person. It will be recalled that the learned Chief Justice in that case added the proviso that, in addition, it must be proved that the acts of the servant were done within the scope of his employment. This test has frequently, in subsequent

[1] (1884) 12 Q.B.D. p. 362. [2] *Ibid.*, p. 364. [3] *Ibid.*, p. 362.

[4] (1888) 21 Q.B.D. 249. See, too, *Massey* v. *Morriss* [1894] 2 Q.B. 412, per Cave, J. at p. 414, in which the learned judge explained the licensing cases thus: "Licences to keep alehouses are only granted to persons of good personal character, and it is obvious that the object of so restricting the grant of licences would be defeated if the licensed person could, by delegating the control and management of the house to another person who was altogether unfit to keep it, free himself from responsibility for the manner in which the house was conducted."

[5] *Ibid.*, p. 256. [6] *Ante* p. 222. [7] [1896] 1 Q.B. 655.

cases, been treated as an alternative to the delegation test, but in no case has it been regarded as an added essential requirement. No reference to it, for example, is to be found in the case of *Worth* v. *Brown*,[1] decided the same year, in which a licensee, who was absent at the time of the offence, was sought to be made vicariously liable for permitting drunkenness. In charge of the bar at the time was a barmaid who, in the opinion of the court, must have been aware of the condition of the drunken man. For the purposes of the Licensing Act 1872, s. 13, Grantham and Collins JJ., considered that the barmaid, by being in charge, was substituted for the licensee himself. "She was not merely his agent" said Grantham, J., "for certain purposes only, she was his agent in the further sense of being his *alter ego*, and the licensee was liable for any misconduct of hers in the management of the business."[2]

Conflict in the application of the respective tests

The problem whether the two tests of delegation and acting within the scope of employment are synonymous, a suggestion approved by Lord Goddard, C.J., in the recent case of *Barker* v. *Levinson*,[3] arises directly in a series of cases which turn on the Intoxicating Liquors (Sale to Children) Act, 1901,[4] s. 2. This section makes it an offence for any licensee to knowingly sell intoxicating liquor to any person under 14 years, in a vessel which is not corked or sealed. In the first of these cases, *Emary* v. *Nolloth*,[5] a decision which the other cases purported to follow, it appeared that a child aged 9 was served by a barman contrary to the express orders, and without the knowledge, of the licensee who was himself in charge of the premises at the time of the sale. There can be little doubt that the barman, as in fact was expressly mentioned in the case stated by the magistrates in *McKenna* v. *Harding*[6] upon precisely similar facts, was acting within the general scope of his employment. He was employed to serve customers and the fact that he acted illegally and contrary to orders does not alter the fact that, if the governing test to be applied was whether he had acted within the scope of his employment, the licensee would have been held liable. By applying the delegation of authority test, however, the court, consisting of Lord Alverstone, C.J., and Channell, J., considered that no offence had been committed by

[1] (1896) 40 Sol. Jo. 515. [2] *Loc. cit.* [3] [1951] 1 K.B. 342.
[4] 64 Vict. & 1 Edw. 7, c. 27, re-enacted in the Licensing Act, 1953, s. 128 (1).
[5] [1903] 2 K.B. 264. [6] (1905) 69 J.P. 354.

the licensee. This ruling was followed by the Irish Divisional Court in *Conlon* v. *Muldowney*,[1] and by the English Divisional Court in *McKenna* v. *Harding*[2] and *Allchorn* v. *Hopkins*.[3] The conflict in the result achieved, according to which governing test is applied, raises two questions: are the respective tests applicable to different categories of statutory offences, and, if not, which of the two principles is to be preferred?

Is the delegation principle confined to offences of absolute prohibition?

Hitherto, it will be noticed, all the cases in which the delegation principle has been invoked have involved proof of knowledge, the servant-in-charge's knowledge or connivance being deemed to be that of his employer. Furthermore, in *Emary* v. *Nolloth*,[4] Lord Alverstone, C.J., in attempting to extract general principles from the cases dealing with vicarious liability, treated the delegation of authority test exclusively in relation to offences involving the epithets, "knowingly allowing", "permitting" and "suffering".[5] That this particular test is not, however, rigidly confined to statutory offences involving knowledge was made apparent, for example, in *Strutt* v. *Clift*,[6] in which the owners of a dairy farm were convicted of using a van without a proper licence, contrary to the Customs and Inland Revenue Duties Act, 1869.[7] By a later enactment in 1888, exemption is granted from the requirement of a carriage licence if the van is used solely for the conveyance of goods in the course of husbandry. On one occasion the bailiff, who was in charge of the dairy farm, used the van for private purposes without the knowledge or authority of the appellants. Upholding the conviction Lord Alverstone, C.J., relied on his judgment in *Emary* v. *Nolloth*, saying:[8] "the appellants, by placing the bailiff in charge of the van, delegated to him their power to prevent its user for the purpose for which it was in fact used, and they are consequently responsible for his act." Pickford and Coleridge, JJ., delivered judgments in a similar strain, stressing the fact that the person who used the van was the person who had charge of it on the appellants' behalf. Applying the same test in *Wilson* v. *Murphy*,[9] another decision based on an offence not involving guilty knowledge, the Court of Criminal Appeal quashed

[1] [1904] 2 Ir. R. 498. [2] (1905) 69 J.P. 354. [3] (1905) 69 J.P. 355.
[4] [1903] 2 K.B. 264. [5] *Ibid.*, at p. 289. [6] [1911] 1 K.B. 1.
[7] 32 & 33 Vict. c. 14, s. 27, as amended by 51 & 52 Vict. c. 8, s. 4 (3).
[8] [1911] 1 K.B. at p. 7. [9] [1937] 1 All E.R. 315.

the conviction of an employer charged with publishing ready money betting coupons, contrary to the Ready Money Football Betting Act, 1920, s. 1.[1] One of the collectors employed by the respondent, in violation of his express instructions, had wrongfully used the coupons, supplied to him by the head office, for purposes of ready money betting. Distinguishing the decision in *Allen* v. *Whitehead*[2] in which, it will be remembered, the licensee had transferred to his manager the responsibility for the conduct of the refreshment house, the court considered that there had been no such delegation of authority to the collector in this case. Consequently, no question of vicarious liability was involved. It is, of course, a moot point whether it could not be said that the collector's illegal conduct occurred in the course of his employment, thus providing additional evidence for the apparent conflict in the application of the respective tests.

Reference has already been made[3] to the decision in *Barker* v. *Levinson*[4] which, also, was concerned with a crime of absolute prohibition. Although the Divisional Court appear to have wavered in their choice of principle when deciding the case, Lord Goddard, C.J., according to the authorised Law Reports, laid greater store on the principle that "if a master chooses to delegate the conduct of his business to a servant who does an act in the course of conducting the business *which is absolutely prohibited*,[5] the master is liable".[6] Having regard to the authorities already cited, this statement purporting to restrict the doctrine of vicarious liability to crimes of absolute liability would seem to be misjudged,[7] but it was repeated by the Lord Chief Justice in *Gardner* v. *Akeroyd* where he declared:[8] "A master who is not particeps in the offence can only be liable criminally for the acts of his servant *if the statute which creates the offence does so in terms which impose an absolute prohibition.*"[9] Lest there be any doubt as to his interpretation of such crimes, Lord Goddard explained: "Where the prohibition is

[1] 10 & 11 Geo. 5, c. 52. [2] [1930] 1 K.B. 211. [3] *Ante*, p. 224.

[4] [1951] 1 K.B. 342; [1950] 2 All E.R. 825.

[5] The writer's italics. [6] *Ibid.*, p. 345.

[7] For a clear enunciation of the distinction between absolute (or strict) liability and vicarious liability see Glanville Williams, *Criminal Law*, pp. 285–286. Vicarious liability may arise in relation to an offence of absolute prohibition, but it does not necessarily arise because the offence is one of absolute prohibition.

[8] [1952] 2 Q.B. 743 at p. 749. More recently, in *James & Son, Ltd.* v. *Smee* [1954] 3 All E.R., at p. 280, we find Slade, J., restricting the doctrine of vicarious liability to "acts which the law absolutely prohibits".

[9] The writer's italics.

absolute no question of knowledge or intent arises, the state of mind of the perpetrator is immaterial."[1] In the light of such cases as *Redgate* v. *Haynes*,[2] *Crabtree* v. *Hole*,[3] *Bond* v. *Evans*,[4] *Worth* v. *Brown*[5] and the *Commissioner of Police* v. *Cartman*,[6] it is respectfully submitted that the above statement of the law is inaccurate and misleading.

Furthermore, two cases, both arising under section 44 of the Metropolitan Police Act, 1839,[7] in which the foundation of criminal liability is knowingly permitting or suffering prohibited conduct, provide conclusive evidence that the doctrine of vicarious liability extends its tentacles into the realm of *mens rea* just as much as it does in the field of offences of absolute liability. The circumstances leading to the first of these cases, *Allen* v. *Whitehead*,[8] have already been stated and it is necessary only to be reminded that the licensee's conviction was upheld for knowingly permitting prostitutes to foregather despite his express instructions to the contrary given to the manager whom he employed to run his business. That *mens rea* in the form of guilty knowledge was essential, and that the master could be held vicariously liable for such an offence is made abundantly clear by Lord Hewart, C.J., who said:[9] ". . . the proprietor, the keeper of the house, had delegated his duty to a manager, so far as the conduct of the house was concerned. He had transferred to the manager the exercise of discretion in the conduct of the business, and it seems to me that the only reasonable conclusion is, regard being had to the purpose of this Act, that the knowledge of the manager was the knowledge of the keeper of the house."

Enunciation of the true principle

This doctrine was followed in slightly different circumstances in *Linnett* v. *Commissioner of Police*,[10] a decision which has been repeatedly cited in recent cases[11] as correctly laying down the principle underlying the application of vicarious liability. The only essential difference in the respective facts was that the appellant in *Linnett* was not the sole licensee, the licence being jointly held by the appellant and the manager who was in charge of the premises. Contrasting oddly with his statement (*supra*) in

[1] *Loc. cit.*
[2] (1876) L.R. 1 Q.B. 89.
[3] (1879) 43 J.P. 799.
[4] (1888) 21 Q.B.D. 249.
[5] (1896) 40 Sol. Jo. 515.
[6] [1896] 1 Q.B. 655.
[7] 2 & 3 Vict. c. 47.
[8] [1930] 1 K.B. 211.
[9] *Ibid.*, p. 221.
[10] [1946] K.B. 290.
[11] See, for example, *Barker* v. *Levinson* [1951] 1 K.B. 342; *Quality Dairies (York) Ltd.* v. *Pedley* [1952] 1 All E.R. 380; and *Ferguson* v. *Weaving* [1951] 1 K.B. 814.

the later case of *Gardner* v. *Akeroyd*,[1] Lord Goddard, C.J., declared in the present case:[2] "There are many cases . . . under the Licensing Acts, the Food and Drugs Acts and various other Acts, in which persons have been held liable because their servants and their managers have done certain acts, knowingly done certain acts, and their knowledge has been imputed to the master. One has to see what the principle is that underlies those decisions. The principle does not, in my opinion, depend merely upon the legal relationship between the two persons, the person who actually permitted with knowledge and the person who is convicted although he had no actual knowledge. The point does not, as I say, depend merely on the fact that the relationship of master and servant exists; it depends on the fact the person who is responsible in law as the keeper of the house, or the licensee of the house if the offence is under the Licensing Acts, has chosen to delegate his duties, powers and authority to somebody else. . . . If he chooses to delegate his powers to some other person, then the knowledge of that other person becomes, to use a convenient expression, the principal's knowledge." By placing his co-licensee in charge of the premises the court held that the appellant, Linnett, was just as much liable for his acts and for his knowledge as if he had been a servant.

Any reference in such circumstances to "acting within the scope of employment" would be entirely inappropriate, and the principle propounded by the Lord Chief Justice would seem to lift the doctrine of vicarious liability above the relationships of master and servant, and of principal and agent. We come back, therefore, to the question whether the delegation test should not prevail in all cases, thus excluding any reference to the alternative tests "acting within the scope of employment" or "acting within the scope of authority". In cases like *Emary* v. *Nolloth*,[3] *Conlon* v. *Muldowney*,[4] *McKenna* v. *Harding*,[5] *Allchorn* v. *Hopkins*,[6] and possibly *Wilson* v. *Murphy*,[7] assuming the course of employment test had been applied it is not unreasonable to suppose that a different decision, contrary to the court's intention, would have been reached. In every other case, it is submitted, where reliance has been placed on the formulae peculiar to servants and agents, the same decision would have been achieved if, instead, the delegation of authority rule had been invoked. To avoid further con-

[1] [1952] 2 Q.B. 743.
[2] [1946] K.B. at pp. 294–295.
[3] [1903] 2 K.B. 264.
[4] [1904] 2 Ir.R. 498.
[5] (1905) 69 J.P. 354.
[6] (1905) 69 J.P. 355.
[7] [1937] 1 All E.R. 315.

flict, therefore, it is suggested that the scope of employment or authority tests be discarded completely, and the doctrine of vicarious liability be aligned with the principle that he who chooses to delegate any duties, powers, or responsibilities, imposed upon him by Act of Parliament, should remain liable for the acts of any person appointed to act in his place. It may well be that master and servant cases will continue to predominate, but it seems inimical to have a special test for such a relationship which may conflict with the wider and more general principle enunciated in *Linnett* v. *Metropolitan Police*.[1] Moreover, it is submitted that the delegation rule should apply irrespective of whether the offence charged is one of absolute prohibition or one requiring proof of *mens rea* in the form of guilty knowledge.

Factors which determine the application of vicarious liability

It must not be thought that the doctrine of vicarious liability is of general application throughout the vast field of statutory crime. As Lord Goddard, C.J., did well to point out in *Gardner* v. *Akeroyd*, vicarious liability does not mean that whenever an Act forbids something a master is liable if his servant does the act forbidden.[2] It is a matter of construction in each individual case and, in the oft-quoted words of Atkin, J. in *Mousell Bros.* v. *L.N.W.Rly. Co.*,[3] "regard must be had to the object of the statute, the words used, the nature of the duty laid down, the person upon whom it is imposed, the person by whom it would in ordinary circumstances be performed, and the person upon whom the penalty is imposed." Similar considerations were outlined by Viscount Reading, C.J., in the same case,[4] by Lord Russell of Killowen, C.J., in *Coppen* v. *Moore*,[5] and by Channell, J., in *Pearks, Gunston and Tee* v. *Ward*.[6] One significant feature dominating each of these judgments is the association of the doctrine of vicarious liability with what Channell, J., described as "quasi-criminal offences, that is to say, where certain acts are forbidden by law under a penalty",[6] and what Atkin, J. defined as offences wherein "the legislature prohibit an act or enforce a duty in such words as to make the prohibition or duty absolute".[3] Cases

[1] [1946] K.B. 290. [2] [1952] 2 Q.B. 743, at p. 749.

[3] [1917] 2 K.B. 836, at p. 845. See, too, the statement by Cave, J. in *Chisholm* v. *Doulton* (1889) 22 Q.B.D. 736, at p. 742.

[4] *Ibid.*, pp. 843, 844. [5] [1898] 2 Q.B. 306, at p. 312.

[6] [1902] 2 K.B. 1, at p. 11.

arising under such statutes as the Food and Drugs Acts, the Merchandise Marks Acts, the Fertilisers and Feeding Stuffs Acts, the Weights and Measures Acts and the Road Traffic Acts are sufficient indication of the type of legislation in which such offences are to be found. As has already been shown, however, vicarious liability may equally be relied upon where the prohibition is not absolute but dependent upon proof of knowledge, such as offences under the Metropolitan Police Act, the Licensing Acts, and certain offences under the Road Traffic Acts. With the ever widening scope of modern legislation, particularly as expressed in delegated legislation with its detailed regulations governing the duties of persons in control of certain industries, trades or professions affecting the general public welfare, it is only to be expected that in future the doctrine of vicarious liability will be increasingly relied upon in an endeavour to secure a well ordered state of society.

Liability for the acts of strangers

So far we have been concerned to ascertain the law governing vicarious liability for the criminal acts of servants, agents or any person to whom another's statutory duties or responsibilities are delegated. What of the position where a third party, not falling within any of these categories, is the primary wrongdoer and it is sought to punish another person for the offence committed? The views of the judges on this question are almost unanimous in rejecting any extension of vicarious liability to cover such a contingency, but there are some notable exceptions. Nearly a century ago in *Hearne* v. *Garton*[1] the court accepted as well-established the rule that "a party cannot be criminally liable for the act of a third person".[2] In that case, the respondents, a firm of carriers were charged with sending goods of a dangerous quality by rail without indicating the nature of the goods on the outside of the package. The original sender had marked the box as containing an innocuous collection of seeds and corks when in fact it contained oil of vitriol. The question, according to Lord Campbell, C.J., was whether the legislature intended that a man should be liable who sent the goods with the most perfect innocence. In his opinion, supported by Wightman, Erle and Crompton, JJ., the justices' finding of acquittal was correct since the respondents were not to be the victims of the third party's wrongdoing. Clearly,

[1] (1859) 28 L.J.M.C. 216.

[2] *Per* Crompton, J., at p. 220.

the decision of the court was influenced considerably by the absence of any moral culpability on the part of the respondents.

Forty years later, in *Parker* v. *Alder*,[1] a radical change in the mood of the judiciary is evidenced, for in that case a strong Divisional Court upheld the conviction of an innocent milk vendor for selling milk which had been adulterated in the course of transit by some person unknown.[2] Prompting this decision, reversing as it did the principle accepted by the court in *Hearne* v. *Garton*, was the view expressed by Wills, J., that "there is no material distinction between the case of adulteration by a servant without the authority, and against the express orders, of his master, and adulteration by the fraudulent act of a stranger".[3] Lord Russell of Killowen, C.J., added the explanation that there is no material difference "because a vendor is no more able to prevent the adulteration by a dishonest servant than he is to prevent adulteration by strangers such as servants of the railway company".[4] But if in such a case, as the learned judge suggested, the respondent ought not to have been prosecuted, what is the purpose served by invoking the doctrine of vicarious liability? Indeed one may ask, if the milk-vendor is prosecuted and convicted, but is unable to prevent a recurrence of the same circumstances, how can it be said that the punishment of the milk-vendor is likely to further the object of the particular statute? No adverse comment on the decision, however, was made by Darling, Avory or Sankey, JJ., in *Andrews* v. *Luckin*,[5] which followed the earlier decision on facts which failed even to disclose how the milk had been tampered with in the course of transit. A few years earlier, on the other hand, in *Strutt* v. *Clift*,[6] where the owners of a farm were

[1] [1899] 1 Q.B. 20.

[2] Contrary to the Food & Drugs Act, 1875, s. 6. This offence is now contained in the Food and Drugs Act, 1938, s. 3 (1), which offence in *Lamb* v. *Sunderland and District Creamery, Ltd.* [1951] 1 All E.R. 923 was construed as one of absolute prohibition.

[3] *Ibid.*, p. 26, citing in support *Brown* v. *Foot* (1892) 66 L.T. (N.S.) 649, a case of master and servant.

[4] *Ibid.*, p. 25.

[5] (1917) 34 T.L.R. 33, and see the observations of Humphreys, J., in *Watson* v. *Coupland* [1945] 1 All E.R. 217, at p. 219. Comparison may also be made with American decisions—collected in Miller, *Criminal Law*, p. 162—in which a defendant has been held criminally liable for an offence caused by the malicious interference of a third person. For example, in *Cowen* v. *N.Y.C. & H.R.R. Co.* (1909) 202 Mass. 394, where a statute prohibited the obstruction of a highway crossing for more than a certain length of time, the facts that a third person maliciously opened the valves of the air brakes of the defendant's train, preventing its being moved, was held to be no defence.

[6] [1911] 1 K.B. 1.

held vicariously liable for the act of their bailiff in driving their van without a proper licence, Lord Coleridge, J., had declared:[1] "This is not like the case of a stranger taking the van out of the appellant's possession and using it for an improper purpose." In the same case, Lord Alverstone, C.J., distinguished the decision in *Egan* v. *Floyde*[2] on the ground that there the accused's infringement of the statutory exemption from having a licence in respect of his sheep dog was due to the wrongful acts of third persons who, he said, could not be compared with the position of a bailiff who had been placed in charge of the farm generally.

Such was the position until the recent decision in *Reynolds* v. *G. H. Austin & Co. Ltd.*[3] In that case, the respondent bus company, it will be recalled, were charged with permitting a coach to be used as an express carriage without a road service licence.[4] Unfortunately, without any knowledge on their part, the hirer of the coach had publicly advertised the trip, which action violated one of the statutory conditions exempting the bus company from having the necessary licence. It was argued that the bus company was liable for the illegal act of the hirer but according to Humphreys, J. the doctrine of vicarious responsibility in criminal law "does not extend to the case of a defendant charged with having done an act lawful in itself but which had become unlawful as the result of some action entirely unknown to him by some person not his servant or agent".[5] Lord Goddard, C.J., was equally emphatic in stating that hitherto the doctrine "has never been applied, as far as I know, to a case where the prohibited act is not that of the defendant, but that of some person over whom he had no control and for whom he had no responsibility".[6] This principle, of course, was not accepted by the judges in *Parker* v. *Alder*[7] or *Andrews* v. *Luckin*,[8] and it is unfortunate that the attention of the Divisional Court in *Reynolds* v. *Austin* was not apparently drawn to the decision in those two cases which, it is respectfully submitted, must be regarded as unsatisfactory authorities. As Devlin, J., in the later case pungently remarked:[9] "If a man is punished because of an act done by another, whom he cannot reasonably be expected to influence or control, the law is engaged, not in punishing thoughtlessness or inefficiency and thereby promoting

[1] *Ibid.*, p. 8. [2] (1910) 74 J.P. 223. [3] [1951] 2 K.B. 135.
[4] An offence under the Road Traffic Act, 1930, s. 72 (10).
[5] *Ibid.*, p. 143. [6] *Ibid.*, p. 145. [7] [1899] 1 Q.B. 20.
[8] (1917) 34 T.L.R. 33. [9] [1951] 2 K.B. at p. 149.

the welfare of the community, but in pouncing on the most convenient victim." Referring to the particular facts before the court, Devlin, J., continued:[1] "No amount of forethought and no degree of efficiency can protect the accused. . . . To punish the owner of the vehicle in such circumstances achieves no object except to make him an underwriter of the good behaviour of the community at large." Apt as these views are to the circumstances in *Reynolds* v. *Austin*, no less do they apply to the situation which existed in *Parker* v. *Alder*. Is it too much to expect that a firm stand will be made against any reversion to the rule as applied in *Parker* v. *Alder?* Certainly there is hope in the general principle advocated by Devlin, J., "that where the punishment of an individual will not promote the observance of the law either by that individual or by others whose conduct he may reasonably be expected to influence, then, in the absence of clear and express words, such punishment is not intended."[2] It is most encouraging to find the strong Divisional Court, consisting of five judges, in the recent case of *James & Son, Ltd.* v. *Smee*[3] lending their full support to the above principles.

Statutory exemptions from vicarious liability

Third-party procedure

This commendable principle finds support not only in the utterances of judges but in the provisions of many statutes during the past sixty odd years. Appreciating the very real possibility that, where a statutory crime is defined in absolute terms, even the most scrupulous and careful of employers is liable to find himself convicted on account of the misconduct of one of his employees, the legislature has frequently made provision for an exemptive clause in penal legislation under which the employer may require the actual wrongdoer to be brought before the court and thus gain for himself total exemption from any punishment. Generally described as "third party procedure" such escape clauses were at first confined to employers and employees, but later statutes extended this salutary provision to cover acts done by persons over whom the defendant had no control. Probably the earliest example of express legislative relaxation of the doctrine of vicarious liability in statutory crime is to be found in the Truck Amendment Act, 1887.[4] In a clause which was to be

[1] [1951] 2 K.B. p. 150. [2] *Loc. cit.* [3] [1954] 3 All E.R. 273, at pp. 278, 279.
[4] 50 & 51 Vict. c. 46.

repeated verbatim in subsequent enactments, section 12 (2) of the 1887 Act provides: "Where an employer is charged with an offence against this Act he shall be entitled, upon information duly laid by him, to have any other person whom he charges as the actual offender brought before the court . . . and, if after the commission of the offence has been proved, the employer proves that he had used due diligence to enforce the execution of the said Acts, and that the said other person had committed the offence without his knowledge, consent or connivance, the said other person shall be convicted of such offence and the employer shall be exempt from any penalty." Although the words "any other person" are used it is fairly clear from the preceding sub-section, which provides for awarding the same penalty to an agent of the employer if it is proved that the agent has in fact committed the offence, that the exemption was restricted to offences perpetrated by persons subject to the control of the employer. In addition, it will be noticed that the employer was required to prove the exercise of due diligence on his own part and a complete absence of any knowledge, consent or connivance that the offence was being committed. This emphasis on personal rather than vicarious responsibility was continued by the inclusion of similar exemptive provisions in the Betting and Loans (Infants) Act, 1892,[1] the Factories and Workshops Act, 1901,[2] and the Shops Act, 1912,[3] the latter being concerned with transgressions committed by some manager, agent or servant of the occupier of a shop.

The comparative ease with which an employer, through the medium of a careless assistant, can commit any one of the manifold offences contained in the various Weights and Measures Acts was offset by the insertion in the Sale of Food (Weights and Measures) Act, 1926,[4] s. 12 (5), of a clause identical with that introduced in the Truck Amendment Act, 1887, but substituting

[1] 55 Vict. c. 4, s. 1 (2). [2] 1 Edw. 7, c. 22, s. 141 (1). [3] 2 Geo. 5, c. 3, s. 14 (3).

[4] 16 & 17 Geo. 5, c. 63, s. 12 (5). Cf. s. 12 (2) which provides: "In any proceedings . . . in respect of an alleged deficiency of weight or measure, if the defendant proves . . . that such deficiency *was due to the action of some person over whom the defendant had no control*, all due diligence [having been] exercised by the defendant to prevent the occurrence of such deficiency, the defendant shall be discharged from the prosecution." For the application of this particular defence see *Brentnall* v. *L.C.C.* [1944] 2 All E.R. 552. It is also worth noting that section 15 (1) of the 1926 Act provides that that statute shall be construed as one with the Weights and Measures Acts, 1878 to 1926. In *Hart* v. *Hudson* [1928] 2 K.B. 629 and *Phillips* v. *Parnaby* [1934] 2 K.B. 299, the Divisional Court have held that the defence under s. 12 (5) of the 1926 Act is available in "coal" prosecutions under s. 21 (2) and s. 29 of the Weights and Measures Act, 1899.

for the words "without his knowledge, consent or connivance" the phrase "without his consent, connivance or wilful default". Presumably, the change was dictated by the realisation that knowledge was essential to consent,[1] and by introducing the words "wilful default" the legislature appear to have intended to tighten rather than relax the exemption.

Another formula was resorted to in the Food and Drugs Act, 1938,[2] s. 83 (1), which, unlike the 1926 Act, does not require the defendant to prove that the third party had actually committed the offence with which he is charged, it being sufficient if he proves that the "contravention was due to the *act or default* of that other person". This recognises the difficulty on occasion of proving that a servant has committed an offence which, from its nature and having regard to the objects of the statute, can normally be committed only by the employer. Moreover, provided the defendant shows that he has used all due diligence in observing the relevant provisions he is not required to negative consent, connivance or wilful default on his part. Yet another difference is that whereas section 83 (1) of the 1938 provides a complete defence, the words used being "[the defendant] shall be acquitted of the offence", section 12 (5) of the 1926 Act merely exempts the accused from penalties, which is quite a different thing. Explaining the application of this defence in *Lamb* v. *Sunderland and District Creamery*,[3] Lord Goddard, C.J., said it was designed to meet the case of a shopkeeper who buys goods in good faith from a wholesaler or a manufacturer, sells them as he receives them, and then finds that they are adulterated or below the required legal standard. In those circumstances the real responsibility lies on the wholesaler or manufacturer and not on the retailer, who, provided he has not failed to exercise due diligence, incurs no criminal liability. Of course, even if the adulteration is occasioned by a servant or total stranger it is still possible for the retailer to escape all responsibility, as was exemplified by the decision in *Malcolm* v. *Cheek*.[4] The respondent in that case, a licensee, was charged with selling gin containing an excessive quantity of water

[1] Cf. the Licensing Act, 1953 (1 & 2 Eliz. 2, c. 46), s. 122 (4), which provides that a licensee shall not be guilty of an offence under the section committed by his servant as agent "if he proves that the offence was committed without his knowledge or consent". See, too, s. 123 (4).

[2] 1 & 2 Geo. 6, c. 56.

[3] [1951] 1 All E.R. 923. See, too, *Lindley* v. *Horner* [1950] 1 All E.R. 234; *Lester* v. *Balfour Williamson Merchant Shippers Ltd.* [1953] 1 All E.R. 1146, and *Fisher* v. *Yardley's London and Provincial Stores* [1953] 3 W.L.R. 469.

[4] [1947] 2 All E.R. 881

contrary to the Food and Drugs Act, 1938, s. 3. Fortunately for the respondent, shortly before the sale was made, a customer had observed his barman pouring water into the gin bottle. The licensee having no knowledge of what had happened, and having exercised all due diligence, was held entitled to avail himself of the defence provided by section 83 (1). More recent statutes, in which a similar defence is provided, include the Wages Councils Act, 1945,[1] the Agricultural Wages Act, 1948,[2] and the Agriculture (Poisonous Substances) Act, 1952.[3]

Vicarious liability of corporation officers

Although the criminal liability of corporations is outside the purview of this study, it is worth observing that an even stronger tendency on the part of Parliament exists to minimise the hardships of vicarious responsibility where it is sought to hold directors, managers and other officers liable for offences committed by servants of a corporation. This is particularly noticeable in the nationalisation statutes, such as the Coal Industry Nationalisation Act, 1946,[4] the Electricity Act, 1947,[5] the Transport Act, 1947,[6] the Gas Act, 1948,[7] the Air Corporations Act, 1949,[8] and the Iron and Steel Act, 1949.[9] In each of these statutes there will be found a provision which enacts that "where an offence under the Act is committed by a body corporate every director, general manager, secretary or other similar officer shall be deemed guilty unless he proves that the offence was committed without his consent or connivance and that he exercised all such due diligence to prevent the commission of the offence as he ought to have exercised having regard to the nature of his functions in that capacity and to all the circumstances".[10] The resemblance between this defence and that provided under such statutes as the

[1] 8 & 9 Geo. 6, c. 17, s. 16.
[2] 11 & 12 Geo. 6, c. 47, s. 10.
[3] 15 & 16 Geo. 6 & 1 Eliz. 2, c. 60, s. 5 (1).
[4] 9 & 10 Geo. 6, c. 59, s. 59 (2).
[5] 10 & 11 Geo. 6, c. 54, s. 62 (2).
[6] 10 & 11 Geo. 6, c. 49, s. 121 (3).
[7] 11 & 12 Geo. 6, c. 67, s. 69 (2).
[8] 12, 13 & 14 Geo. 6, c. 91, s. 36 (2).
[9] 12, 13 & 14 Geo. 6, c. 72, s. 55.
[10] Other recent enactments containing a similar provision are the Civil Aviation Act, 1946 (9 & 10 Geo. 6, c. 70), s. 47 (2); Exchange Control Act, 1947 (10 & 11 Geo. 6, c. 14), Sch. V, Part II, para 1 (2); Statistics of Trade Act, 1947 (10 & 11 Geo. 6, c. 39), s. 13 (2); Monopolies and Restrictive Practices Act, 1948 (11 & 12 Geo. 6, c. 66), s. 18 (3). Comparison may be made with the Betting and Lotteries Act, 1934 (24 & 25 Geo. 5, c. 58), s. 29, in which the provision related solely to directors and who, to rebut the presumption of guilt, were only required to show that the offence was committed without their knowledge.

Sale of Food (Weights and Measures) Act, 1926, and the Food and Drugs Act, 1938, is self-evident, and underlying both provisions is the apparent desire of the legislature to impose vicarious liability only on proof of personal deviation by the defendant from the requisite standard of care. A similar provision in the Borrowing (Control and Guarantees) Act, 1946,[1] evoked strong words from Upjohn, J., in the recent case of *London Property Investments Ltd.* v. *A.G.*,[2] where the learned judge declared that "it represents the high-water mark of the Parliamentary invasion of the traditional rights of the subjects of this realm".[3] It is clear that what Upjohn, J., had in mind was the reversal of the fundamental rule in criminal law that the burden of proving the guilt of the accused is upon the prosecution, but a careful examination of the statute book will reveal the existence of a wide range of similar exceptions[4] to the general rule. Moreover, these exceptions are by no means a recent innovation, extending back to such statutes as the Customs Consolidation Act, 1876,[5] the Merchandise Marks Act, 1887,[6] and the Stamp Act, 1891.[7] The strong feelings which the particular incursion evoked from Upjohn, J., were shared by at least one private member of the House of Commons who, in 1951, introduced the Directors etc. Burden of Proof Bill with the object of transferring the burden of proof, in a scheduled list of offences, on to the prosecution. Owing to the pressure of Parliamentary business the bill was shelved, but it is worth noting that in other statutes, such as the Factories Act, 1937,[8] the Prevention of Fraud (Investments) Act, 1939,[9] the Adoption Act, 1950,[10] the Agriculture (Poisonous Substances) Act, 1952,[11]

[1] 9 & 10 Geo. 6, c. 58, s. 4 (2) (3).

[2] [1953] 1 All E.R. 436. [3] *Ibid.*, p. 441.

[4] In addition to the examples given above, reference may be made to the Public Stores Act, 1875 (38 & 39 Vict. c. 25), ss. 4 and 7; Customs and Inland Revenue Act, 1878 (41 & 42 Vict. c. 15), s. 19; Official Secrets Act, 1911 (1 & 2 Geo. 5, c. 28), s.1 (2) & s.2; Forgery Act, 1913 (3 & 4 Geo. 5, c. 27), ss. 8, 9 & 10; Bankruptcy Act, 1914 (4 & 5 Geo. 5, c. 59), s. 154; Prevention of Corruption Act, 1916 (6 & 7 Geo. 5, c. 64), s. 2; Larceny Act, 1916 (6 & 7 Geo. 5, c. 50), s. 28 (2); Coinage Offences Act, 1936 (26 Geo. 5 and 1 Edw. 8, c. 16) ss. 6, 7, 8, 9 & 10; Companies Act, 1948 (11 & 12 Geo. 6, c. 38), s. 417; and the Vehicles (Excise) Act, 1949 (12, 13 & 14 Geo. 6, c. 89), s. 22.

[5] 39 & 40 Vict. c. 36, ss. 191 & 259. See *R.* v. *Cohen* [1951] 1 K.B. 505, and *Petty* v. *Biggerstaff* [1954] N.I. 70.

[6] 50 & 51 Vict. c. 28, ss. 2 (2) & 5, as amended by the Patents (International Conventions) Act, 1938, s. 10.

[7] 54 & 55 Vict. c. 39, s. 13. [8] 1 Edw. 8 & 1 Geo. 6, c.67, s. 130 (5).

[9] 2 & 3 Geo. 6, c. 16, s. 18. [10] 14 Geo. 6, c. 26, s. 41 (1).

[11] 15 & 16 Geo. 6 & 1 Eliz. 2, c. 60, s. 4 (4).

and the Food and Drugs (Amdt.) Act, 1954,[1] the legislature has placed the burden on the prosecution of proving consent, connivance or negligence on the part of a director, manager or other officer, before such person can be held vicariously liable. Why Parliament should choose in some such cases to place the burden of proof upon the prosecution and in others upon the defence is difficult to understand, but for our present purposes suffice it to say that the legislature's increasing accent on personal responsibility portrays a welcome and significant attitude. Again in *Gardner* v. *Akeroyd* we find the present Lord Chief Justice declaring that "Just as in former days the term 'odious' was applied to some forms of estoppel, so might it be to vicarious liability".[2] So long as modern legislation continues to intrude itself into every sphere of trading, business, health and social welfare activities, laying down elaborate codes of conduct to be observed by responsible officials, so, too, the doctrine of vicarious liability will continue to be an evil necessity. But each gesture on the part of the judiciary and of the legislature which refuses to extend this obnoxious principle is to be applauded.

[1] 2 & 3 Eliz. 2, c. 67, s. 26(3). It is also significant and encouraging to note that in the Interpretation Act (N.I.), 1954, s. 20(2), a general clause appears in which the burden of proof is placed upon the prosecution in any such statutory offence involving the officers of a company.

[2] [1952] 2 Q.B. at p. 751.

XI

GENERAL OUTLINE OF *MENS REA* IN STATUTORY OFFENCES AND CONCLUDING REMARKS

THEORIES OF LIABILITY

JUDICIAL interpretation of statutory offences is a matter which, in the past, has generally been treated solely in relation to the particular offence before the court. Thus, it has long been maintained that there is a sound basic rule of interpretation which ordains that each individual offence must be looked at by itself, and that it is either unjustifiable or irrelevant to consider the construction adopted in other cases involving analogous offences, either within the same statute or in similar enactments. The alternative view, which is now put forward, is that there are certain general principles which should be taken into account when construing any statutory offence based on one of the epithets studied in the earlier chapters of this work. It would seem that there are three possible lines of interpreting such offences and it is proposed to summarise them.

Absolute liability untrammelled by references to mens rea

Sometimes, it has been seen, the court adopts the full-blooded theory of absolute prohibition, under which liability is said to be incurred by the mere intentional doing of the forbidden act. No reference is made to the doctrine of *mens rea*, and to all intents and purposes the court treats the offence in exactly the same way as if the legislature had, in defining the offence, used a form of language which was couched in absolute terms. There is no evidence that this line of interpretation has ever been adopted in malicious crimes, but instances will be recalled in which crimes of "wilfulness" or "permitting" or "suffering" or "causing" or "with intent to defraud" have been so interpreted.

Many different considerations may be seen contributing to this result. In the first place, it is frequently said that the doctrine of absolute liability is supported by the comparative unimportance of the offence and by the fact that only a monetary penalty is involved. In fact, the penalty in many such cases is far from being a trivial amount and, moreover, to the individual concerned the consequences may not be limited to the imposition of a fine or penalty. The local publicity following the conviction of a shopkeeper, chemist, or coal merchant for an offence, say, under the Weights and Measures Acts or the Merchandise Marks Acts may be far reaching and possibly disastrous to the future success of his business. The important point is that these reasons, often put forward in support of construing offences as being of absolute prohibition, are no less applicable if the offences are, instead, held to require proof of guilty knowledge. It is difficult, therefore, to see any basis for advancing these arguments in favour of an interpretation which leads to the former, rather than the latter, result.

Another reason sometimes put forward for abrogating the doctrine of *mens rea* when interpreting a statutory offence is the difficulty of procuring adequate proof of guilty knowledge. There is considerable force in this argument, which is recognised by the legislature itself. It is becoming quite common to find a proviso inserted in an offence of seemingly absolute liability to the effect that it is a defence if the accused can prove that the offence was committed without his knowledge or connivance. Although transferring the burden of proof on to the defendant the legislature is observed to be still maintaining the principle that liability depends on proof of a guilty mind. Where, on the other hand, key-words like "wilfully" or "fraudulently" or "permits" are inserted in an offence, the intention, it is submitted, is to impose upon the prosecution the task of establishing guilty knowledge in the accused.

Then again, according to many judges it is of paramount importance to take into account the social purpose behind the statute which, it is said, should be interpreted in the way which is most likely to give effect to the intention of Parliament. This line of reasoning, perhaps by coincidence, is almost invariably resorted to when it is proposed to exclude the doctrine of *mens rea*. Now, it is not suggested that in construing a statutory offence regard should not be had to the objects of a statute, but what is criticised is the lop-sided emphasis which is frequently given to this tenet of interpretation. Take, for example, any piece of social legislation like the Licensing Acts, the Fertilisers and Feeding Stuffs Acts, or the Food and Drugs Acts. A careful analysis of all the offences created in any one such enactment will invariably reveal the fact that, whereas some are deliberately framed in a form designed to absolutely forbid any infringement, others are made dependent on the prohibited events being done wilfully or maliciously or knowingly, or being suffered, or allowed or permitted.

In some statutes this process of defining offences is carried still further, and often it will be found that in a single section, or even sub-section, different forms of wording are used to define two or more separate offences. It would be going much too far to suggest that the draftsman's choice of phrasing is indiscriminate, and there is no evidence that this is so. But in the face of such diverse definitions within a single enactment, it is difficult to see the justification for using the objects of the statute as a panacea for ignoring the salient words "wilfully", "permits" or "suffers" and concluding that the offence is one of absolute prohibition. If carried to its logical conclusion it would follow that since social welfare legislation is enacted primarily for the benefit of the general public, its objects must be achieved by laying down a presumption that criminal liability under such enactments is independent of *mens rea*. By the end of the last century, as we have seen, certain of the judges were prepared to recognise and act upon this presumption. Gradually, however, in the past fifty years there has been re-established the principle that in statutory crimes, as with common law crimes, there is still a presumption in favour of the requirement of a guilty mind, and that to overcome such presumption there must be strong indications of the legislature's intention to exclude its operation.

Although the court is not entitled to look beyond the words of a statute, no such restrictions are placed upon the writer. The question is whether at the present day sufficient, if indeed any, attention is given by Parliament to the problem whether, in laying down prescribed standards of conduct in the fields of public health, the sale of food and drugs, weights and measures, licensing, or nationalised industries, it is necessary that the fundamental maxim of criminal liability should be ignored or thrown overboard. How often, for instance, is this question considered by Parliament when it is debating new social legislation? As often as not the matter appears to be left entirely in the hands of the draftsman who, faced with the creation of a fresh batch of offences to ensure that the aims of a new bill are fulfilled, quite understandably finds himself repeating verbatim clauses which have been accepted in other enactments of an analogous nature. This process is repeated over and over again and is apparently accepted without demur by the legislature. In other spheres, when the attention of Parliament is drawn to an alleged inroad on established principle, public interest has been awakened and an opportunity given for judging such a policy on its merits. One day, perhaps, some enterprising member will perform a valuable service by calling attention to the widespread practice of imposing criminal liability independent of any moral fault. Sometimes it is clearly necessary but if this practice is allowed to continue unabated, and supplemented by judicial interpretations which are influenced by the same attitude, there is a very real danger that the criminal law will come to be regarded with contempt. The process of basing criminal liability upon a theory of absolute prohibition may well have the opposite effect to that intended and lead to a weakening respect for the law.[1]

Absolute liability with lip-service to the doctrine of mens rea

According to this doctrine of liability the court considers that where the legislature absolutely prohibits the doing of an act, the doing of it supplies the *mens rea*. Throughout this book, attention has been drawn to the increasingly frequent use of this principle in recent years.[2] Of course, where the statutory offence is defined in absolute terms—in other words, where the language used in the enactment permits of no equivocation and the offence is rightly construed as one of absolute liability—no danger to the accused exists by adopting this unfamiliar meaning of *mens rea*. The introduction of any reference to *mens rea* in such circumstances can amount to nothing more than paying lip-service to a principle which is essentially concerned with the mind of the accused. The real danger arises if the above principle is invoked when construing offences which are based on any one of the terms examined

[1] Writing in 1933, Sayre, *Public Welfare Offences* (1933) 33 *Col. L.R.* 55, said much the same thing in these words: "when the law begins to permit convictions for serious offences of men who are morally innocent and free from fault, who may even be respected and useful members of the community, its restraining power becomes undermined. Once it becomes respectable to be convicted, the vitality of the criminal law has been sapped. It is no answer that judges convinced of the actual moral innocence of the defendant may impose only a nominal punishment. The harm is wrought through the conviction itself." Similar warnings have been given by such writers as Hall, *General Principles of Criminal Law*, p. 280 *et seq.*; Turner and Radzinowicz, *The Language of Criminal Science* (1939) 7 *C.L.J.*, p. 234, n. 32; Stallybrass, *The Eclipse of Mens Rea*, 52 *L.Q.R.* 57.

[2] A collection of recent utterances to this effect are given *ante* p. 38, n. 2.

in this study. It has been shown repeatedly in the chapters devoted to offences involving malice and wilfulness how, by the courts concentrating on the mere doing of the forbidden act, the necessity for establishing a guilty mind is pushed farther and farther into the background. Indeed, this line of construction has often proved instrumental in an offence embodying the words "wilfully" or "permits" or "causes" being interpreted as one of absolute liability.

There may be good reasons for advocating complete freedom of action for the judiciary in interpreting new offences, and for saying that there is nothing illogical in offences, say of wilfulness, sometimes being interpreted in absolute terms and sometimes with reference to guilty knowledge. What is undesirable is the practice of construing such offences as being absolutely prohibited and at the same time maintaining that the doctrine of *mens rea* is thereby fulfilled. If, as is submitted, *mens rea* is still fundamentally based upon a blameworthy state of mind,[1] then it is time careful consideration was given to the desirability of continuing this other unreal application of the *mens rea* principle.

Liability based upon mens rea

This, the third alternative line of interpretation, gives effect to the old common law meaning of *mens rea* as indicating a guilty mind. Although, for the sake of brevity and as a generalisation, it

[1] It is, of course, true that writers in recent years have varied considerably in their attitude towards this fundamental problem. Thus, Lord Justice Denning in his book *The Changing Law*, p. 112 wrote: "In order to hold a person individually responsible for his crime, so as to be liable to punishment, it is obviously necessary that he should have a guilty mind. . . . In order that an act should be punishable, it must be morally blameworthy. It must be a sin." Dr. Goodhart, *English Law and the Moral Law*, p. 83 *et seq.*, on the other hand, considers that the danger in criminal law is not that we may underrate the influence of the moral law, but that we may exaggerate it. He proceeds to make the sweeping statement (p. 85) that to define *mens rea* in terms of moral guilt is a misinterpretation because in most crimes *mens rea* means nothing more than that the person has intentionally done the prohibited act. Sayre, *Public Welfare Offences* (1933) 33 *Col. L.R.* 55, 69 considers that the criminal law, designed to try the subjective blameworthiness of individual offenders, is not adapted for exercising petty regulation on a wholesale scale . . . what is badly needed is some form of administrative control which will prove quick, objective and comprehensive. Jerome Hall, *General Principles* (see Chapters 5 & 6) is a strong advocate of moral culpability as the foundation of criminal liability and severely criticises Holmes, *The Common Law*, who advanced the view that criminal law was based on an objective, non-moral foundation. See, too, Paton, *Jurisprudence* (2nd ed.), pp. 310–311, Miller, *Criminal Law*, p. 73, Friedmann, *Law and Social Change in Contemporary Britain*, pp. 261–262, Stallybrass, *The Eclipse of Mens Rea* (1936) 52 *L.Q.R.* 60.

may be permissible to refer simply to "a guilty mind", a closer analysis of this concept is now called for. What does it connote? At least one thing is crystal clear, namely, that it does not involve proof that the accused knew that he was committing a criminal offence. It has always been accepted as an axiomatic principle that ignorance of the law is no excuse. Were the position otherwise it is obvious that the legislature's handiwork could be flouted indiscriminately, an offender taking care to ensure that he did not make himself cognisant with the law.

Leaving aside this well-established rule, it may be as well to explain further the dubious explanation of *mens rea* as the intentional doing of the forbidden act, and to distinguish it from the common law interpretation of *mens rea* as a guilty mind. In recent years, there has been a marked tendency to invoke the former interpretation when dealing with statutory offences which, by their very wording, are absolutely prohibited. Now, insofar as the intentional doing of the act involves the process of the accused's mind prompting and controlling his doing of the act, it is of course true that a certain mental element is involved. But that mental element is not judged according to whether or not it is a morally blameworthy state of mind. Where all that is meant is that the accused's conduct must be a voluntary expression of his will, this is a basic principle which runs throughout the whole field of criminal liability, whether the crime originated at common law or by statutory enactment, and whether the crime is one of absolute prohibition or one involving proof of a guilty mind. All that it involves is the principle that the act must be attributable to the accused, i.e., it must have been done intentionally and not accidentally.

It is important, however, to realise that the word "act", when used by the judges in this context, is generally regarded as referring only to the initial act which sets in motion a series of consequences. For example, suppose a person is charged with selling to a purchaser an article of food which is adulterated. Assuming this is an offence of absolute prohibition, all that the court is generally concerned with is proof that the act of selling was intentional and that it was not done, say, in a state of somnambulism or automatism. Now, the consequences of the accused shopkeeper's intentionally performing the act of selling is that he thereby transfers an article of food, to a purchaser, the article being adulterated. If the offence is construed as one of absolute prohibition it is not necessary to show that the shopkeeper knew that the article was adulterated. Provided the article sold was, in fact, adulterated the shopkeeper is criminally liable if he intentionally performs the act of selling. Where, on the other hand, the statutory offence is intended to prohibit a shopkeeper from "wilfully" or "knowingly" selling an article of food which is adulterated, different considerations apply. In such a case, it is submitted, proof is required not only of the intentional act of selling but also of knowledge on the part of the shopkeeper of the consequences of the act of selling, viz., knowledge that the article sold was in fact adulterated. There must, in other words, be not only an intentional selling but an intentional selling of an article which is known to be adulterated. It is this so-called guilty knowledge which represents the true meaning of *mens rea* as a blameworthy state of mind.

It is possible, of course, that the word "act" is used synonymously with the *actus reus* of a crime and, therefore, as embracing all the elements which constitute the *actus reus*. If this is so, then the definition of *mens rea* as the intentional doing of the forbidden act requires the accused's intention to extend to both the initial act and also the ensuing consequences which together make up the *actus reus*. Inasmuch as intention presupposes the existence of knowledge or foresight it would seem that absence of knowledge of any one of the elements of the *actus reus* operates as a complete defence. This principle would be quite satisfactory in statutory offences involving *mens rea* in the form of wilfully, knowingly, permitting, suffering, allowing or causing. However, since it is this same test of intentionally doing the forbidden act which is said to suffice in crimes of absolute prohibition, it would seem to follow that equating the word "act" with *actus reus* as explained above must result in such crimes being interpreted as involving proof of guilty knowledge. Such an interpretation would undermine the whole theory of absolute liability. It is for this reason that it seems apparent that, when speaking of the intentional doing of the forbidden act in relation to either kind of offence, the judges have in mind the primary or initial act only.

There is, perforce, no single, general blameworthy state of mind, and reference must be made to the wording of the particular statutory offence. Thus, the guilty mind embodied in the words "maliciously" or "fraudulently" is distinguishable from that incorporated in the verbs "suffers" or "allows". But what the foregoing study does establish is the general acceptance, with occasional unsatisfactory exceptions, of the principle that, where any of the relevant epithets appears in the definition of an offence, the prosecution must prove that the accused had a guilty mind, and that it is not enough simply to prove that the defendant intentionally did the act prohibited. Moreover, it is submitted that a guilty mind in each of these instances connotes the idea of a knowingly wrongful act, varying in the degree of culpability according to the particular epithet used by the legislature when framing the statutory offence. It may be helpful to review the conclusions reached when analysing the cases dealing with the respective words and phrases.

Summary of the Analysis of Individual Epithets

Maliciously

The study which has been carried out of the statutes and cases dealing with malicious crimes shows how the meaning to be attributed to the word malice has developed over the centuries. Whereas, originally, malice was associated exclusively with wickedness and, in particular, with a wicked mind, the view has been expressed by some modern writers that malice no longer has any such association with the idea of wickedness. The concept of express malice, in the form of evil intention, may not be given so much prominence by the judges as in the past, but this is partly due to the introduction of the doctrine of implied malice. According to this doctrine the notion of ill-will, inherent in the meaning of malice, is inferred from the doing of the wrongful act. It is of course, well recognised that the state of a man's mind is generally ascertained from his conduct, but unless the liability for malicious crime is to be made absolute it is obvious that the accused's conduct is not the sole criterion of liability. Circumstances may exist wherein the imputation of ill-will or wickedness arising from the accused's conduct may be negatived as, for example, by proof that the accused acted in pursuance of a bona fide mistaken belief or claim of right. This defence, if judged subjectively, provides added weight to the view that "maliciously", when inserted in a statutory offence, still denotes the moral concept of wickedness or the wanton interference with another person's rights. Moreover, according to this view, the problems arising in connection with transferred malice—where the kind of harm intended is the same or different from that which is occasioned—merely involve special applications of the doctrine of implied malice.

Wilfully

Viewed in isolation from the offences in which this word appears, it might be thought that "wilfully" was a less forceful expression than the word "maliciously". Certainly, it has given rise to greater doubt as to the part it plays in the application of *mens rea*. Some judges, as has been shown, have regarded the term "wilfully" as entirely divorced from the mind of the person charged and have interpreted the epithet as meaning simply the conscious or intentional doing of the prohibited act. On the other hand, it is evident that the great majority of the judges look upon "wilfully"as denoting the necessity for proving that the accused had a guilty mind, in the sense of knowing all the circumstances which constitute the offence. Here, once more, is the perennial and all important problem. Must the fact be faced that both interpretations are permissible and that the choice must be left to the judge according to the nature of the offence involved? The task of the judge is a difficult one and a fairly independent attitude has been adopted by the courts. The result has been the crop of unsatisfactory and sometimes conflicting decisions which were considered in the chapter devoted to wilfulness. As to the solution of this quandary, it lies in the hands of the legislature, or, to be more practical, in the hands of the draftsman. Where the offence is intended to be one of absolute prohibition, the word "wilfully" should be omitted altogether. Where, on the other hand, the offence is intended to be dependent on a blameworthy mind in the form of knowledge of the facts constituting the offence, then the term "wilfully" should be included to denote this requirement.

Knowingly

When considering this equally familiar expression it will be recalled that two principal problems emerged. The first involved the practice of importing the element "knowingly" into an offence which ostensibly was framed in absolute terms. The second problem concerned the question, if the word "knowingly" already appeared in the definition or was introduced by a piece of judicial legislation, to what extent was proof of guilty knowledge required? As to the first of these problems, the tendency today, led by the invigorating influence of the present Lord Chief Justice, is to construe any doubtfully worded offences in favour of the accused. The pendulum of judicial opinion has swung to and fro, with cases like *Woodrow*,[1] *Prince*,[2] *Tolson*,[3] *Wheat and Stocks*,[4] *Brend* v. *Wood*,[5] and *Younghusband* v. *Luftig*[6] standing out as landmarks by which the tone of judicial thought in particular eras may be ascertained. Whereas, at one time, the position had been reached when a judge was prepared to state that in construing a modern statute the presumption as to *mens rea* did not exist, the present attitude is happily the exact reverse and, it is to be hoped, will long continue in the same vein.

As to the extent to which the word "knowingly" in an offence requires proof of *mens rea*, it is important to stress again that guilty knowledge is required not only of the doing of the primary act but also of all the various elements which together constitute the statutory offence. One qualification to this principle may exist, viz., where the legislature provides an exculpatory clause to the offence. It becomes then the task of the court to decide whether the word "knowingly" extends to this escape clause or whether the clause is to be treated separately as being of an absolute character. The presumption, it is submitted, should be in favour of the former construction, while at the same time realising that the intention of Parliament, as expressed in the wording of the enactment, may be to close the door to any such presumption.

Permits: Suffers: Allows

Unlike the terms "maliciously" and "wilfully", these three epithets do not convey the same positive notion of moral culpability. Yet it would be wrong to assume that, in consequence, they fall into a separate category in which no question of a guilty mind is involved. Indeed, all three verbs illustrate the point that in statutory offences there are degrees of anti-social wrongdoing. Whereas malice, wilfulness and fraud constitute a group at the top of the scale, permitting, suffering, allowing, together with the term knowingly, form another group at the lower end of the scale.

Examination of the cases in which each of the words "permits", "suffers" and "allows" has been analysed shows quite clearly, it is submitted, that the same conditions of liability pertain whichever word is inserted by the draftsman. These conditions, it will

[1] (1846) 15 M. & W. 404. [2] (1875) 1 C.C.R. 154. [3] (1889) 23 Q.B.D. 168.
[4] [1921] 2 K.B. 119. [5] (1946) 62 T.L.R. 462 [6] [1949] 2 K.B. 354.

be recalled, are twofold. First, the accused must be shown to have had guilty knowledge that the forbidden event is happening, which means proving that the accused knew of all the facts which constitute the forbidden event. Secondly, that the accused, with such knowledge and being in a position to prevent the event happening, does nothing about it. Only one judge has attempted to distinguish between the respective words—which attempt, with respect, was not very satisfactory—and subsequent cases have tended to regard the three verbs as interchangeable. It must, however, be remembered that opinion on the first of the above conditions is not unanimous, and this is especially so in cases of permitting. The minority view has adopted the interpretation—which spasmodically rears itself in cases of "maliciously", "wilfully" and even "knowingly"—whereby knowledge of the wrongfulness of the event is limited to only one of the several facts constituting the forbidden event. The net result is to treat the remaining elements as absolutely prohibited, a construction which, it is submitted, is erroneous and contrary to the intention of the legislature.

Causes

This word is in a category of its own, for it is used in two senses. In some enactments it is inserted to denote such participation in crime as would, in the case of a felony, amount to being an accessory before the fact. When used in this context the position, as exemplified in a crop of recent cases, is that there can be no liability unless it is shown that the defendant had knowledge of the essential matters which constitute the offence. This principle maintains in full vigour the common law conception of *mens rea*. In other enactments, on the other hand, the word "causes" appears as the particular basis of liability or, occasionally, as an alternative to either one or other of the epithets "permits", "suffers" or "allows". It will be recalled that "causing" is by no means identical with conduct envisaged by words like permitting or suffering. Whereas, as stated above, "permits," "suffers" and "allows" all denote passive acquiescence in the commission of the prohibited act, "causes" is a far more positive epithet and indicates an express authorisation of the forbidden event.

Considerable divergence of judicial opinion is, however, also seen in this field as to the requirement of a guilty mind. What has been said earlier as to the alternative courses which can be adopted in a situation like this is equally pertinent here. Either the variety of interpretations can be accepted and justified on the ground that each offence must be construed according to the individual judge's assessment of the key word; or the principle can be accepted that the expression "causes", in the sense of express authorisation, points to the necessity of guilty knowledge of the different elements which make up the prohibited event. The suggestion made in this work is that the latter solution is preferable.

Fraudulently: Intent to defraud

Equalled only by the word "maliciously" in its emphasis on knowingly wrongful conduct is the word "fraudulently". Used in its widest sense the accent in fraud is upon dishonesty, and, so understood, there should be no doubt as to the application of *mens rea* in crimes based on the epithet "fraudulently" or on the phrase "with intent to defraud". Certainly, throughout the field of offences like larceny, forgery, false pretences, fraudulent conversion, embezzlement and obtaining credit by fraud, there is unanimity of opinion on the necessity for a guilty mind as defined above.

However, it may be remembered that in a series of cases arising under the Merchandise Marks Acts the courts adopted the "absolutist" theory of liability. True, these cases were principally concerned with the analogous phrase "acting innocently", but the same attitude was taken more recently when the defence of "without intent to defraud" was before the court. It is all very well to argue that in offences designed to protect the public the question of *mens rea* should be subordinated to the interests of the common weal. The view now put forward is that, permissible though this attitude may be in cases where the offence is defined in unequivocably absolute terms, no justification exists for the same approach to offences wherein the legislature has inserted the significant words "fraudulently" and "with intent to defraud".

Another similarity between the expressions "fraudulently" and "maliciously" lies in the application of the defence of claim of right or mistaken belief, the general consensus of judicial opinion recognising the validity of such a plea in the more familiar offences involving fraud. Moreover, in acknowledging that such a defence must be judged according to the subjective standard of whether or not the belief was honestly held, it will be seen that a guilty mind is accepted as the foundation of liability. Perhaps, above all the epithets used in statutory offences, the word "fraudulently" most clearly illustrates the retention of a morally or anti-social blameworthy mind as the true meaning of *mens rea*.

The guiding principle

With this bird's eye view of the whole field, is it possible to point to any single thread connecting the various statutory offences? The danger of putting forward any general principle is recognised but it is felt that an attempt should be made. Viewed from the day-to-day practice in the courts the present attitude of the judiciary can hardly claim any measure of coherence either in the direction of the "absolutist" theory of liability or in the direction of the "guilty mind" theory of liability. The power of the legislature to create crimes of absolute prohibition is accepted without cavil. But it is felt that some of the judges, both in the past and at present, have occasionally tended to interpret along absolutist lines offences wherein Parliament has inserted words denoting a contrary intention. These instances are not many but the importance attached to them is apt to assume undue proportions. It is important, therefore, that they be seen in proper perspective. These exceptional cases apart, it is submitted that throughout the cases dealing with one or other of the various epithets the courts have emphasised the requirement of *mens rea* in the form of a guilty mind. The nearest approach to a general definition of *mens rea* in such statutory offences is where a person intentionally does the forbidden act with knowledge of all the wrongful circumstances which the statute seeks to prohibit. It is in the occasioning of a knowingly wrongful event that liability is incurred under a statutory offence based on *mens rea*.

The degrees of knowledge and vicarious liability

It may be useful to recall that, in establishing such guilty knowledge, actual or direct knowledge is not absolutely essential, there being no doubt that a person who deliberately shuts his eyes to an obvious means of knowledge is equally liable. Less certainty is felt in regard to negligence when used in the sense of blameful inadvertence. Thus interpreted, negligence describes the state of mind of a person who ought to have known, and is obviously not so reprehensible as the state of mind of a person who wilfully shuts his eyes to the obvious. Hitherto, strong objection has been voiced to basing criminal liability upon mere inadvertence. But where the choice before Parliament or the courts lies between the two extremes of liability—on the one hand, liability based upon a guilty mind in the form of actual knowledge or connivance, and on the other hand absolute prohibition—it will be apparent that in between there exists a considerable gap. Is it better for the legislature and the courts to be left with the task of making up their minds between these two exclusive forms of liability? Or is it preferable to put forward, as another alternative to absolute prohibition, an intermediate theory of liability based on blameful inadvertence. There is evidence that in modern enactments the latter solution is gaining favour and, insofar as it preserves even at its lowest degree the doctrine of *mens rea*, the acceptance of negligence as a culpable state of mind need not cause so much concern. Of course, regard must be had to the nature of the offence involved. Acceptance of negligence as a sufficient degree of *mens rea*, it is submitted, should be restricted to those statutory offences in which the legislature intends to use the criminal law as a means of securing and maintaining a certain standard of behaviour in such matters as road traffic, food and drugs, weights and measures, licensing and public health.

In seeking to achieve this same purpose it is considered that it is legitimate to have recourse to the principle of vicarious liability. Some measure of conflict in applying this doctrine is, however, bound to arise so long as the courts continue to test such liability by the alternative "scope of employment" and "delegation" formulae. Reasons have been given in the chapter devoted to this subject for preferring the principle that he who chooses to delegate any duties, powers or responsibilities imposed upon him by statute should remain liable for the acts of any person appointed to act in his place. It is suggested that this general principle should supersede the "course of employment" formula which, in addition to sometimes conflicting with the wider principle, presents the obvious danger of equating criminal with tortious responsibility.

Any attempt at extending the application of vicarious liability beyond the realm of statutory offences which are concerned with enforcing legislative standards of correct trading, business and other public welfare behaviour, must be resisted. It is heartening to note the tight hold which the judiciary in recent years has exercised over sorties to extend the principle *respondeat superior* into the field of aiding and abetting, criminal attempts, and also to cover the acts of one who is not a servant or agent but a complete stranger. Times have changed in this respect and it is doubtful whether some of the judges during the early part of the last century would have taken such a firm stand. Parliament, too,—a fact insufficiently realised—since the end of the last century has frequently shown its concern not to punish a person who is morally innocent. Many examples will be recalled in which the legislature has shown its preference for personal rather than vicarious liability. Perhaps the most common method is the insertion in an enactment of "third-party" clauses, whereby the accused, usually an employer, may escape liability if he can prove that he exercised proper care and that the contravention was in fact committed through the act or default of a third person. This tendency towards insistence on personal liability based upon moral fault is also repeatedly seen in statutes when the issue is the criminal responsibility of company officers for offences committed by servants of the corporation. For too long the spirit has prevailed in which the general public interest is regarded as overriding any considerations designed to protect the accused. The time has come to redress the balance.

TABLE OF STATUTES

TABLE OF CASES

BIBLIOGRAPHY

Allen, C. K. *Law in the Making* (1946 ed.) 75
Archbold, *Criminal Pleading and Practice* (33rd ed.) 48
Austin, *Jurisprudence* (3rd ed.), Vol. 1 202

Barry & Paton, *An Introduction to Criminal Law in Australia* 85
Baty, *Vicarious Liability* 217, 227
Bentham, *Collected Works*, Vol. 6 168
Blackstone, *Commentaries* (8th ed.), Vol. 2 44; Vol. 4 63, 75, 138, 179
Bracton, *De Corona* 179
Bracton, *De Legibus* 2
Bridge, *Presumptions and Burdens* (1949), 12 M.L.R. 273 91

Coke, *Third Institute* 2, 179
Cross, *Larceny by an Owner and Animus Furandi* (1952), 68 L.Q.R. 99 181
Criminal Code of Queensland 23, 50
Criminal Code of Tasmania 50
Criminal Code of Western Australia 23, 50

Dean, *Manslaughter and Dangerous Driving* (1937), 53 L.Q.R. 380 202
Denning, *Presumption and Burdens* (1945), 61 L.Q.R. 379 91
Denning, *The Changing Law* 75, 248
Devlin, *Criminal Responsibility and Punishment* (1954), Crim. L.R. 661 203
Dicey, *Conflict of Laws* (5th ed.) 71

East, *Pleas of the Crown*, Vol. 1 3
East, *Pleas of the Crown*, Vol. 2 2, 12, 179, 185
Eversley, *Domestic Relations* (6th ed.) 72

Foster, *Crown Cases* 3, 8
Friedmann, *Law and Social Change in Contemporary Britain* 86, 248

Glanville Williams, *Bigamy and the Third Marriage* (1950), 13 M.L.R. 417 64
Glanville Williams, *Criminal Law—The General Part* 11, 12, 14, 16, 26, 27, 33, 42, 48, 59, 61, 68, 70, 75, 89, 117, 118, 175, 177, 180, 188, 189, 190, 192, 202, 203, 205, 206, 213, 215, 217, 225, 231
Glanville Williams, *Liability for Animals* 44
Glanville Williams, *Mens Rea and Negligence* (1953), 16 M.L.R. 231 191, 201
Glanville Williams, *Merchandise Marks Act—Intent to Defraud* (1952), 15 15 M.L.R. 77 174
Glanville Williams, *Mistake in Criminal Law* (1951), 14 M.L.R. 485 49
Goodhart, *English Law and the Moral Law* 217, 248

Hale, *Pleas of the Crown*, Vol. 1 12, 75, 179, 181
Hall, *General Principles of Criminal Law* 17, 48, 68, 75, 80, 202, 205, 206, 216, 227, 247, 248
Hall, *Revision of Criminal Law* (1954), 33 Nebraska L.R. 3 216
Hanbury, *The Principles of Agency* 217
Hawkins, *Pleas of the Crown* 179
Holdsworth, *History of English Law*, Vol. 7 44
Holmes, *The Common Law* 8, 75, 248

Keedy, *Ignorance and Mistake in the Criminal Law* (1908), 22 Harv. L.R. 75 48, 75
Kenny, *Outlines of Criminal Law* (1st ed.) 14
Kenny, *Outlines of Criminal Law* (15th ed.) 48, 204
Kenny, *Outlines of Criminal Law* (16th ed.) 4, 11, 24, 38, 48, 50, 133, 136, 177, 188, 192, 194, 204, 205, 219

Markby, *Elements of English Law* 8, 53
Michael & Wechsler, *Criminal Law and its Administration* 48, 69
Miller, *Criminal Law* 4, 6, 9, 29, 48, 64, 236, 248
Modern Approach to Criminal Law 8, 58, 59, 70, 202, 205, 206
Montgomerie, *Aiding and Abetting Statutory Offences* (1950), 66 L.Q.R. 228 191

Nino Levi, *A Note on Mistake in Italian Criminal Law*, quoted in Michael and Wechsler's *Criminal Law and its Administration* 48
Nokes, *Introduction to Evidence* 91

Paton, *Jurisprudence* (2nd ed.) 14, 248
Perkins, *Rationale of Mens Rea* (1939), 52 Harv. L.R. 905 11
Pollock and Maitland, *History of English Law*, Vol. 2 2
Pound, *The Spirit of the Common Law* 218
Powell, *The Law of Agency* (2nd ed.) 217

Radzinowicz, *A History of English Criminal Law*, Vol. 1 2
Radzinowicz, *The Language of Criminal Science* (1939), 7 C.L.J. 224 247
Randall, *A Sketch of the Earlier History of the Licensing Laws* (1904), 20 L.Q.R. 316 55
Report of H.M.'s Commissioners of Criminal Law (1843), (7th Report) 202
Report of the Goddard Committee on the Law of Civil Liability for Damage done to Animals (Cmd. 5746) 25
Royal Commission on Capital Punishment (Cmd. 8392) 203
Russell, *Crime* (10th ed.) 4, 18, 20, 24, 26, 48, 68, 177, 179, 202

Salmond, *Jurisprudence* (7th ed.) 202
Salmond, *Jurisprudence* (9th ed.) 12
Salmond, *Jurisprudence* (10th ed.) 205
Sayre, *Criminal Responsibility for the Acts of Another* (1930), 43 Harv. L.R. 689 217

Sayre, *Mens Rea* (1932), 45 Harv. L.R. 974 8
Sayre, *Public Welfare Offences* (1933), 33 Col. L.R. 55 80, 247, 248
Sayre, *The Present Significance of Mens Rea in the Criminal Law* (1934), Harvard Legal Essays, pp. 399–417 80
Stallybrass, *The Eclipse of Mens Rea* (1936), 52 L.Q.R. 57 44, 247, 248
Stephen, *General View of English Criminal Law* 1, 8
Stephen, *History of Criminal Law*, Vol. 2 1, 7, 164, 168
Stephen, *History of Criminal Law*, Vol. 3 2, 5, 165, 166, 168, 176, 179, 185
Stephen, Herbert, *Intent to Deceive or Defraud* (1904), 20 L.Q.R. 186 186

Trowbridge, *Criminal Intent and Bigamy*, 7 Calif. L.R. 1 69

Webb, *History of Liquor Licensing in England* (1903) 55

INDEX

PRINTED IN GREAT BRITAIN
BY ROBERT MACLEHOSE AND CO. LTD
THE UNIVERSITY PRESS, GLASGOW

WITHDRAWN
FROM STOCK
QMUL LIBRARY